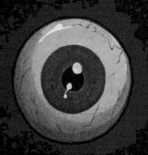

MEGUMI OSUGA

THANK YOU SO MUCH FOR BUYING *MAOH: JUVENILE REMIX*. I NEVER IMAGINED THAT I'D BE ABLE TO ADAPT WORKS WRITTEN BY THE GREAT KOTARO ISAKA. LIFE IS AMAZING SOMETIMES!

MEGUMI OSUGA

BORN DECEMBER 21 IN CHIBA PREFECTURE, MEGUMI OSUGA MADE HER DEBUT WITH *TONPACHI*, WHICH RAN IN *SHONEN SUNDAY R*, AND HAD A SHORT SERIES IN *SHONEN SUNDAY SUPER* CALLED *HONOU NO ANA NO YOMI*. IN 2007, HER SERIALIZATION OF *MAOH: JUVENILE REMIX* STARTED IN *SHONEN SUNDAY*.

KOTARO ISAKA

BORN IN 1971 IN CHIBA PREFECTURE, KOTARO ISAKA IS ONE OF THE MOST POPU... ...NESE NOVELISTS AND HAS RECEIVED NUMEROUS AWARDS. HE H... ...MOST OF WHICH HAVE BEEN TUR...

D1041281

MAOH
JUVENILE REMIX

MAOH: JUVENILE REMIX
Volume 01

Shonen Sunday Edition

Original Story by **Kotaro ISAKA**
Story and Art by **Megumi OSUGA**

Logo and cover design created by Isao YOSHIMURA & Bay Bridge Studio.

Translation/Stephen Paul
Touch-up Art & Lettering/James Dashiell
Design/Sam Elzway
Editor/Alexis Kirsch

VP, Production/Alvin Lu
VP, Sales & Product Marketing/Gonzalo Ferreyra
VP, Creative/Linda Espinosa
Publisher/Hyoe Narita

The rights of the author(s) of the work(s) in this publication to be so identified have been asserted in accordance with Copyright, Designs and Patents Act 1988. A CIP catalogue record for this book is available from the British Library.

Printed in the U.S.A.

Published by VIZ Media, LLC
P.O. Box 77010
San Francisco, CA 94107

10 9 8 7 6 5 4 3 2 1
First printing, May 2010

viz media
www.viz.com

SHONEN SUNDAY
www.shonensunday.com

MAOH
JUVENILE REMIX

ORIGINAL STORY BY
KOTARO ISAKA

STORY AND ART BY
MEGUMI OSUGA

CONTENTS

CHAPTER 1   FIRST CONTACT   005

CHAPTER 2   THE FIVE-YEAR PLAN   069

CHAPTER 3   THE BYSTANDER   105

CHAPTER 4   SEEPING DISCORD...   125

CHAPTER 5   WHAT I CAN DO   143

CHAPTER 6   THE BOOK OF EVERYONE'S DEATH   161

CHAPTER 7   THE WORD THAT CHANGES THE WORLD   179

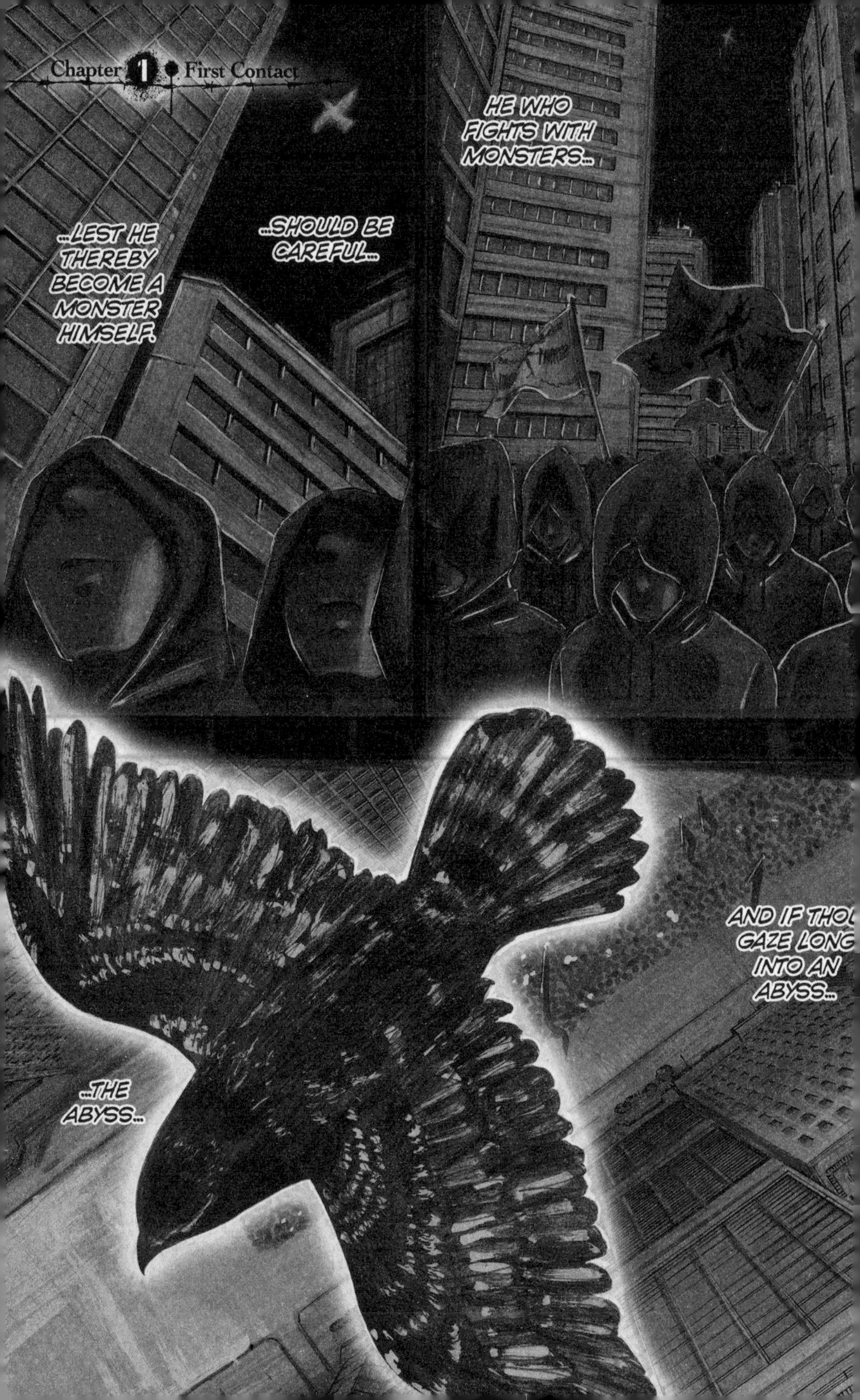
Chapter 1 First Contact
HE WHO FIGHTS WITH MONSTERS...
...SHOULD BE CAREFUL...
...LEST HE THEREBY BECOME A MONSTER HIMSELF.
AND IF THOU GAZE LONG INTO AN ABYSS...
...THE ABYSS...

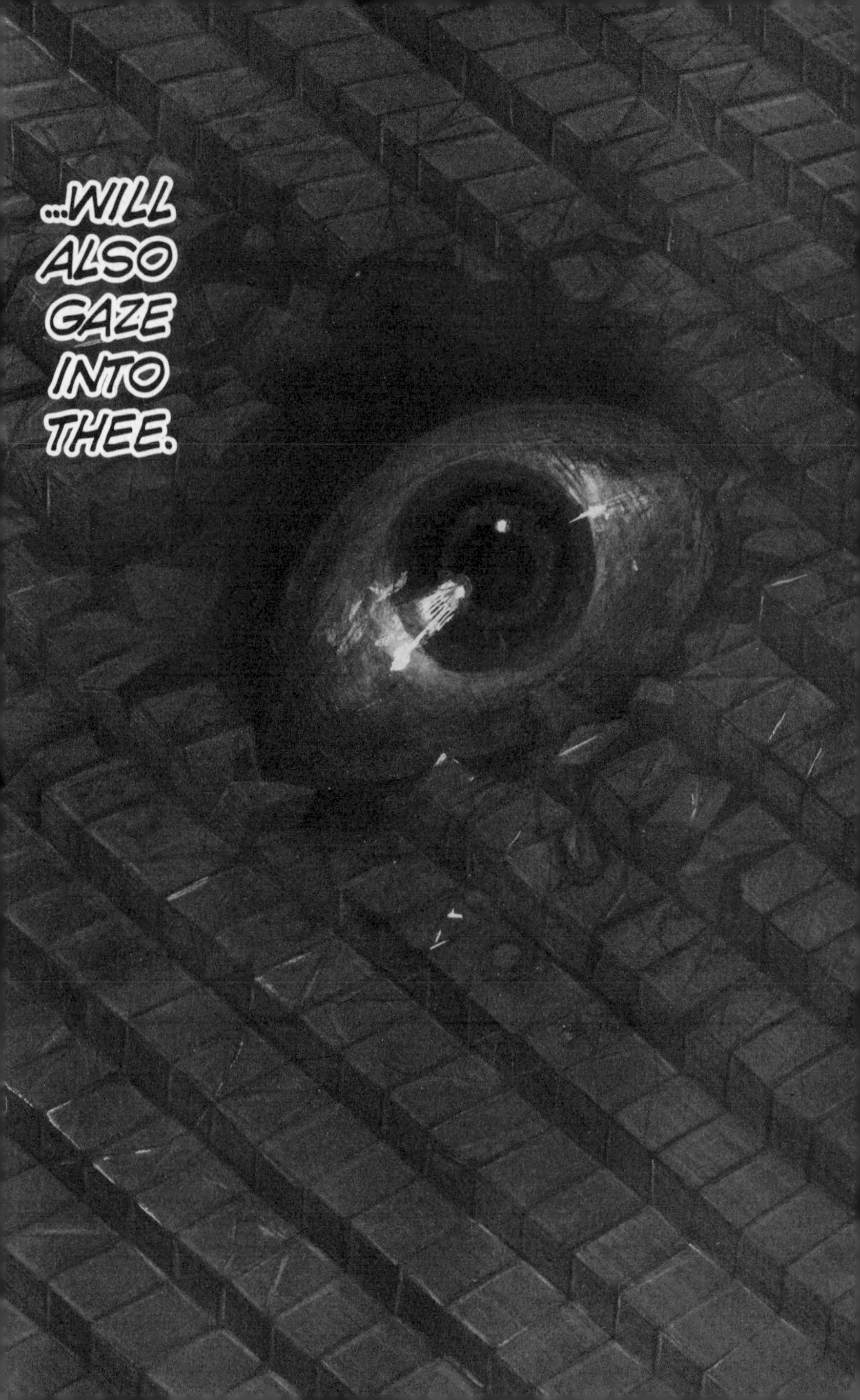
...WILL ALSO GAZE INTO THEE.

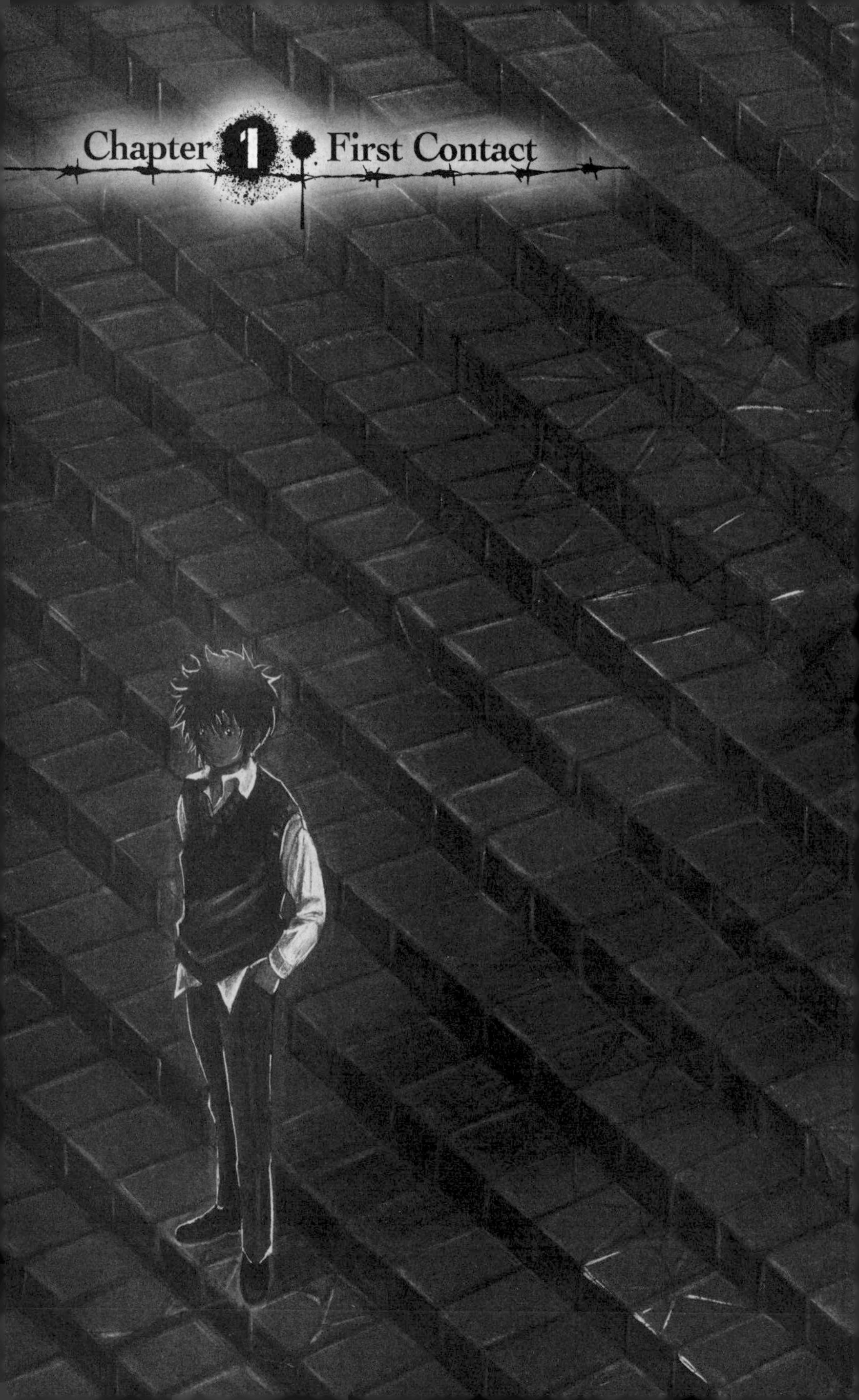
Chapter 1 First Contact

MAOH
JUVENILE REMIX

Act One
Ando

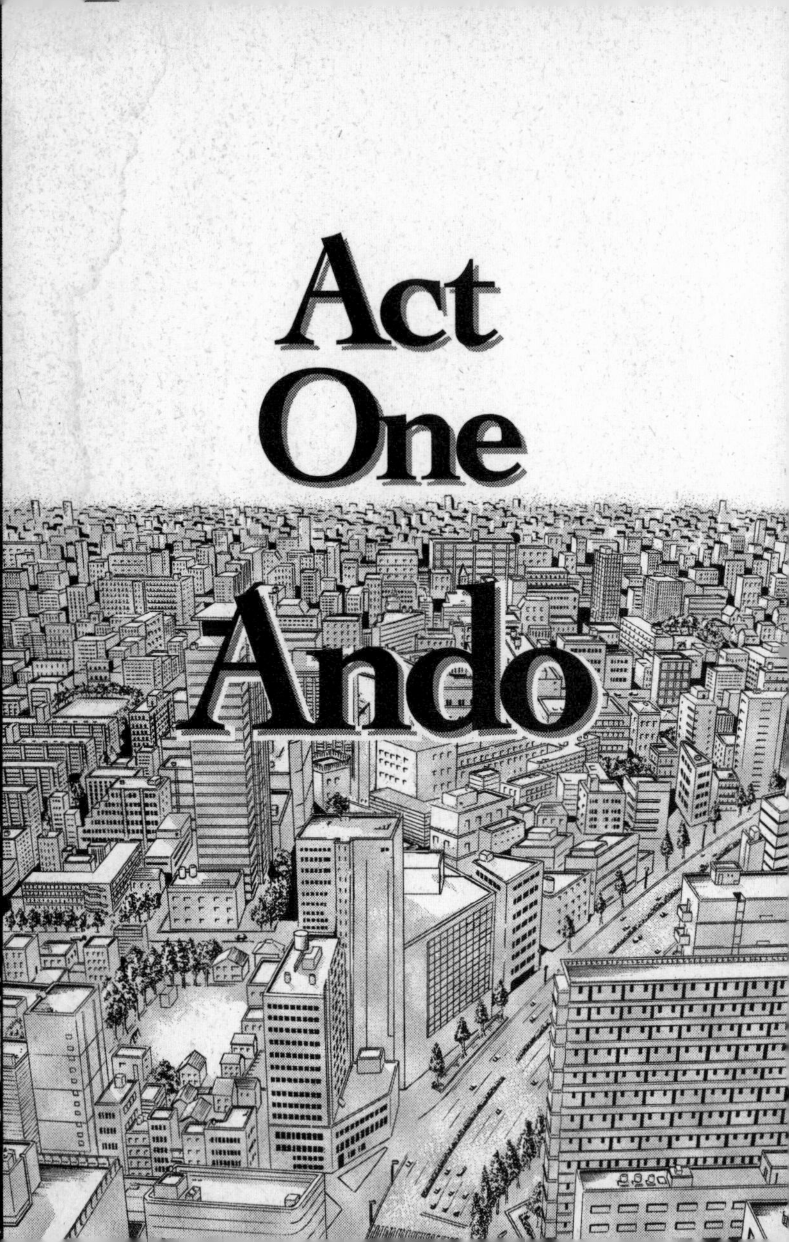

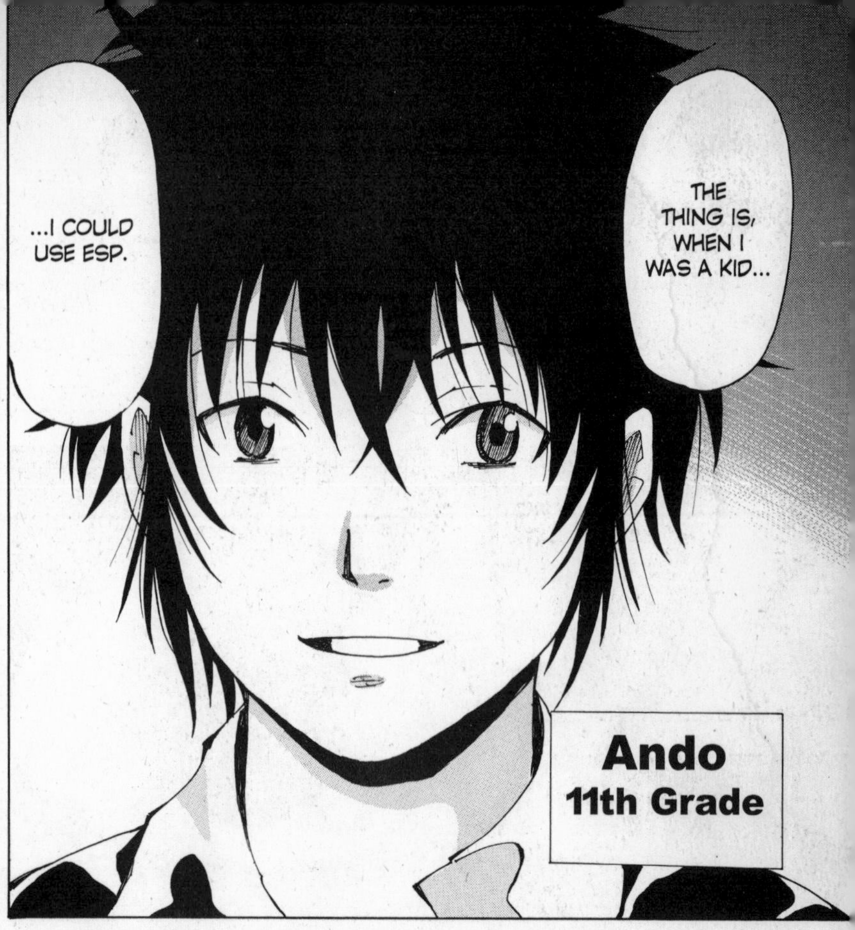
THE THING IS, WHEN I WAS A KID...
...I COULD USE ESP.
Ando
11th Grade
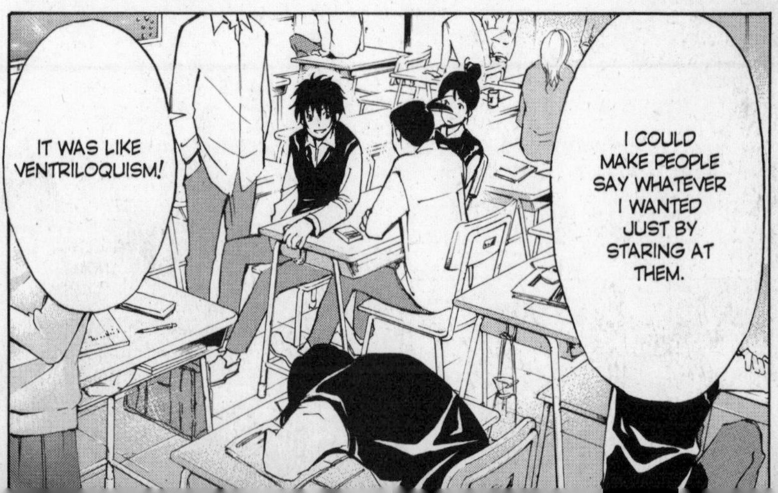
I COULD MAKE PEOPLE SAY WHATEVER I WANTED JUST BY STARING AT THEM.
IT WAS LIKE VENTRILOQUISM!

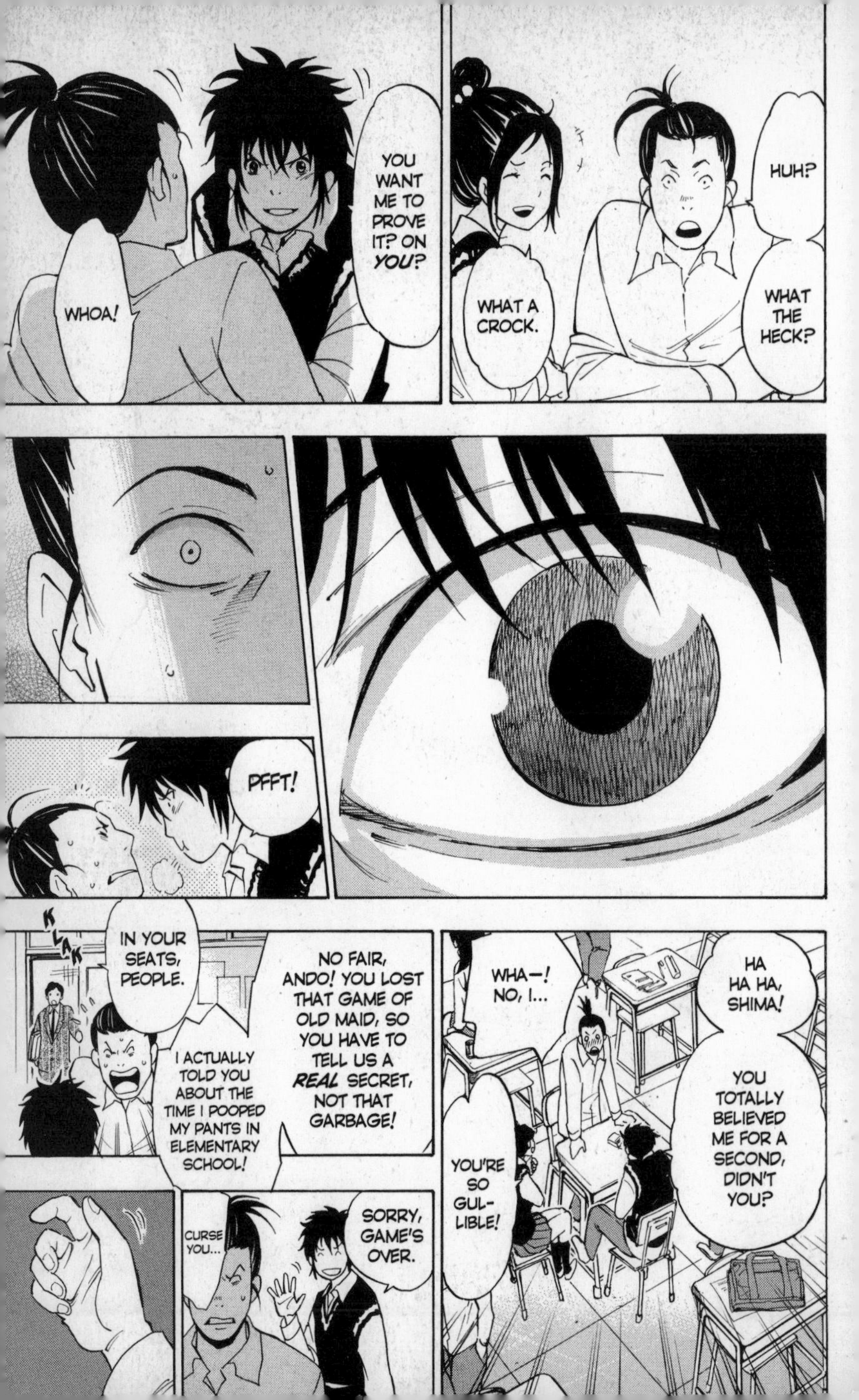
HUH?
WHAT THE HECK?
WHAT A CROCK.
YOU WANT ME TO PROVE IT? ON *YOU*?
WHOA!
PFFT!
HA HA HA, SHIMA!
YOU TOTALLY BELIEVED ME FOR A SECOND, DIDN'T YOU?
WHA—! NO, I...
YOU'RE SO GUL-LIBLE!
NO FAIR, ANDO! YOU LOST THAT GAME OF OLD MAID, SO YOU HAVE TO TELL US A *REAL* SECRET, NOT THAT GARBAGE!
I ACTUALLY TOLD YOU ABOUT THE TIME I POOPED MY PANTS IN ELEMENTARY SCHOOL!
KLAK
IN YOUR SEATS, PEOPLE.
SORRY, GAME'S OVER.
CURSE YOU...

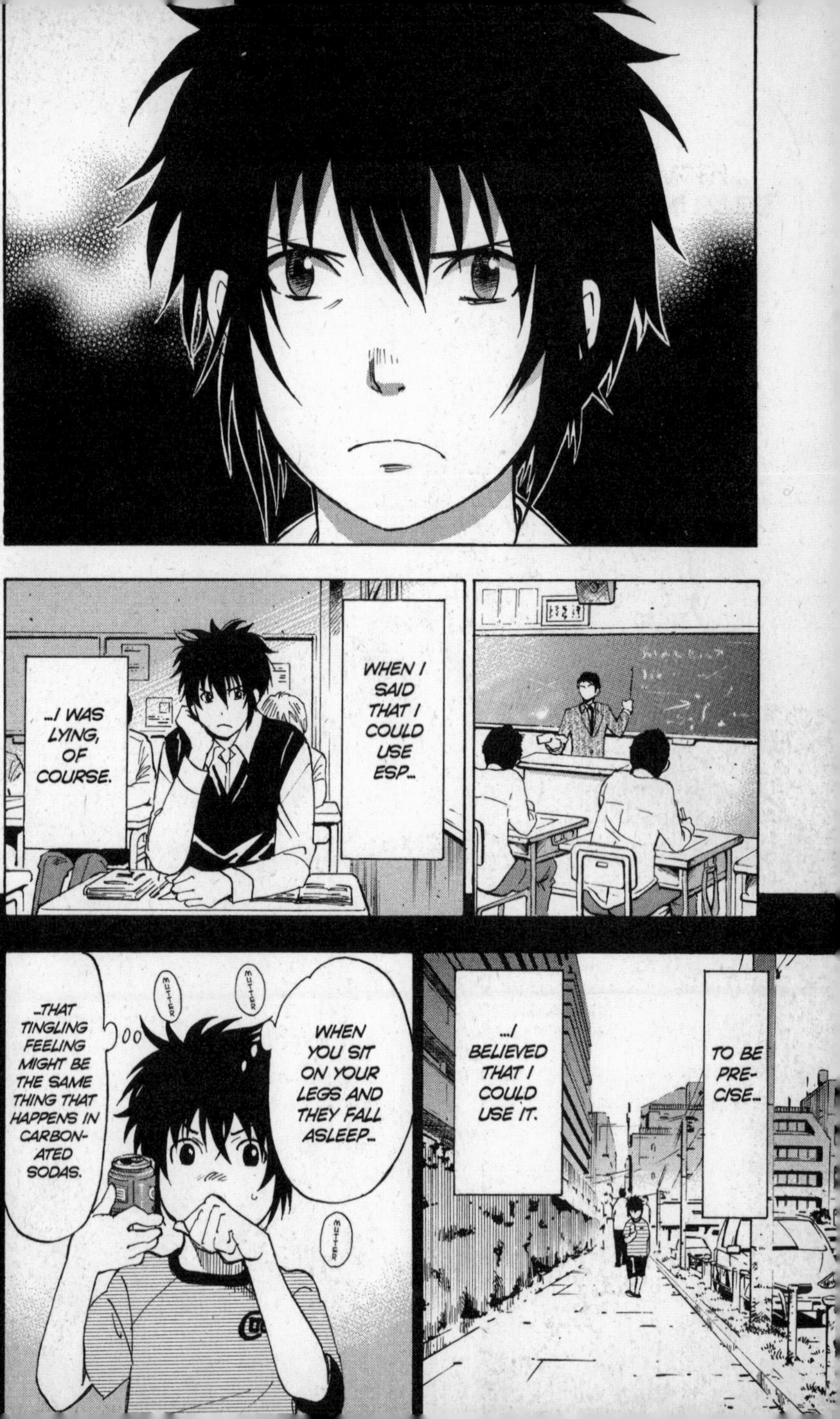
WHEN I SAID THAT I COULD USE ESP...
...I WAS LYING, OF COURSE.
TO BE PRE-CISE...
...I BELIEVED THAT I COULD USE IT.
MUTTER
MUTTER
WHEN YOU SIT ON YOUR LEGS AND THEY FALL ASLEEP...
...THAT TINGLING FEELING MIGHT BE THE SAME THING THAT HAPPENS IN CARBON-ATED SODAS.
MUTTER

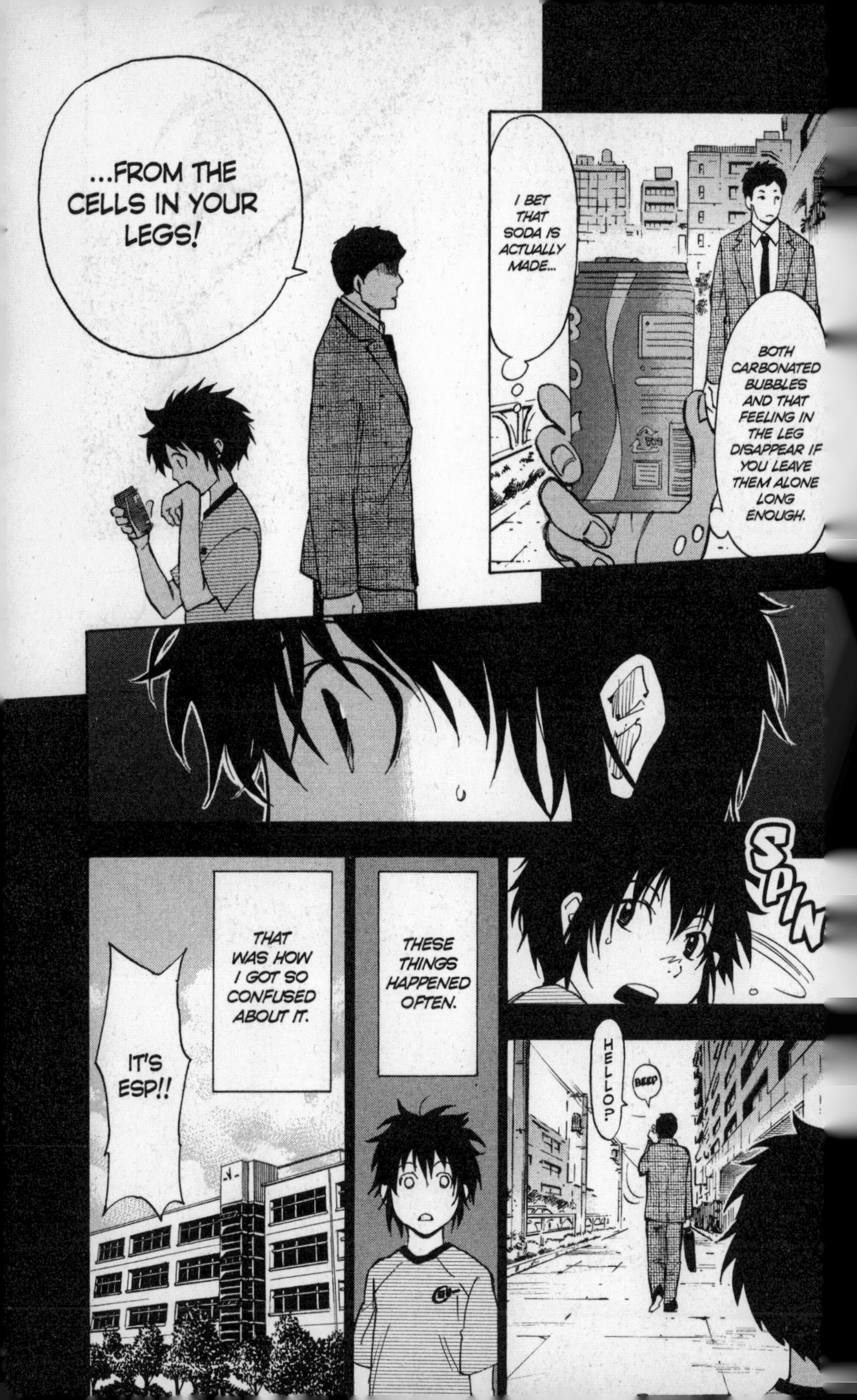
BOTH CARBONATED BUBBLES AND THAT FEELING IN THE LEG DISAPPEAR IF YOU LEAVE THEM ALONE LONG ENOUGH.
I BET THAT SODA IS ACTUALLY MADE...
...FROM THE CELLS IN YOUR LEGS!
SPIN
HELLO?
BEEP
THESE THINGS HAPPENED OFTEN.
THAT WAS HOW I GOT SO CONFUSED ABOUT IT.
IT'S ESP!!

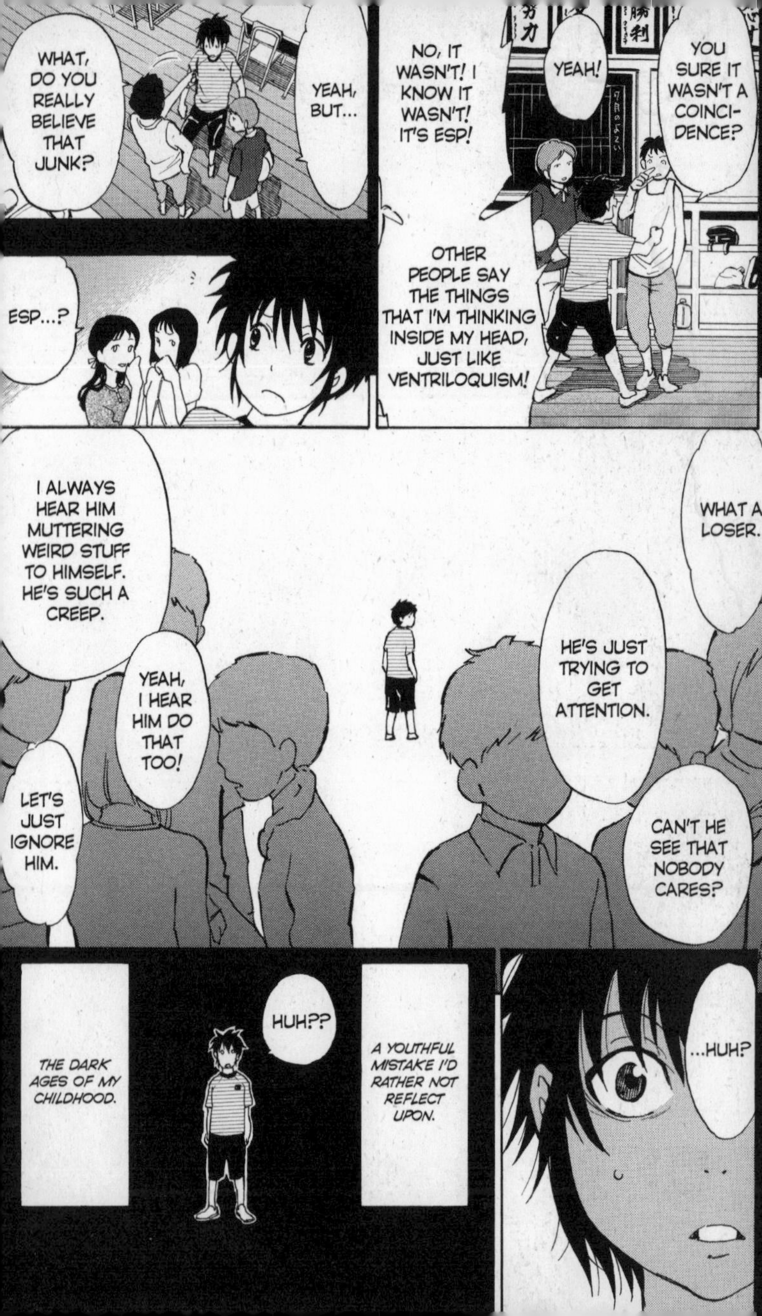
YOU SURE IT WASN'T A COINCIDENCE?
YEAH!
NO, IT WASN'T! I KNOW IT WASN'T! IT'S ESP!
OTHER PEOPLE SAY THE THINGS THAT I'M THINKING INSIDE MY HEAD, JUST LIKE VENTRILOQUISM!
YEAH, BUT...
WHAT, DO YOU REALLY BELIEVE THAT JUNK?
ESP...?
WHAT A LOSER.
HE'S JUST TRYING TO GET ATTENTION.
CAN'T HE SEE THAT NOBODY CARES?
I ALWAYS HEAR HIM MUTTERING WEIRD STUFF TO HIMSELF. HE'S SUCH A CREEP.
YEAH, I HEAR HIM DO THAT TOO!
LET'S JUST IGNORE HIM.
...HUH?
A YOUTHFUL MISTAKE I'D RATHER NOT REFLECT UPON.
HUH??
THE DARK AGES OF MY CHILDHOOD.

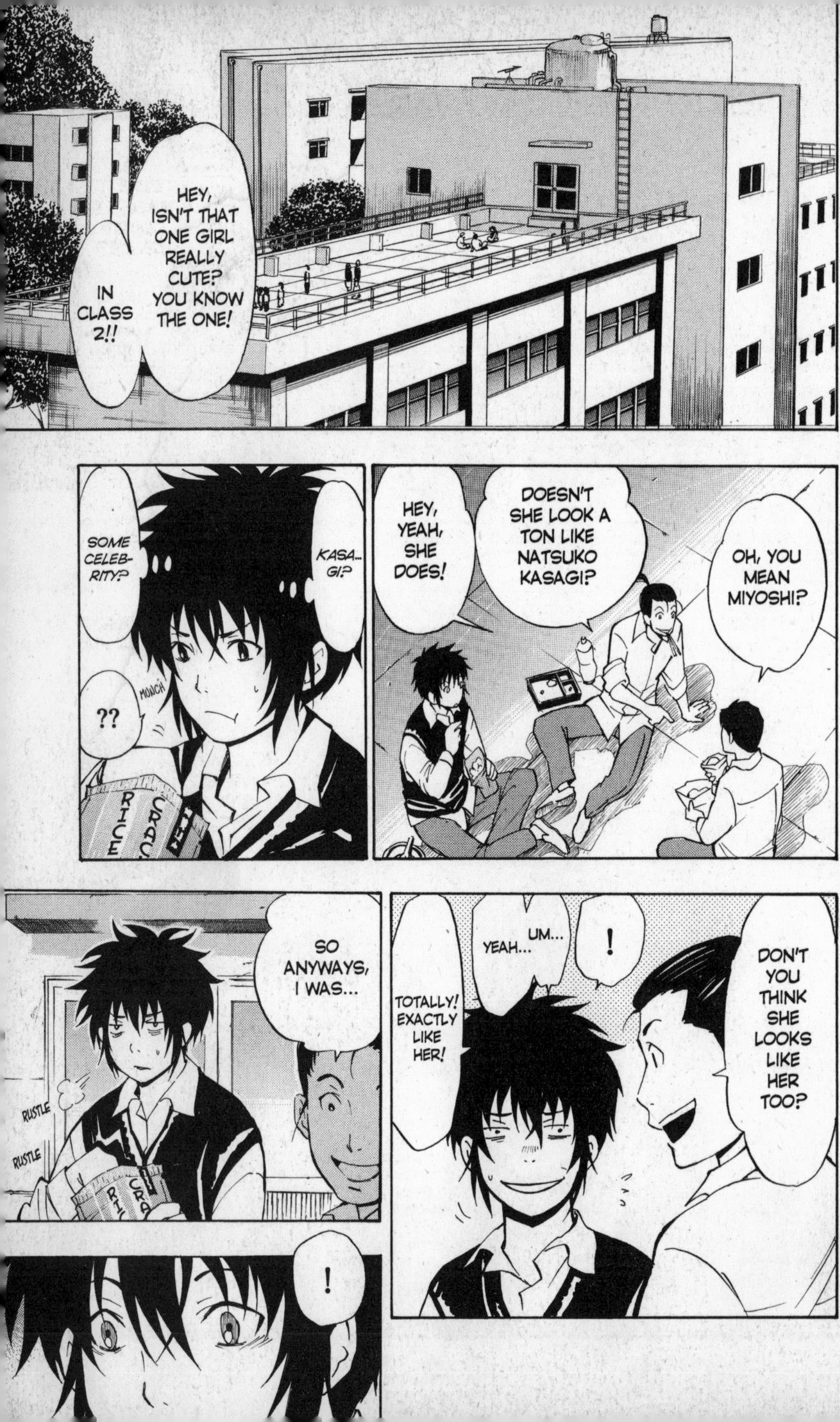
HEY, ISN'T THAT ONE GIRL REALLY CUTE? YOU KNOW THE ONE!
IN CLASS 2!!
OH, YOU MEAN MIYOSHI?
DOESN'T SHE LOOK A TON LIKE NATSUKO KASAGI?
HEY, YEAH, SHE DOES!
KASA... GI?
SOME CELEBRITY?
MUNCH
??
DON'T YOU THINK SHE LOOKS LIKE HER TOO?
!
UM... YEAH...
TOTALLY! EXACTLY LIKE HER!
SO ANYWAYS, I WAS...
RUSTLE
RUSTLE
!

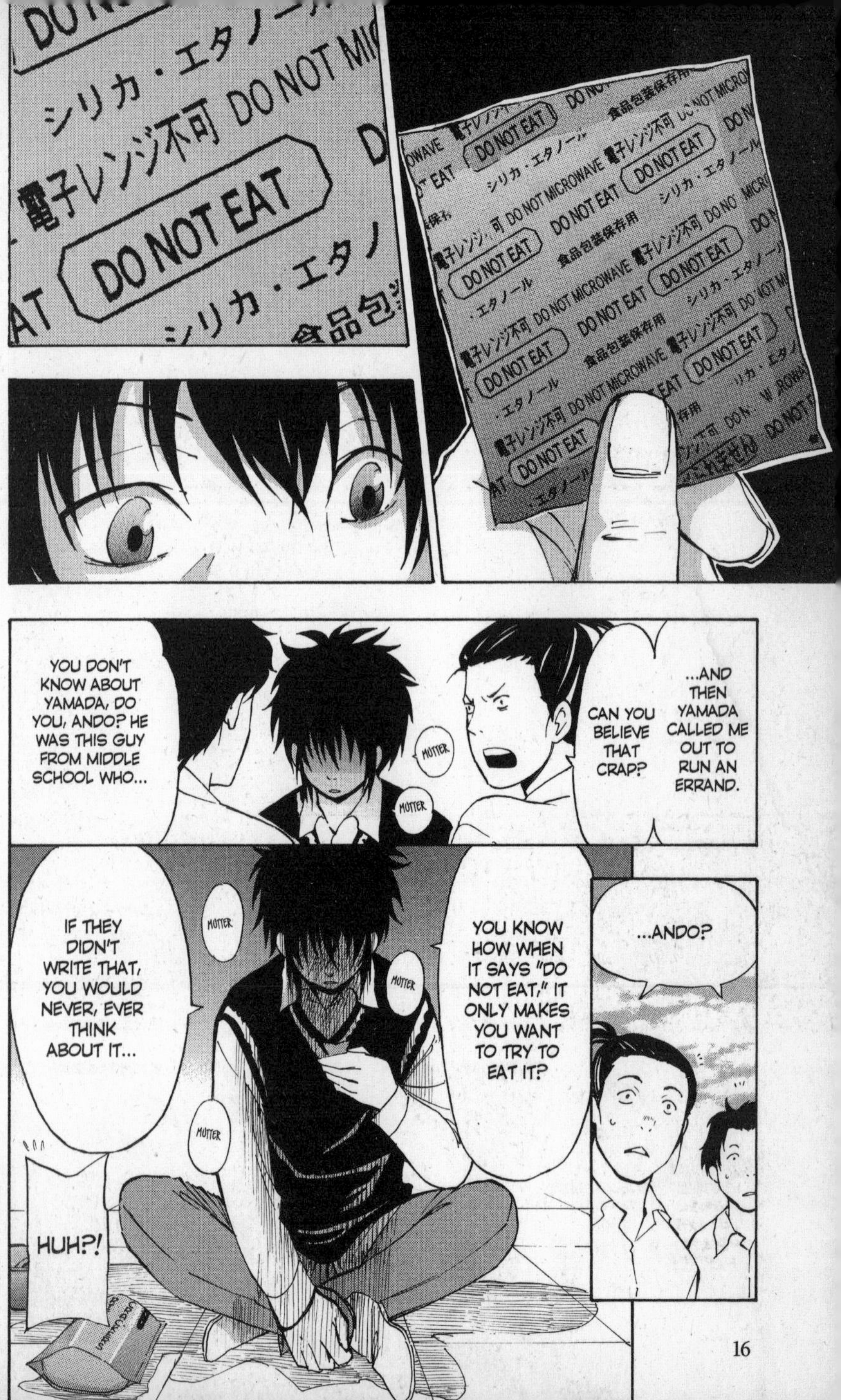
DO NOT EAT
DO NOT MICROWAVE
電子レンジ不可
食品包装保存用
シリカ・エタノール
シリカ・エタノ
電子レンジ不可 DO NOT MIC
DO NOT EAT
...AND THEN YAMADA CALLED ME OUT TO RUN AN ERRAND.
CAN YOU BELIEVE THAT CRAP?
MUTTER
MUTTER
YOU DON'T KNOW ABOUT YAMADA, DO YOU, ANDO? HE WAS THIS GUY FROM MIDDLE SCHOOL WHO...
...ANDO?
YOU KNOW HOW WHEN IT SAYS "DO NOT EAT," IT ONLY MAKES YOU WANT TO TRY TO EAT IT?
MUTTER
MUTTER
IF THEY DIDN'T WRITE THAT, YOU WOULD NEVER, EVER THINK ABOUT IT...
MUTTER
HUH?!

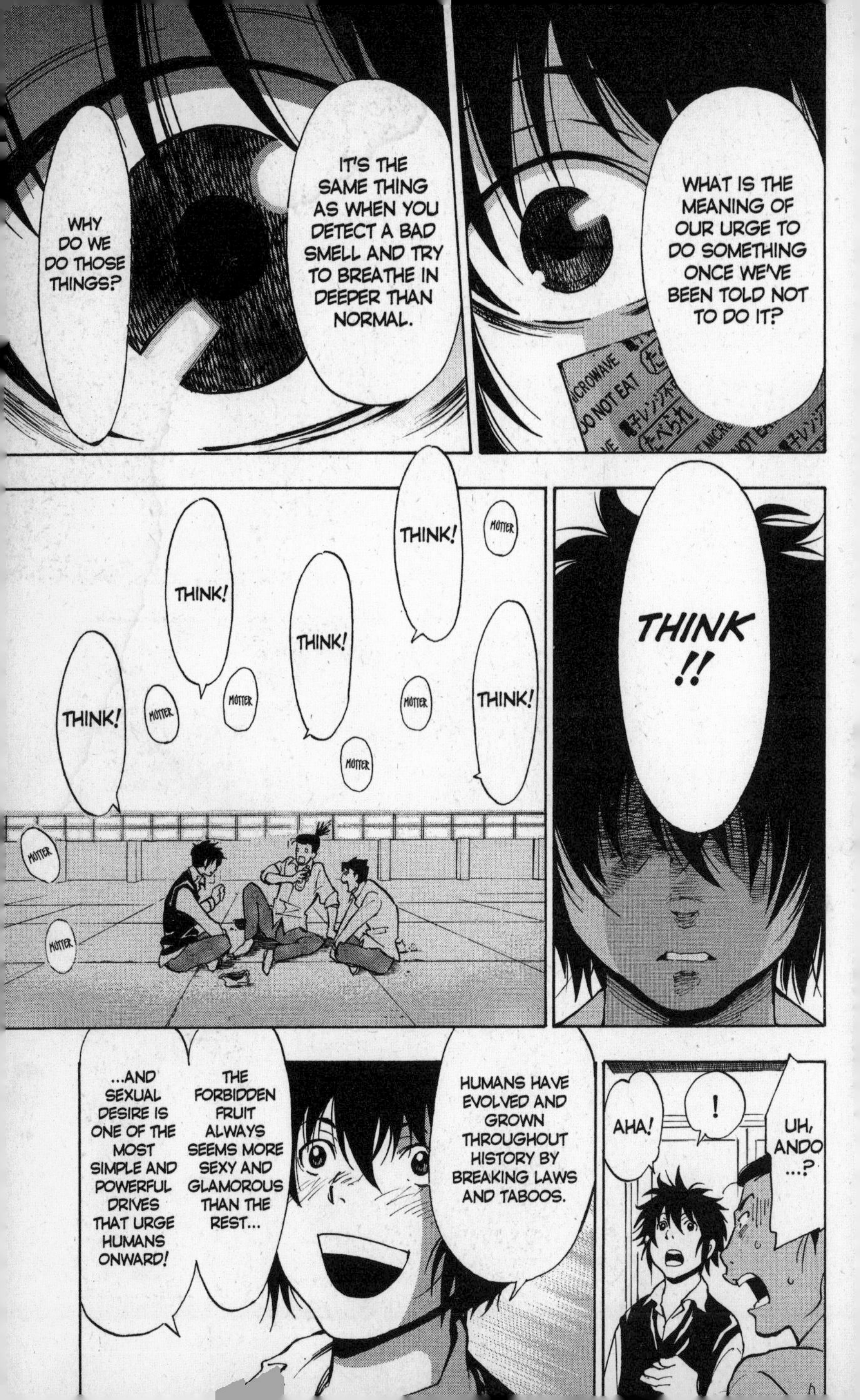
WHAT IS THE MEANING OF OUR URGE TO DO SOMETHING ONCE WE'VE BEEN TOLD NOT TO DO IT?
MICROWAVE
DO NOT EAT
IT'S THE SAME THING AS WHEN YOU DETECT A BAD SMELL AND TRY TO BREATHE IN DEEPER THAN NORMAL.
WHY DO WE DO THOSE THINGS?
THINK!!
MUTTER
THINK!
THINK!
MUTTER
THINK!
MUTTER
THINK!
MUTTER
MUTTER
THINK!
MUTTER
MUTTER
MUTTER
UH, ANDO ...?
!
AHA!
HUMANS HAVE EVOLVED AND GROWN THROUGHOUT HISTORY BY BREAKING LAWS AND TABOOS.
THE FORBIDDEN FRUIT ALWAYS SEEMS MORE SEXY AND GLAMOROUS THAN THE REST...
...AND SEXUAL DESIRE IS ONE OF THE MOST SIMPLE AND POWERFUL DRIVES THAT URGE HUMANS ONWARD!

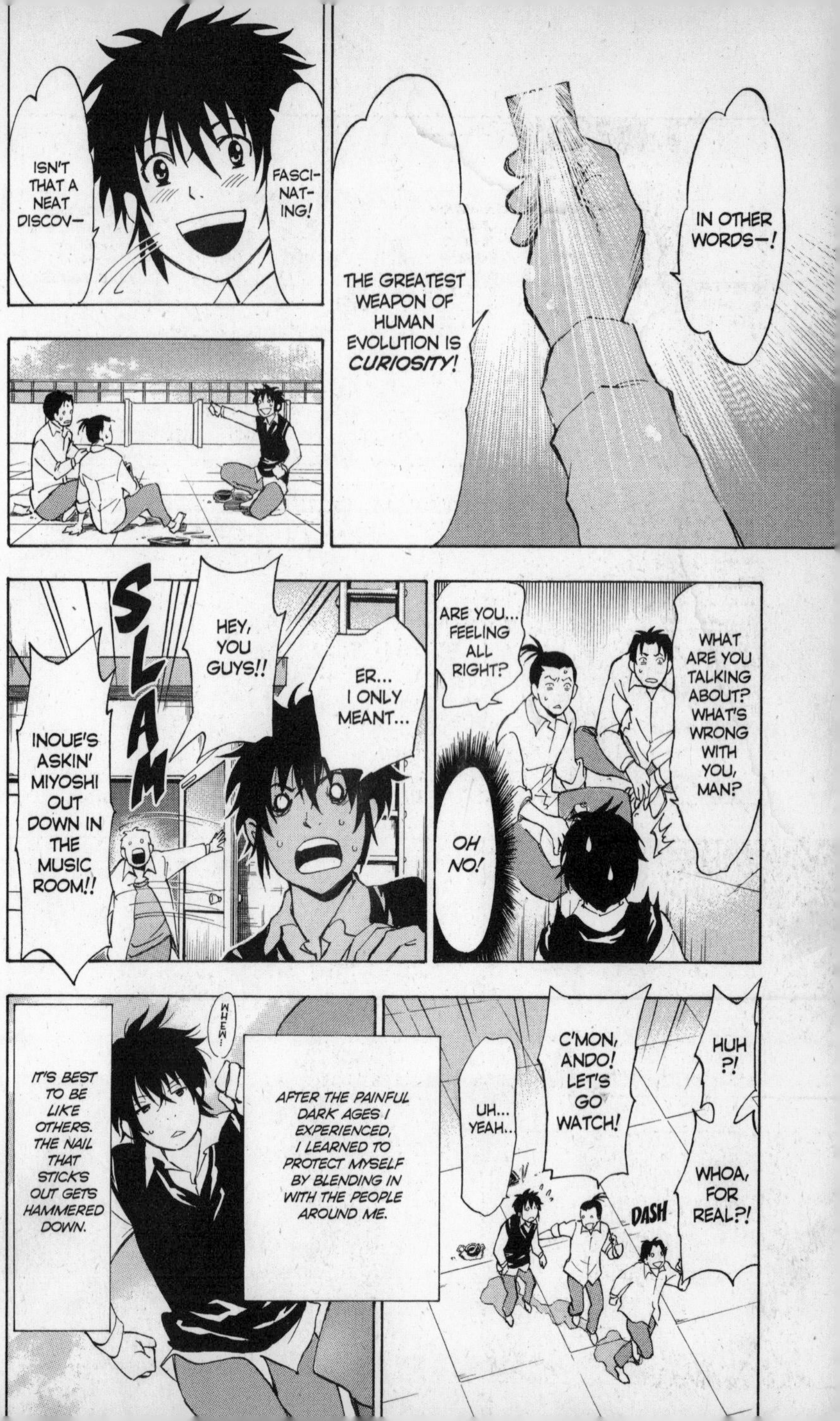
IN OTHER WORDS—!
THE GREATEST WEAPON OF HUMAN EVOLUTION IS *CURIOSITY!*
FASCI-NAT-ING!
ISN'T THAT A NEAT DISCOV—
WHAT ARE YOU TALKING ABOUT? WHAT'S WRONG WITH YOU, MAN?
ARE YOU... FEELING ALL RIGHT?
OH NO!
ER... I ONLY MEANT...
HEY, YOU GUYS!!
SLAM
INOUE'S ASKIN' MIYOSHI OUT DOWN IN THE MUSIC ROOM!!
HUH?!
C'MON, ANDO! LET'S GO WATCH!
WHOA, FOR REAL?!
UH... YEAH..
DASH
WHEW...
AFTER THE PAINFUL DARK AGES I EXPERIENCED, I LEARNED TO PROTECT MYSELF BY BLENDING IN WITH THE PEOPLE AROUND ME.
IT'S BEST TO BE LIKE OTHERS. THE NAIL THAT STICKS OUT GETS HAMMERED DOWN.

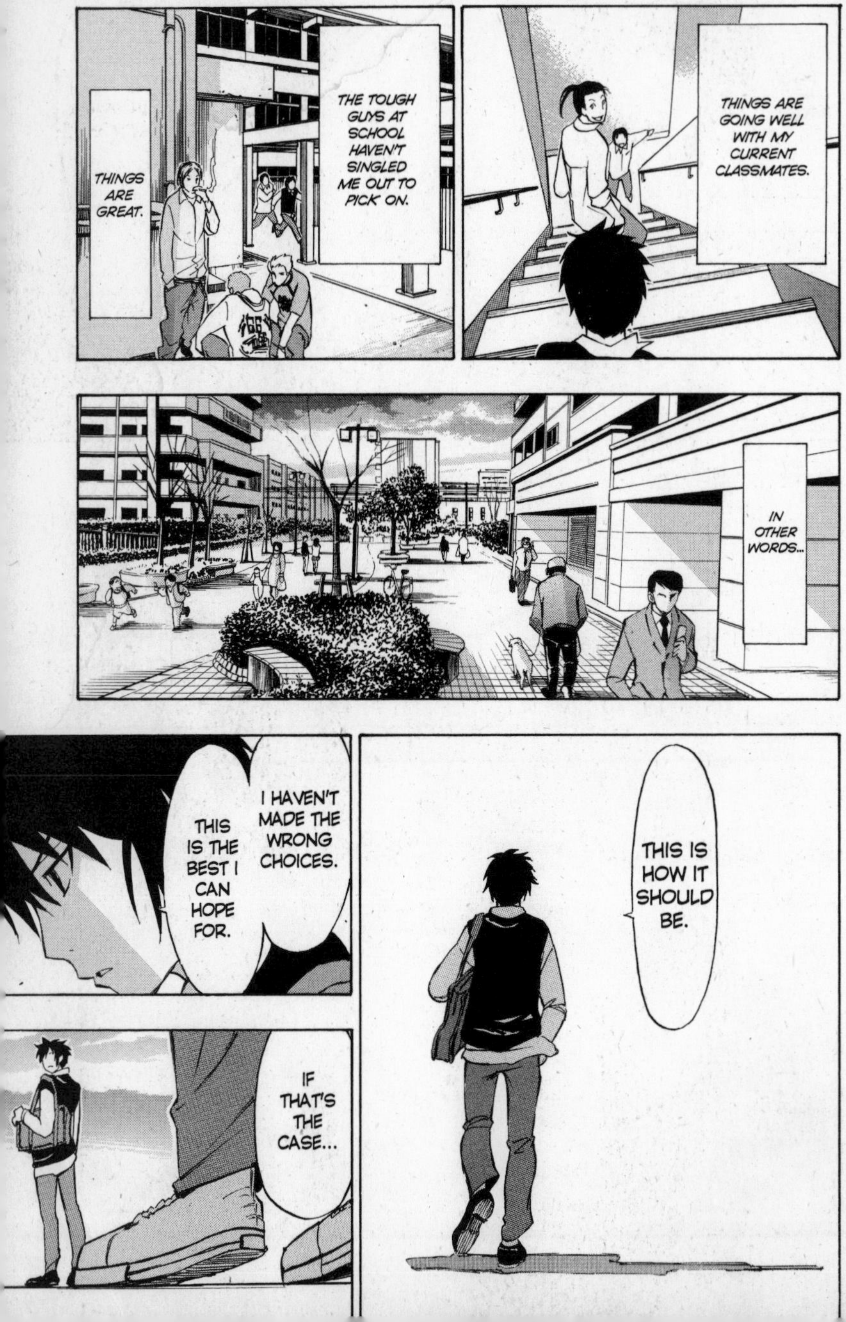
THINGS ARE GOING WELL WITH MY CURRENT CLASSMATES.
THE TOUGH GUYS AT SCHOOL HAVEN'T SINGLED ME OUT TO PICK ON.
THINGS ARE GREAT.
IN OTHER WORDS...
THIS IS HOW IT SHOULD BE.
I HAVEN'T MADE THE WRONG CHOICES.
THIS IS THE BEST I CAN HOPE FOR.
IF THAT'S THE CASE...

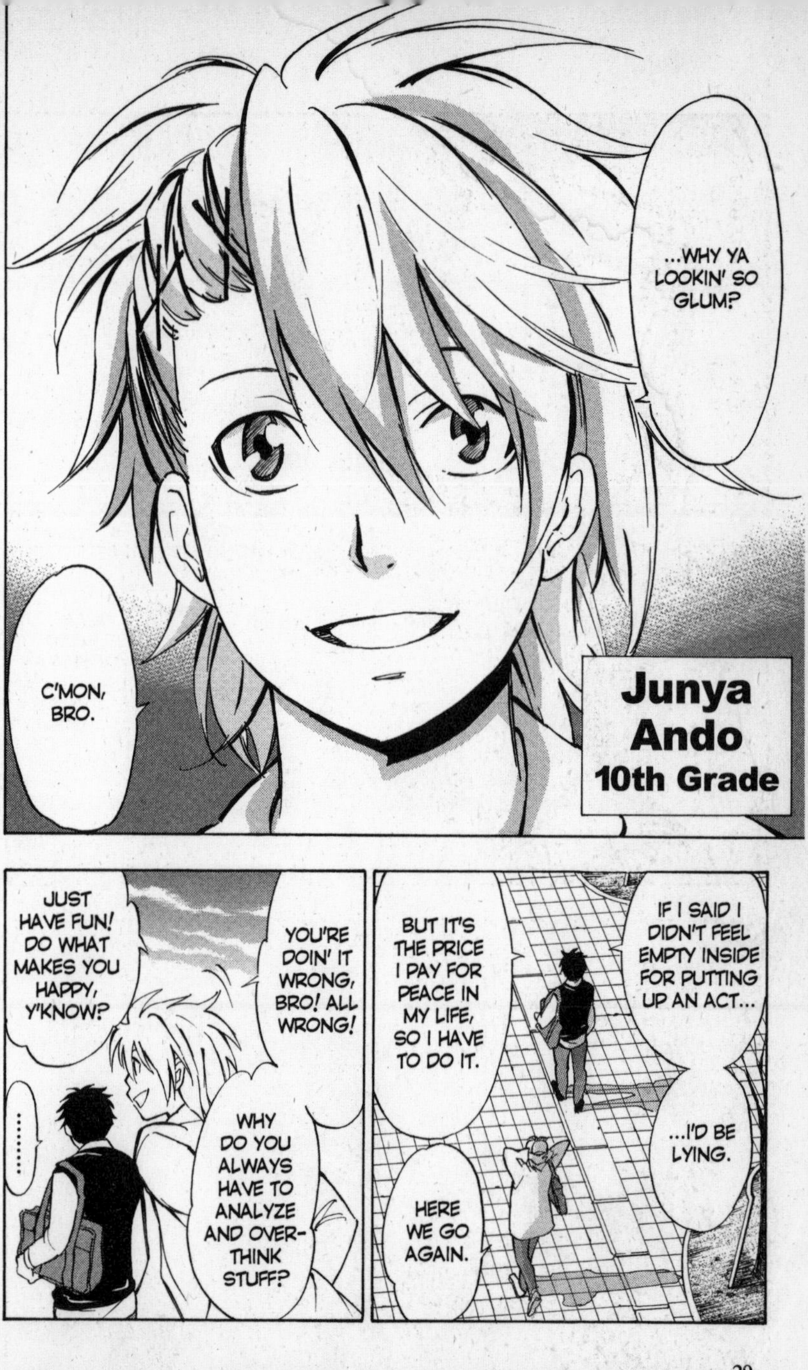
...WHY YA LOOKIN' SO GLUM?
C'MON, BRO.
Junya Ando 10th Grade
IF I SAID I DIDN'T FEEL EMPTY INSIDE FOR PUTTING UP AN ACT...
...I'D BE LYING.
BUT IT'S THE PRICE I PAY FOR PEACE IN MY LIFE, SO I HAVE TO DO IT.
HERE WE GO AGAIN.
YOU'RE DOIN' IT WRONG, BRO! ALL WRONG!
JUST HAVE FUN! DO WHAT MAKES YOU HAPPY, Y'KNOW?
WHY DO YOU ALWAYS HAVE TO ANALYZE AND OVER-THINK STUFF?
....

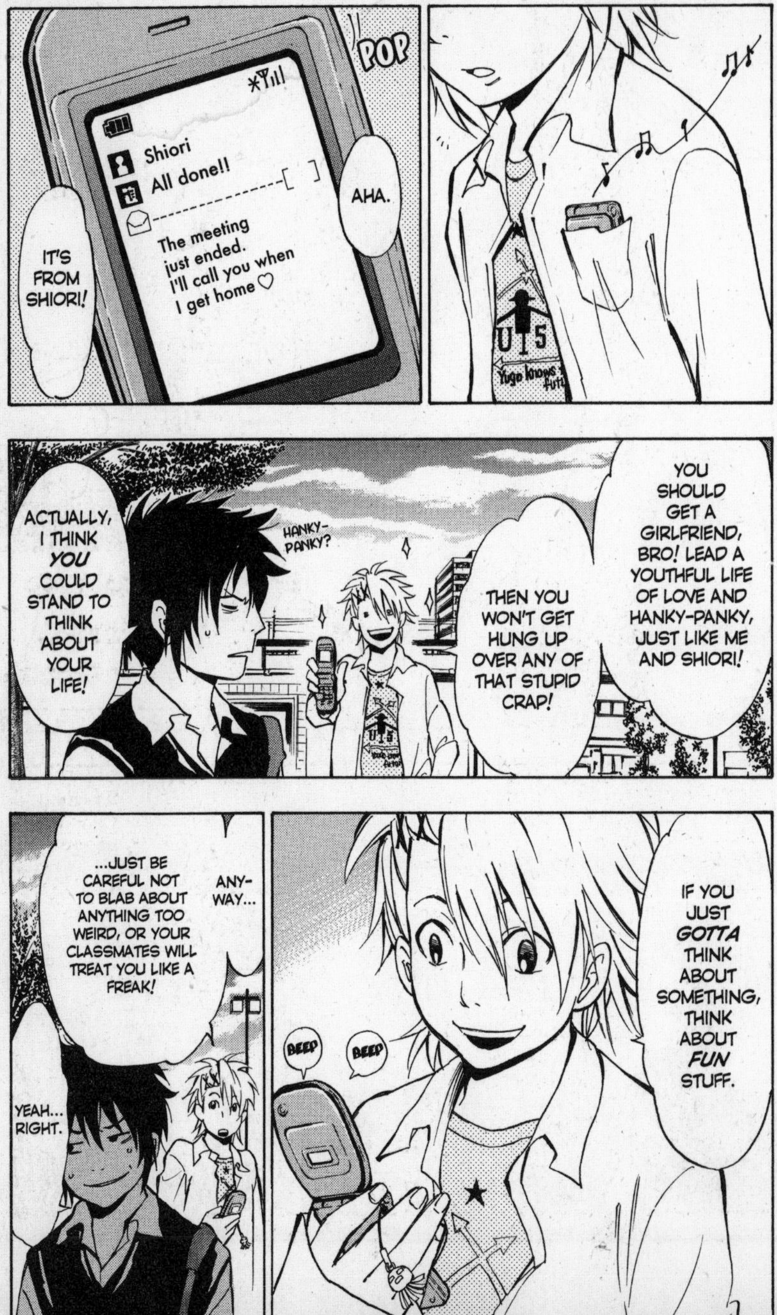
POP
AHA.
Shiori
All done!!
The meeting just ended. I'll call you when I get home ♡
IT'S FROM SHIORI!
YOU SHOULD GET A GIRLFRIEND, BRO! LEAD A YOUTHFUL LIFE OF LOVE AND HANKY-PANKY, JUST LIKE ME AND SHIORI!
THEN YOU WON'T GET HUNG UP OVER ANY OF THAT STUPID CRAP!
HANKY-PANKY?
ACTUALLY, I THINK YOU COULD STAND TO THINK ABOUT YOUR LIFE!
IF YOU JUST GOTTA THINK ABOUT SOMETHING, THINK ABOUT FUN STUFF.
BEEP
BEEP
ANY-WAY...
...JUST BE CAREFUL NOT TO BLAB ABOUT ANYTHING TOO WEIRD, OR YOUR CLASSMATES WILL TREAT YOU LIKE A FREAK!
YEAH... RIGHT.

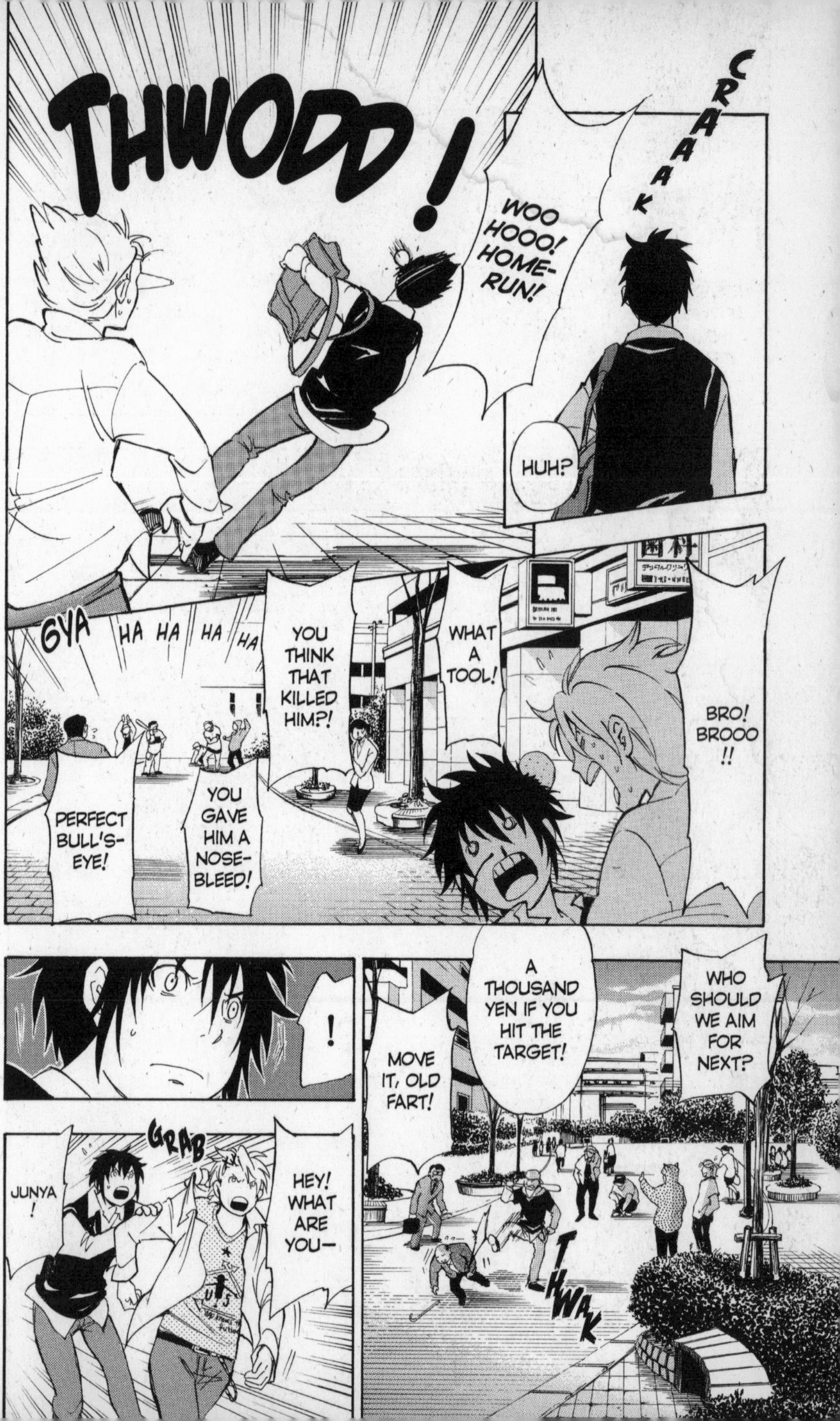
CRAAAK
WOO HOOO! HOME-RUN!
HUH?
THWODD!
BRO! BROOO!!
WHAT A TOOL!
YOU THINK THAT KILLED HIM?!
GYA HA HA HA HA
YOU GAVE HIM A NOSE-BLEED!
PERFECT BULL'S-EYE!
WHO SHOULD WE AIM FOR NEXT?
A THOUSAND YEN IF YOU HIT THE TARGET!
MOVE IT, OLD FART!
THWAK
!
GRAB
HEY! WHAT ARE YOU—
JUNYA!

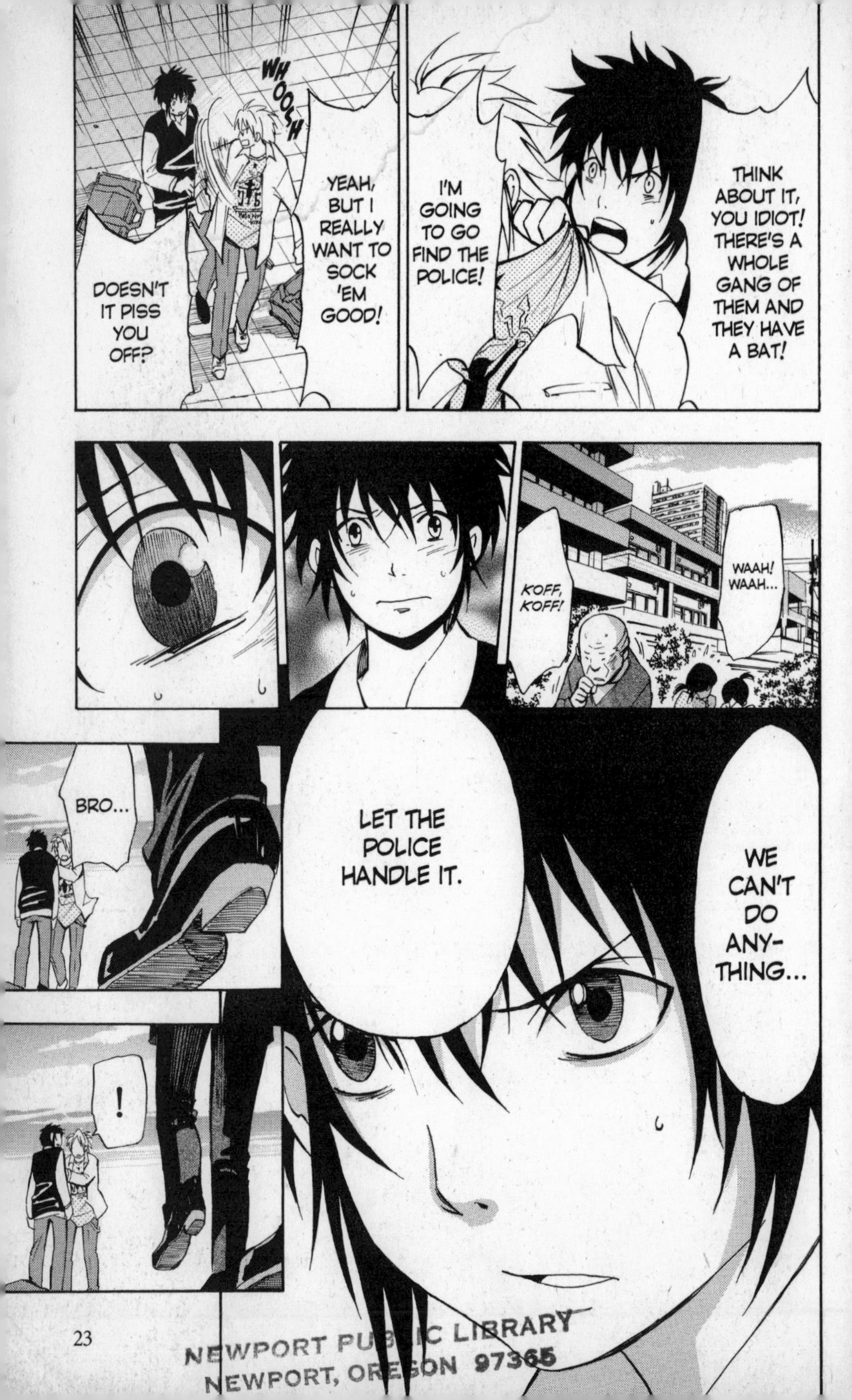
THINK ABOUT IT, YOU IDIOT! THERE'S A WHOLE GANG OF THEM AND THEY HAVE A BAT!
I'M GOING TO GO FIND THE POLICE!
WHOOOSH
YEAH, BUT I REALLY WANT TO SOCK 'EM GOOD!
DOESN'T IT PISS YOU OFF?
WAAH! WAAH...
KOFF, KOFF!
WE CAN'T DO ANY-THING...
LET THE POLICE HANDLE IT.
BRO...
!

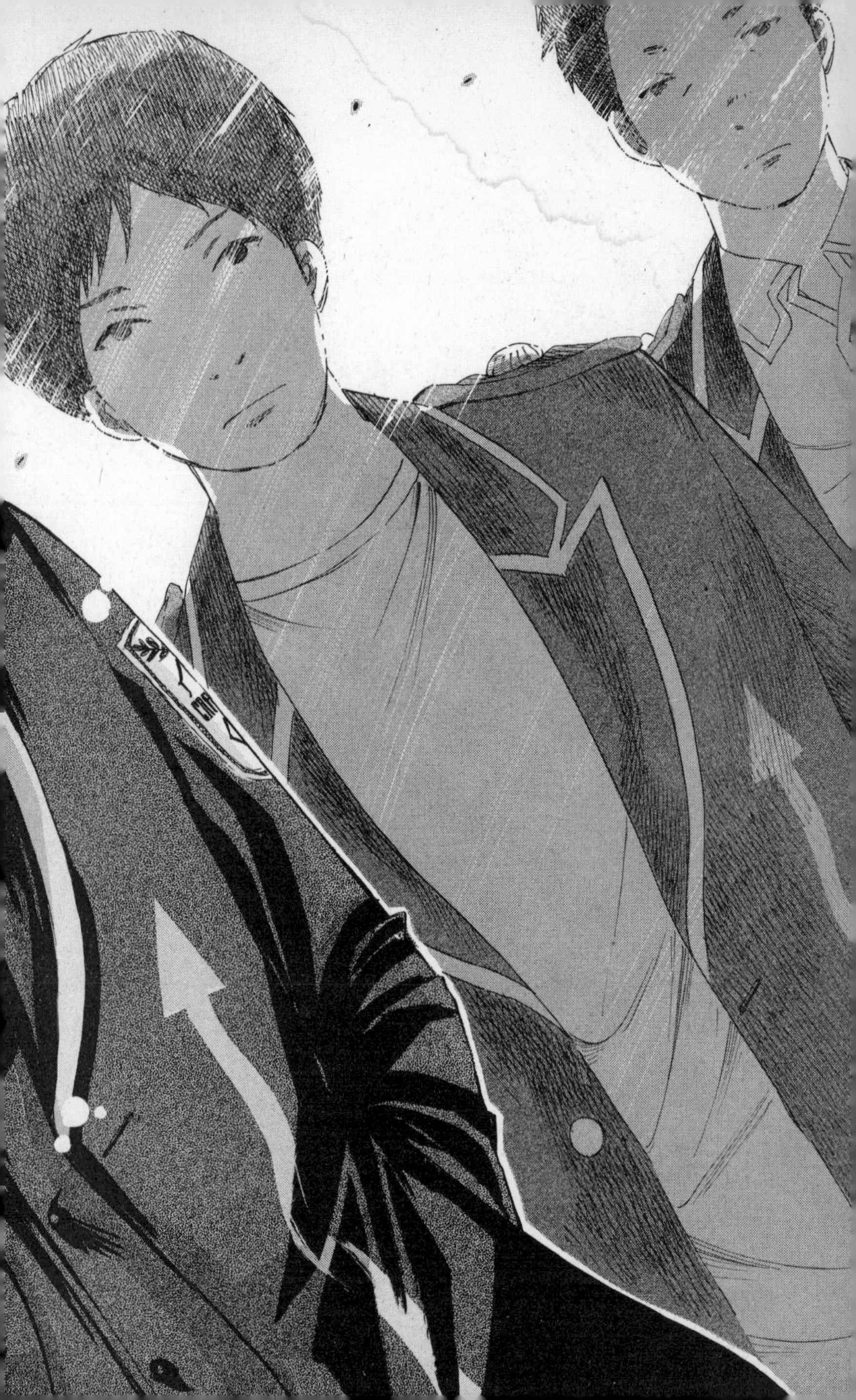

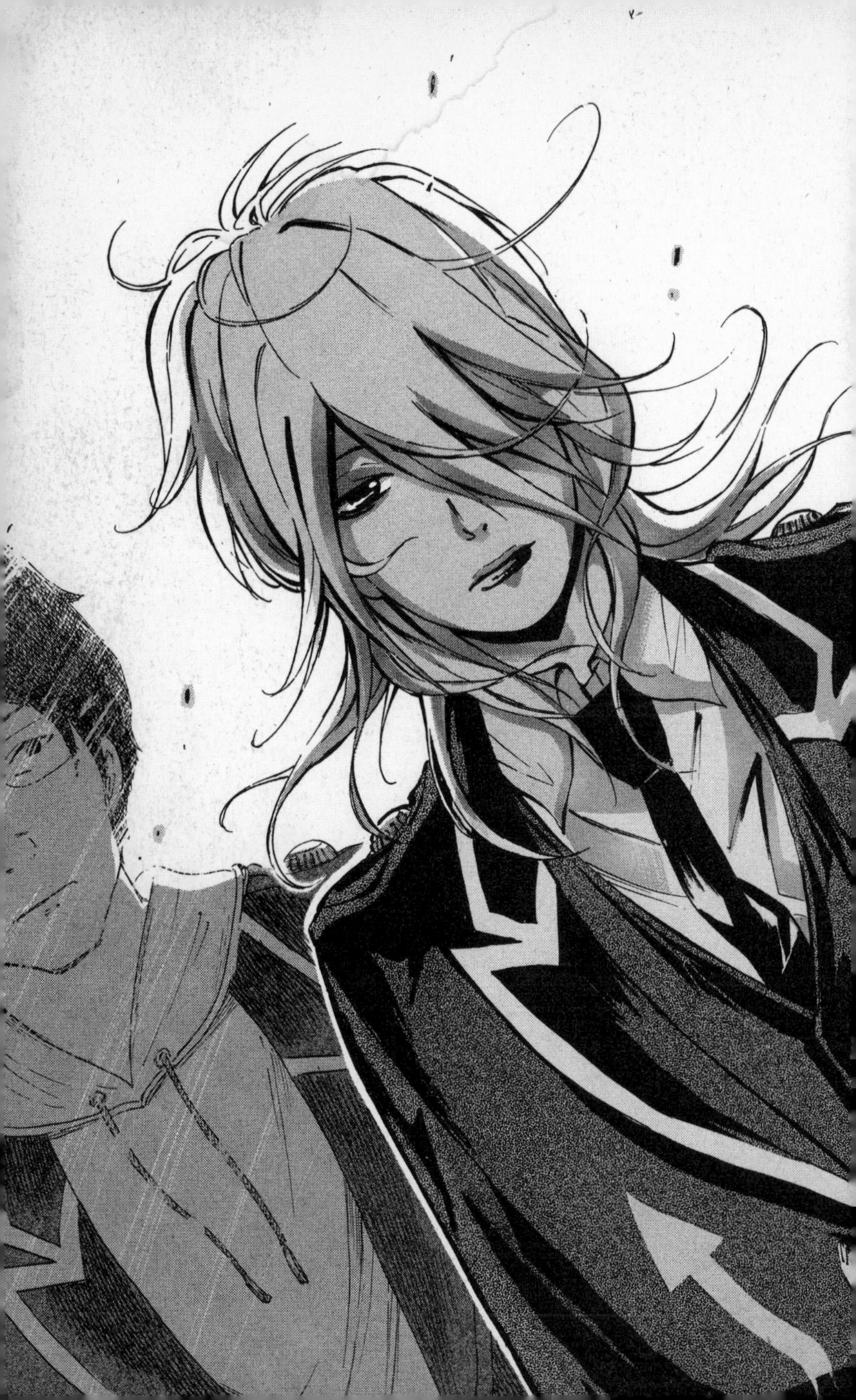

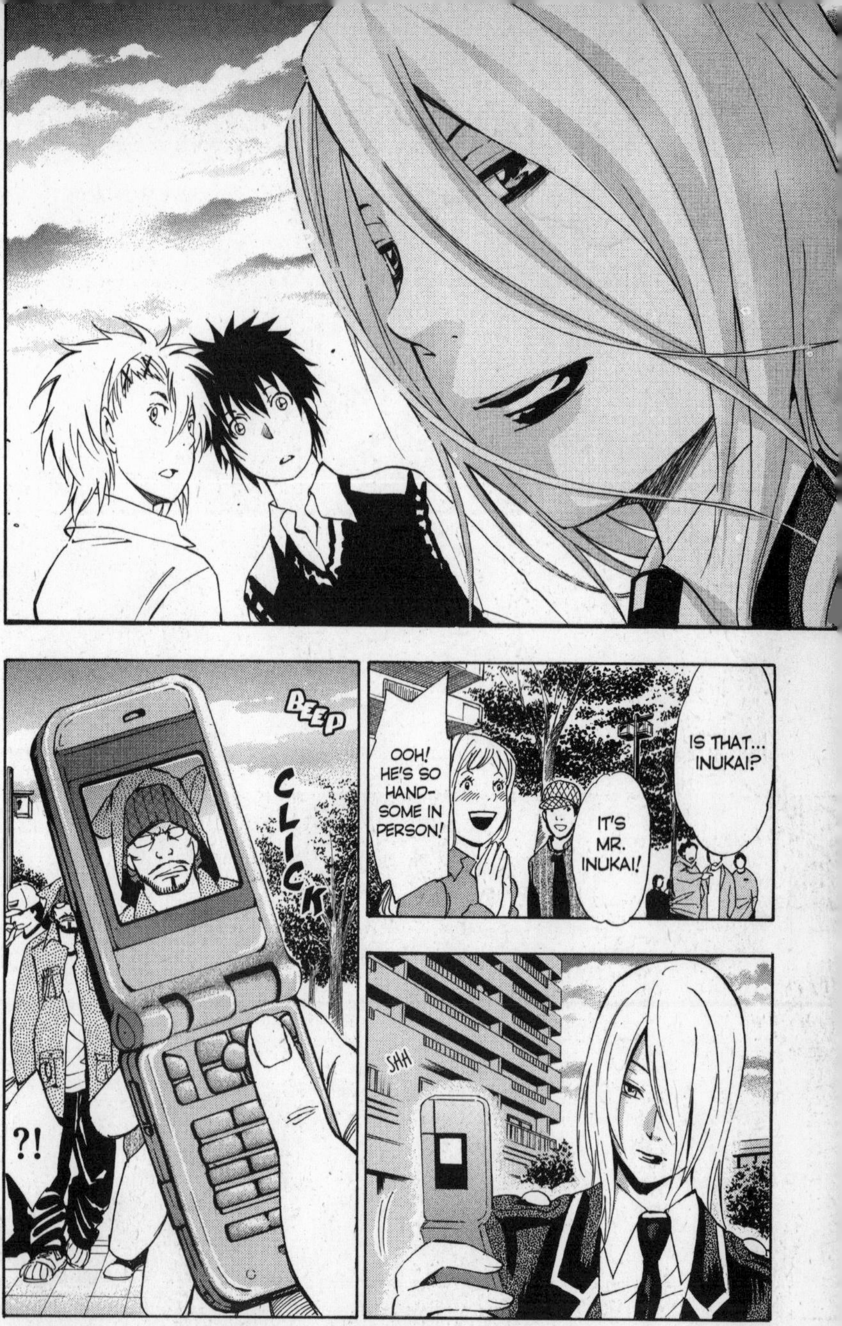
IS THAT... INUKAI?
IT'S MR. INUKAI!
OOH! HE'S SO HANDSOME IN PERSON!
SHH
BEEP
CLICK
?!

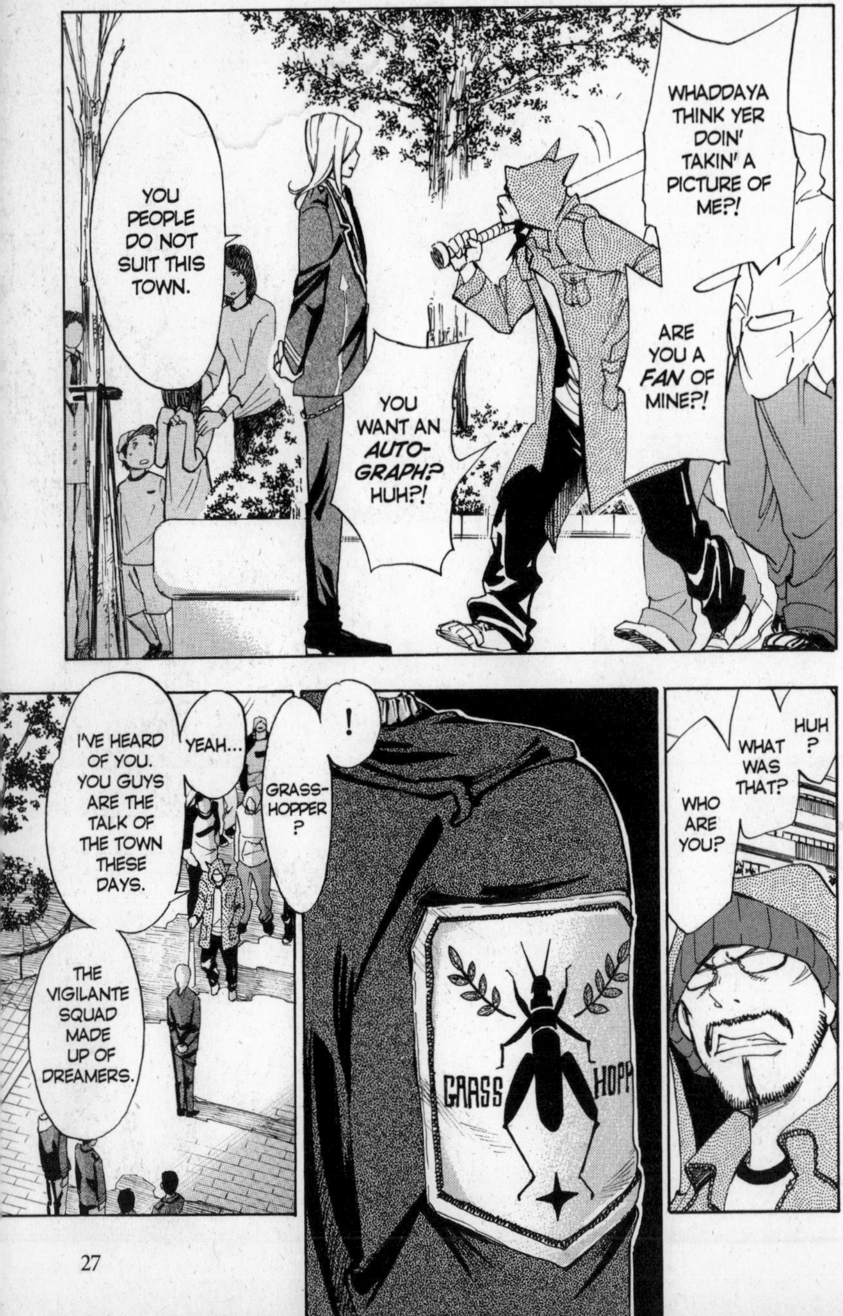
WHADDAYA THINK YER DOIN' TAKIN' A PICTURE OF ME?!
ARE YOU A *FAN* OF MINE?!
YOU WANT AN *AUTOGRAPH?* HUH?!
YOU PEOPLE DO NOT SUIT THIS TOWN.
HUH?
WHAT WAS THAT?
WHO ARE YOU?
!
GRASS
HOPP
GRASSHOPPER?
YEAH...
I'VE HEARD OF YOU. YOU GUYS ARE THE TALK OF THE TOWN THESE DAYS.
THE VIGILANTE SQUAD MADE UP OF DREAMERS.

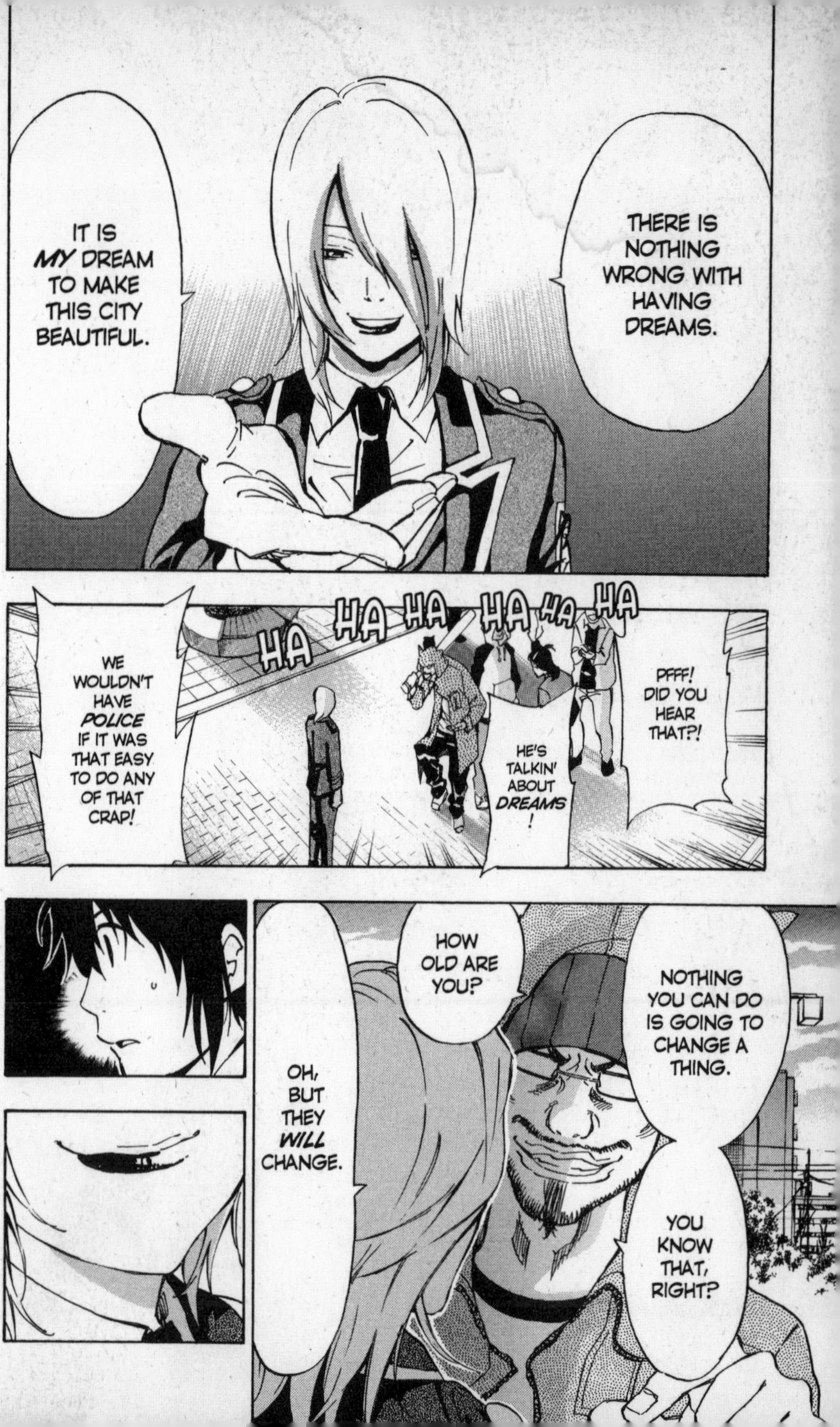
THERE IS NOTHING WRONG WITH HAVING DREAMS.
IT IS MY DREAM TO MAKE THIS CITY BEAUTIFUL.
HA HA HA HA HA HA
PFFF! DID YOU HEAR THAT?!
HE'S TALKIN' ABOUT DREAMS!
WE WOULDN'T HAVE POLICE IF IT WAS THAT EASY TO DO ANY OF THAT CRAP!
NOTHING YOU CAN DO IS GOING TO CHANGE A THING.
HOW OLD ARE YOU?
YOU KNOW THAT, RIGHT?
OH, BUT THEY WILL CHANGE.

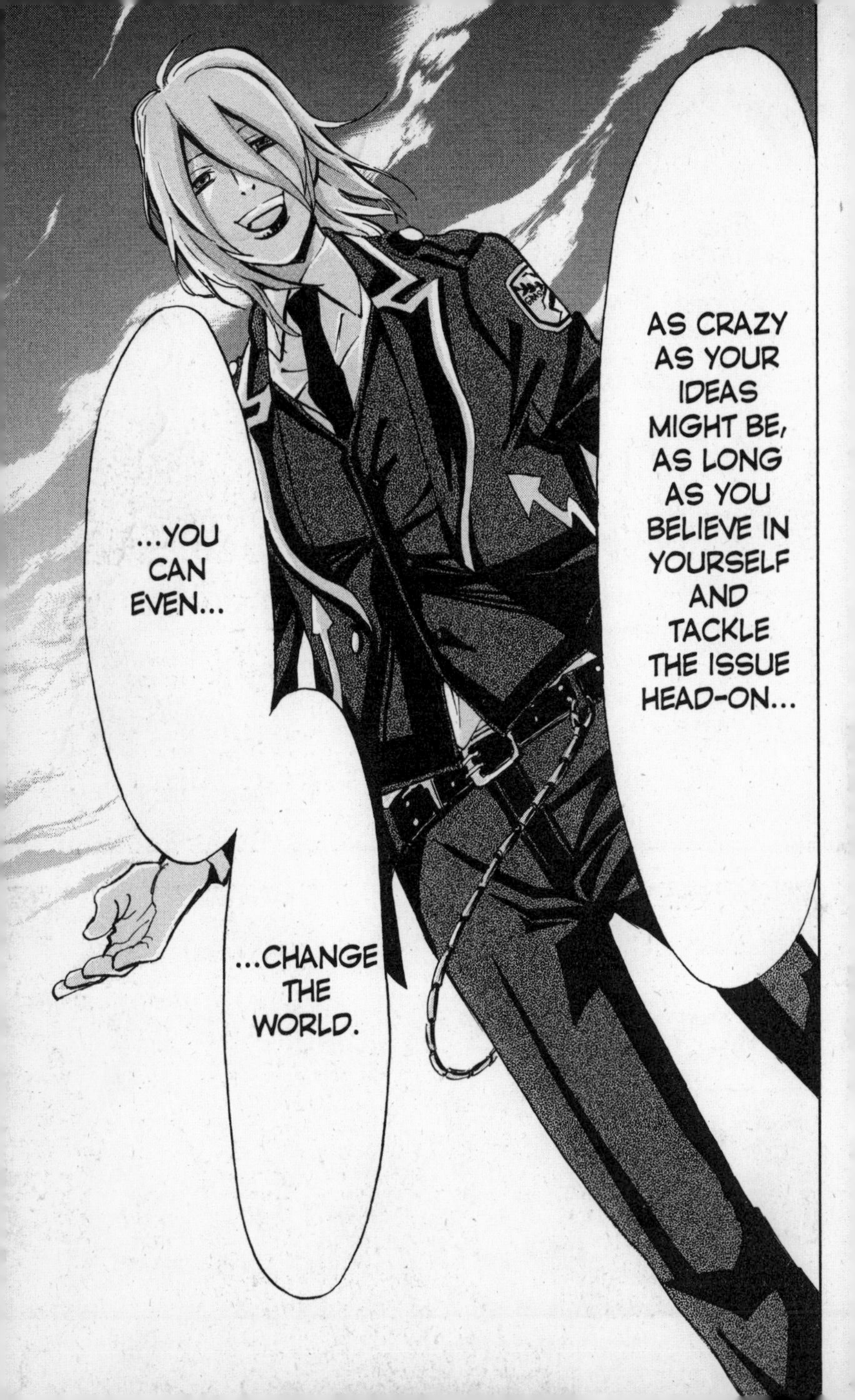
AS CRAZY AS YOUR IDEAS MIGHT BE, AS LONG AS YOU BELIEVE IN YOURSELF AND TACKLE THE ISSUE HEAD-ON...
...YOU CAN EVEN...
...CHANGE THE WORLD.

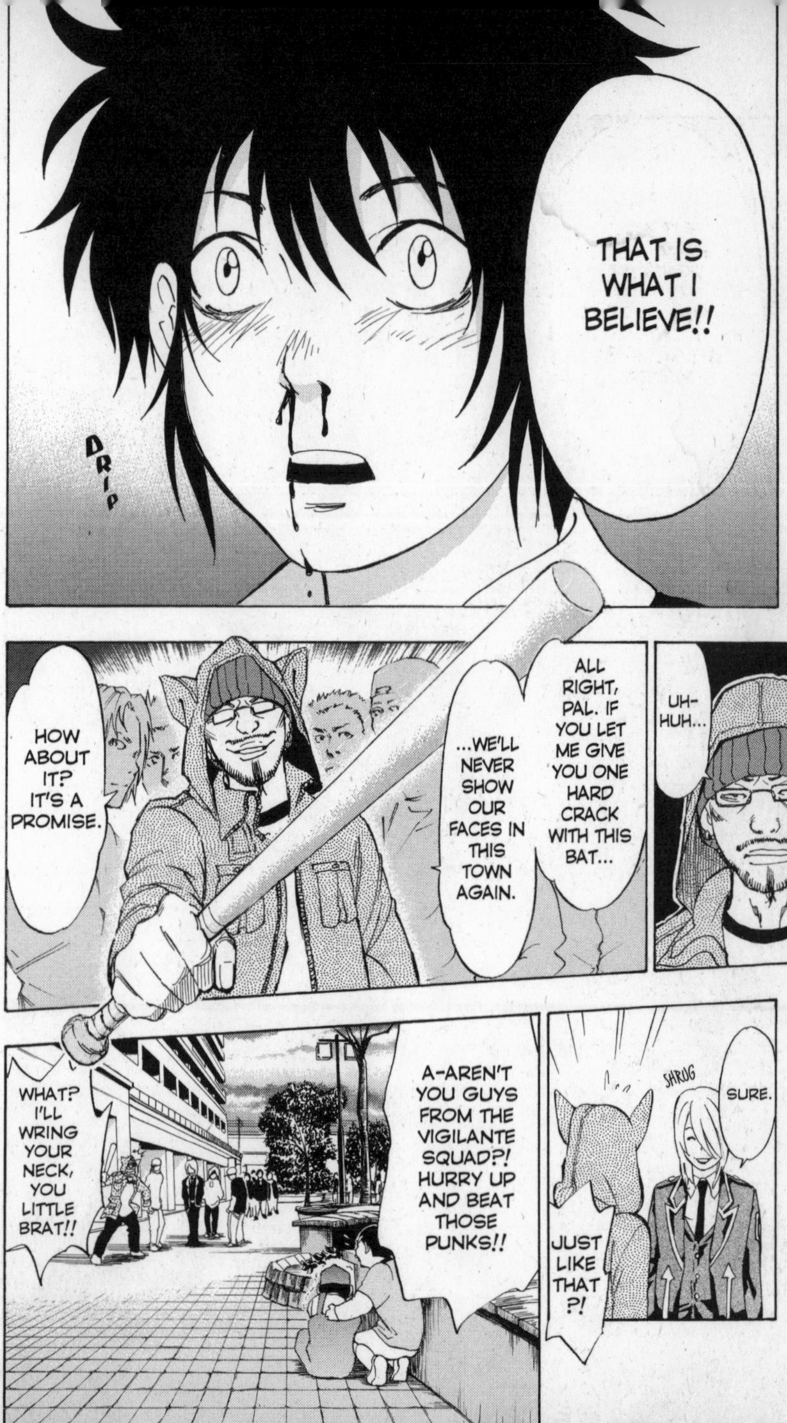
THAT IS WHAT I BELIEVE!!
DRIP
UH-HUH...
ALL RIGHT, PAL. IF YOU LET ME GIVE YOU ONE HARD CRACK WITH THIS BAT...
...WE'LL NEVER SHOW OUR FACES IN THIS TOWN AGAIN.
HOW ABOUT IT? IT'S A PROMISE.
SURE.
SHRUG
JUST LIKE THAT?!
A-AREN'T YOU GUYS FROM THE VIGILANTE SQUAD?! HURRY UP AND BEAT THOSE PUNKS!!
WHAT? I'LL WRING YOUR NECK, YOU LITTLE BRAT!!

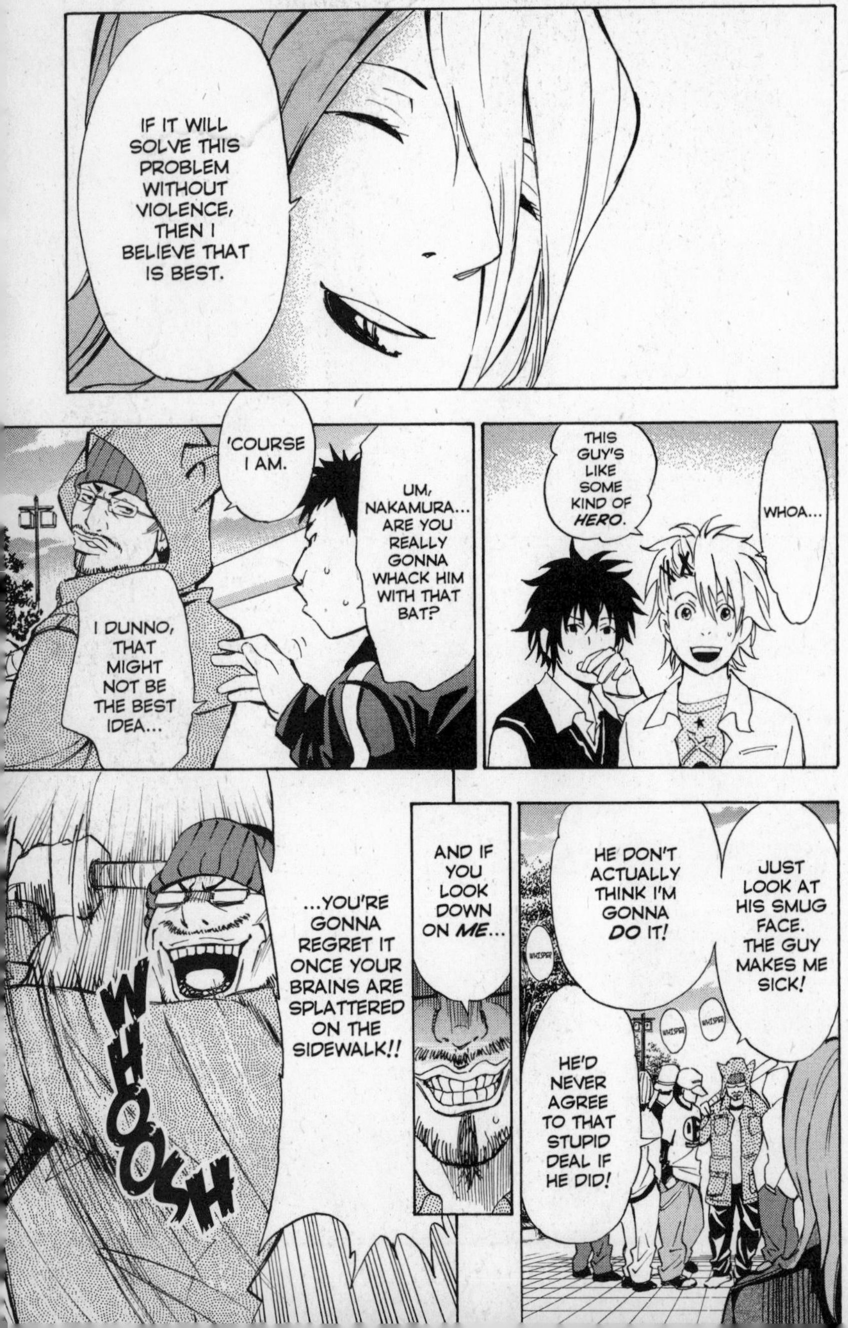
IF IT WILL SOLVE THIS PROBLEM WITHOUT VIOLENCE, THEN I BELIEVE THAT IS BEST.
WHOA...
THIS GUY'S LIKE SOME KIND OF HERO.
UM, NAKAMURA... ARE YOU REALLY GONNA WHACK HIM WITH THAT BAT?
'COURSE I AM.
I DUNNO, THAT MIGHT NOT BE THE BEST IDEA...
JUST LOOK AT HIS SMUG FACE. THE GUY MAKES ME SICK!
HE DON'T ACTUALLY THINK I'M GONNA DO IT!
WHISPER
WHISPER
WHISPER
HE'D NEVER AGREE TO THAT STUPID DEAL IF HE DID!
AND IF YOU LOOK DOWN ON ME...
...YOU'RE GONNA REGRET IT ONCE YOUR BRAINS ARE SPLATTERED ON THE SIDEWALK!!
WHOOSH

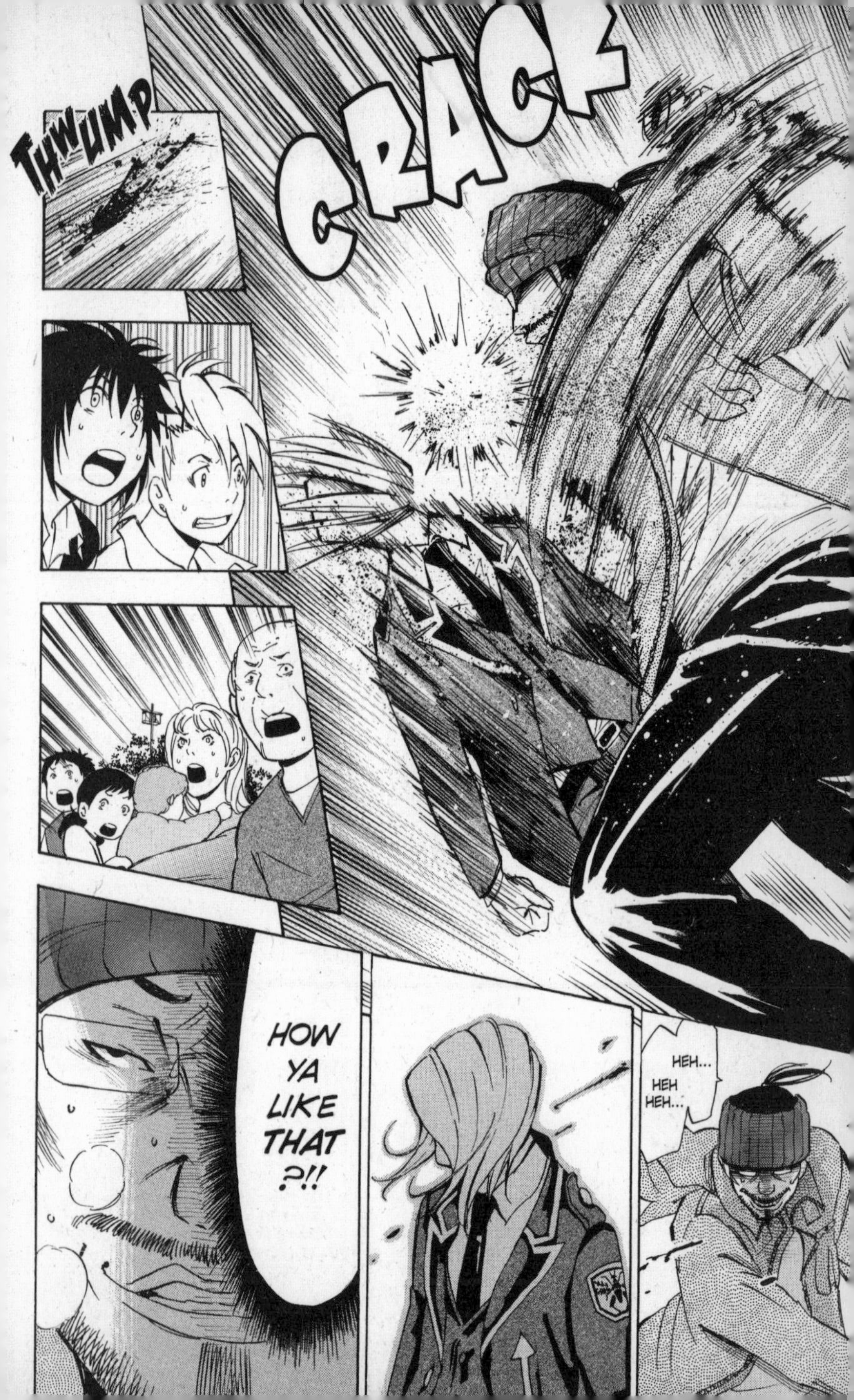
CRACK
THWUMP
HEH... HEH HEH...
HOW YA LIKE THAT?!!

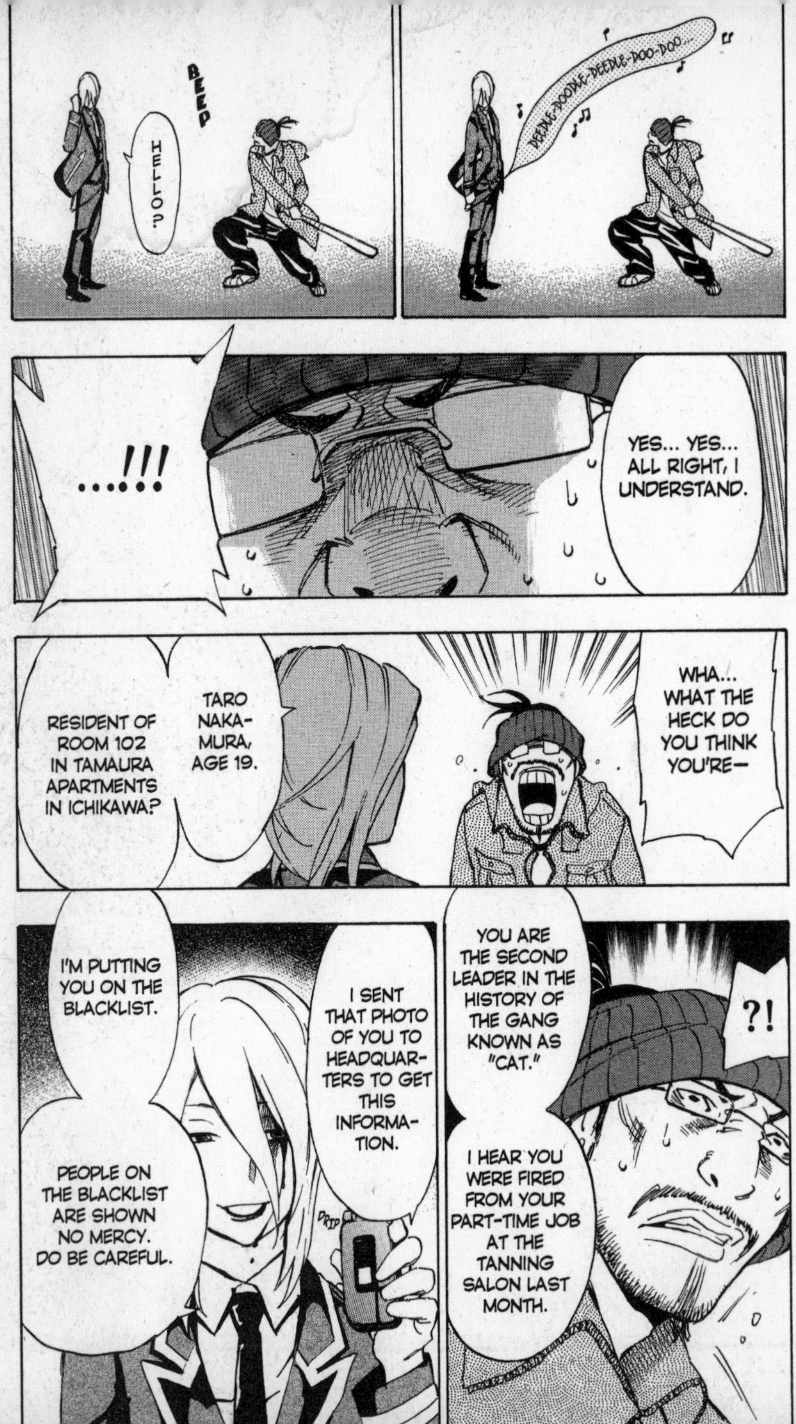
DEEDLE-DOODLE-DEEDLE-DOO-DOO...
BEEP
HELLO?
YES... YES... ALL RIGHT, I UNDERSTAND.
...!!!
WHA... WHAT THE HECK DO YOU THINK YOU'RE—
TARO NAKAMURA, AGE 19.
RESIDENT OF ROOM 102 IN TAMAURA APARTMENTS IN ICHIKAWA?
?!
YOU ARE THE SECOND LEADER IN THE HISTORY OF THE GANG KNOWN AS "CAT."
I HEAR YOU WERE FIRED FROM YOUR PART-TIME JOB AT THE TANNING SALON LAST MONTH.
I SENT THAT PHOTO OF YOU TO HEADQUARTERS TO GET THIS INFORMATION.
DRIP
I'M PUTTING YOU ON THE BLACKLIST.
PEOPLE ON THE BLACKLIST ARE SHOWN NO MERCY. DO BE CAREFUL.

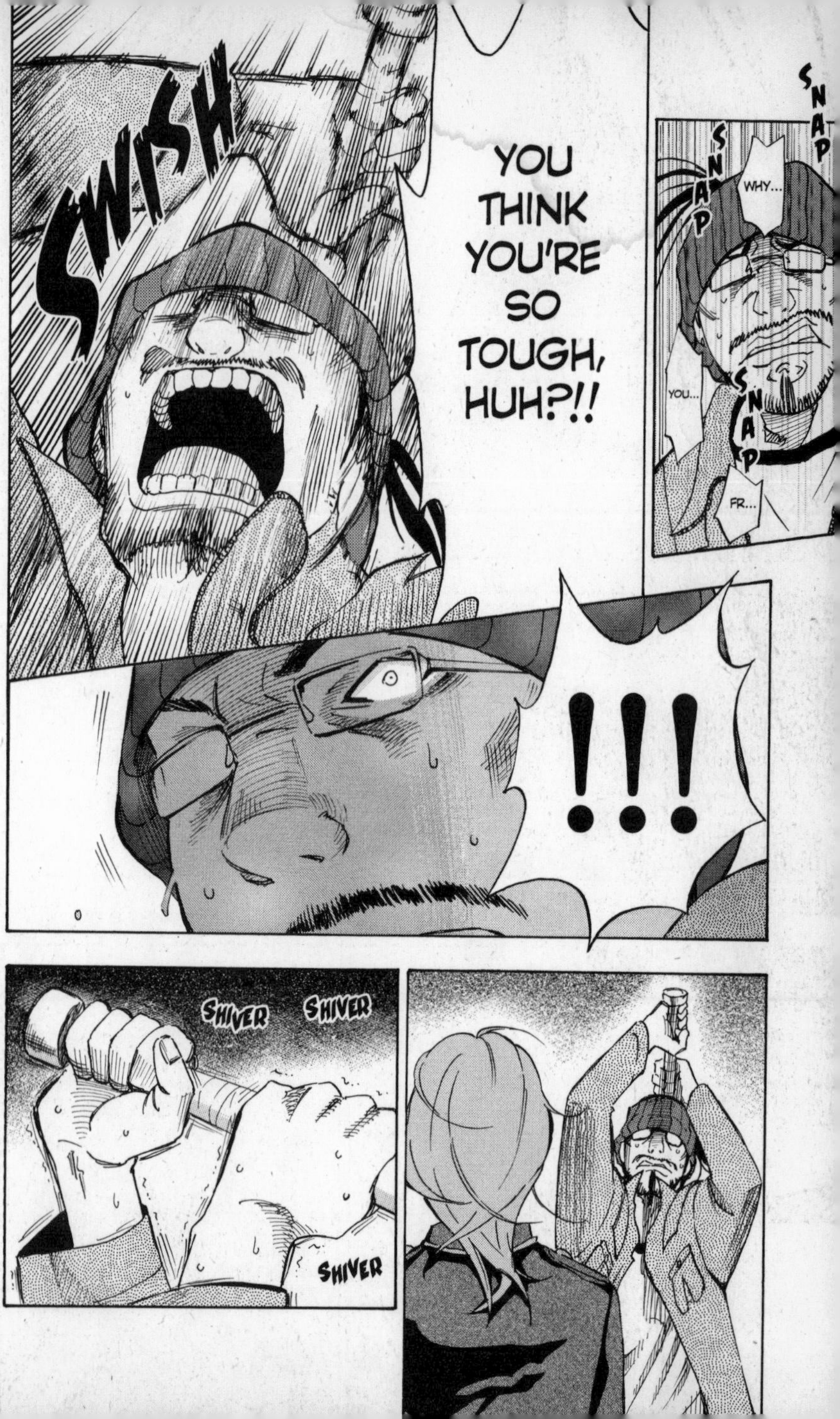
SNAP
SNAP
WHY...
YOU...
SNAP
FR...
SWISH
YOU THINK YOU'RE SO TOUGH, HUH?!!
!!!
SHIVER
SHIVER
SHIVER

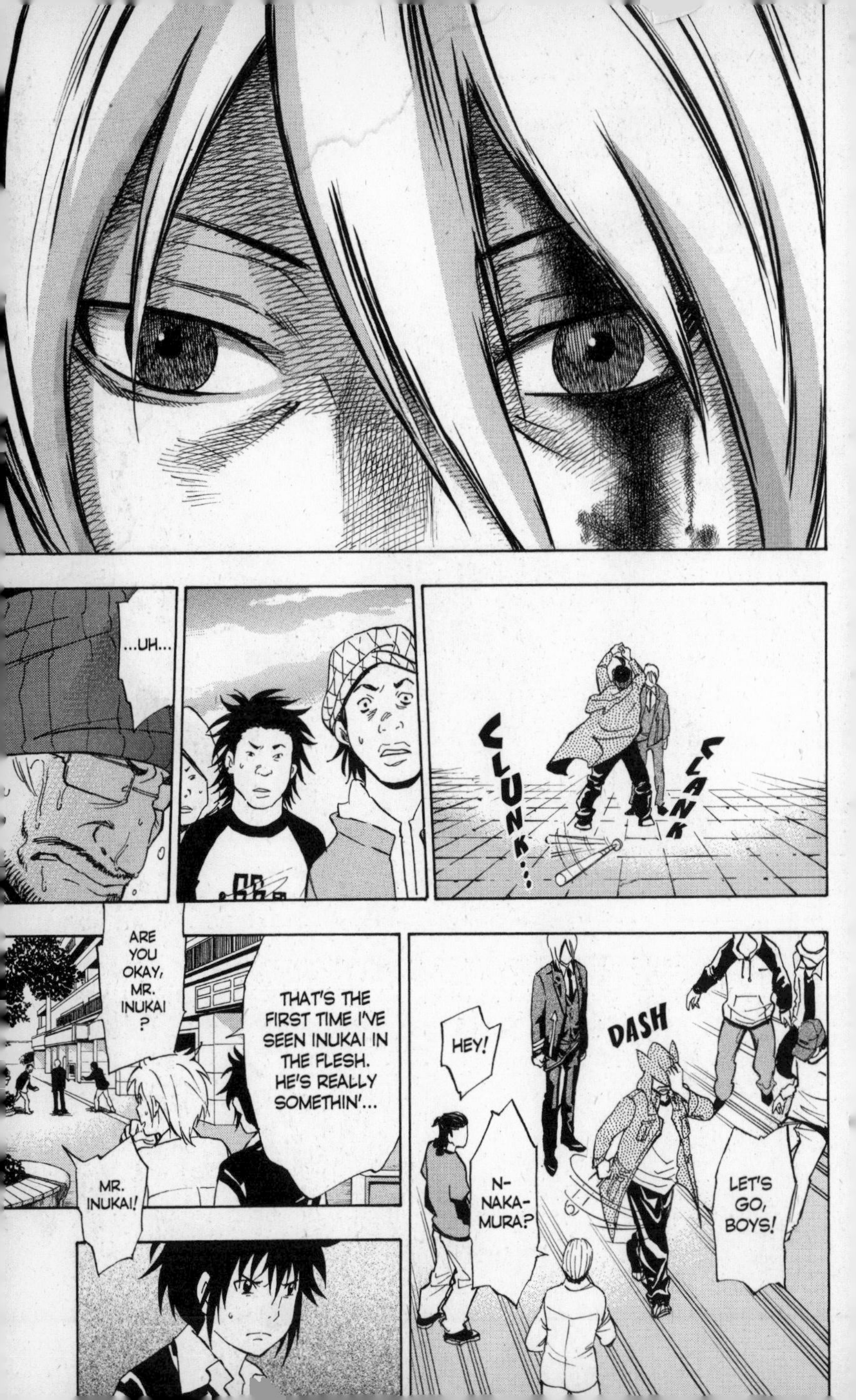
CLANK
CLUNK...
...UH...
DASH
HEY!
LET'S GO, BOYS!
N-NAKAMURA?
ARE YOU OKAY, MR. INUKAI?
THAT'S THE FIRST TIME I'VE SEEN INUKAI IN THE FLESH. HE'S REALLY SOMETHIN'...
MR. INUKAI!

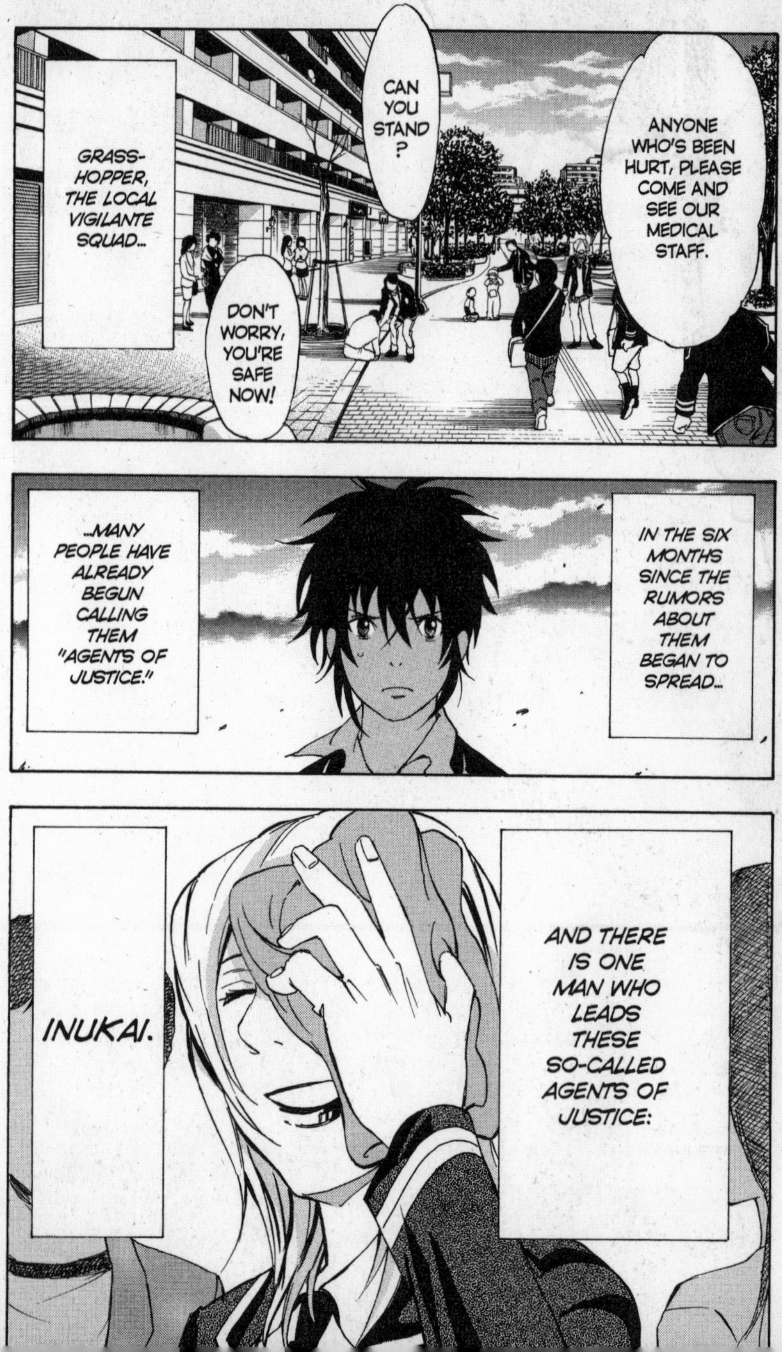
ANYONE WHO'S BEEN HURT, PLEASE COME AND SEE OUR MEDICAL STAFF.
CAN YOU STAND?
GRASS-HOPPER, THE LOCAL VIGILANTE SQUAD...
DON'T WORRY, YOU'RE SAFE NOW!
IN THE SIX MONTHS SINCE THE RUMORS ABOUT THEM BEGAN TO SPREAD...
...MANY PEOPLE HAVE ALREADY BEGUN CALLING THEM "AGENTS OF JUSTICE."
AND THERE IS ONE MAN WHO LEADS THESE SO-CALLED AGENTS OF JUSTICE:
INUKAI.

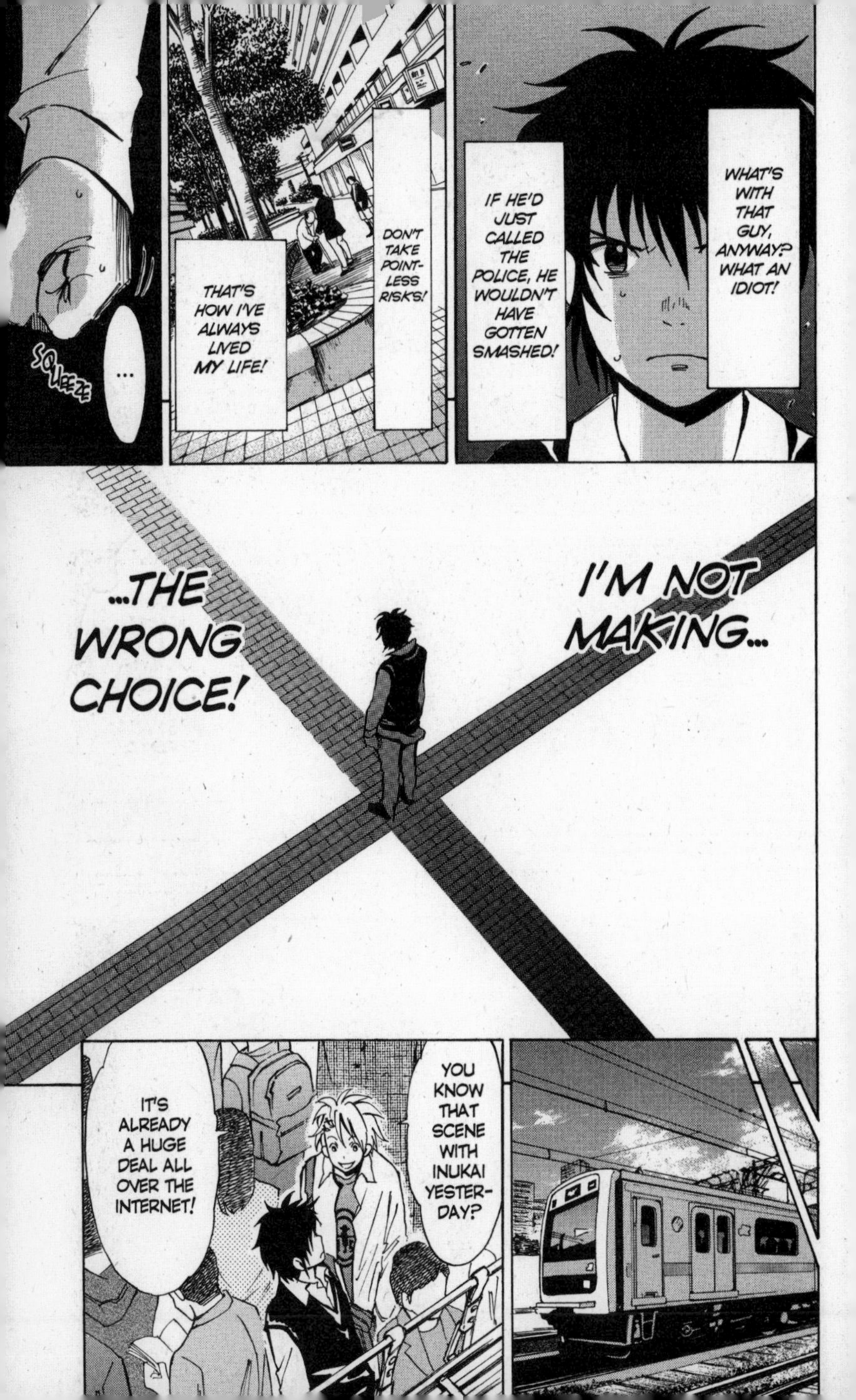
WHAT'S WITH THAT GUY, ANYWAY? WHAT AN IDIOT!
IF HE'D JUST CALLED THE POLICE, HE WOULDN'T HAVE GOTTEN SMASHED!
DON'T TAKE POINT-LESS RISKS!
THAT'S HOW I'VE ALWAYS LIVED MY LIFE!
SQUEEZE
...
I'M NOT MAKING...
...THE WRONG CHOICE!
YOU KNOW THAT SCENE WITH INUKAI YESTER-DAY?
IT'S ALREADY A HUGE DEAL ALL OVER THE INTERNET!

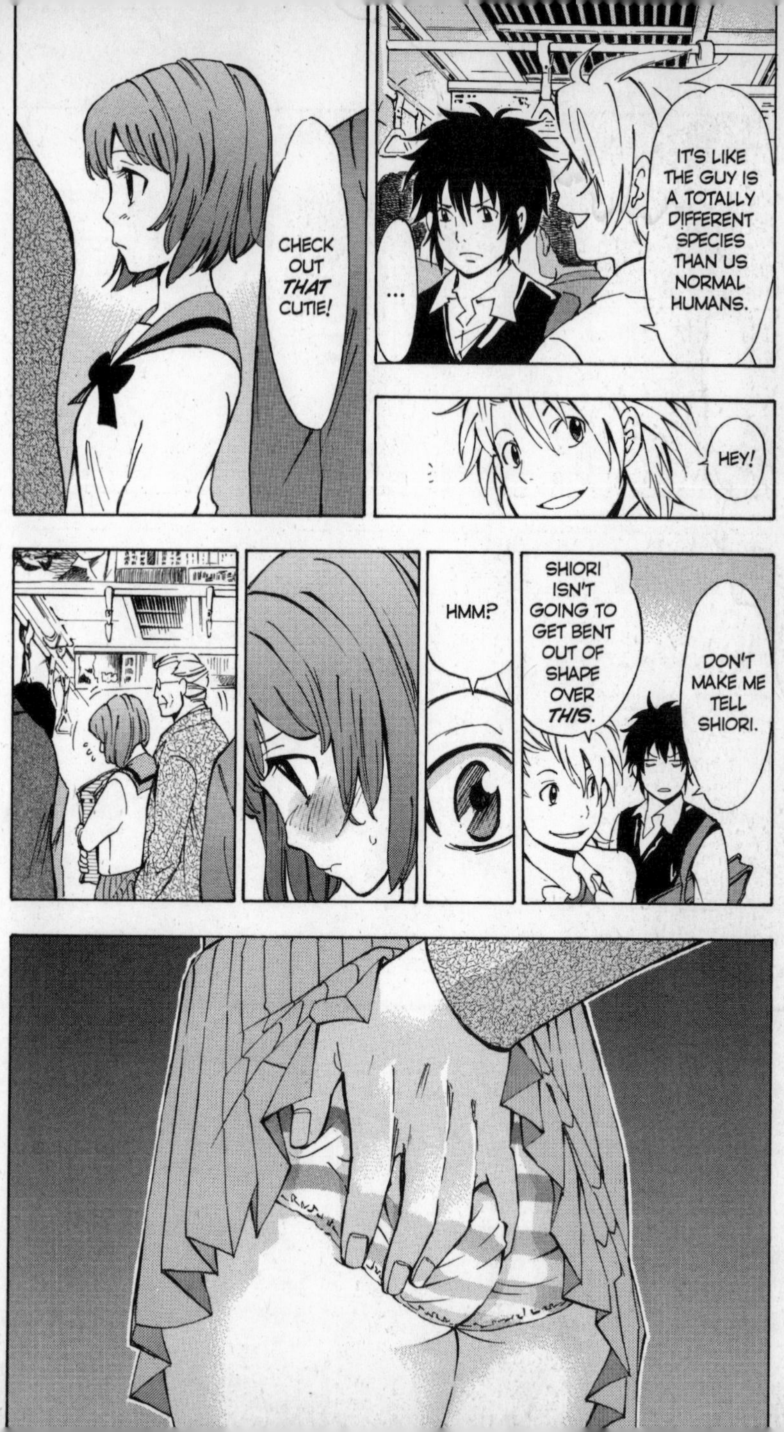
IT'S LIKE THE GUY IS A TOTALLY DIFFERENT SPECIES THAN US NORMAL HUMANS.
...
HEY!
CHECK OUT *THAT* CUTIE!
DON'T MAKE ME TELL SHIORI.
SHIORI ISN'T GOING TO GET BENT OUT OF SHAPE OVER *THIS*.
HMM?

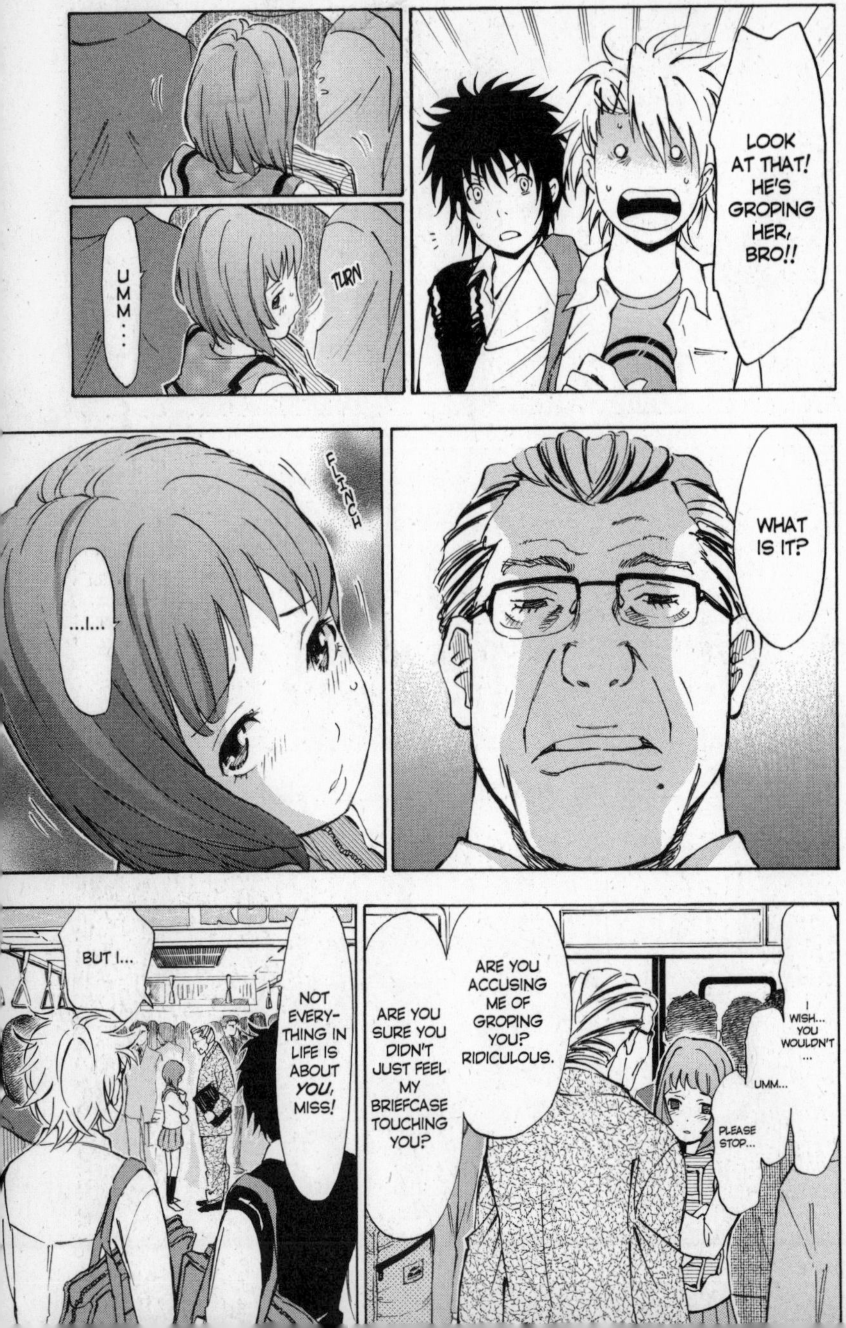
LOOK AT THAT! HE'S GROPING HER, BRO!!
UMM...
TURN
WHAT IS IT?
FLINCH
...I...
I WISH... YOU WOULDN'T ...
UMM...
PLEASE STOP...
ARE YOU ACCUSING ME OF GROPING YOU? RIDICULOUS.
ARE YOU SURE YOU DIDN'T JUST FEEL MY BRIEFCASE TOUCHING YOU?
NOT EVERYTHING IN LIFE IS ABOUT *YOU*, MISS!
BUT I...

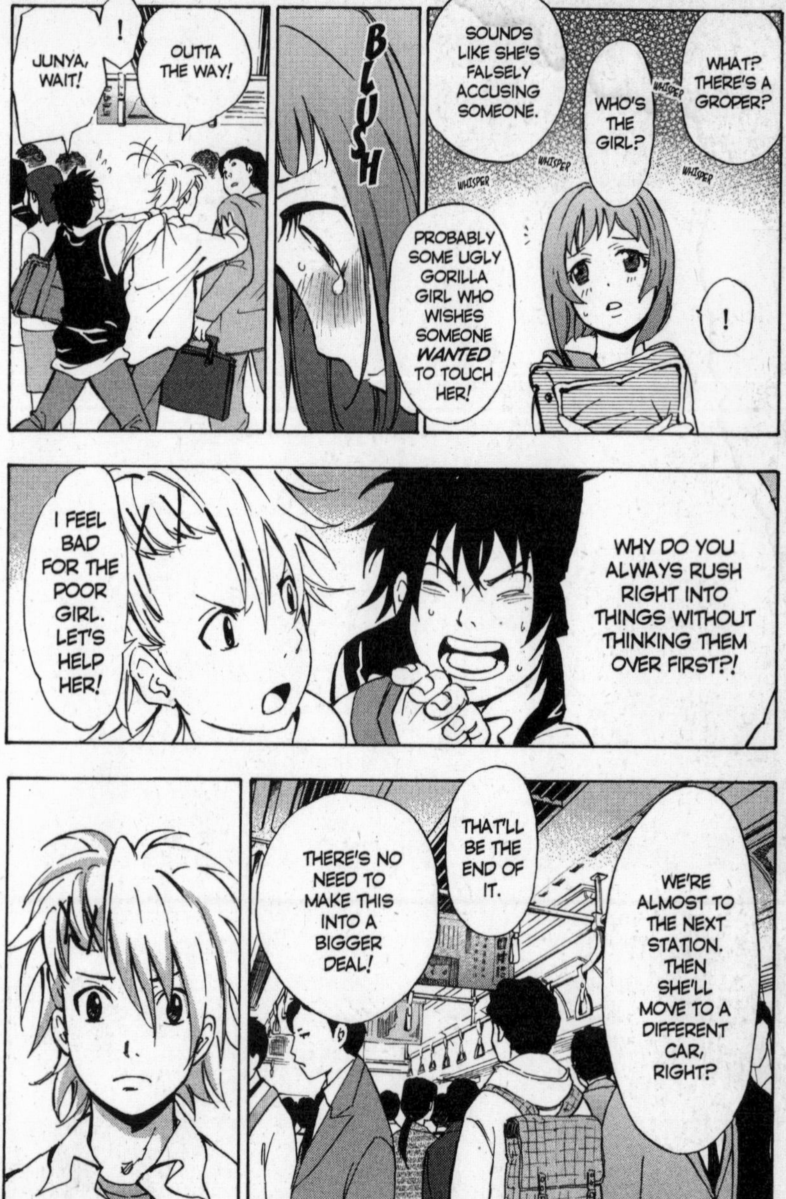
WHAT? THERE'S A GROPER?
WHISPER
WHO'S THE GIRL?
WHISPER
SOUNDS LIKE SHE'S FALSELY ACCUSING SOMEONE.
WHISPER
WHISPER
PROBABLY SOME UGLY GORILLA GIRL WHO WISHES SOMEONE *WANTED* TO TOUCH HER!
!
BLUSH
!
OUTTA THE WAY!
JUNYA, WAIT!
WHY DO YOU ALWAYS RUSH RIGHT INTO THINGS WITHOUT THINKING THEM OVER FIRST?!
I FEEL BAD FOR THE POOR GIRL. LET'S HELP HER!
WE'RE ALMOST TO THE NEXT STATION. THEN SHE'LL MOVE TO A DIFFERENT CAR, RIGHT?
THAT'LL BE THE END OF IT.
THERE'S NO NEED TO MAKE THIS INTO A BIGGER DEAL!

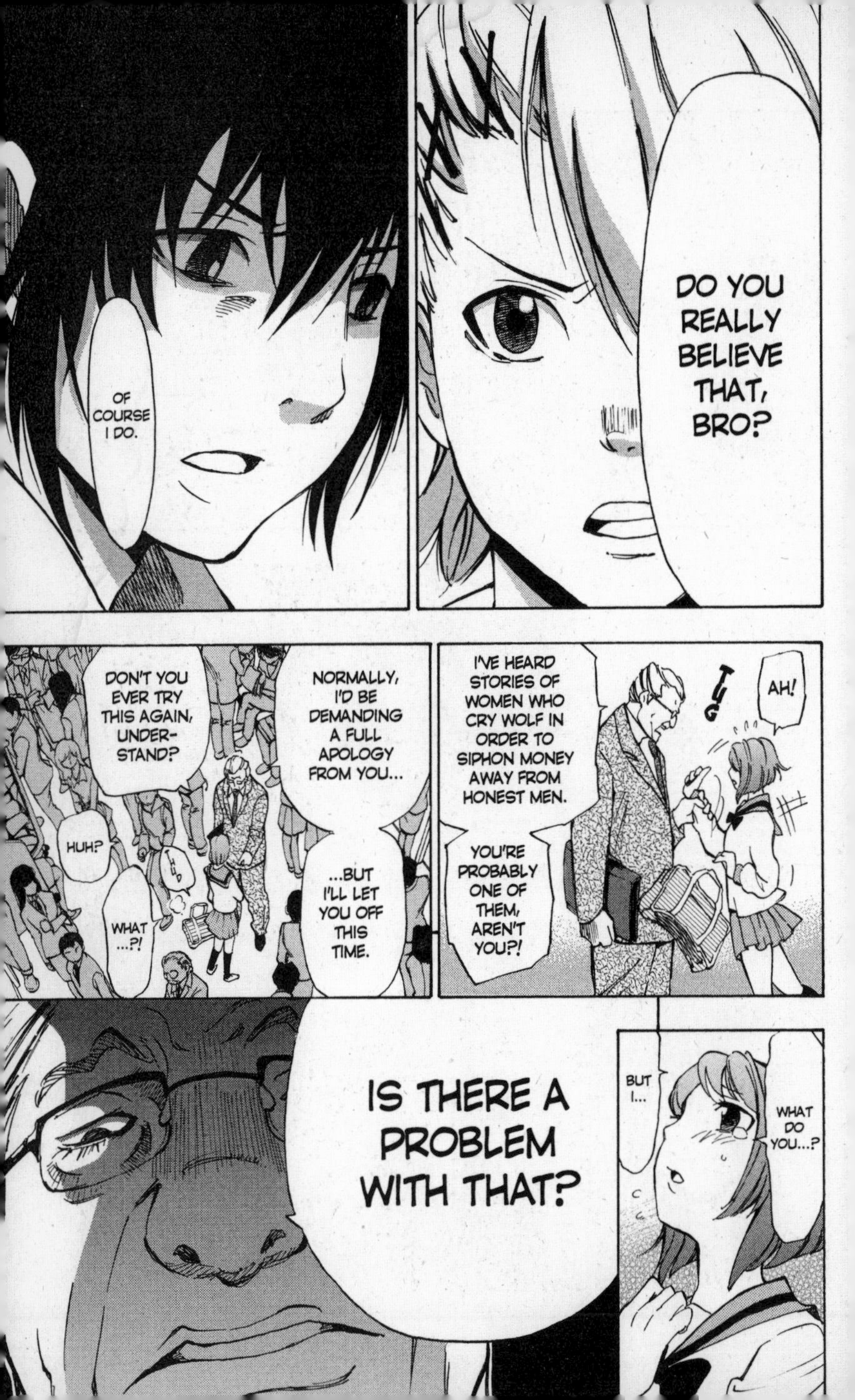
DO YOU REALLY BELIEVE THAT, BRO?
OF COURSE I DO.
AH!
TUG
I'VE HEARD STORIES OF WOMEN WHO CRY WOLF IN ORDER TO SIPHON MONEY AWAY FROM HONEST MEN.
YOU'RE PROBABLY ONE OF THEM, AREN'T YOU?!
NORMALLY, I'D BE DEMANDING A FULL APOLOGY FROM YOU...
...BUT I'LL LET YOU OFF THIS TIME.
DON'T YOU EVER TRY THIS AGAIN, UNDER-STAND?
HUH?
THUD
WHAT ...?!
WHAT DO YOU...?
BUT I...
IS THERE A PROBLEM WITH THAT?

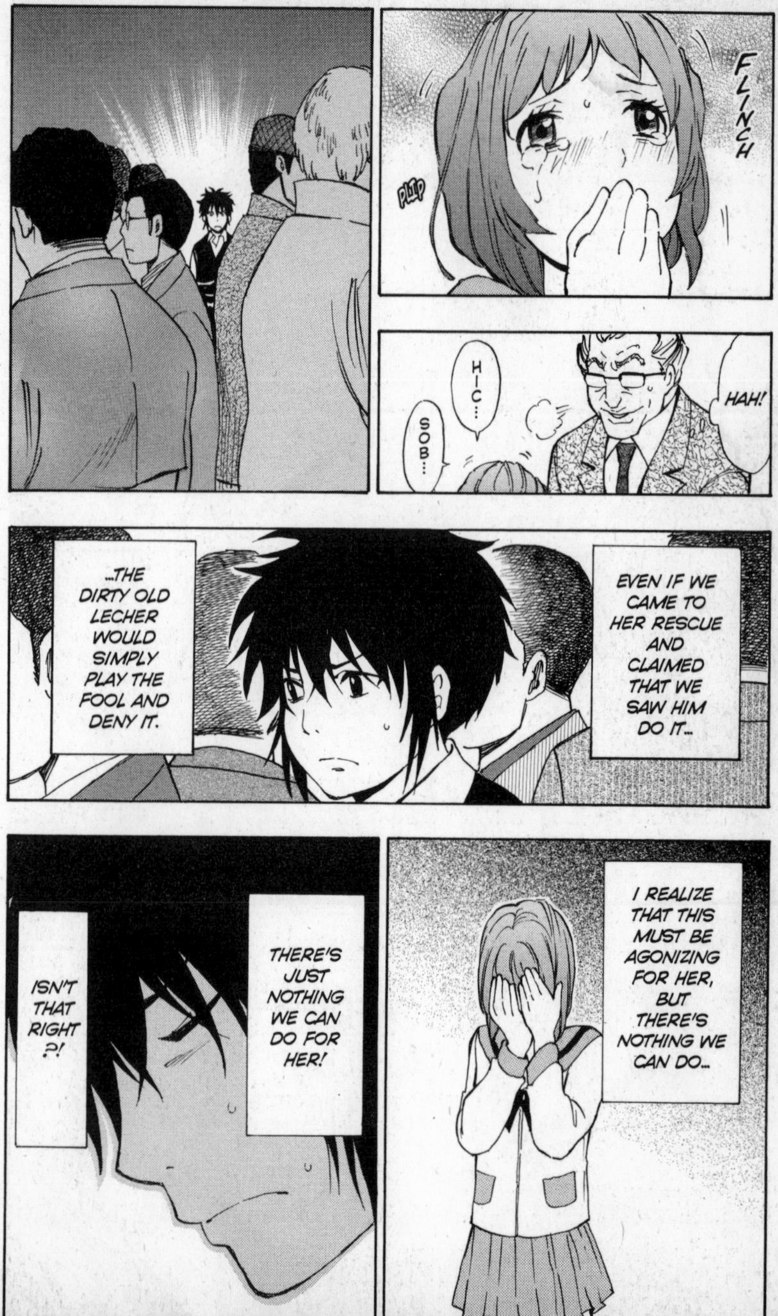
FLINCH
PLIP
HAH!
HIC...
SOB...
EVEN IF WE CAME TO HER RESCUE AND CLAIMED THAT WE SAW HIM DO IT...
...THE DIRTY OLD LECHER WOULD SIMPLY PLAY THE FOOL AND DENY IT.
I REALIZE THAT THIS MUST BE AGONIZING FOR HER, BUT THERE'S NOTHING WE CAN DO...
THERE'S JUST NOTHING WE CAN DO FOR HER!
ISN'T THAT RIGHT?!

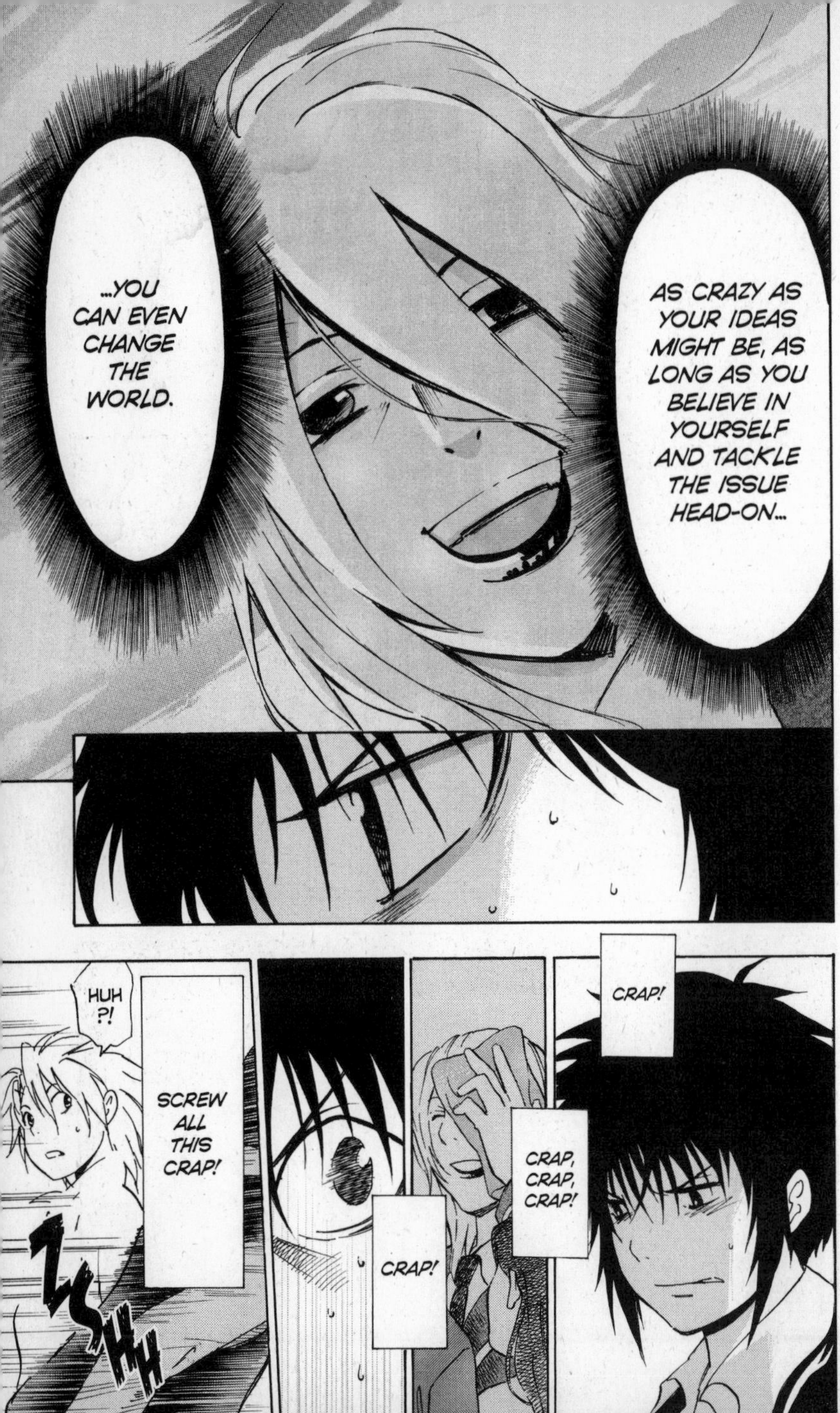
AS CRAZY AS YOUR IDEAS MIGHT BE, AS LONG AS YOU BELIEVE IN YOURSELF AND TACKLE THE ISSUE HEAD-ON...
...YOU CAN EVEN CHANGE THE WORLD.
CRAP!
CRAP, CRAP, CRAP!
CRAP!
SCREW ALL THIS CRAP!
HUH ?!
ZSHH

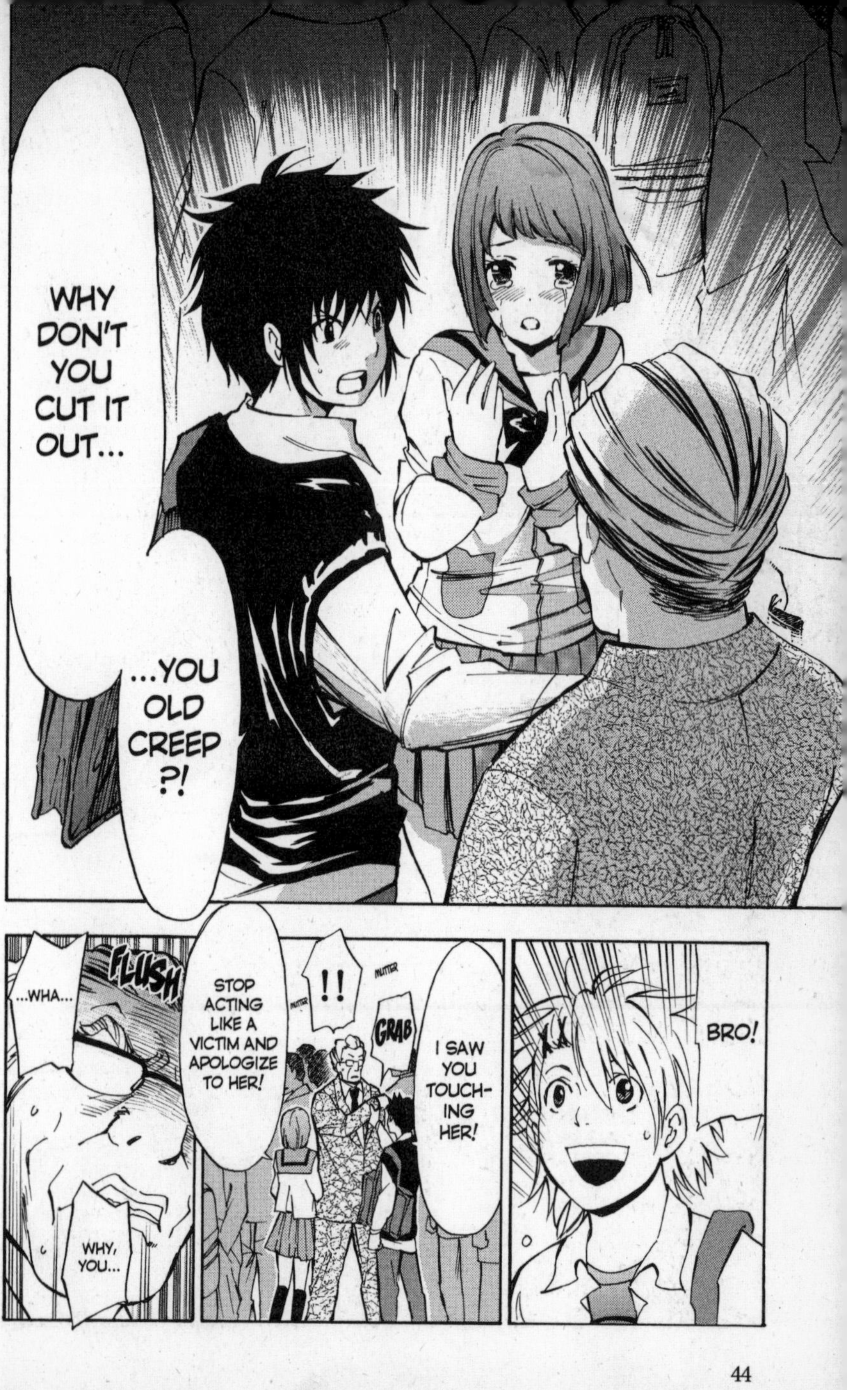
WHY DON'T YOU CUT IT OUT...
...YOU OLD CREEP?!
BRO!
I SAW YOU TOUCHING HER!
GRAB
MUTTER
!!
MUTTER
STOP ACTING LIKE A VICTIM AND APOLOGIZE TO HER!
FLUSH
...WHA...
WHY, YOU...

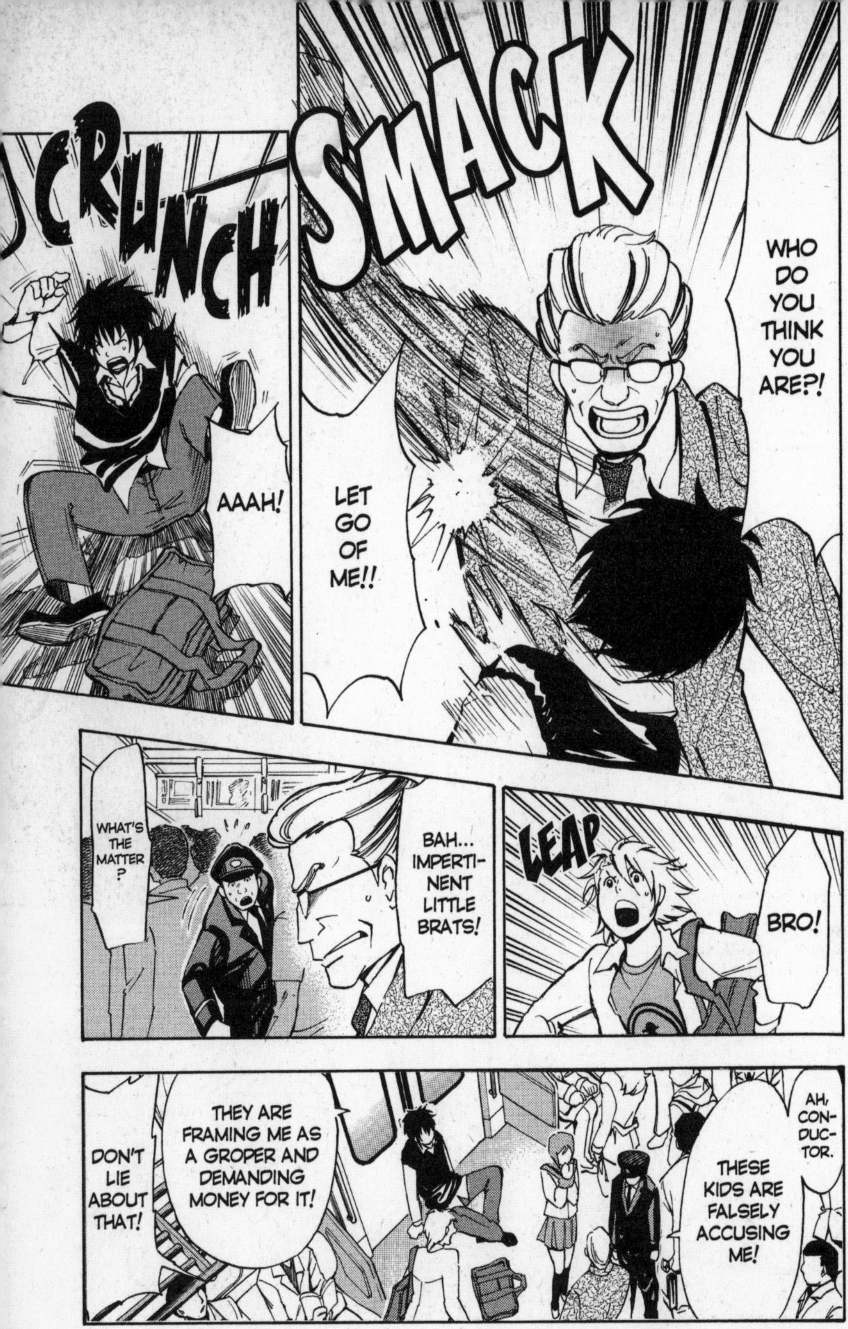
WHO DO YOU THINK YOU ARE?!
SMACK
LET GO OF ME!!
CRUNCH
AAAH!
BRO!
LEAP
BAH... IMPERTI-NENT LITTLE BRATS!
WHAT'S THE MATTER?
AH, CON-DUC-TOR.
THESE KIDS ARE FALSELY ACCUSING ME!
THEY ARE FRAMING ME AS A GROPER AND DEMANDING MONEY FOR IT!
DON'T LIE ABOUT THAT!

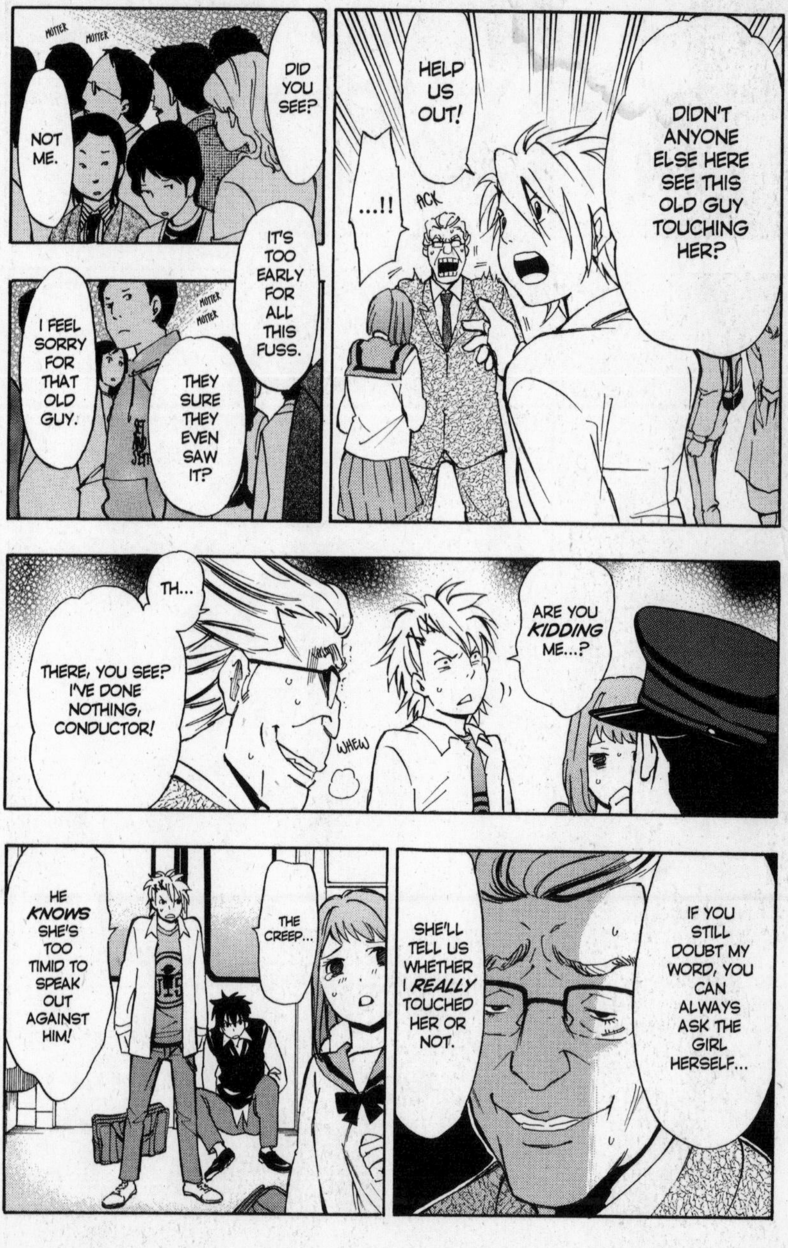
DIDN'T ANYONE ELSE HERE SEE THIS OLD GUY TOUCHING HER?
HELP US OUT!
ACK
...!!
MUTTER MUTTER
DID YOU SEE?
NOT ME.
IT'S TOO EARLY FOR ALL THIS FUSS.
MUTTER MUTTER
THEY SURE THEY EVEN SAW IT?
I FEEL SORRY FOR THAT OLD GUY.
ARE YOU *KIDDING* ME...?
TH...
THERE, YOU SEE? I'VE DONE NOTHING, CONDUCTOR!
WHEW
IF YOU STILL DOUBT MY WORD, YOU CAN ALWAYS ASK THE GIRL HERSELF...
SHE'LL TELL US WHETHER I *REALLY* TOUCHED HER OR NOT.
THE CREEP...
HE *KNOWS* SHE'S TOO TIMID TO SPEAK OUT AGAINST HIM!

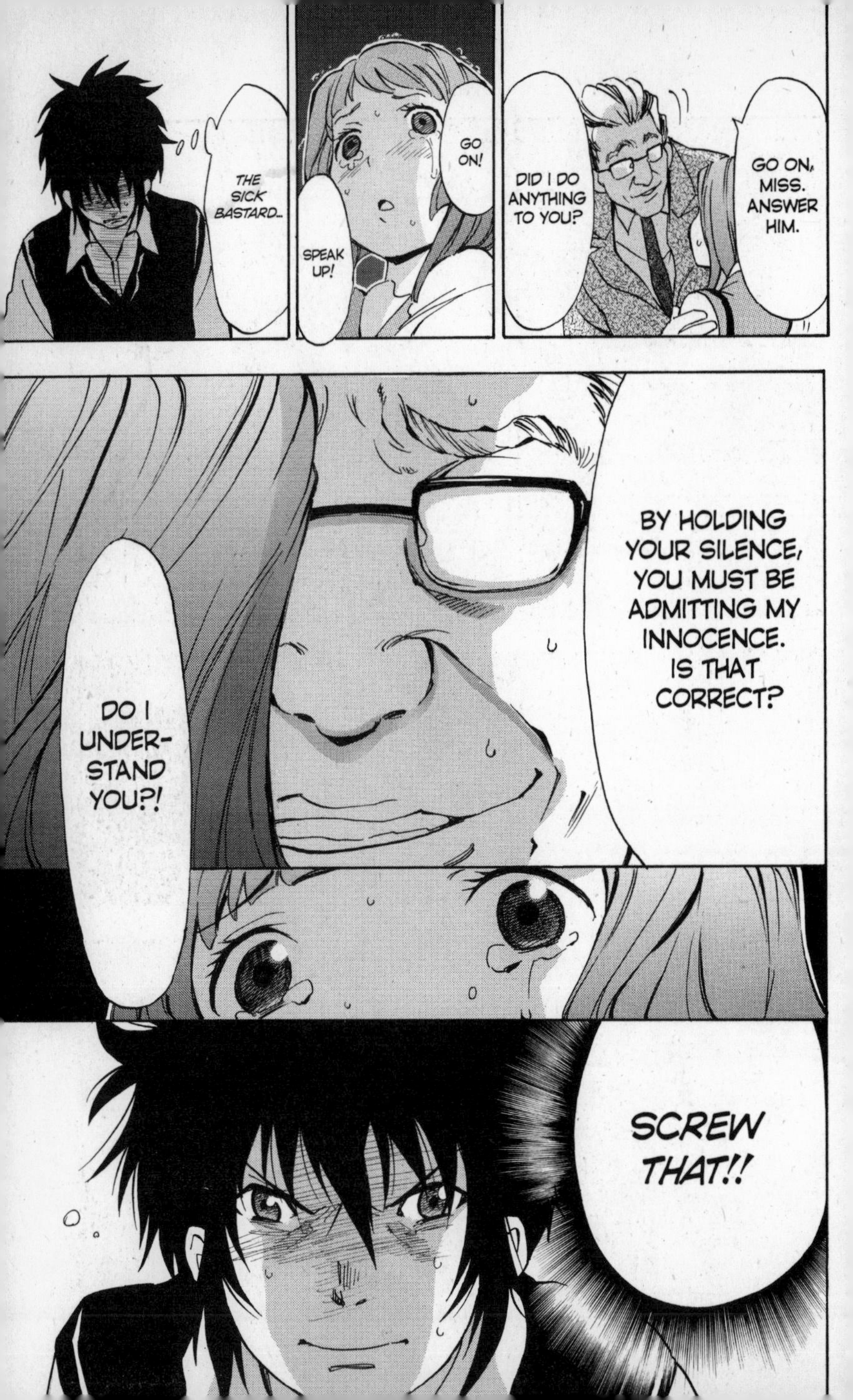
GO ON, MISS. ANSWER HIM.
DID I DO ANYTHING TO YOU?
GO ON!
SPEAK UP!
THE SICK BASTARD...
BY HOLDING YOUR SILENCE, YOU MUST BE ADMITTING MY INNOCENCE. IS THAT CORRECT?
DO I UNDER-STAND YOU?!
SCREW THAT!!

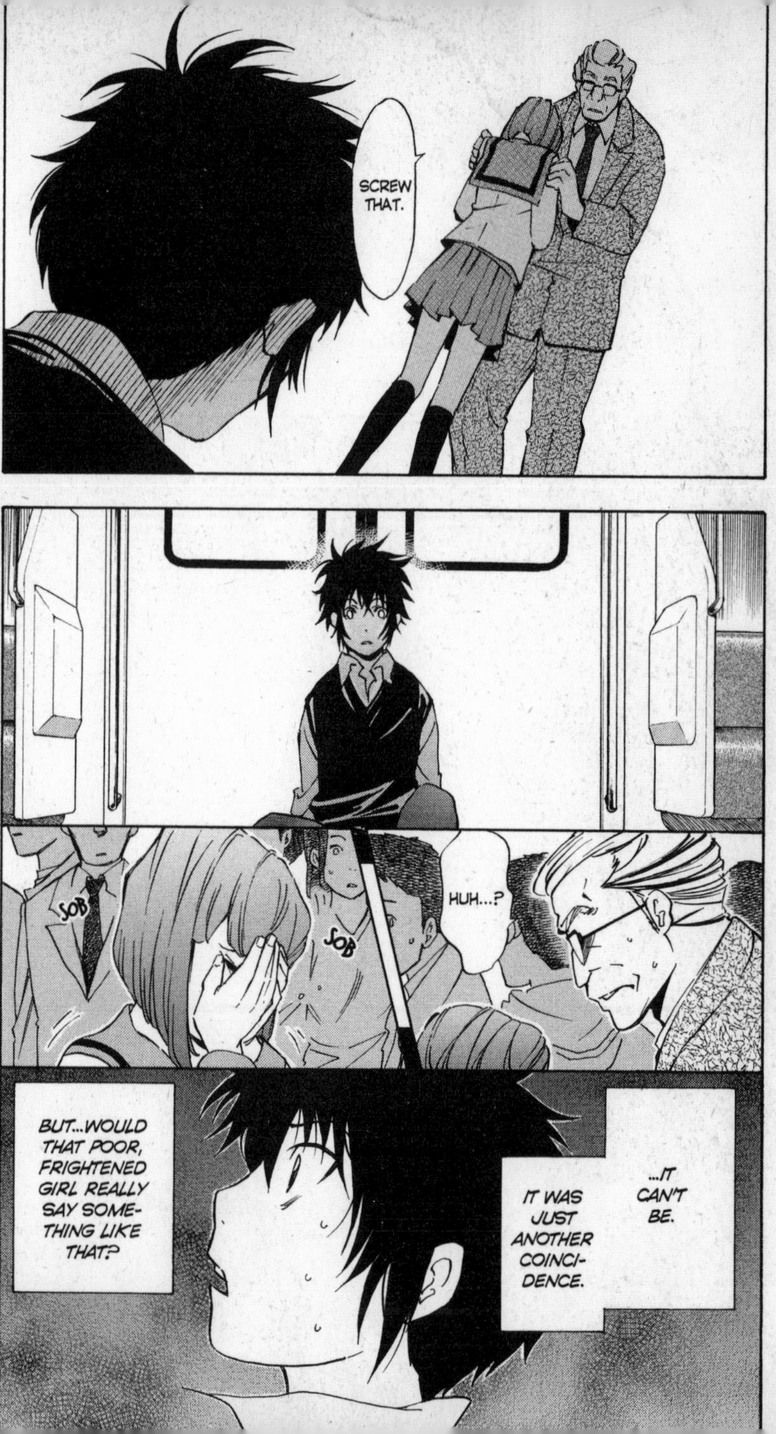
SCREW THAT.
HUH...?
SOB
SOB
...IT CAN'T BE.
IT WAS JUST ANOTHER COINCI-DENCE.
BUT...WOULD THAT POOR, FRIGHTENED GIRL REALLY SAY SOME-THING LIKE THAT?

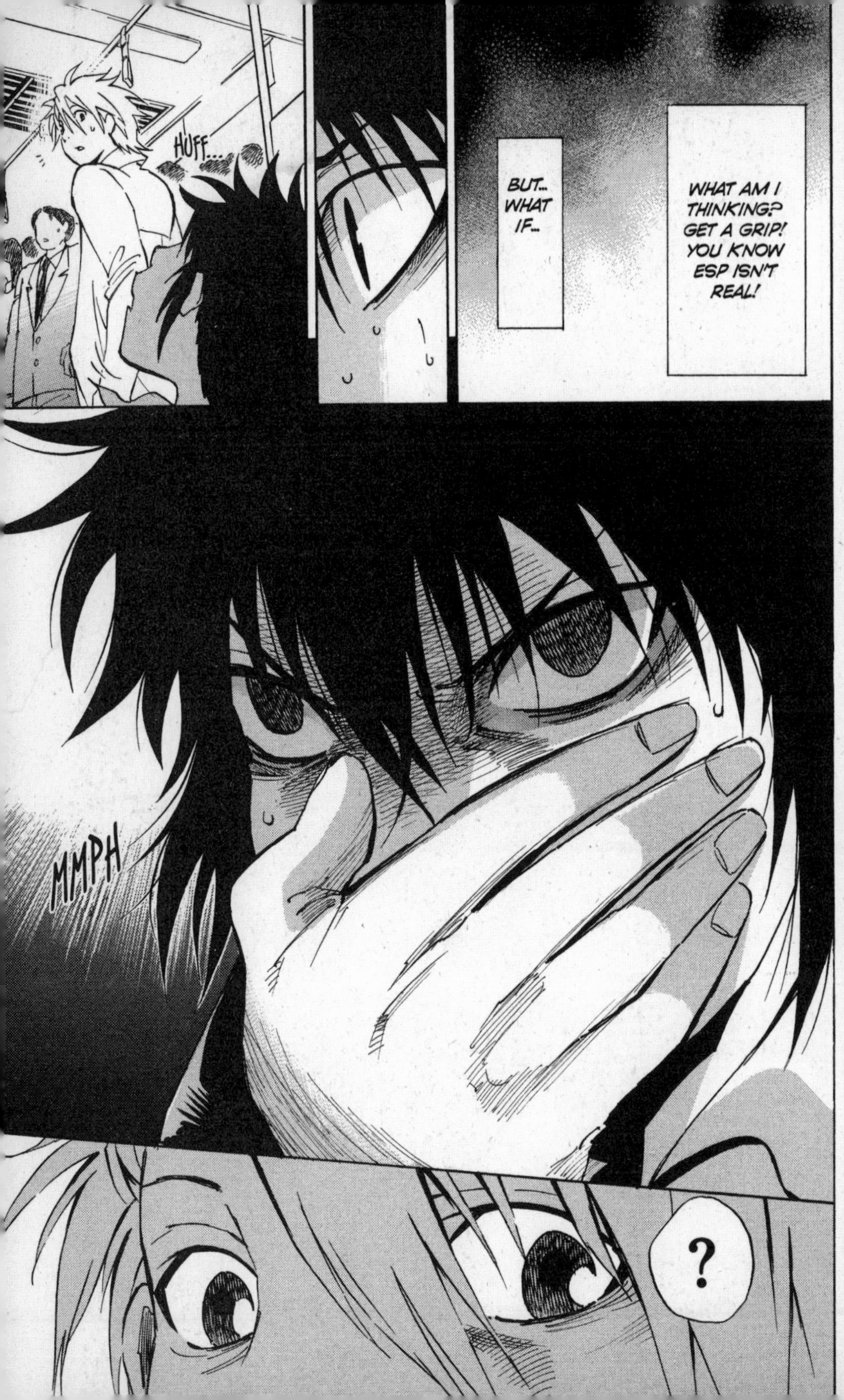
WHAT AM I THINKING? GET A GRIP! YOU KNOW ESP ISN'T REAL!
BUT... WHAT IF...
HUFF...
MMPH
?

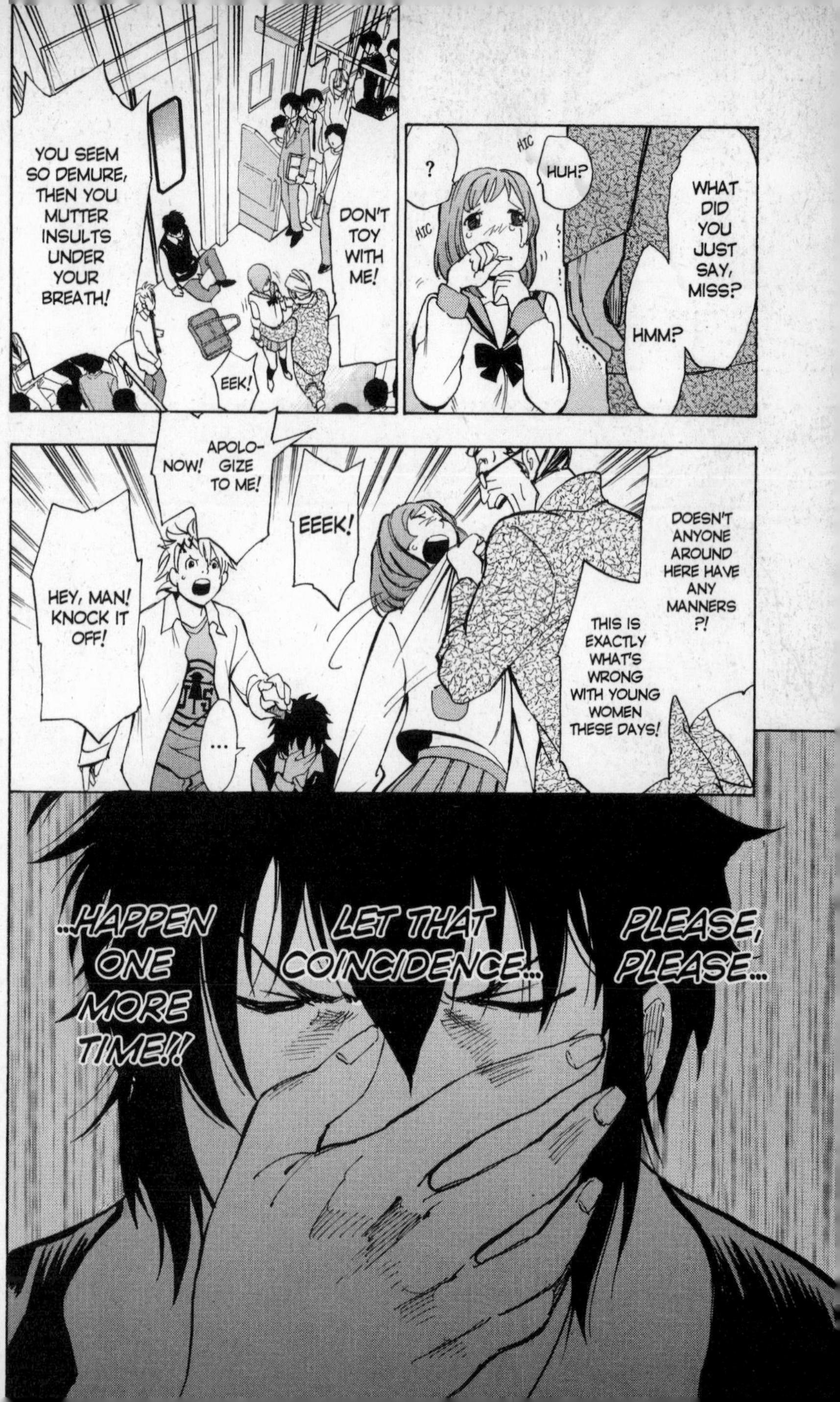
WHAT DID YOU JUST SAY, MISS?
HMM?
HUH?
HIC
?
HIC
YOU SEEM SO DEMURE, THEN YOU MUTTER INSULTS UNDER YOUR BREATH!
DON'T TOY WITH ME!
EEK!
DOESN'T ANYONE AROUND HERE HAVE ANY MANNERS?!
THIS IS EXACTLY WHAT'S WRONG WITH YOUNG WOMEN THESE DAYS!
EEEK!
APOLO- GIZE TO ME!
NOW!
HEY, MAN! KNOCK IT OFF!
...
PLEASE, PLEASE...
LET THAT COINCIDENCE...
...HAPPEN ONE MORE TIME!!

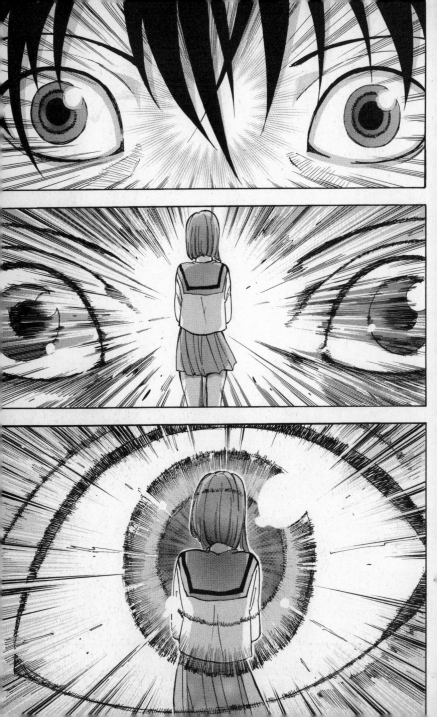

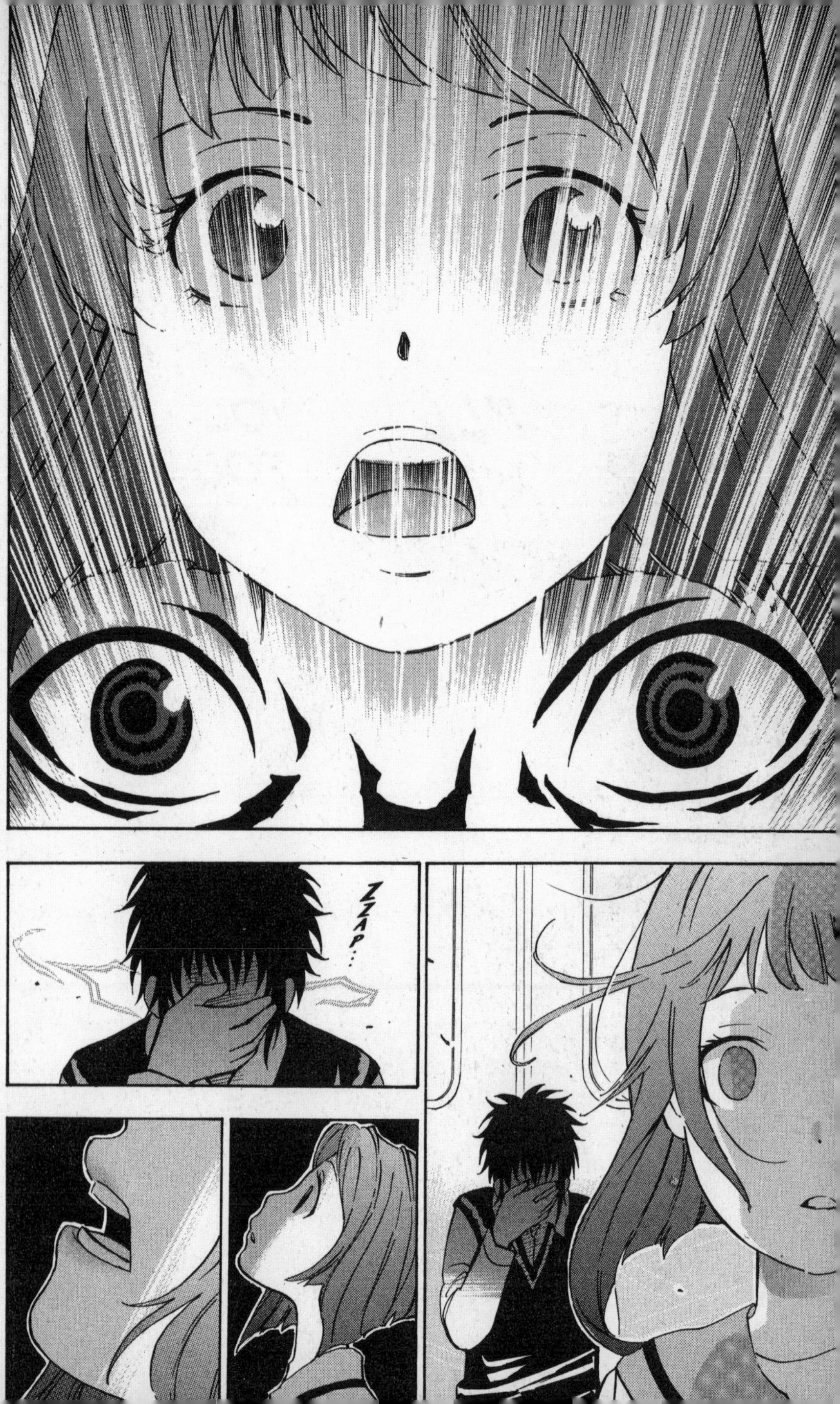
ZZAP...

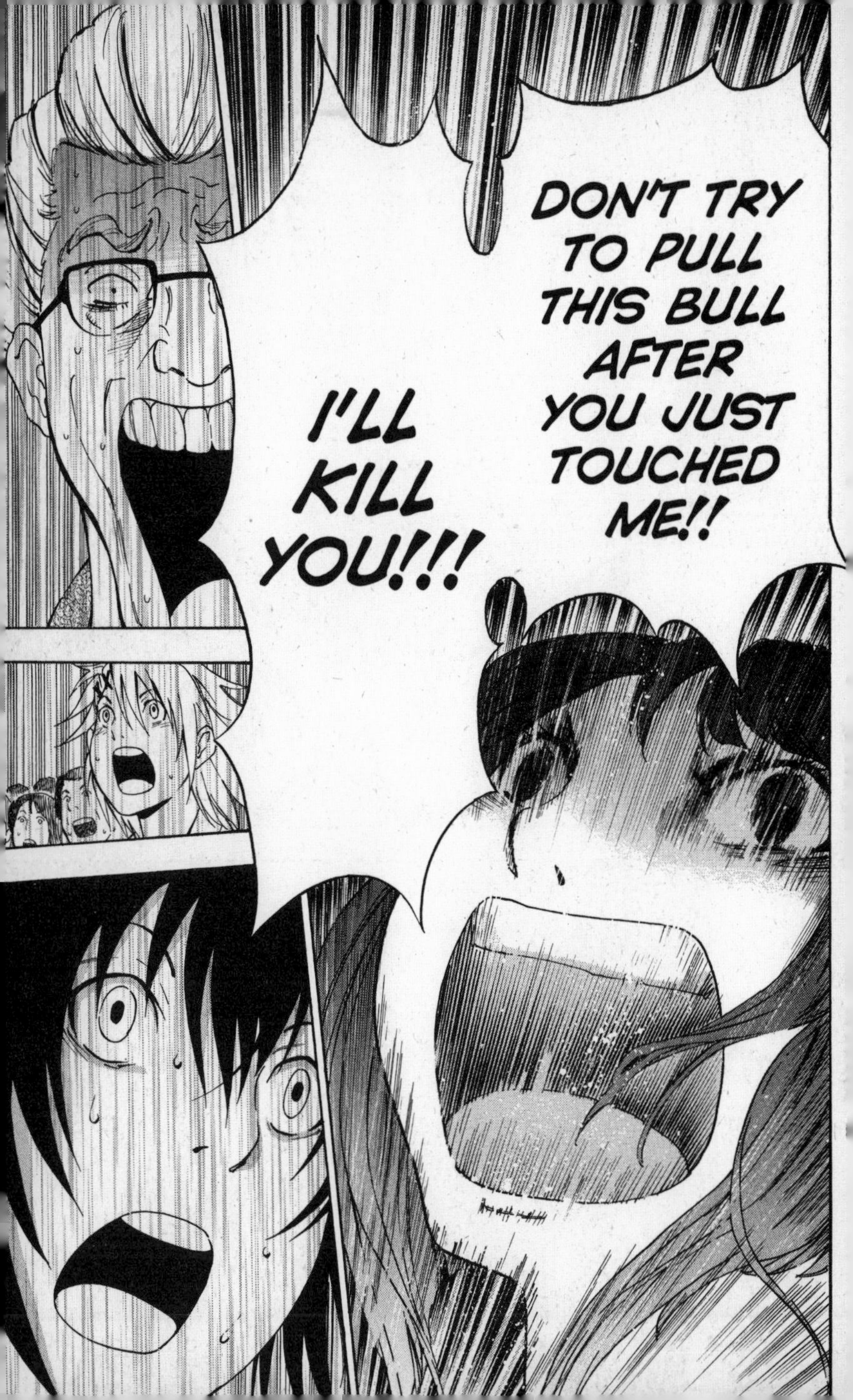
DON'T TRY TO PULL THIS BULL AFTER YOU JUST TOUCHED ME!!
I'LL KILL YOU!!!

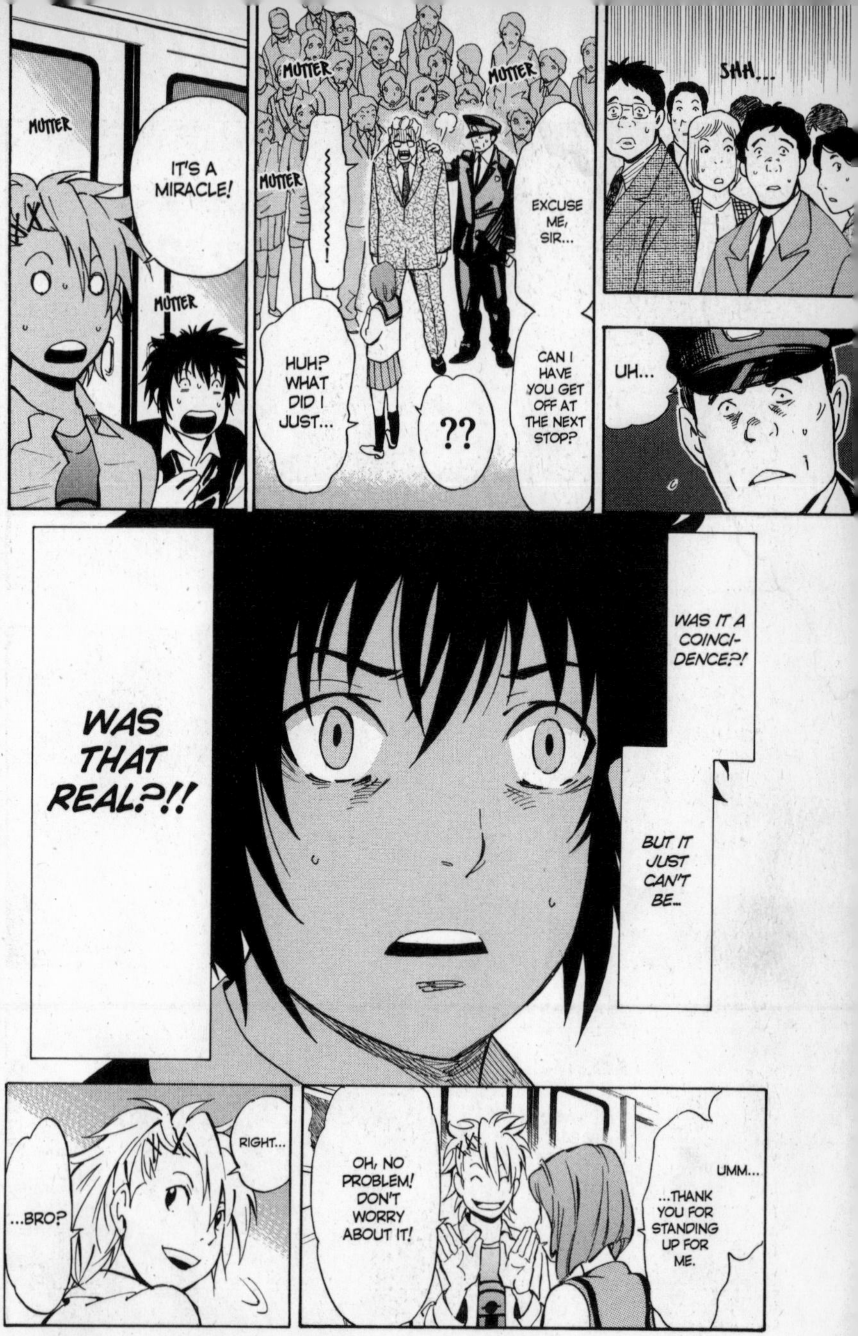
SHH...
UH...
MUTTER
MUTTER
EXCUSE ME, SIR...
CAN I HAVE YOU GET OFF AT THE NEXT STOP?
MUTTER
??
HUH? WHAT DID I JUST...
IT'S A MIRACLE!
MUTTER
MUTTER
WAS IT A COINCIDENCE?!
BUT IT JUST CAN'T BE...
WAS THAT REAL?!!
UMM...
...THANK YOU FOR STANDING UP FOR ME.
OH, NO PROBLEM! DON'T WORRY ABOUT IT!
RIGHT...
...BRO?

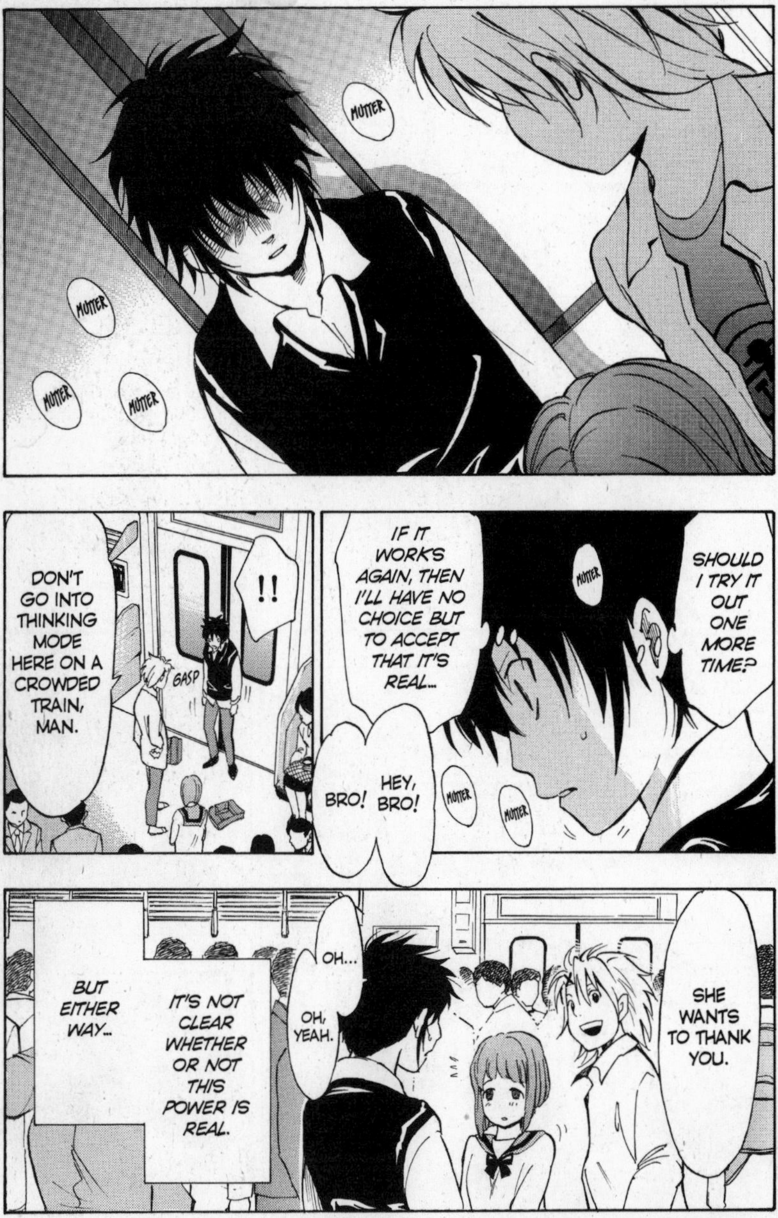
MUTTER
MUTTER
MUTTER
MUTTER
SHOULD I TRY IT OUT ONE MORE TIME?
MUTTER
IF IT WORKS AGAIN, THEN I'LL HAVE NO CHOICE BUT TO ACCEPT THAT IT'S REAL...
HEY, BRO!
BRO!
MUTTER
MUTTER
!!
GASP
DON'T GO INTO THINKING MODE HERE ON A CROWDED TRAIN, MAN.
SHE WANTS TO THANK YOU.
OH...
OH, YEAH.
IT'S NOT CLEAR WHETHER OR NOT THIS POWER IS REAL.
BUT EITHER WAY...

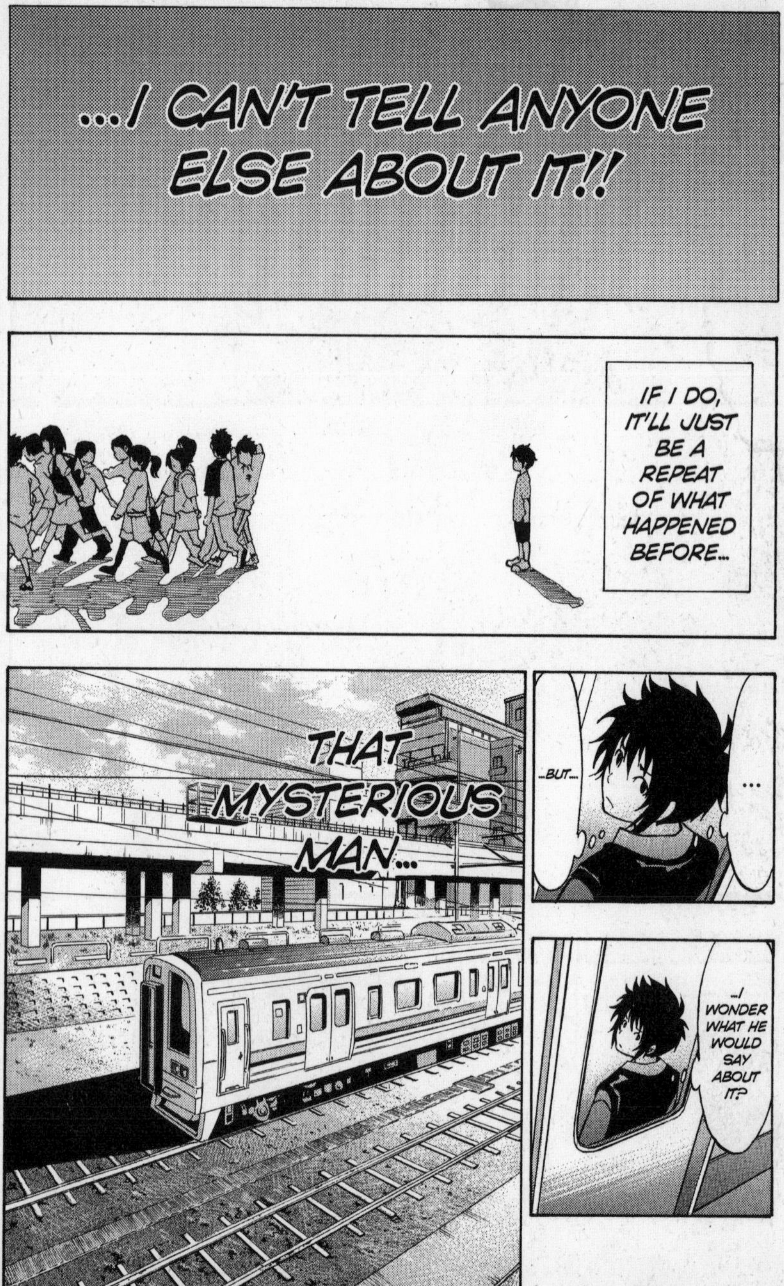
...I CAN'T TELL ANYONE ELSE ABOUT IT!!
IF I DO, IT'LL JUST BE A REPEAT OF WHAT HAPPENED BEFORE...
...
...BUT...
...I WONDER WHAT HE WOULD SAY ABOUT IT?
THAT MYSTERIOUS MAN...

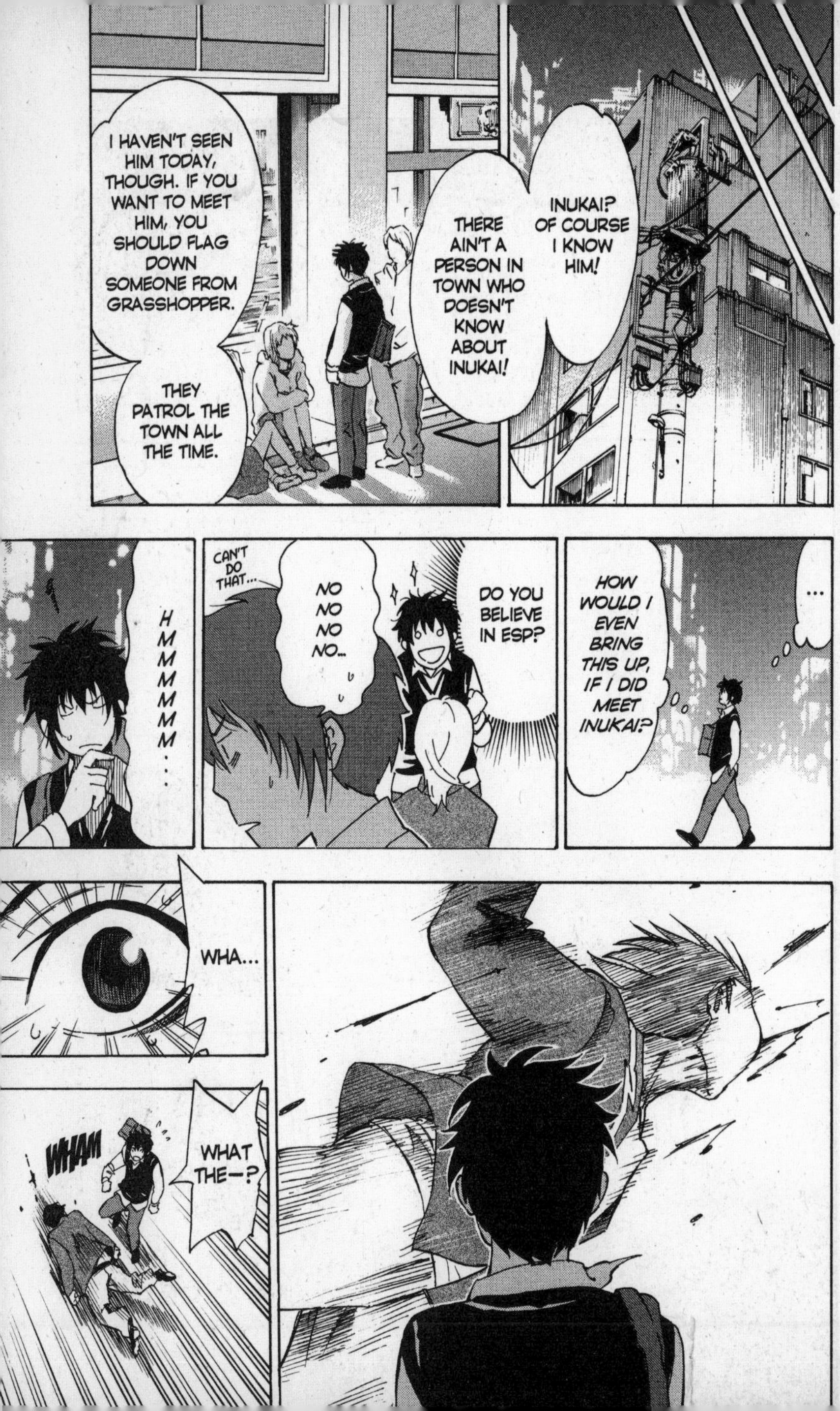
INUKAI? OF COURSE I KNOW HIM!
THERE AIN'T A PERSON IN TOWN WHO DOESN'T KNOW ABOUT INUKAI!
I HAVEN'T SEEN HIM TODAY, THOUGH. IF YOU WANT TO MEET HIM, YOU SHOULD FLAG DOWN SOMEONE FROM GRASSHOPPER.
THEY PATROL THE TOWN ALL THE TIME.
...
HOW WOULD I EVEN BRING THIS UP, IF I DID MEET INUKAI?
DO YOU BELIEVE IN ESP?
NO NO NO NO...
CAN'T DO THAT...
HMMMMMMM...
WHA...
WHAM
WHAT THE—?

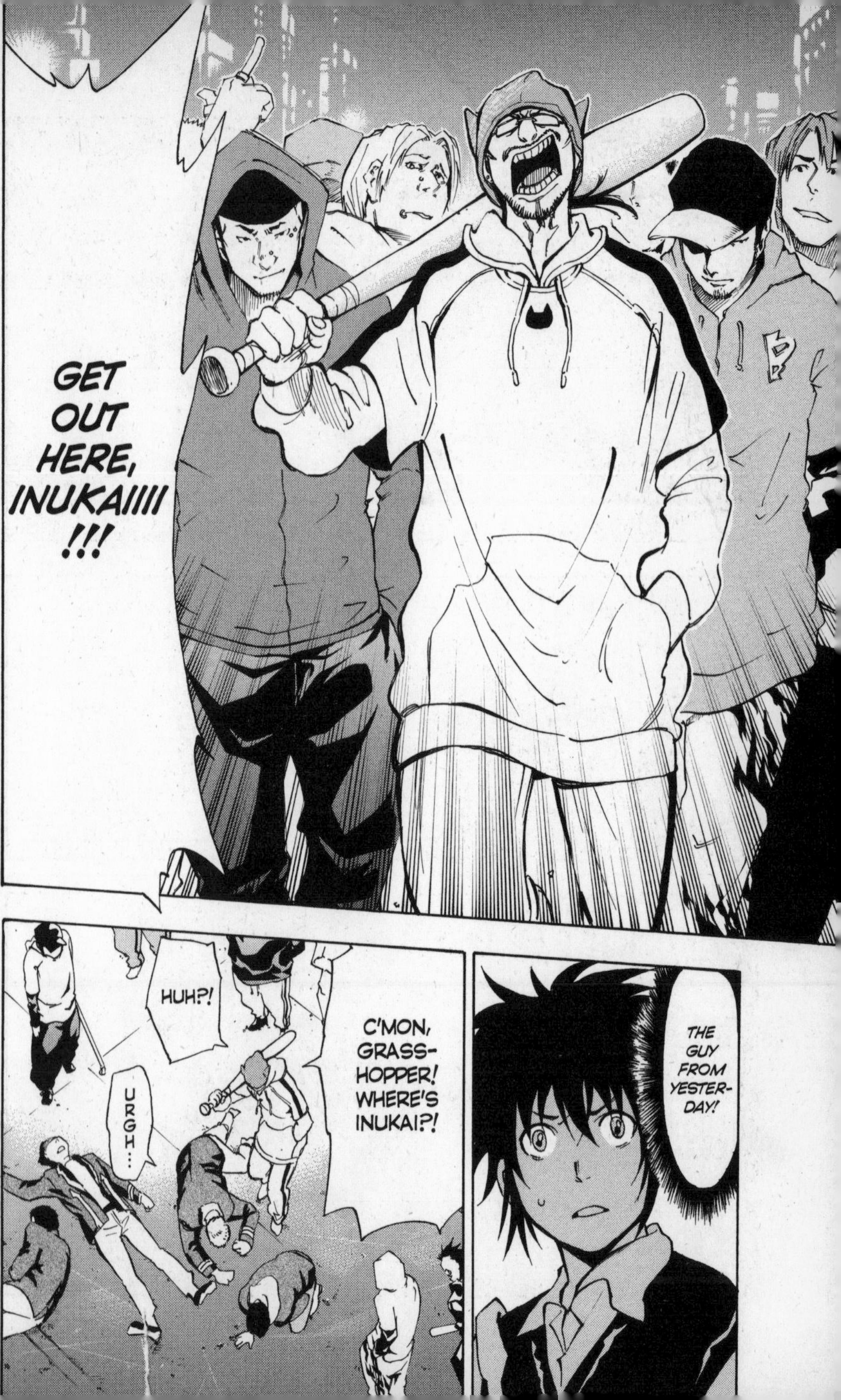
GET OUT HERE, INUKAIIII !!!
THE GUY FROM YESTER-DAY!
C'MON, GRASS-HOPPER! WHERE'S INUKAI?!
HUH?!
URGH...

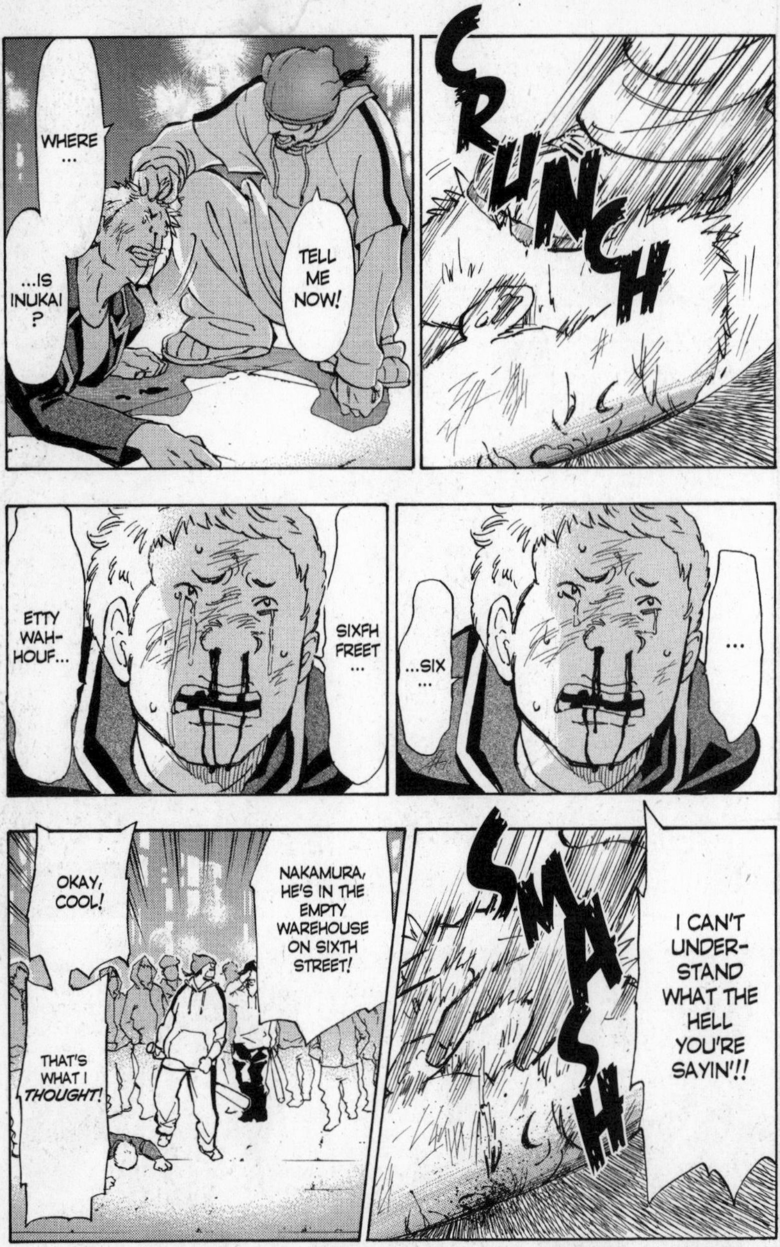
CRUNCH
WHERE ...
...IS INUKAI ?
TELL ME NOW!
...
...SIX ...
SIXFH FREET ...
ETTY WAH-HOUF...
SMASH
I CAN'T UNDER-STAND WHAT THE HELL YOU'RE SAYIN'!!
NAKAMURA, HE'S IN THE EMPTY WAREHOUSE ON SIXTH STREET!
OKAY, COOL!
THAT'S WHAT I THOUGHT!

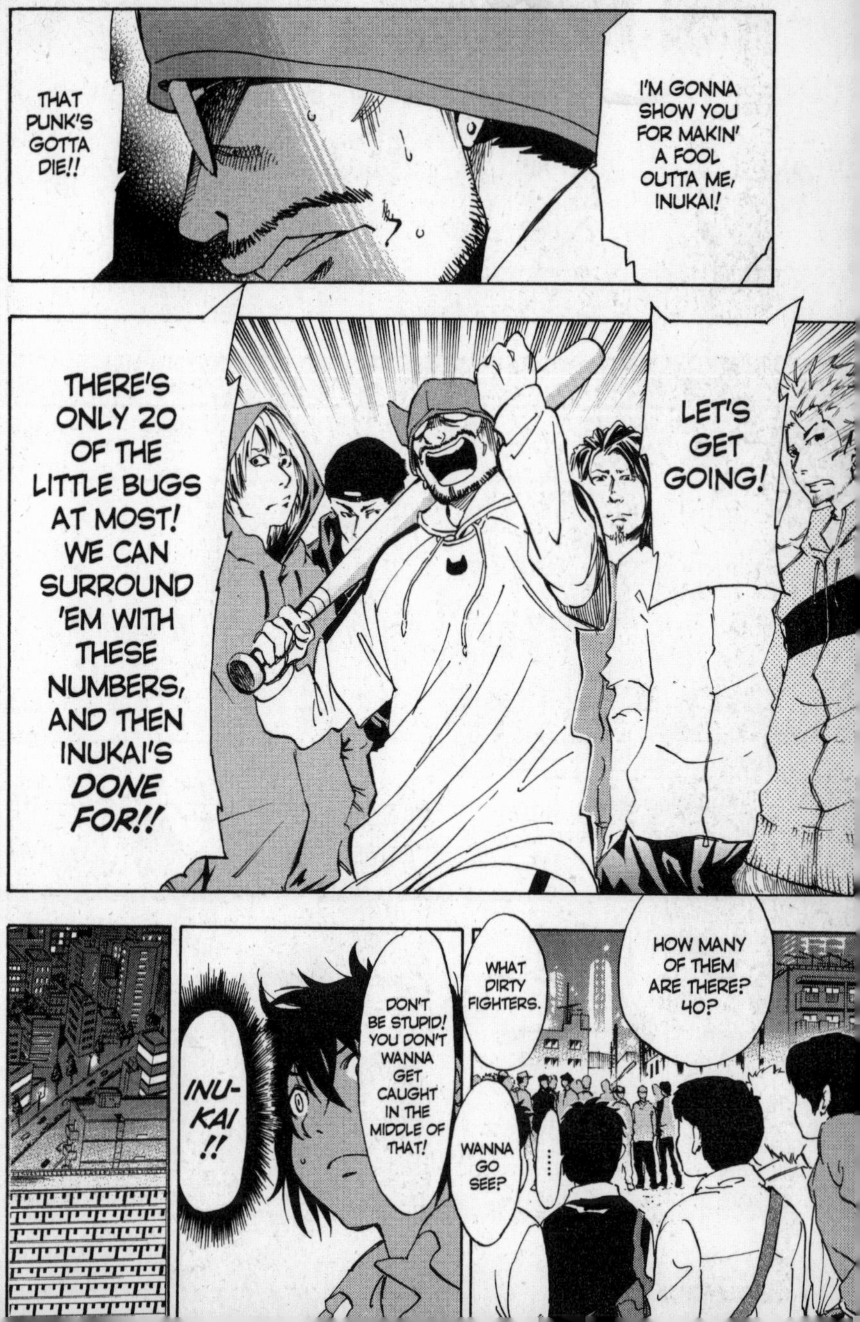
I'M GONNA SHOW YOU FOR MAKIN' A FOOL OUTTA ME, INUKAI!
THAT PUNK'S GOTTA DIE!!
LET'S GET GOING!
THERE'S ONLY 20 OF THE LITTLE BUGS AT MOST! WE CAN SURROUND 'EM WITH THESE NUMBERS, AND THEN INUKAI'S *DONE FOR!!*
HOW MANY OF THEM ARE THERE? 40?
WHAT DIRTY FIGHTERS.
.....
WANNA GO SEE?
DON'T BE STUPID! YOU DON'T WANNA GET CAUGHT IN THE MIDDLE OF THAT!
INU-KAI!!

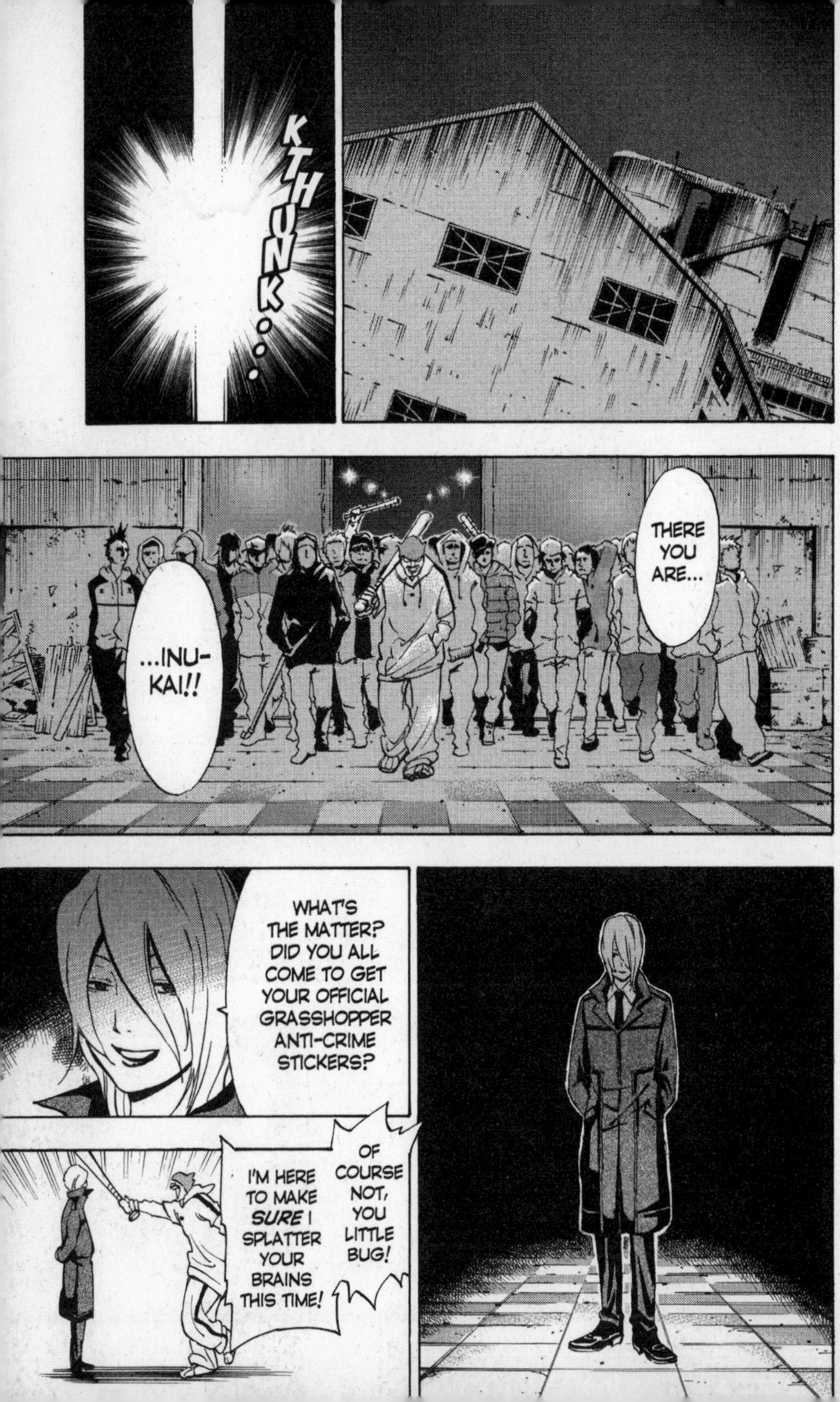
KTHUNK...
THERE YOU ARE...
...INU-KAI!!
WHAT'S THE MATTER? DID YOU ALL COME TO GET YOUR OFFICIAL GRASSHOPPER ANTI-CRIME STICKERS?
OF COURSE NOT, YOU LITTLE BUG!
I'M HERE TO MAKE *SURE* I SPLATTER YOUR BRAINS THIS TIME!

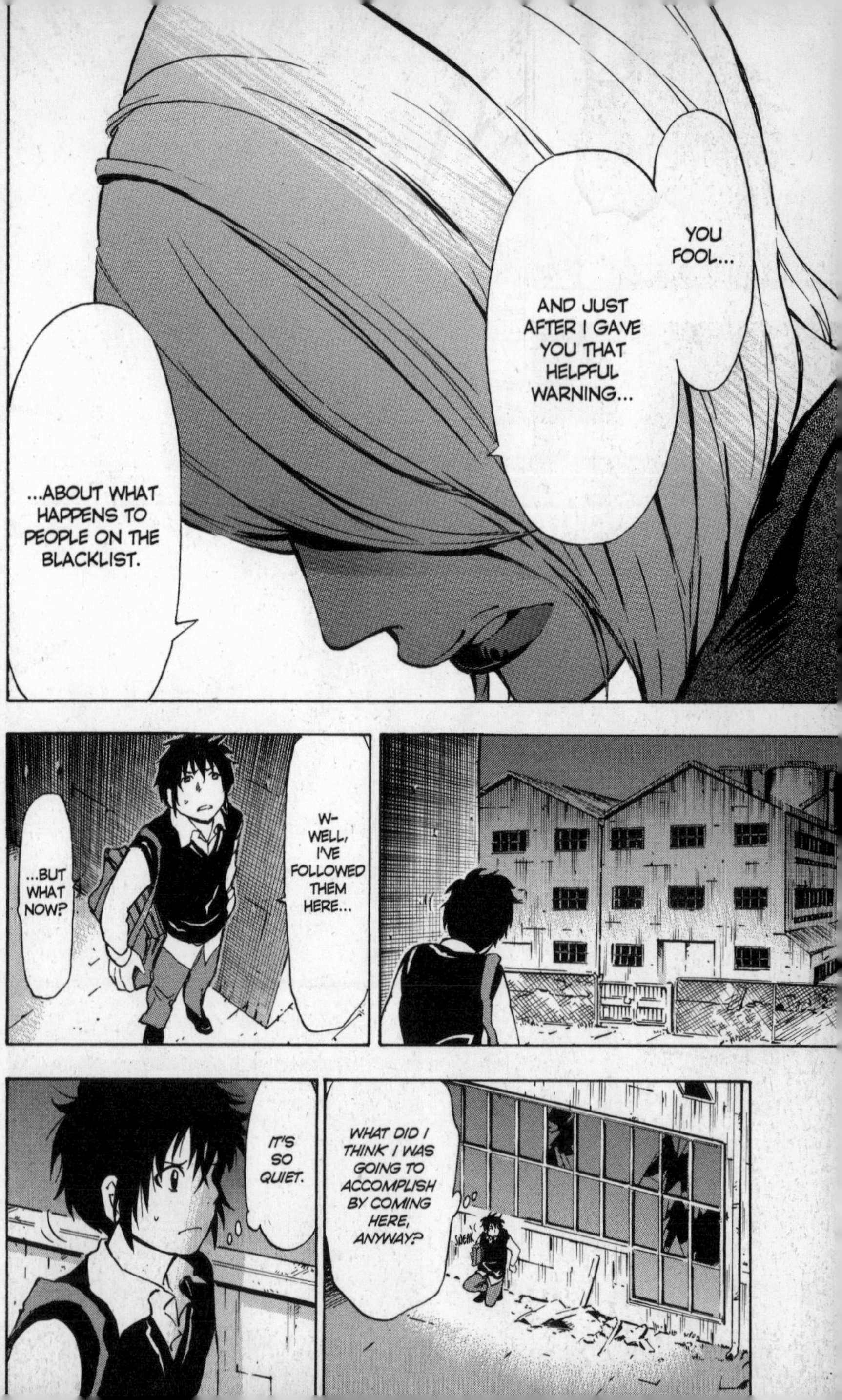
YOU FOOL...
AND JUST AFTER I GAVE YOU THAT HELPFUL WARNING...
...ABOUT WHAT HAPPENS TO PEOPLE ON THE BLACKLIST.
W-WELL, I'VE FOLLOWED THEM HERE...
...BUT WHAT NOW?
WHAT DID I THINK I WAS GOING TO ACCOMPLISH BY COMING HERE, ANYWAY?
IT'S SO QUIET.

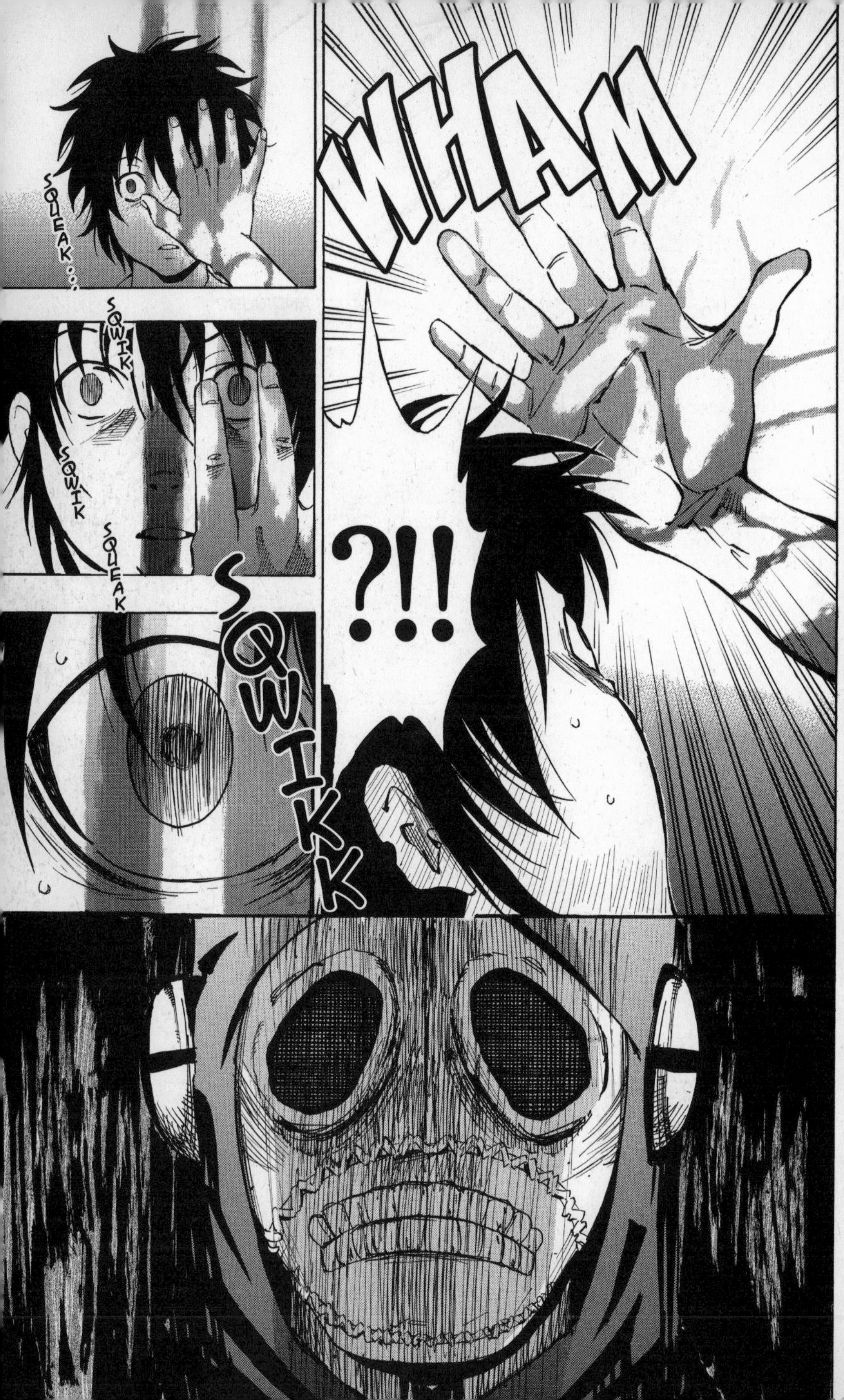
WHAM
?!!
SQUEAK...
SQWIK
SQWIK
SQUEAK
SQWIKK

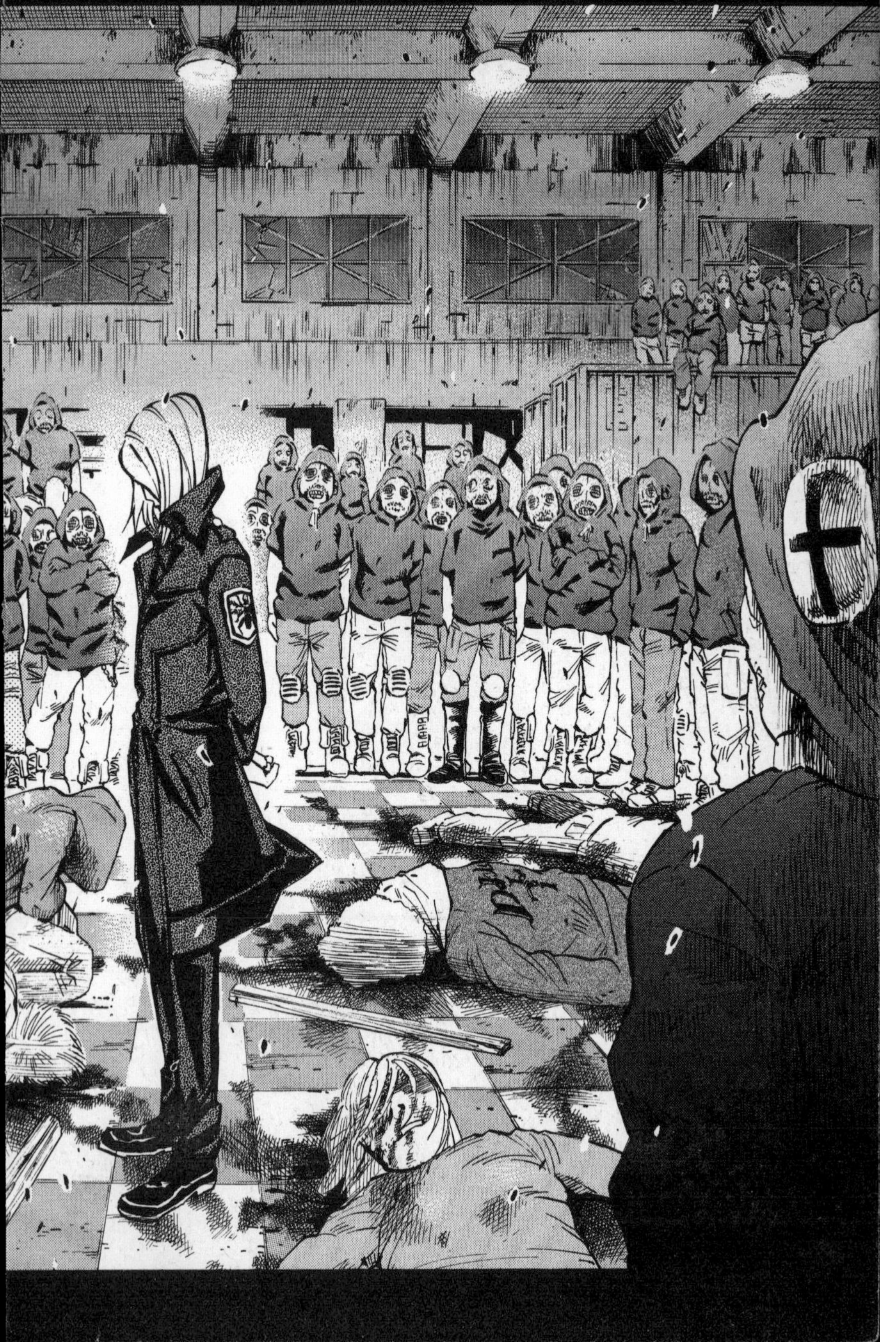

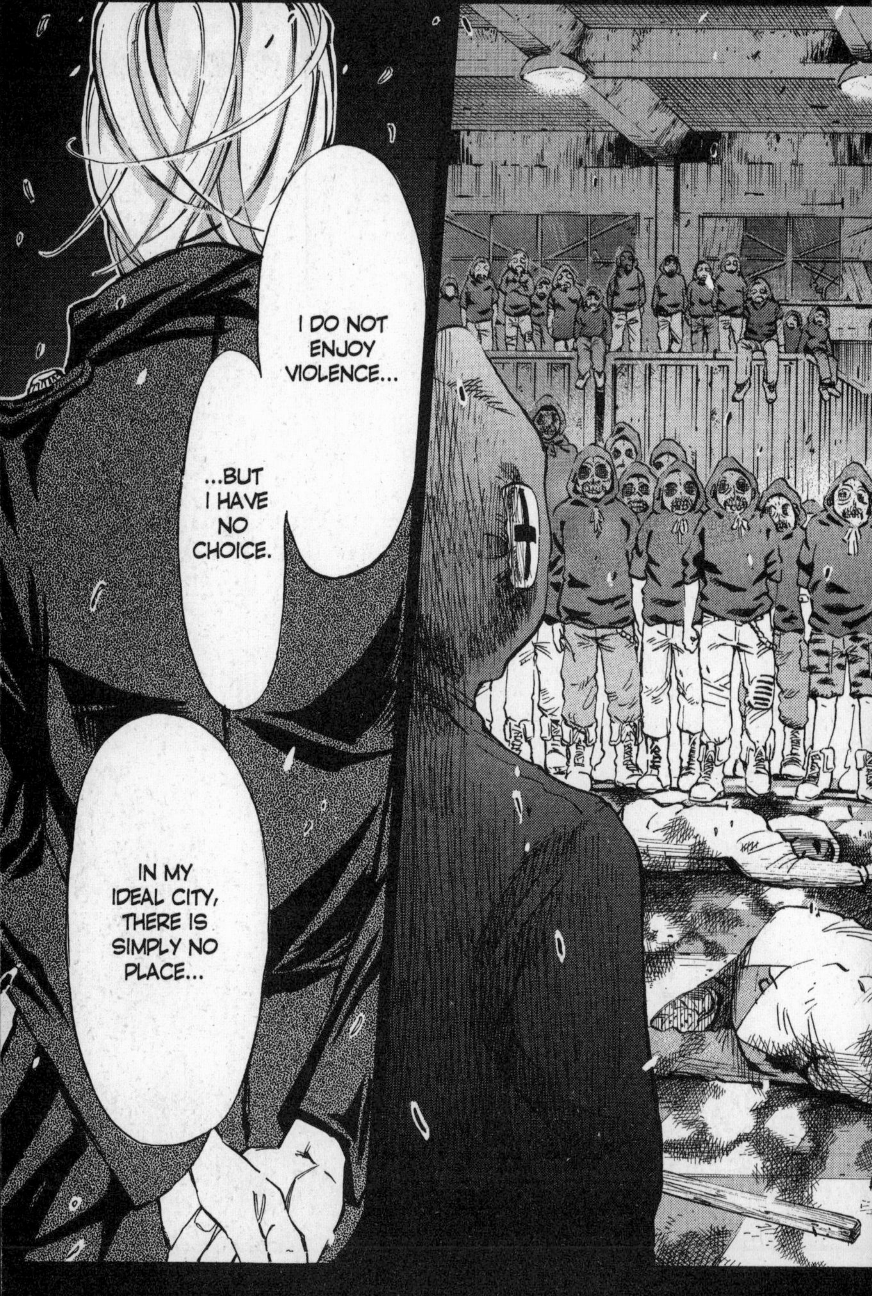
I DO NOT ENJOY VIOLENCE...
...BUT I HAVE NO CHOICE.
IN MY IDEAL CITY, THERE IS SIMPLY NO PLACE...

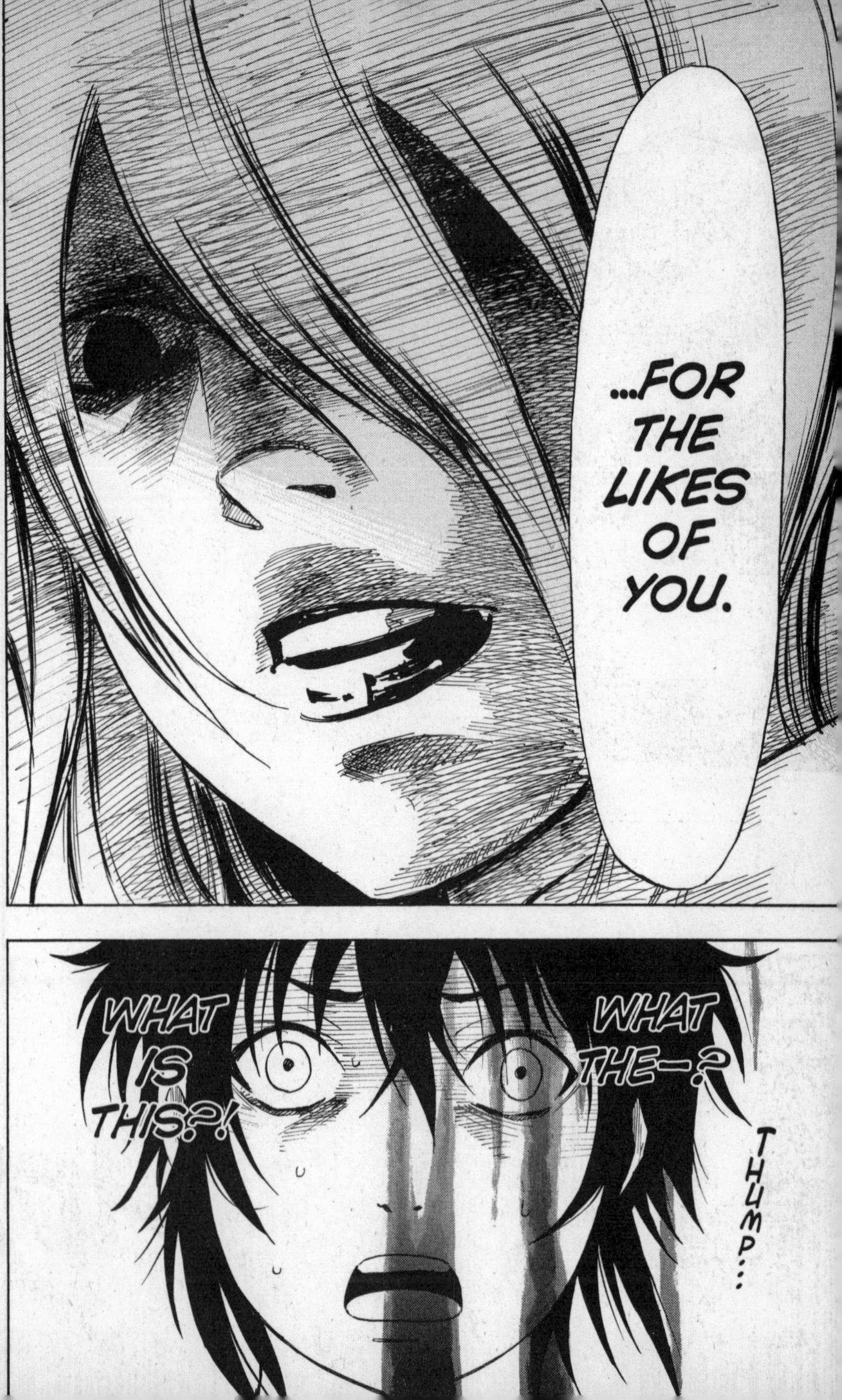
...FOR THE LIKES OF YOU.
WHAT THE--?
WHAT IS THIS?!
THUMP...

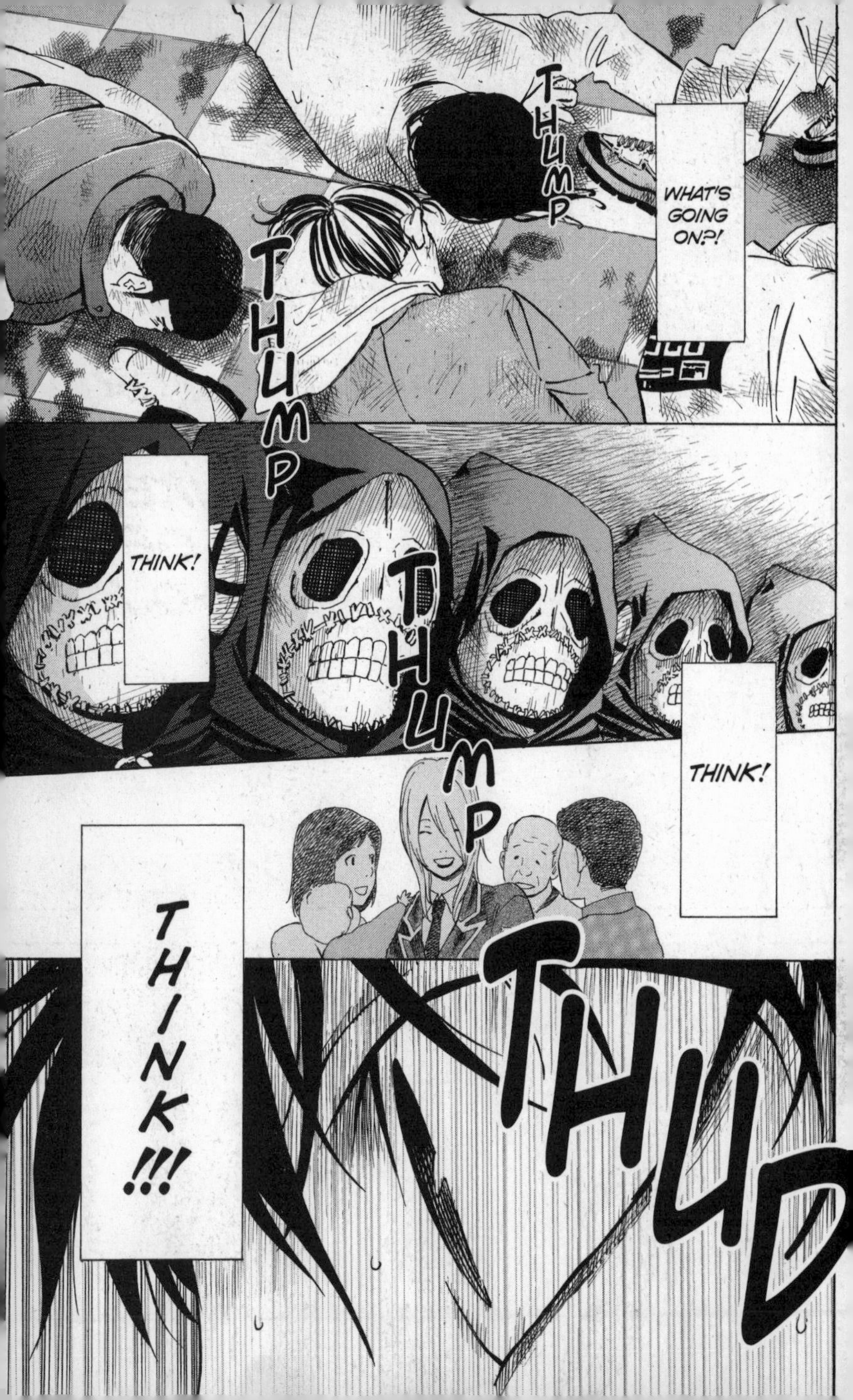
THUMP
WHAT'S GOING ON?!
THUMP
THUMP
THINK!
THINK!
THUD
THINK!!!

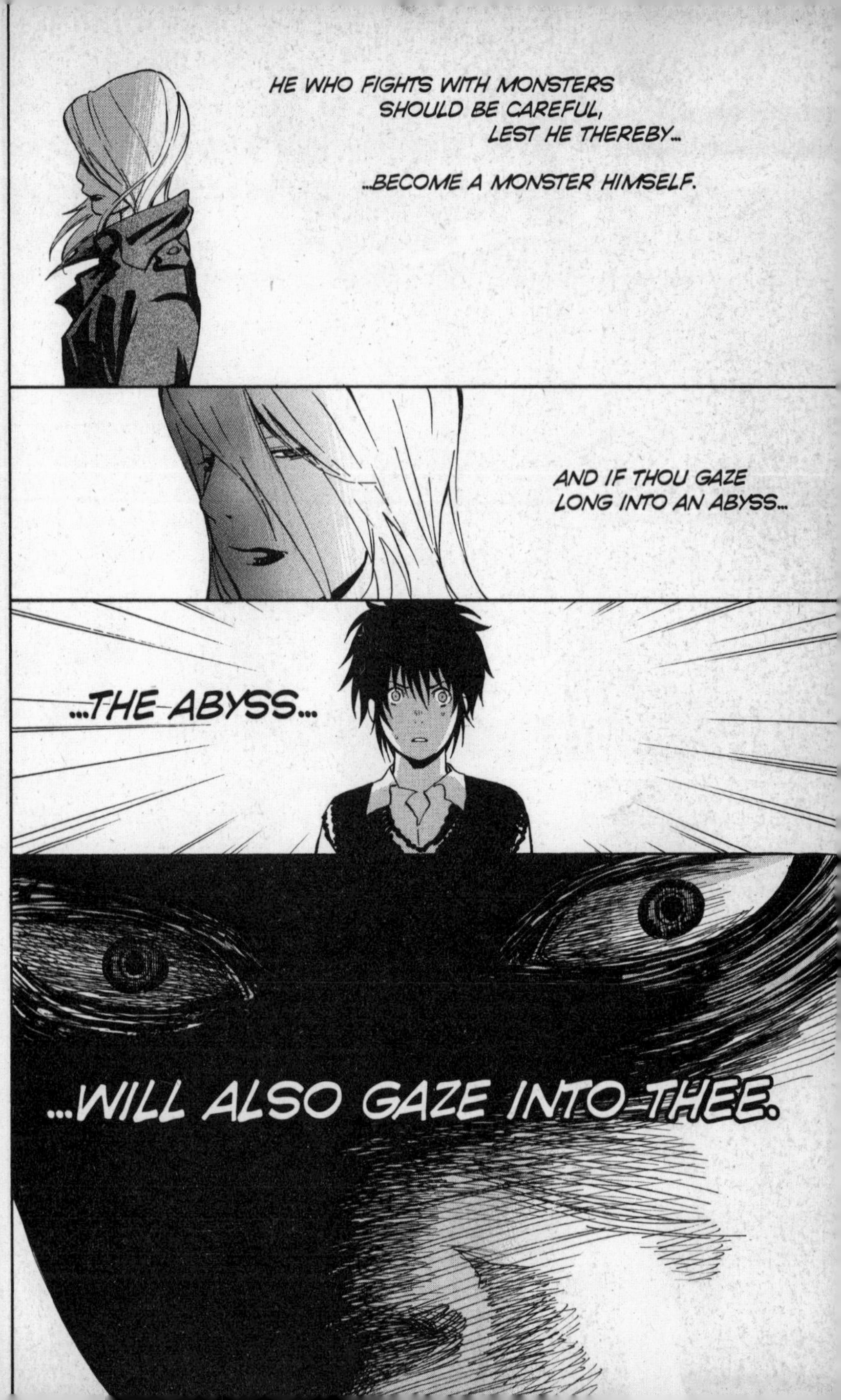
HE WHO FIGHTS WITH MONSTERS SHOULD BE CAREFUL, LEST HE THEREBY...
...BECOME A MONSTER HIMSELF.
AND IF THOU GAZE LONG INTO AN ABYSS...
...THE ABYSS...
...WILL ALSO GAZE INTO THEE.

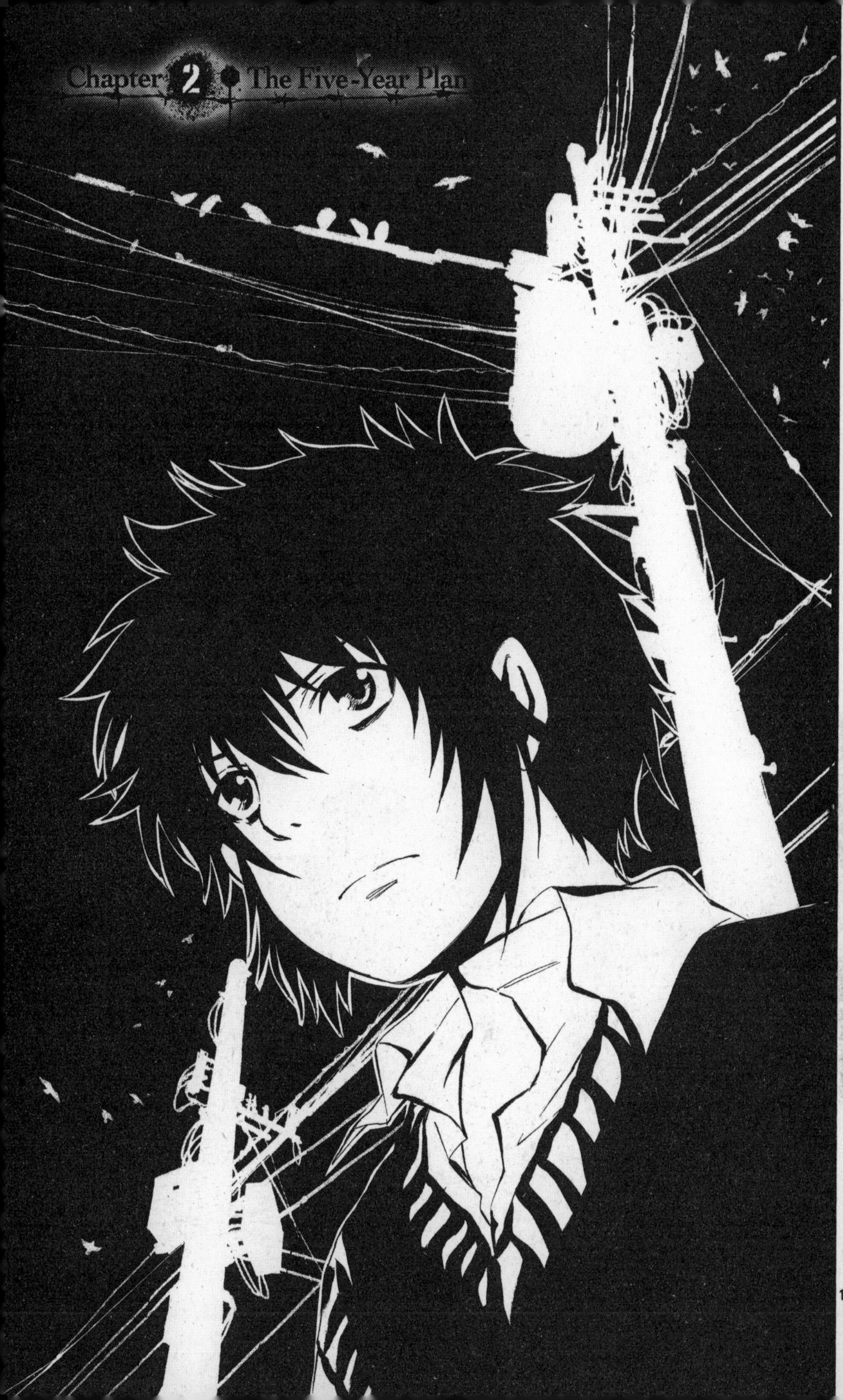
Chapter 2 The Five-Year Plan

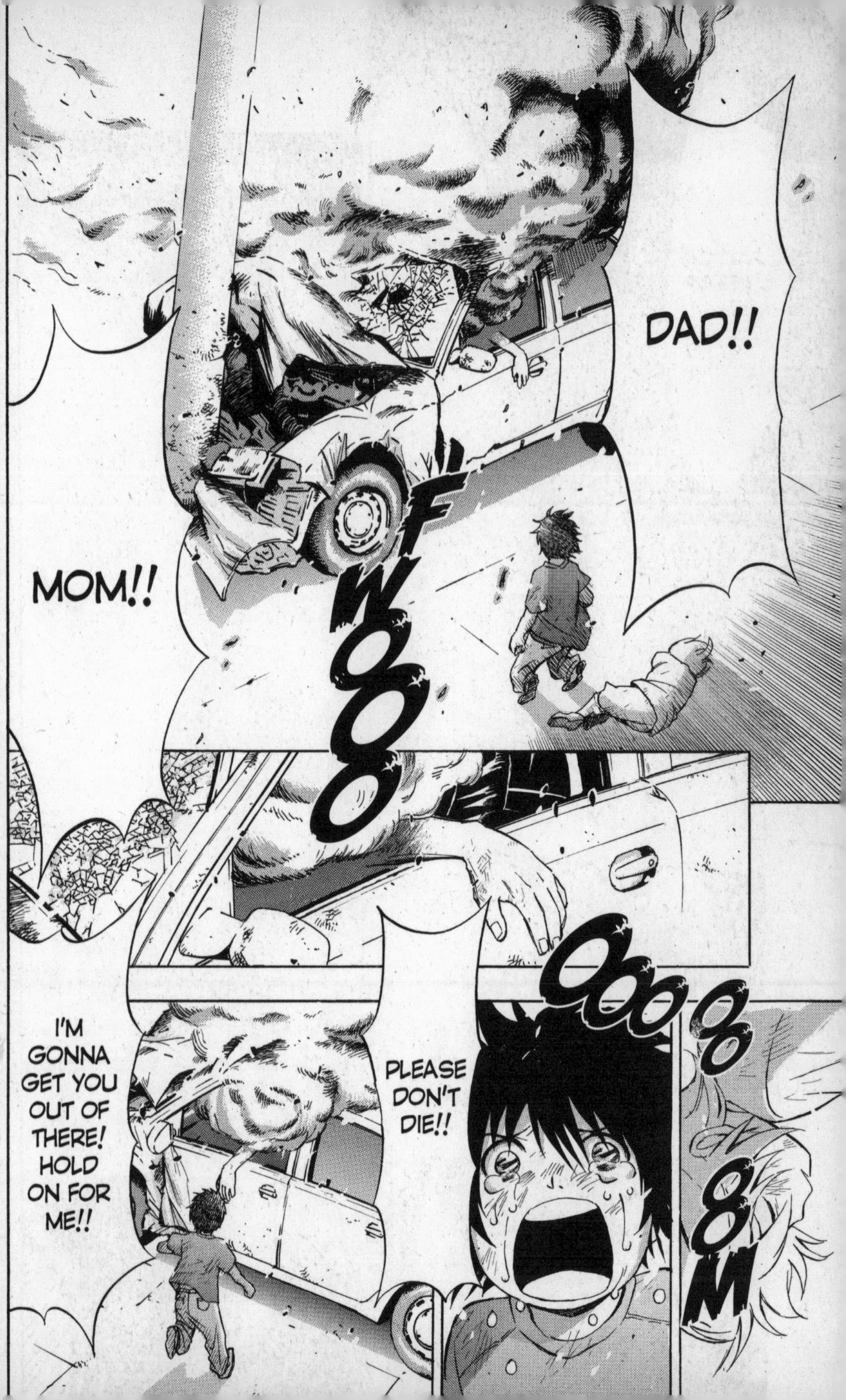
DAD!!
MOM!!
FWOOOOOOOOM
PLEASE DON'T DIE!!
I'M GONNA GET YOU OUT OF THERE! HOLD ON FOR ME!!

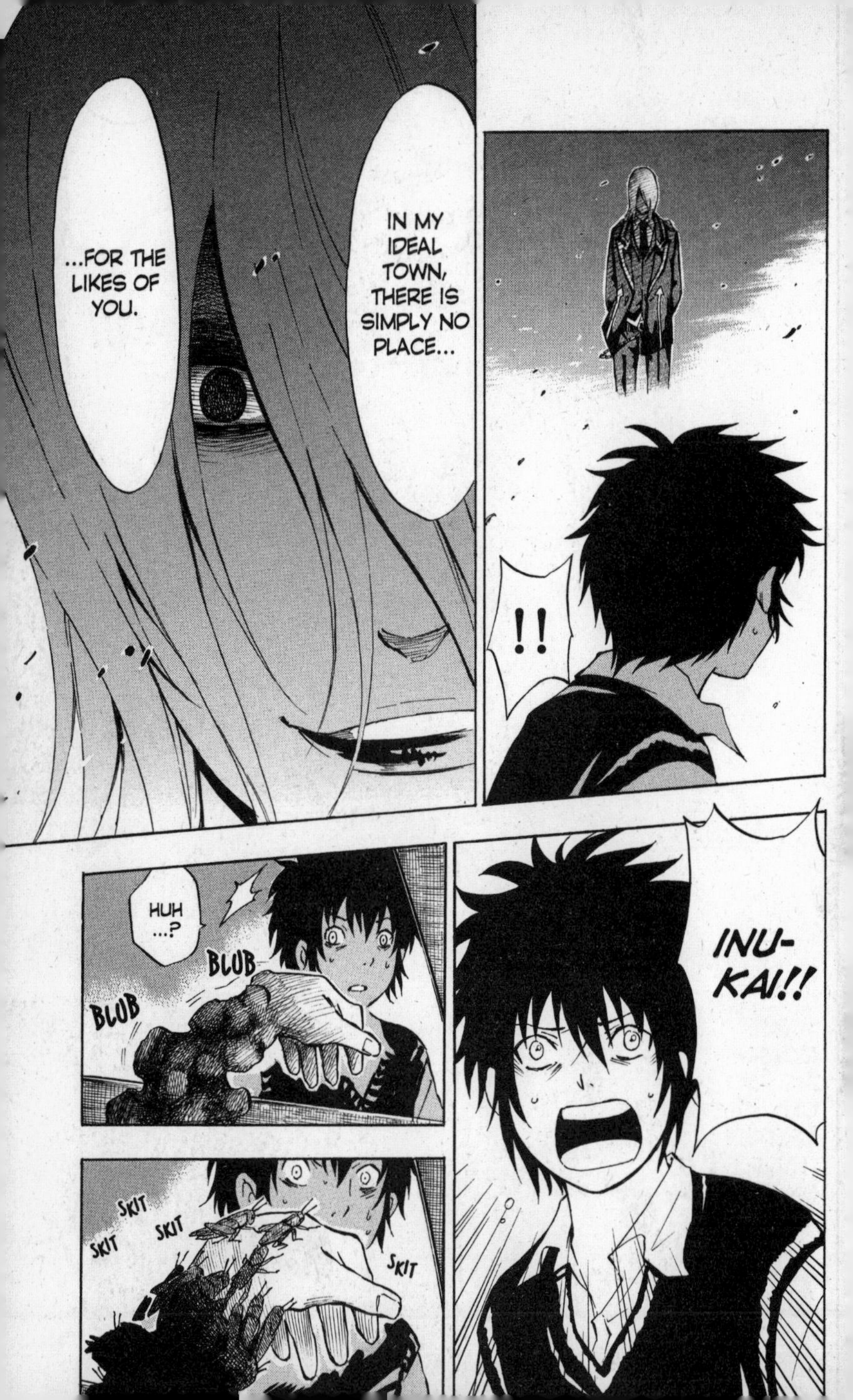
!!
IN MY IDEAL TOWN, THERE IS SIMPLY NO PLACE...
...FOR THE LIKES OF YOU.
INU-KAI!!
HUH ...?
BLUB
BLUB
SKIT
SKIT
SKIT
SKIT

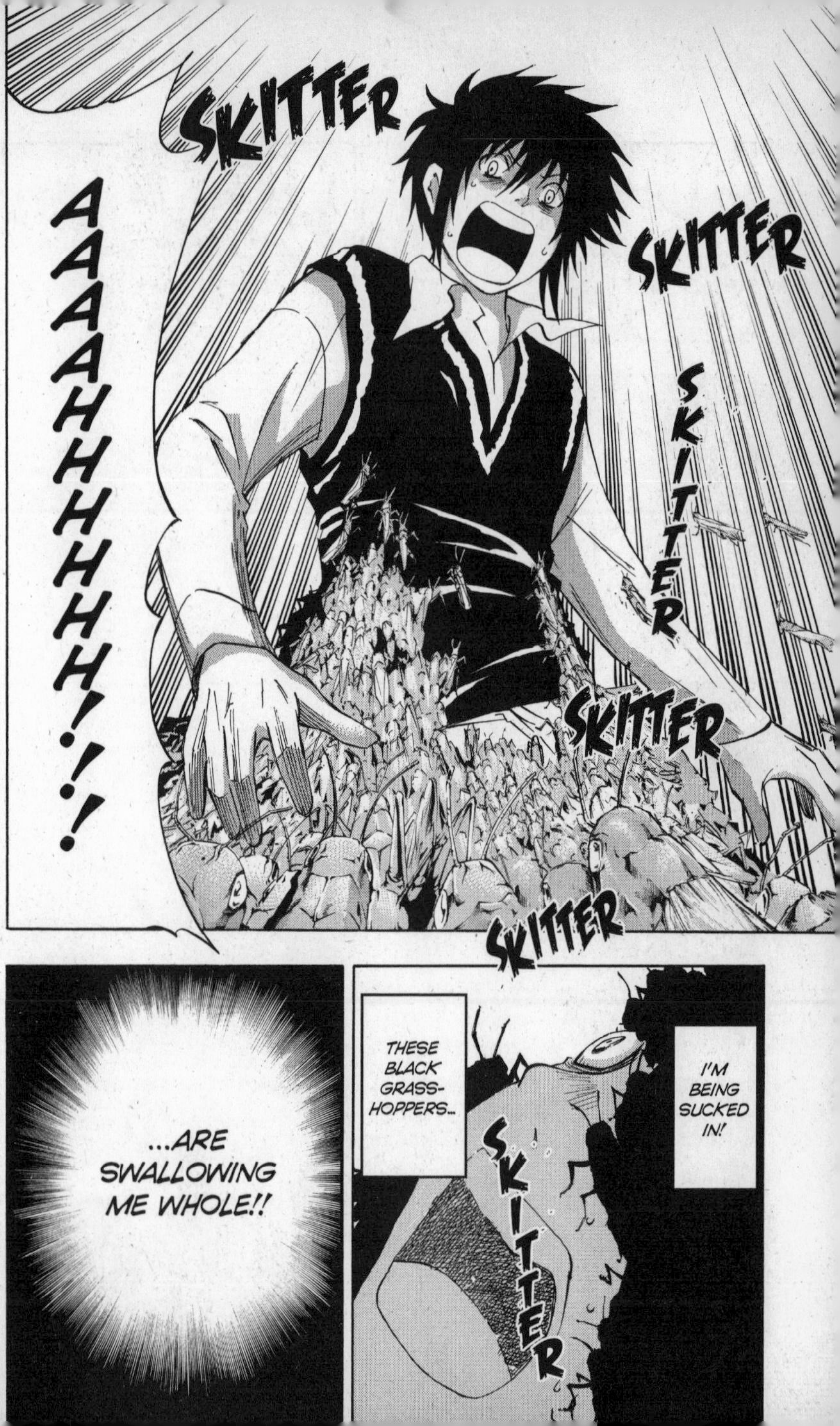
SKITTER
SKITTER
SKITTER
AAAAHHHHHHH!!!
SKITTER
SKITTER
I'M BEING SUCKED IN!
THESE BLACK GRASS-HOPPERS...
SKITTER
...ARE SWALLOWING ME WHOLE!!

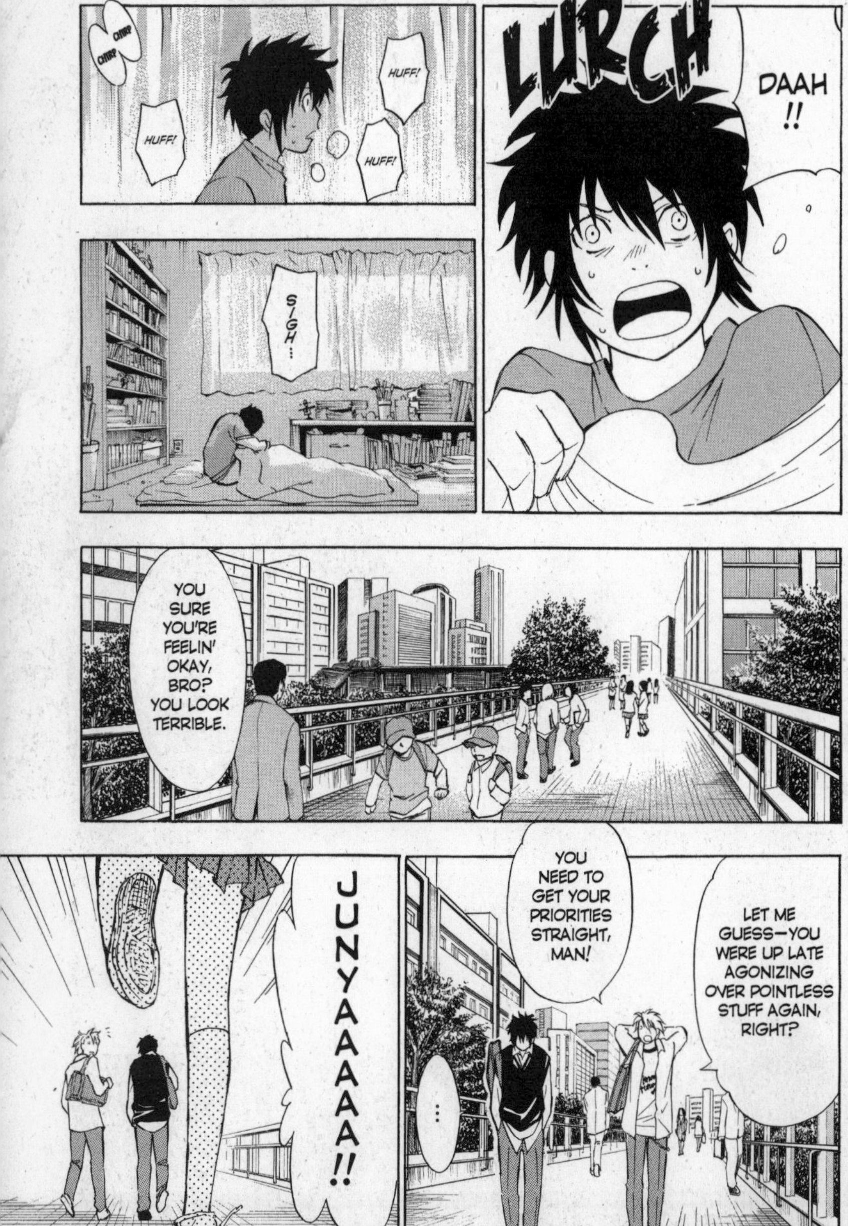
LURCH
DAAH!!
HUFF!
HUFF!
CHIRP CHIRP
HUFF!
SIGH…
YOU SURE YOU'RE FEELIN' OKAY, BRO? YOU LOOK TERRIBLE.
LET ME GUESS—YOU WERE UP LATE AGONIZING OVER POINTLESS STUFF AGAIN, RIGHT?
YOU NEED TO GET YOUR PRIORITIES STRAIGHT, MAN!
…
JUNYAAAAAA!!

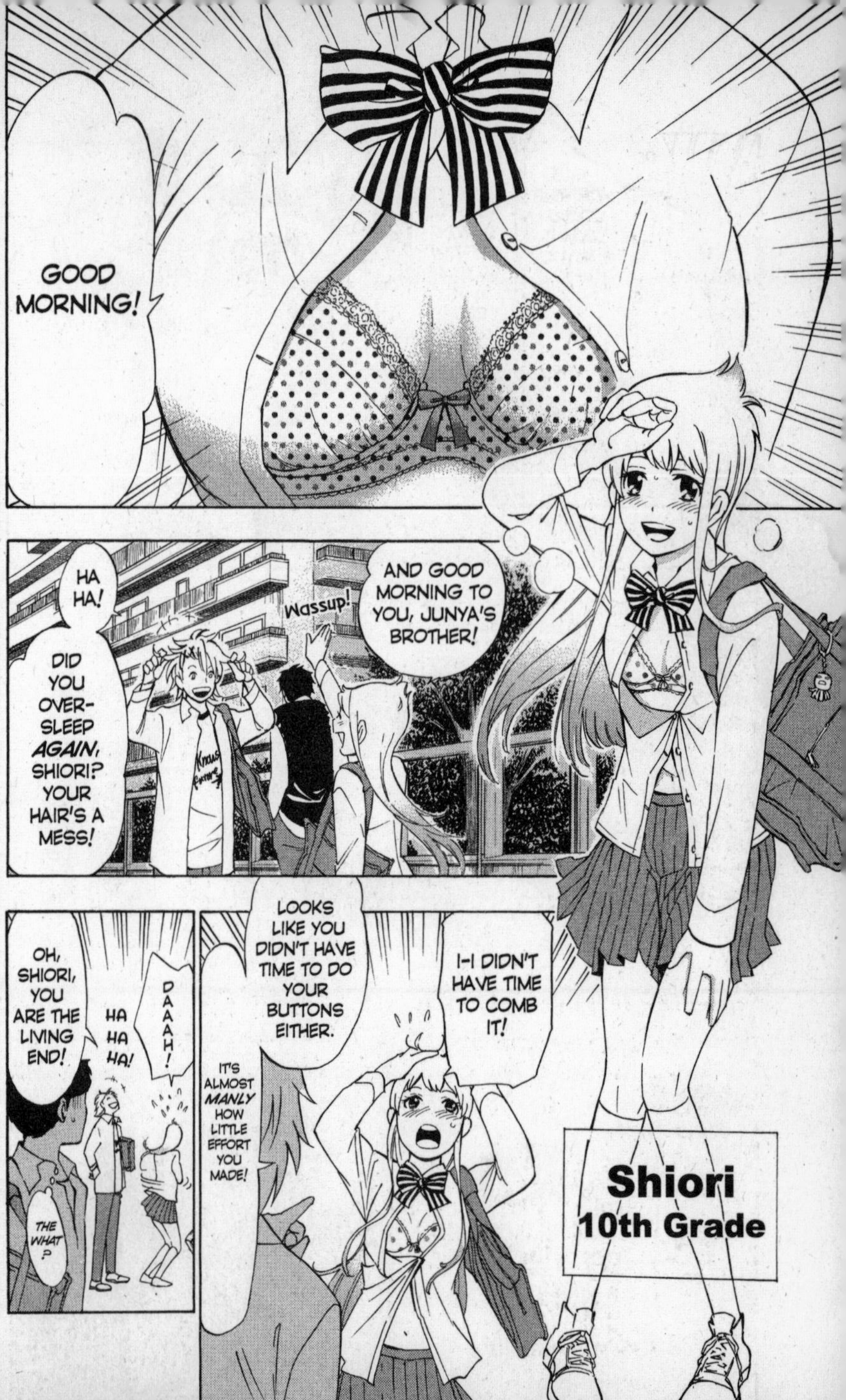
GOOD MORNING!
AND GOOD MORNING TO YOU, JUNYA'S BROTHER!
Wassup!
HA HA!
DID YOU OVER-SLEEP AGAIN, SHIORI? YOUR HAIR'S A MESS!
Shiori 10th Grade
I-I DIDN'T HAVE TIME TO COMB IT!
LOOKS LIKE YOU DIDN'T HAVE TIME TO DO YOUR BUTTONS EITHER.
IT'S ALMOST MANLY HOW LITTLE EFFORT YOU MADE!
DAAAAH!
HA HA HA!
OH, SHIORI, YOU ARE THE LIVING END!
THE WHAT?

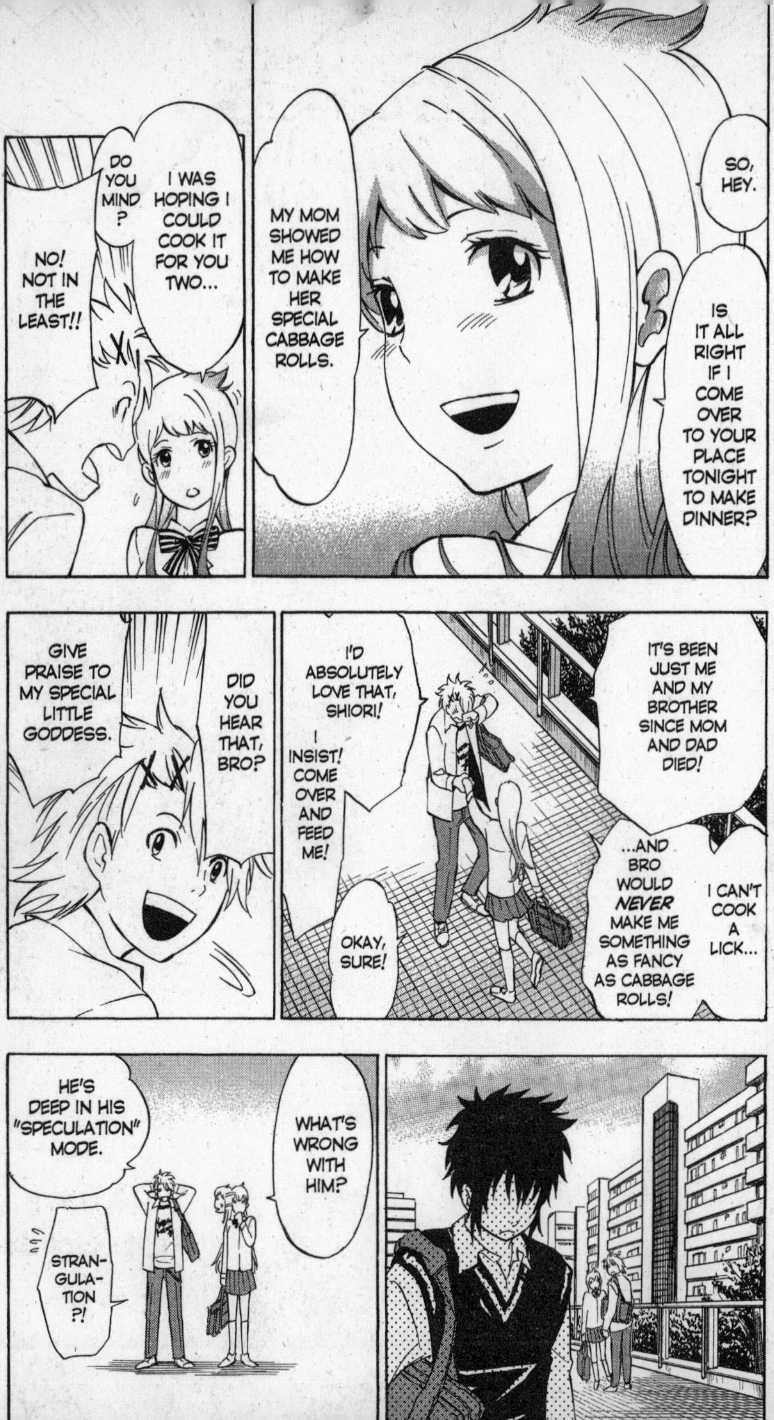
SO, HEY.
IS IT ALL RIGHT IF I COME OVER TO YOUR PLACE TONIGHT TO MAKE DINNER?
MY MOM SHOWED ME HOW TO MAKE HER SPECIAL CABBAGE ROLLS.
I WAS HOPING I COULD COOK IT FOR YOU TWO...
DO YOU MIND?
NO! NOT IN THE LEAST!!
IT'S BEEN JUST ME AND MY BROTHER SINCE MOM AND DAD DIED!
I CAN'T COOK A LICK...
...AND BRO WOULD *NEVER* MAKE ME SOMETHING AS FANCY AS CABBAGE ROLLS!
I'D ABSOLUTELY LOVE THAT, SHIORI!
I INSIST! COME OVER AND FEED ME!
OKAY, SURE!
DID YOU HEAR THAT, BRO?
GIVE PRAISE TO MY SPECIAL LITTLE GODDESS.
WHAT'S WRONG WITH HIM?
HE'S DEEP IN HIS "SPECULATION" MODE.
STRANGULATION?!

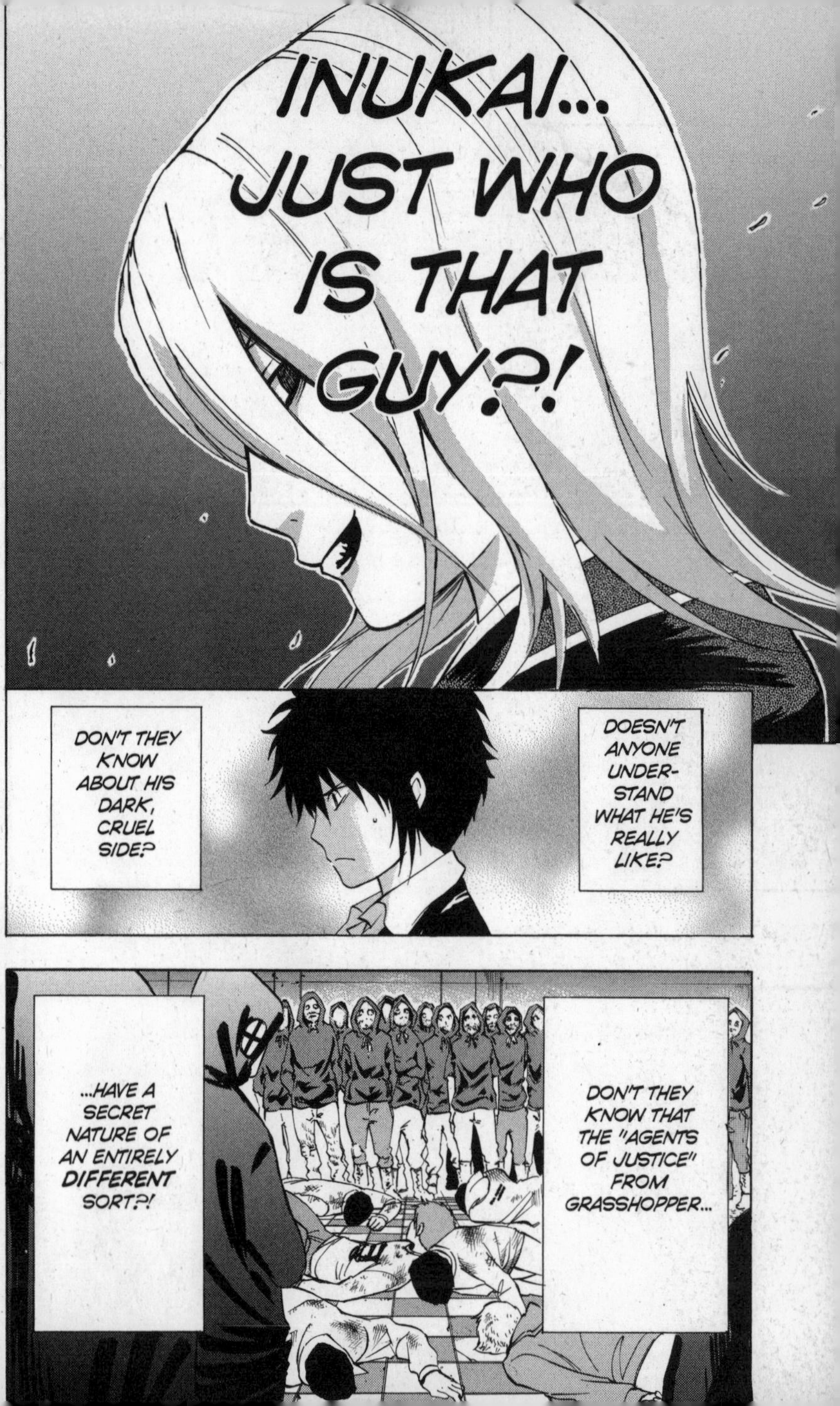
INUKAI... JUST WHO IS THAT GUY?!
DOESN'T ANYONE UNDER-STAND WHAT HE'S REALLY LIKE?
DON'T THEY KNOW ABOUT HIS DARK, CRUEL SIDE?
DON'T THEY KNOW THAT THE "AGENTS OF JUSTICE" FROM GRASSHOPPER...
...HAVE A SECRET NATURE OF AN ENTIRELY DIFFERENT SORT?!

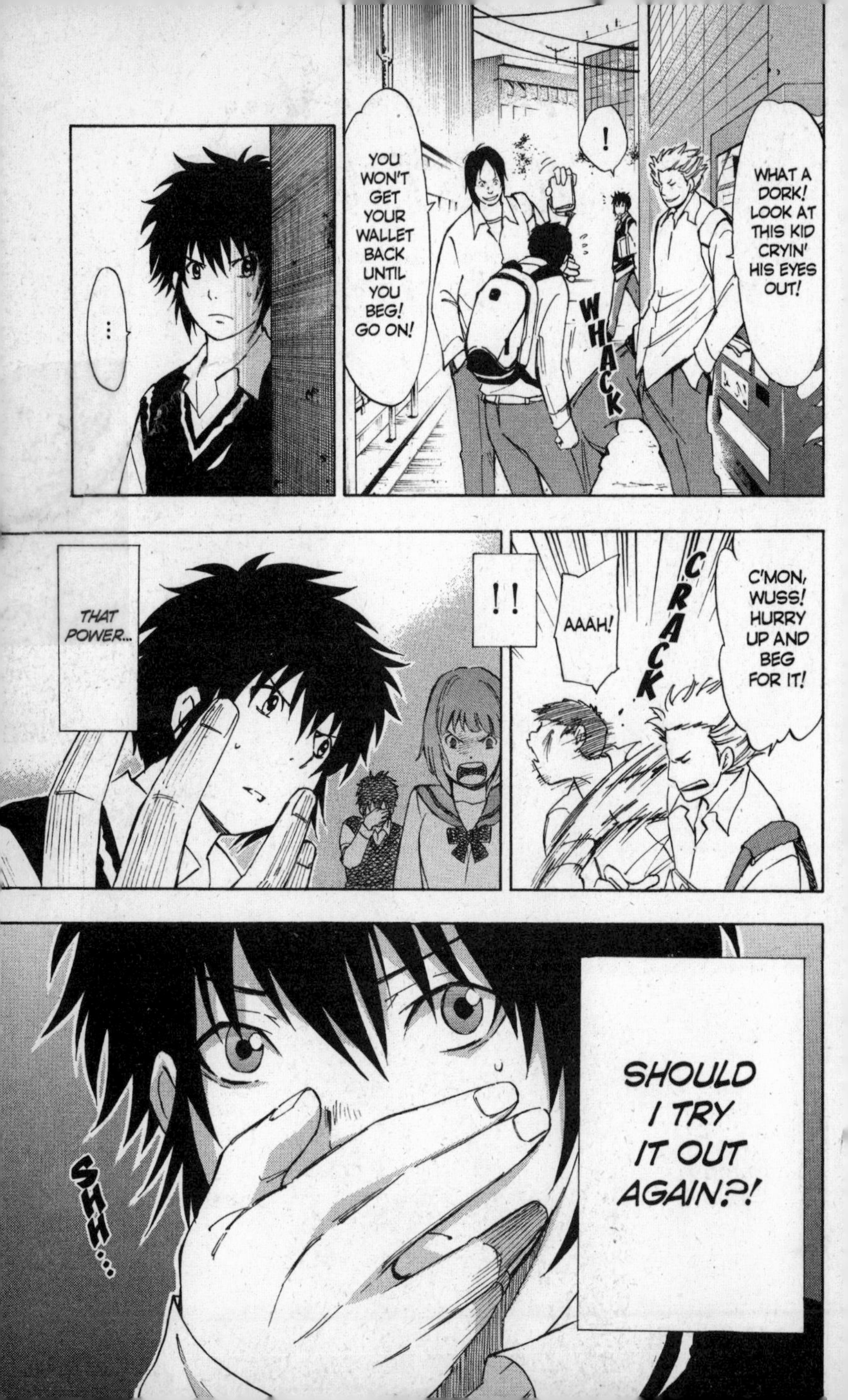
WHAT A DORK! LOOK AT THIS KID CRYIN' HIS EYES OUT!
!
YOU WON'T GET YOUR WALLET BACK UNTIL YOU BEG! GO ON!
WHACK
...
C'MON, WUSS! HURRY UP AND BEG FOR IT!
CRACK
AAAH!
!!
THAT POWER...
SHOULD I TRY IT OUT AGAIN?!
SHH...

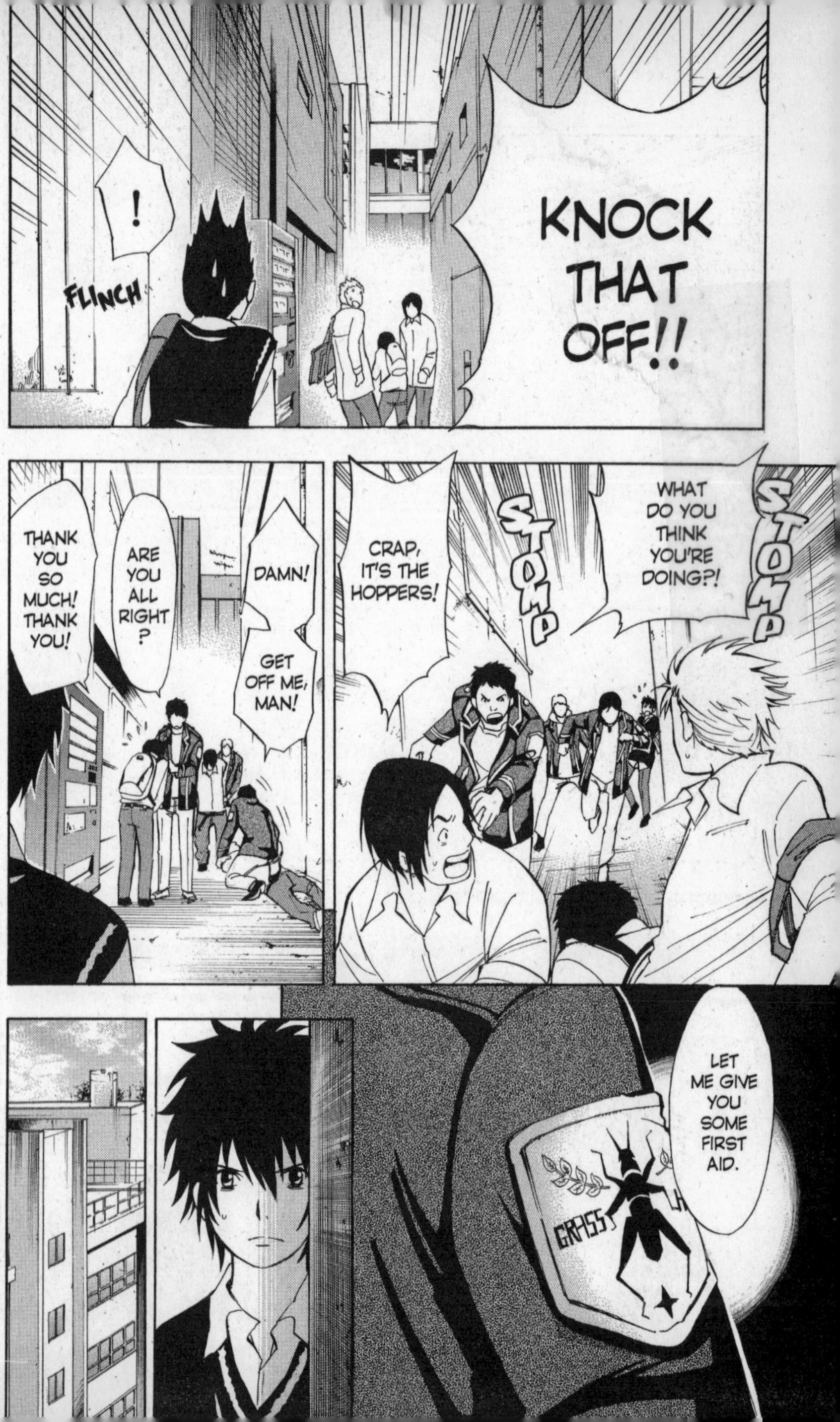
KNOCK THAT OFF!!
!
FLINCH
WHAT DO YOU THINK YOU'RE DOING?!
STOMP
STOMP
CRAP, IT'S THE HOPPERS!
DAMN!
GET OFF ME, MAN!
ARE YOU ALL RIGHT?
THANK YOU SO MUCH! THANK YOU!
LET ME GIVE YOU SOME FIRST AID.
GRASS

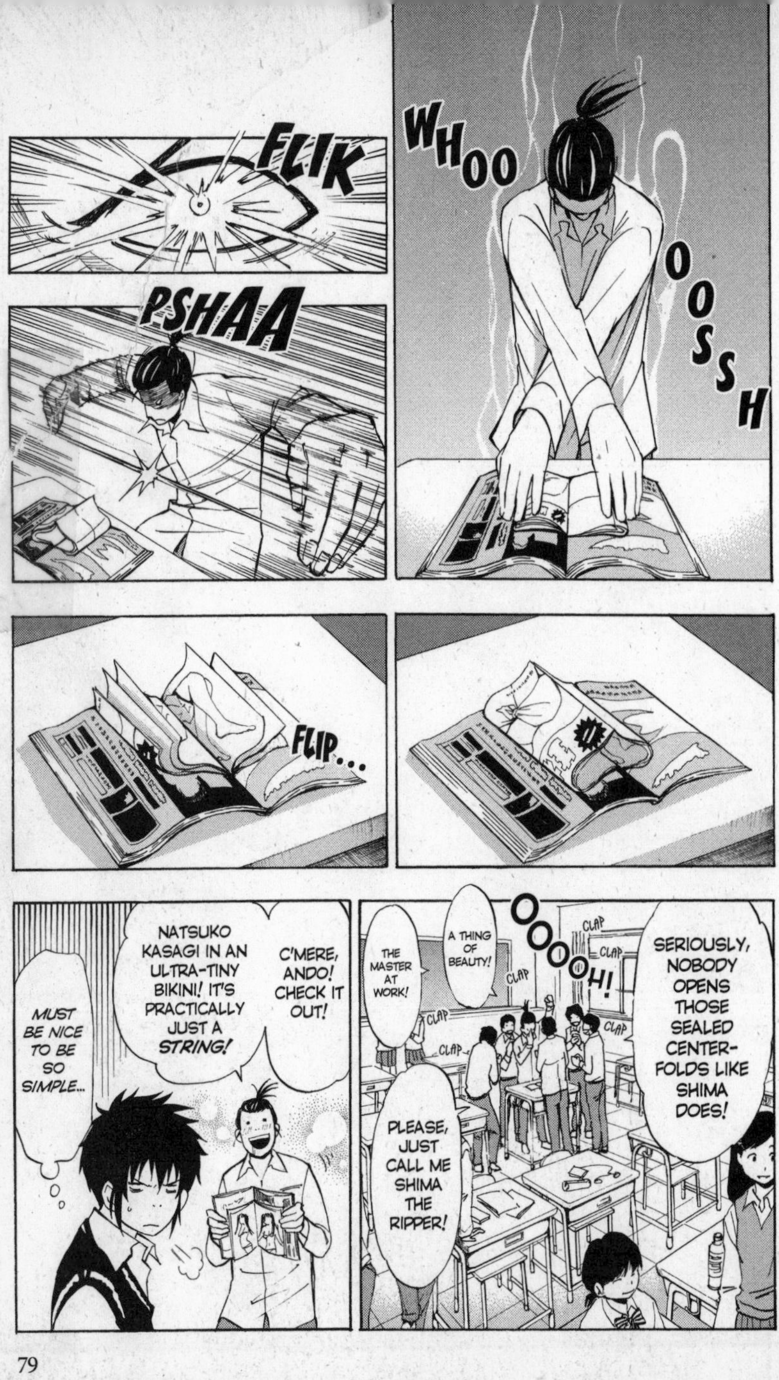
WHOOOOOSSH
FLIK
PSHAA
FLIP...
OOOOOH!
CLAP
CLAP
CLAP
CLAP
CLAP
SERIOUSLY, NOBODY OPENS THOSE SEALED CENTER-FOLDS LIKE SHIMA DOES!
A THING OF BEAUTY!
THE MASTER AT WORK!
PLEASE, JUST CALL ME SHIMA THE RIPPER!
C'MERE, ANDO! CHECK IT OUT!
NATSUKO KASAGI IN AN ULTRA-TINY BIKINI! IT'S PRACTICALLY JUST A STRING!
MUST BE NICE TO BE SO SIMPLE...

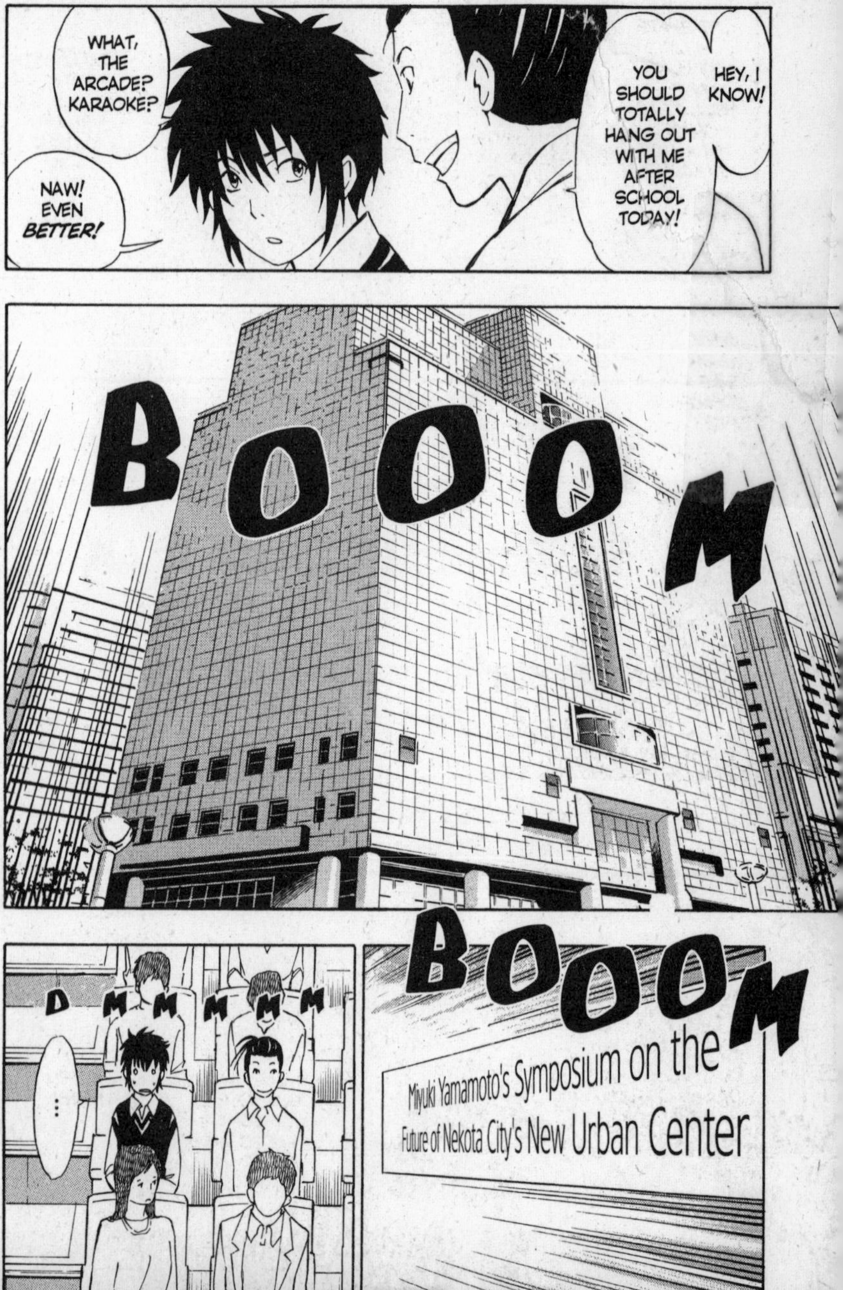
HEY, I KNOW!
YOU SHOULD TOTALLY HANG OUT WITH ME AFTER SCHOOL TODAY!
WHAT, THE ARCADE? KARAOKE?
NAW! EVEN *BETTER!*
BOOOM
BOOOM
Miyuki Yamamoto's Symposium on the Future of Nekota City's New Urban Center
DMMMMMM
...

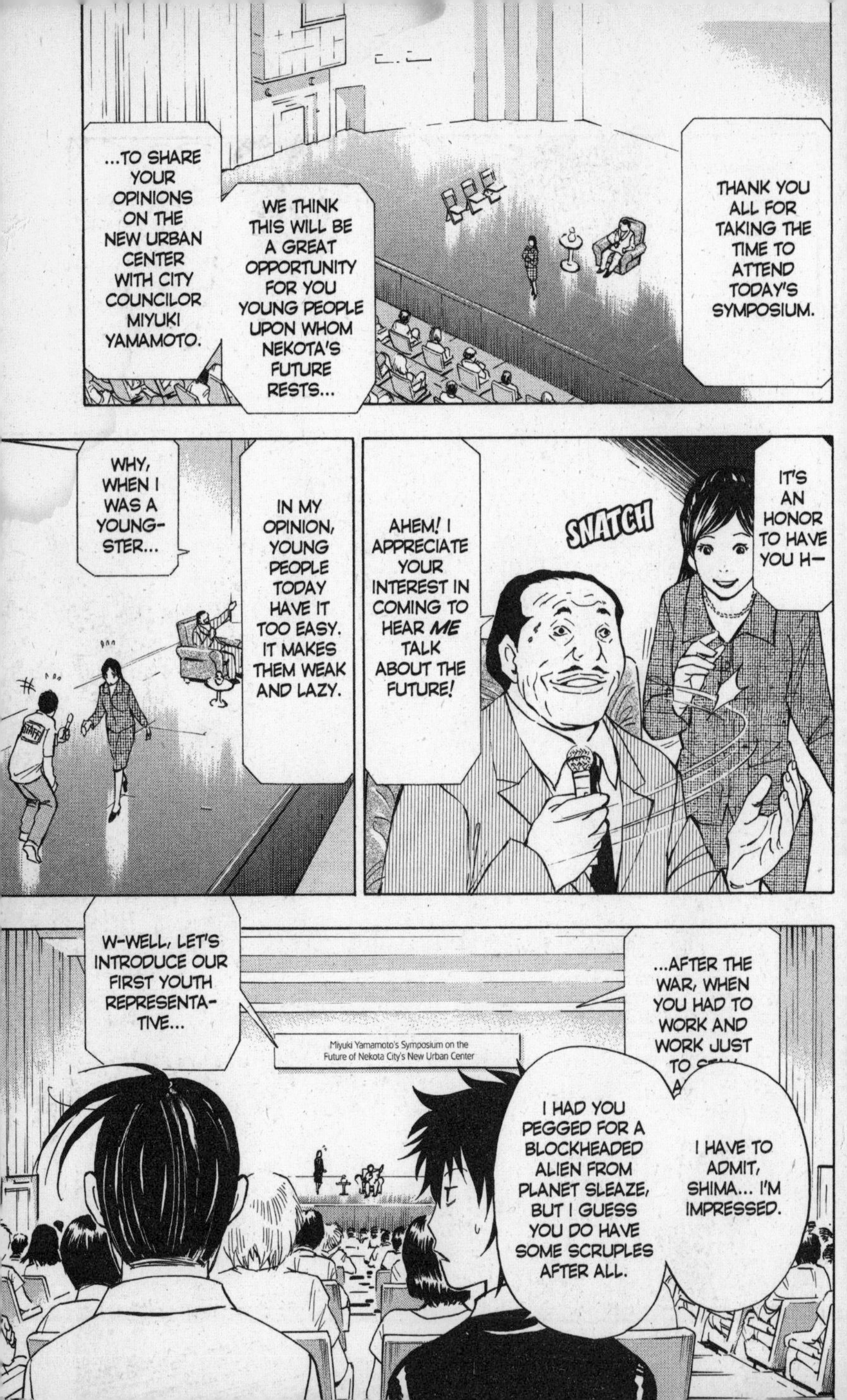
THANK YOU ALL FOR TAKING THE TIME TO ATTEND TODAY'S SYMPOSIUM.
WE THINK THIS WILL BE A GREAT OPPORTUNITY FOR YOU YOUNG PEOPLE UPON WHOM NEKOTA'S FUTURE RESTS...
...TO SHARE YOUR OPINIONS ON THE NEW URBAN CENTER WITH CITY COUNCILOR MIYUKI YAMAMOTO.
IT'S AN HONOR TO HAVE YOU H—
SNATCH
AHEM! I APPRECIATE YOUR INTEREST IN COMING TO HEAR *ME* TALK ABOUT THE FUTURE!
IN MY OPINION, YOUNG PEOPLE TODAY HAVE IT TOO EASY. IT MAKES THEM WEAK AND LAZY.
WHY, WHEN I WAS A YOUNGSTER...
...AFTER THE WAR, WHEN YOU HAD TO WORK AND WORK JUST
W-WELL, LET'S INTRODUCE OUR FIRST YOUTH REPRESENTATIVE...
Miyuki Yamamoto's Symposium on the Future of Nekota City's New Urban Center
I HAVE TO ADMIT, SHIMA... I'M IMPRESSED.
I HAD YOU PEGGED FOR A BLOCKHEADED ALIEN FROM PLANET SLEAZE, BUT I GUESS YOU DO HAVE SOME SCRUPLES AFTER ALL.

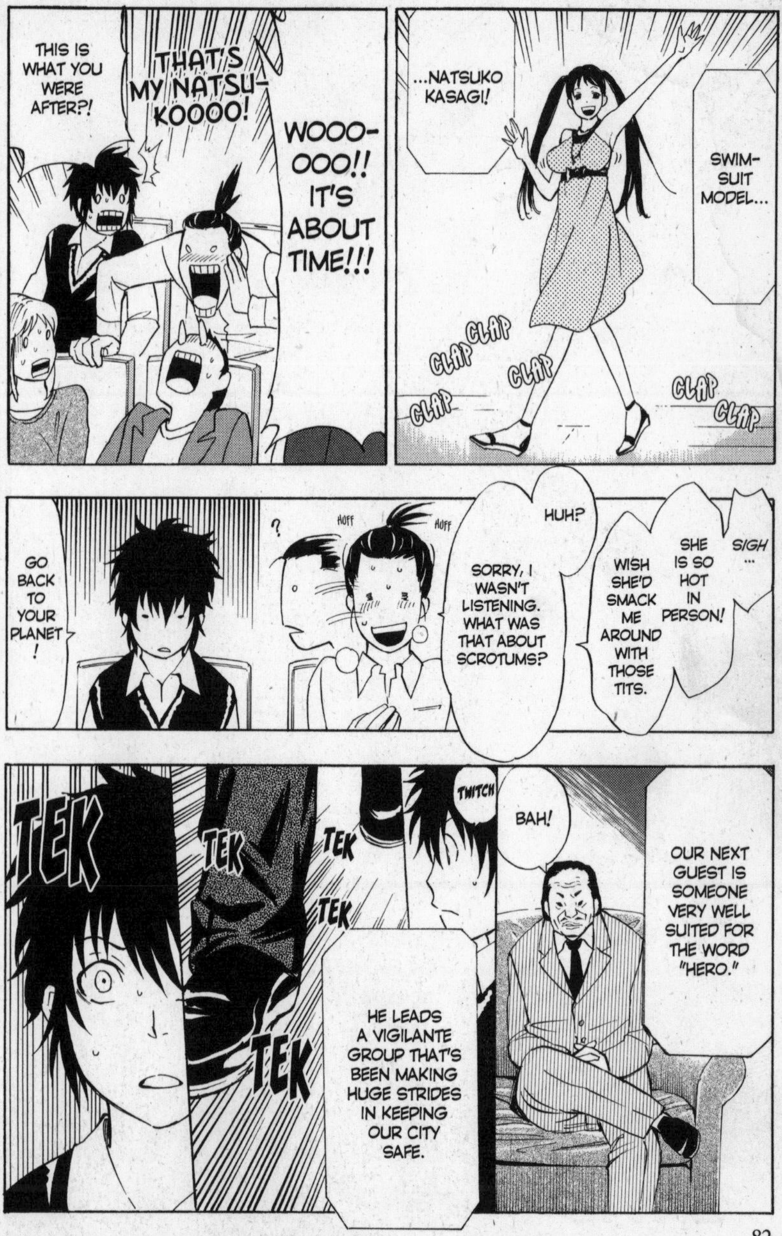
SWIM-SUIT MODEL...
...NATSUKO KASAGI!
CLAP
CLAP
CLAP
CLAP
CLAP
CLAP
WOOO-OOO!! IT'S ABOUT TIME!!!
THAT'S MY NATSU-KOOOO!
THIS IS WHAT YOU WERE AFTER?!
SIGH...
SHE IS SO HOT IN PERSON!
WISH SHE'D SMACK ME AROUND WITH THOSE TITS.
HUH?
SORRY, I WASN'T LISTENING. WHAT WAS THAT ABOUT SCROTUMS?
HUFF
HUFF
?
GO BACK TO YOUR PLANET!
OUR NEXT GUEST IS SOMEONE VERY WELL SUITED FOR THE WORD "HERO."
BAH!
TWITCH
HE LEADS A VIGILANTE GROUP THAT'S BEEN MAKING HUGE STRIDES IN KEEPING OUR CITY SAFE.
TEK
TEK
TEK
TEK
TEK

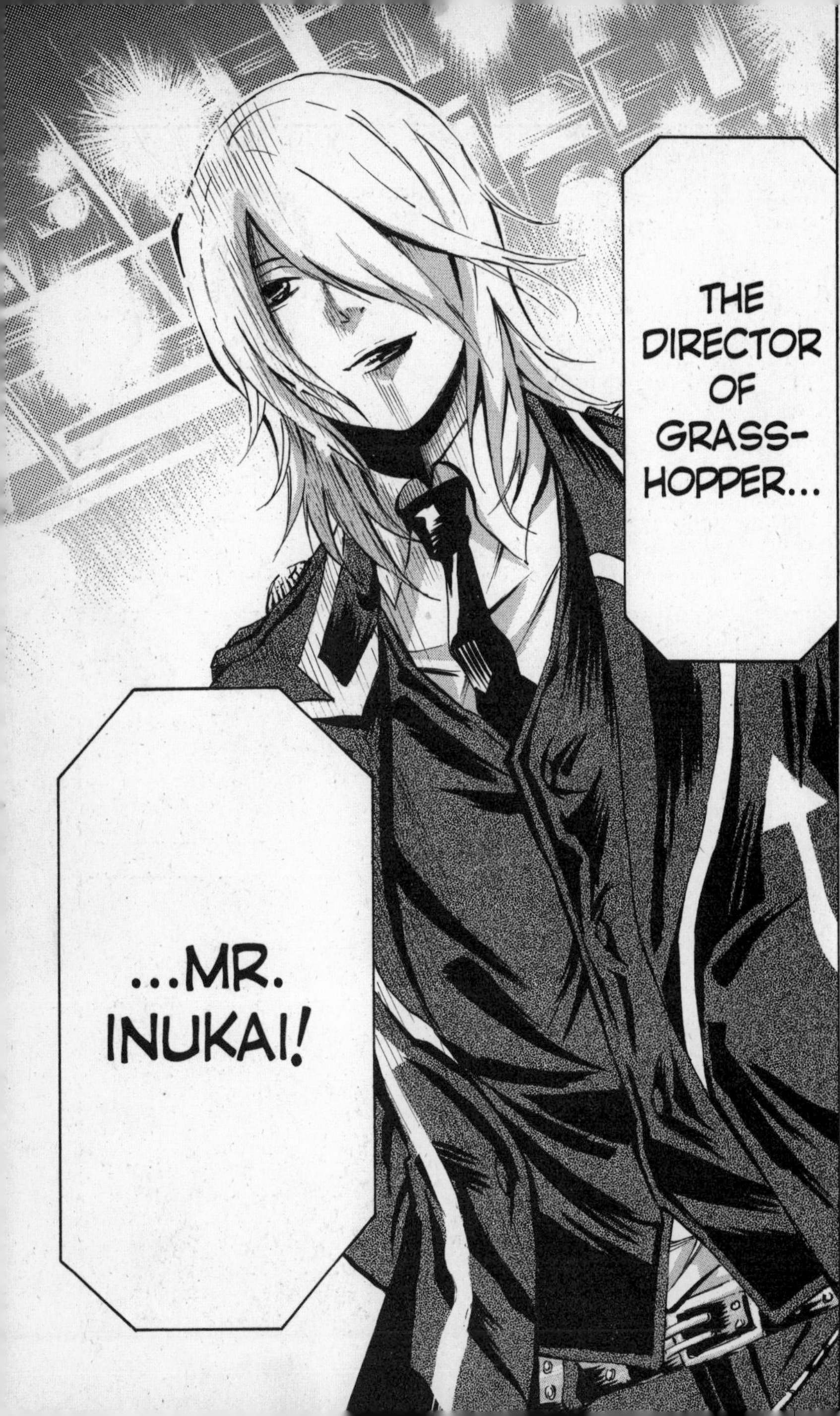
THE DIRECTOR OF GRASS-HOPPER...
...MR. INUKAI!

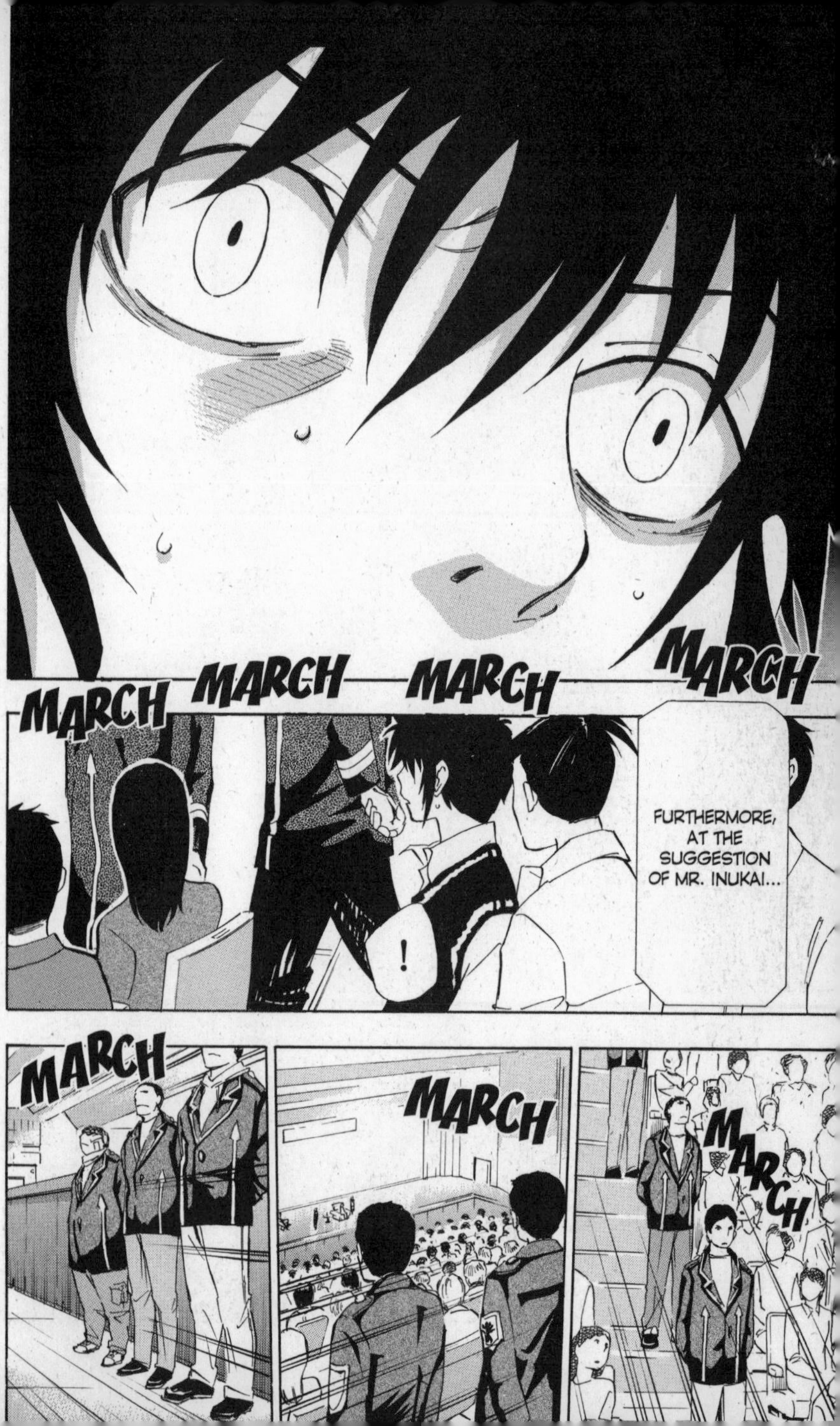
MARCH
MARCH
MARCH
MARCH
FURTHERMORE, AT THE SUGGESTION OF MR. INUKAI...
!
MARCH
MARCH
MARCH

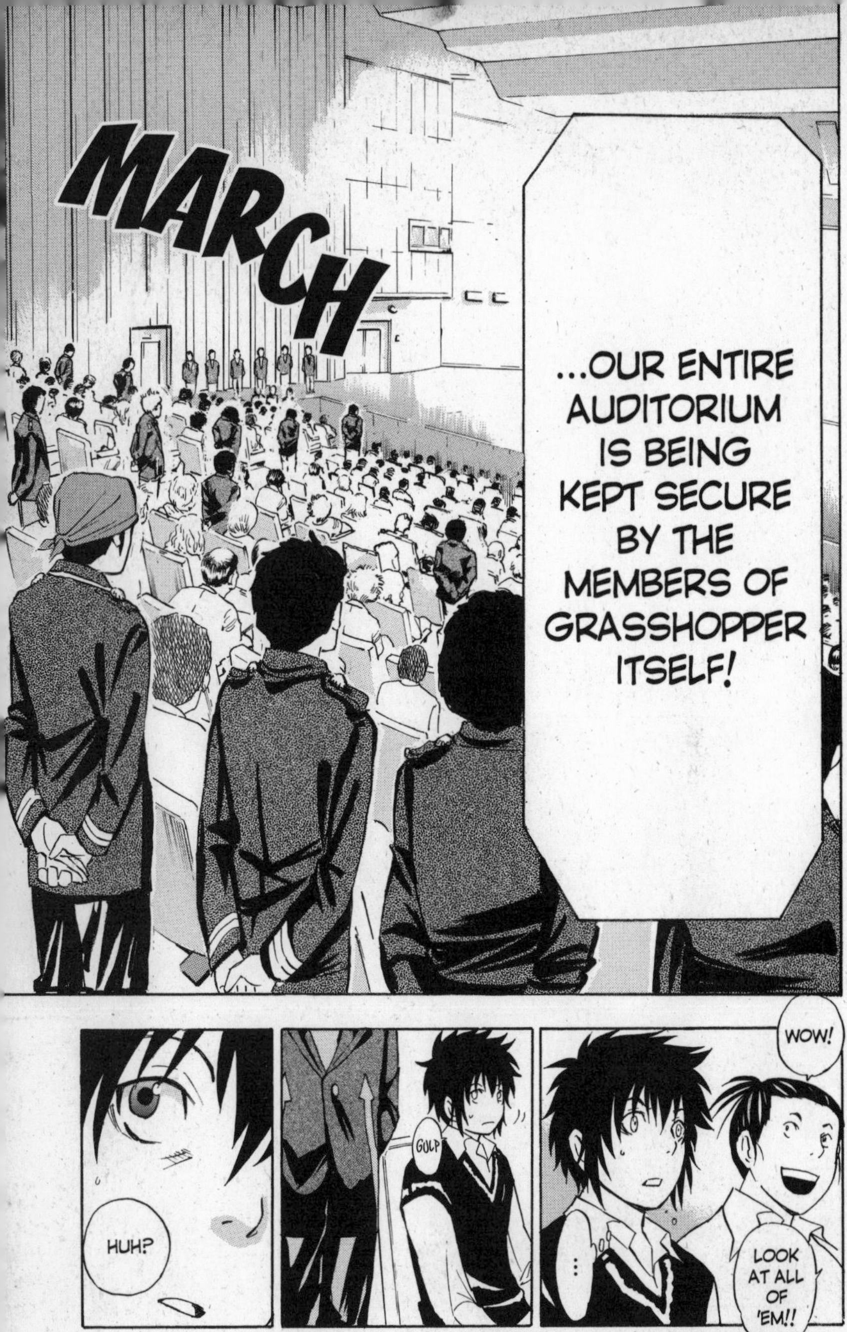
MARCH
...OUR ENTIRE AUDITORIUM IS BEING KEPT SECURE BY THE MEMBERS OF GRASSHOPPER ITSELF!
WOW!
LOOK AT ALL OF 'EM!!
...
GULP
HUH?

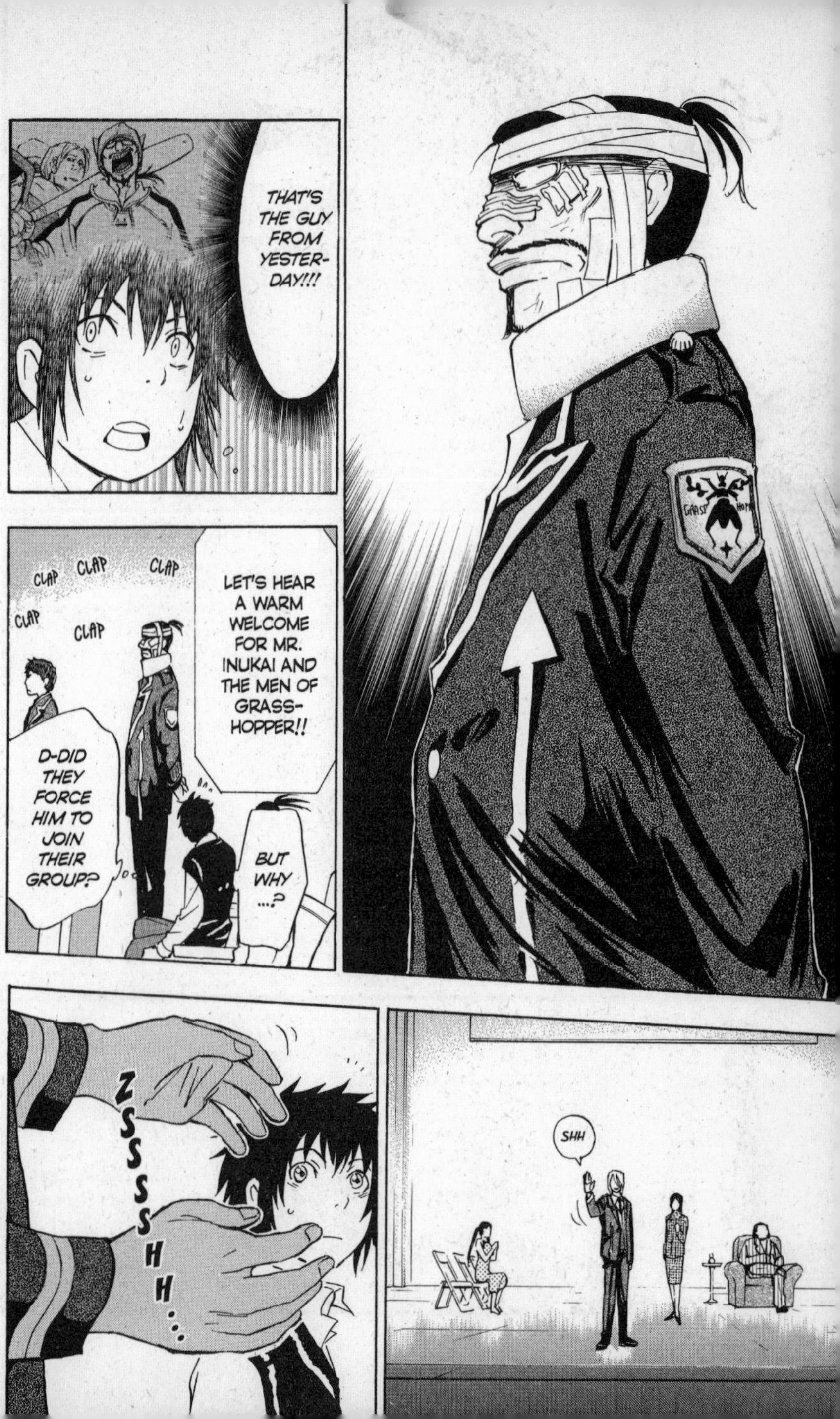
THAT'S THE GUY FROM YESTER-DAY!!!
CLAP CLAP CLAP CLAP CLAP
LET'S HEAR A WARM WELCOME FOR MR. INUKAI AND THE MEN OF GRASS-HOPPER!!
BUT WHY ...?
D-DID THEY FORCE HIM TO JOIN THEIR GROUP?
SHH
ZSSSSHH...

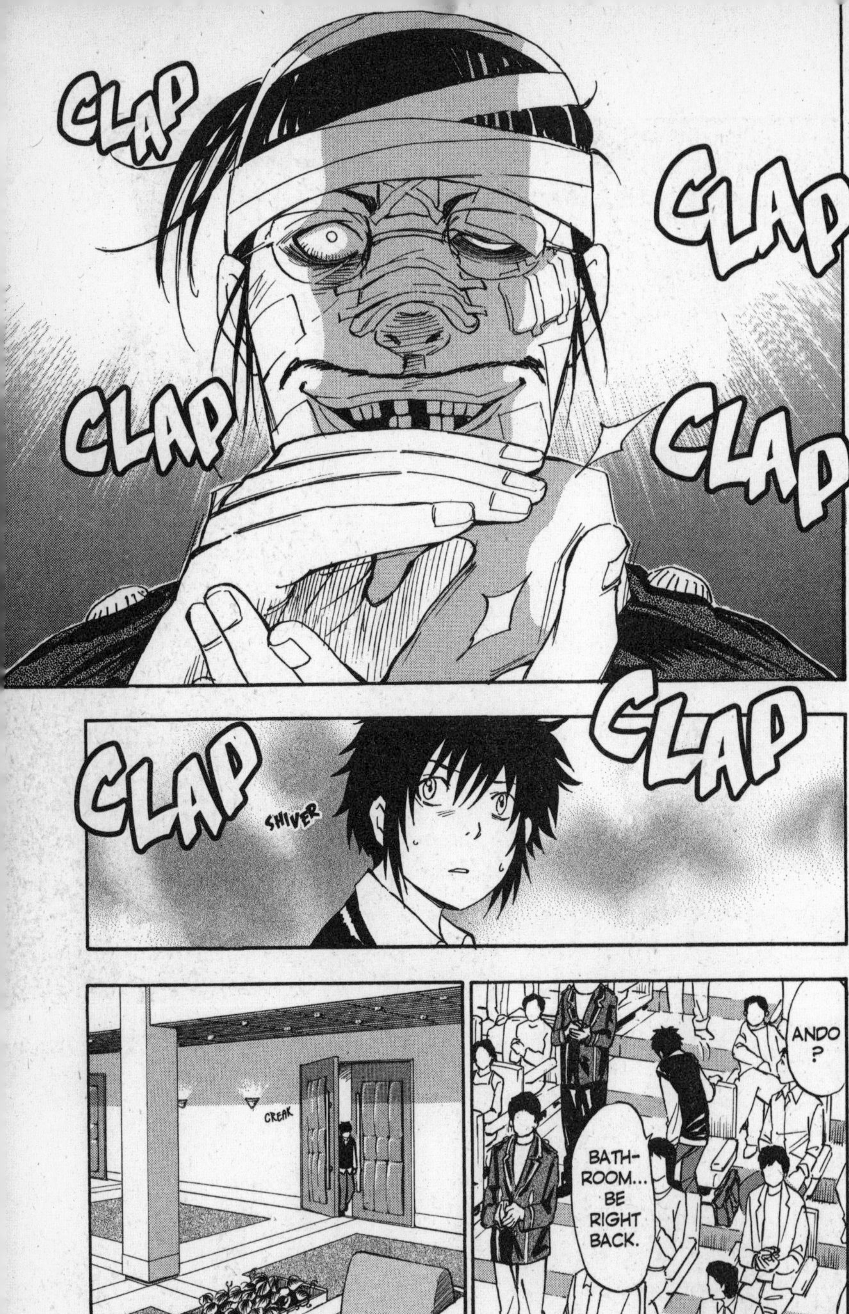
CLAP
CLAP
CLAP
CLAP
CLAP
CLAP
SHIVER
ANDO?
BATHROOM... BE RIGHT BACK.
CREAK

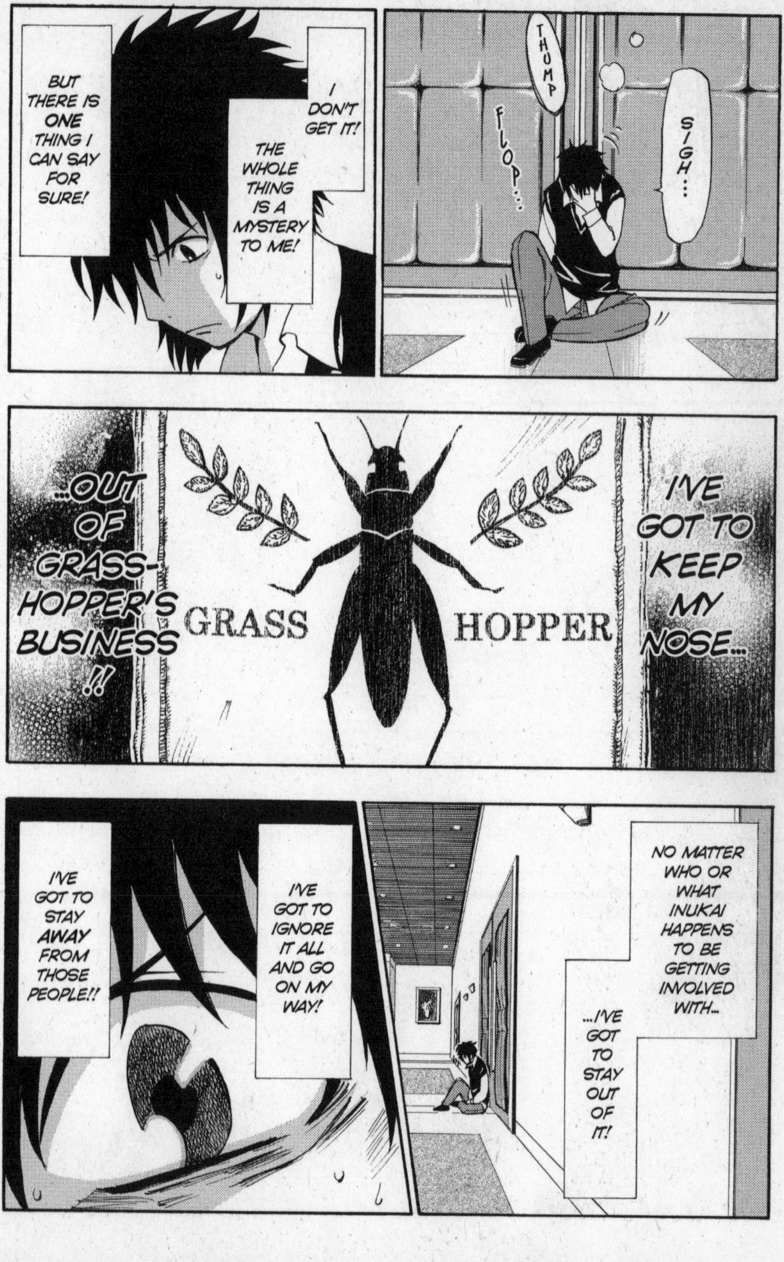
SIGH...
THUMP
FLOP...
I DON'T GET IT!
THE WHOLE THING IS A MYSTERY TO ME!
BUT THERE IS ONE THING I CAN SAY FOR SURE!
I'VE GOT TO KEEP MY NOSE...
HOPPER
GRASS
...OUT OF GRASS-HOPPER'S BUSINESS!!
NO MATTER WHO OR WHAT INUKAI HAPPENS TO BE GETTING INVOLVED WITH...
...I'VE GOT TO STAY OUT OF IT!
I'VE GOT TO IGNORE IT ALL AND GO ON MY WAY!
I'VE GOT TO STAY AWAY FROM THOSE PEOPLE!!

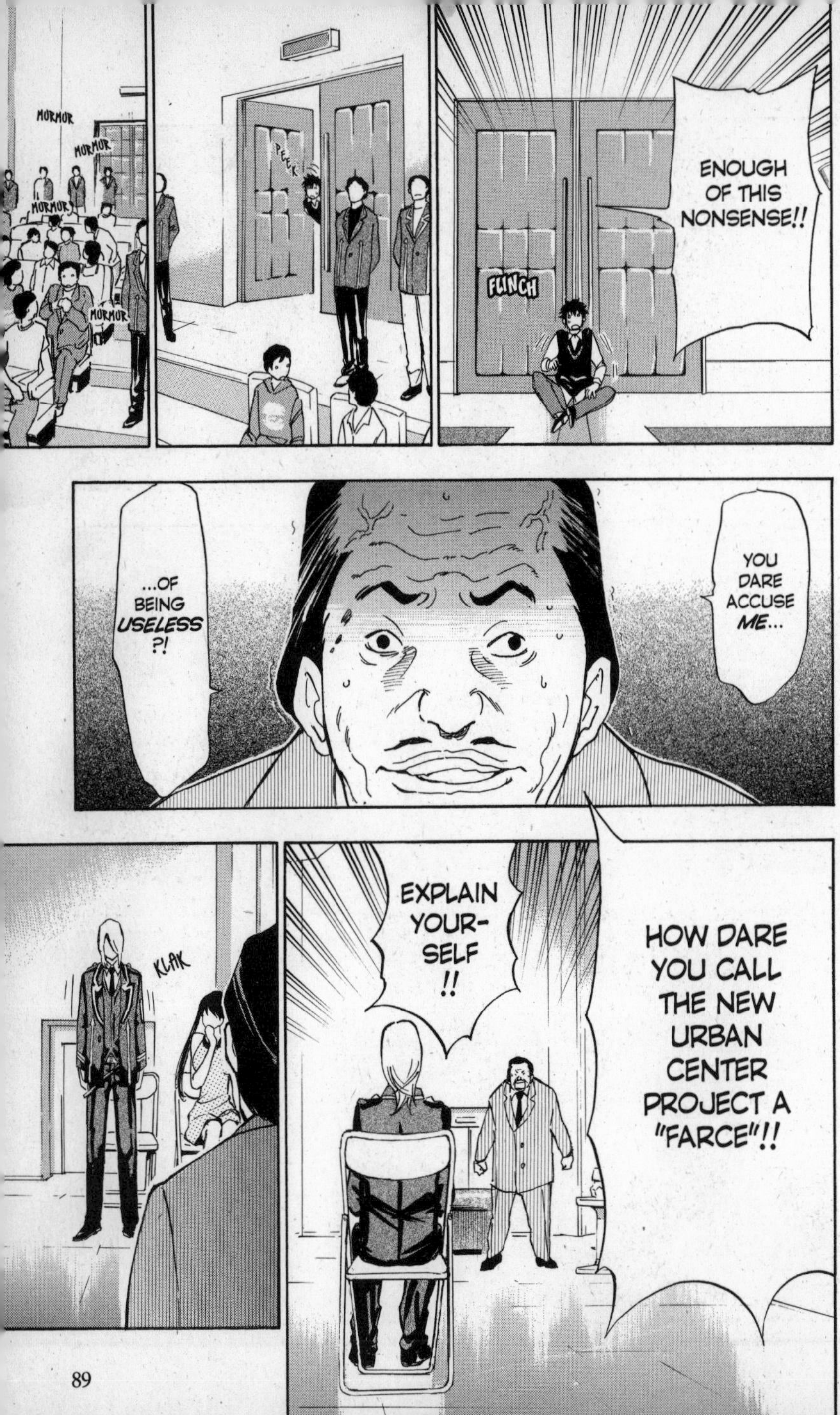
ENOUGH OF THIS NONSENSE!!
FLINCH
PEEK
MURMUR
MURMUR
MURMUR
MURMUR
YOU DARE ACCUSE *ME*...
...OF BEING *USELESS* ?!
HOW DARE YOU CALL THE NEW URBAN CENTER PROJECT A "FARCE"!!
EXPLAIN YOUR-SELF !!
KLAK

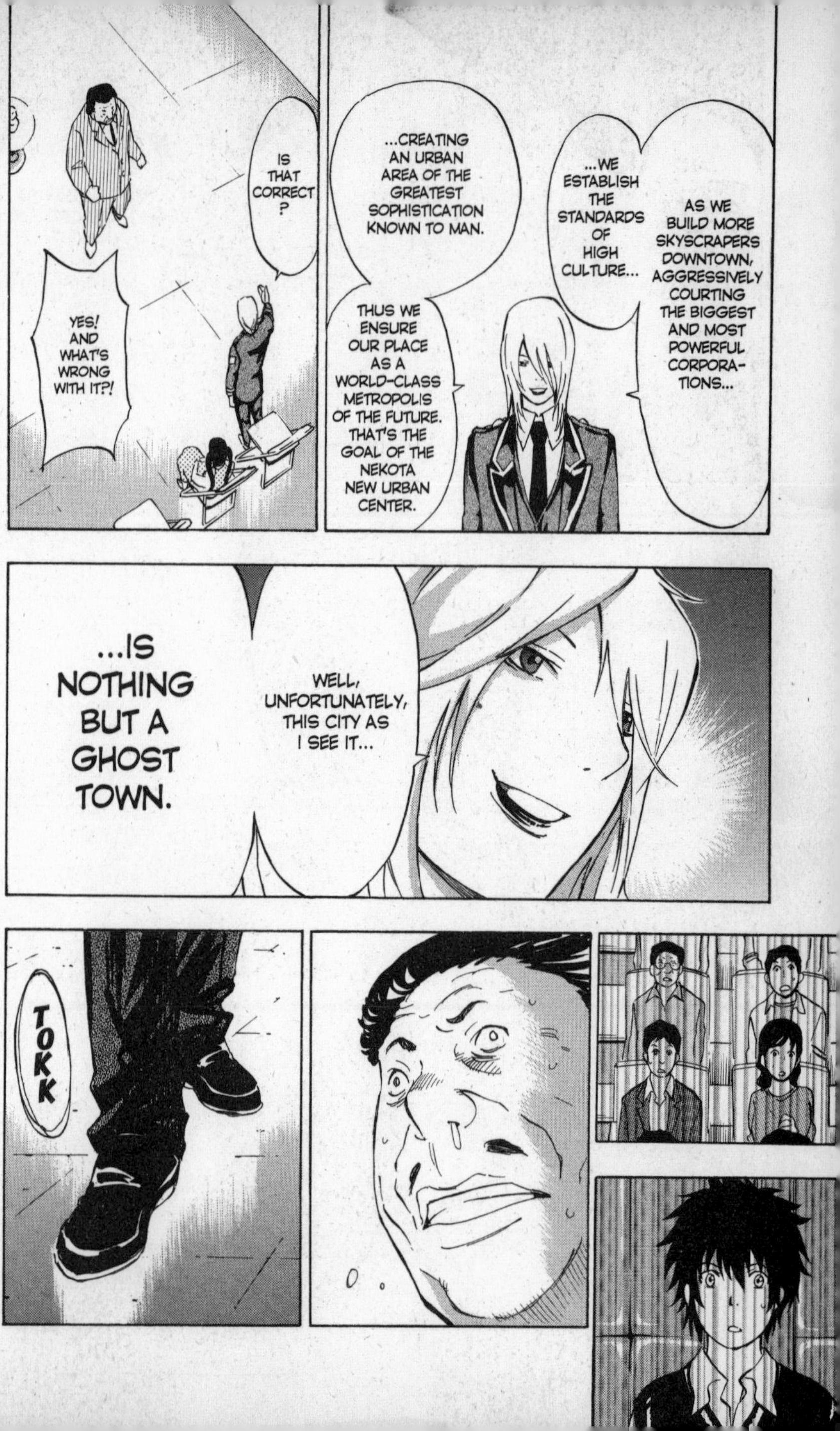
AS WE BUILD MORE SKYSCRAPERS DOWNTOWN, AGGRESSIVELY COURTING THE BIGGEST AND MOST POWERFUL CORPORA-TIONS...
...WE ESTABLISH THE STANDARDS OF HIGH CULTURE...
...CREATING AN URBAN AREA OF THE GREATEST SOPHISTICATION KNOWN TO MAN.
THUS WE ENSURE OUR PLACE AS A WORLD-CLASS METROPOLIS OF THE FUTURE. THAT'S THE GOAL OF THE NEKOTA NEW URBAN CENTER.
IS THAT CORRECT?
YES! AND WHAT'S WRONG WITH IT?!
WELL, UNFORTUNATELY, THIS CITY AS I SEE IT...
...IS NOTHING BUT A GHOST TOWN.
TOKK

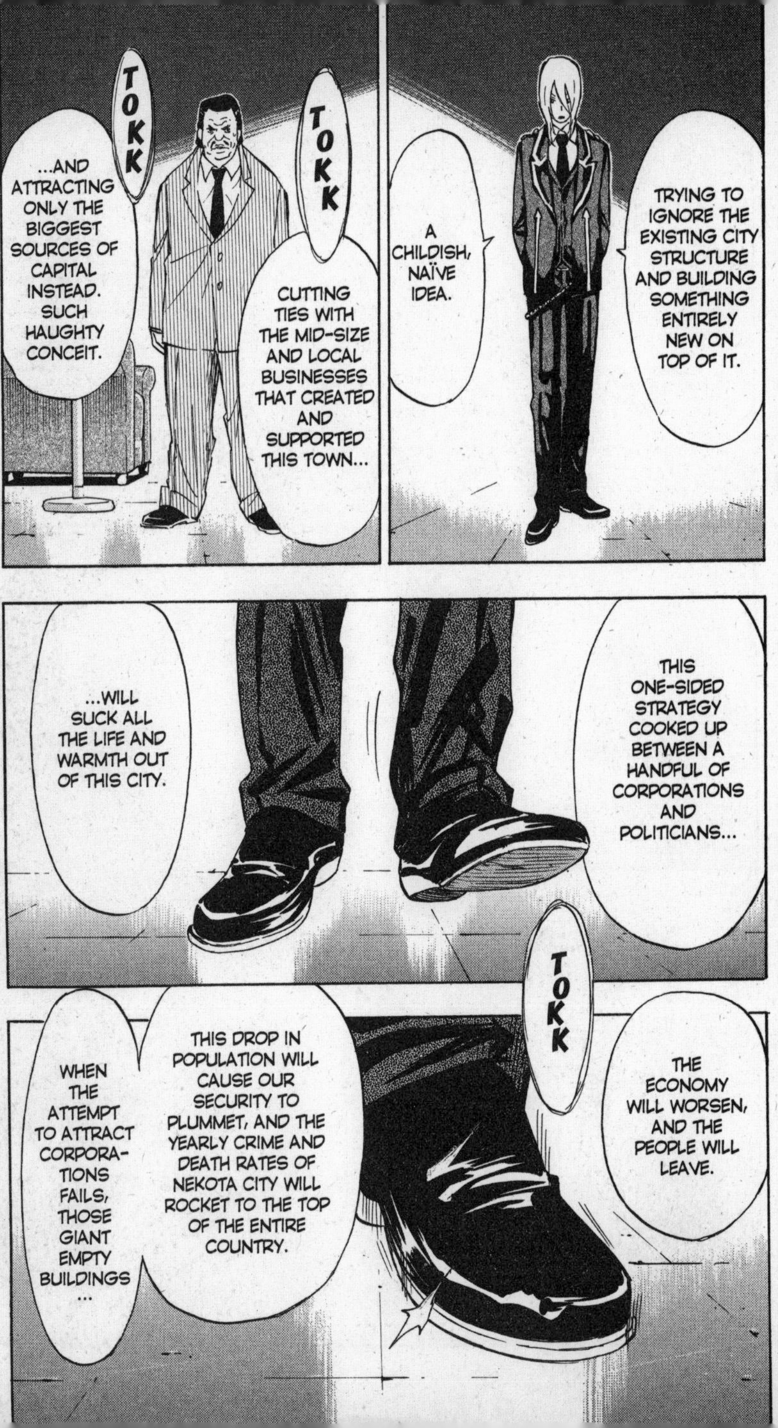
TRYING TO IGNORE THE EXISTING CITY STRUCTURE AND BUILDING SOMETHING ENTIRELY NEW ON TOP OF IT.
A CHILDISH, NAÏVE IDEA.
TOKK
CUTTING TIES WITH THE MID-SIZE AND LOCAL BUSINESSES THAT CREATED AND SUPPORTED THIS TOWN...
TOKK
...AND ATTRACTING ONLY THE BIGGEST SOURCES OF CAPITAL INSTEAD. SUCH HAUGHTY CONCEIT.
THIS ONE-SIDED STRATEGY COOKED UP BETWEEN A HANDFUL OF CORPORATIONS AND POLITICIANS...
...WILL SUCK ALL THE LIFE AND WARMTH OUT OF THIS CITY.
TOKK
THE ECONOMY WILL WORSEN, AND THE PEOPLE WILL LEAVE.
THIS DROP IN POPULATION WILL CAUSE OUR SECURITY TO PLUMMET, AND THE YEARLY CRIME AND DEATH RATES OF NEKOTA CITY WILL ROCKET TO THE TOP OF THE ENTIRE COUNTRY.
WHEN THE ATTEMPT TO ATTRACT CORPORA-TIONS FAILS, THOSE GIANT EMPTY BUILDINGS ...

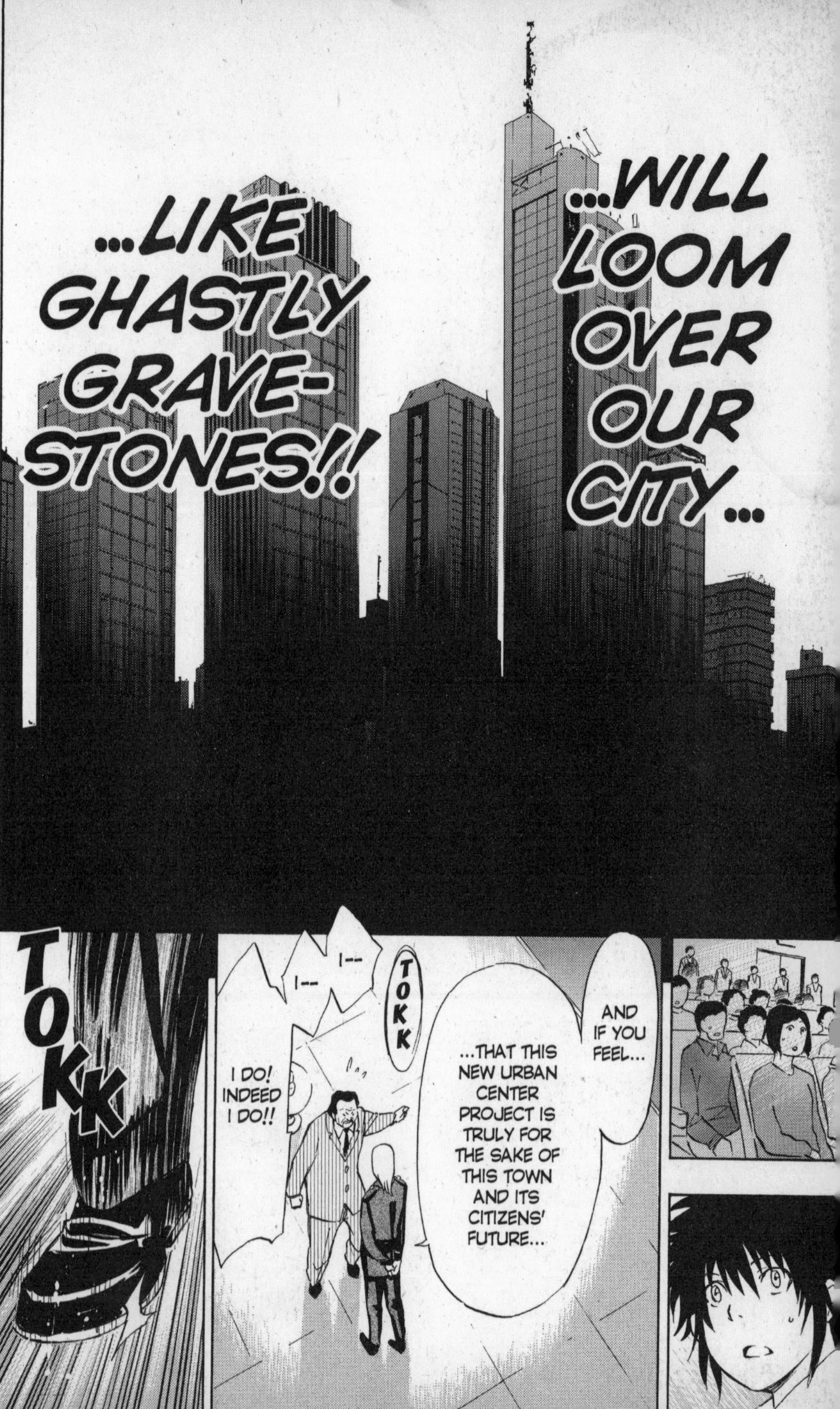
...WILL LOOM OVER OUR CITY...
...LIKE GHASTLY GRAVE-STONES!!
AND IF YOU FEEL...
...THAT THIS NEW URBAN CENTER PROJECT IS TRULY FOR THE SAKE OF THIS TOWN AND ITS CITIZENS' FUTURE...
TOKK
I--
I--
I DO! INDEED I DO!!
TOKK

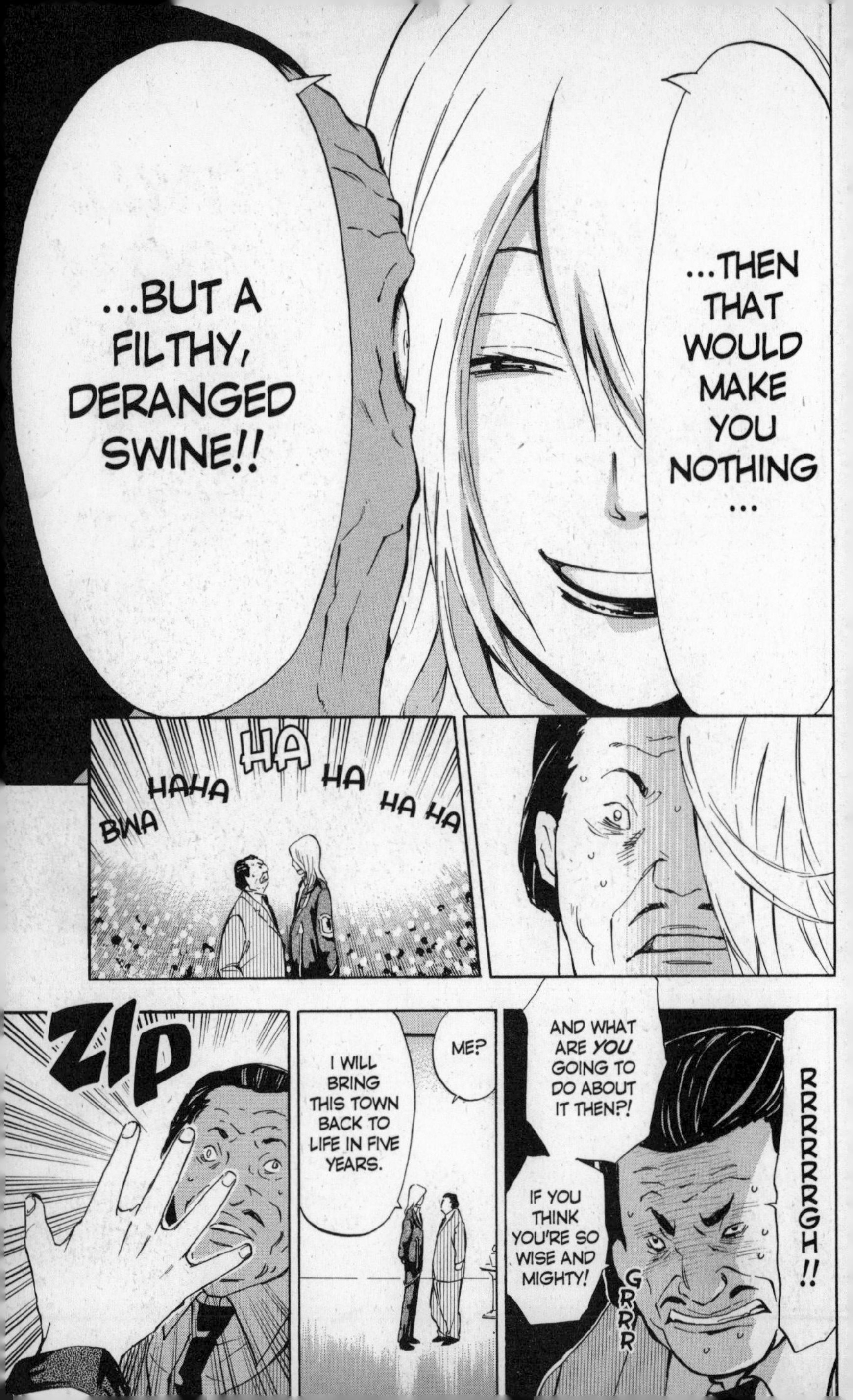
...THEN THAT WOULD MAKE YOU NOTHING...
...BUT A FILTHY, DERANGED SWINE!!
BWA HAHA HA HA HA HA
RRRRRRRGH!!
AND WHAT ARE YOU GOING TO DO ABOUT IT THEN?!
IF YOU THINK YOU'RE SO WISE AND MIGHTY!
GRRR
ME?
I WILL BRING THIS TOWN BACK TO LIFE IN FIVE YEARS.
ZIP

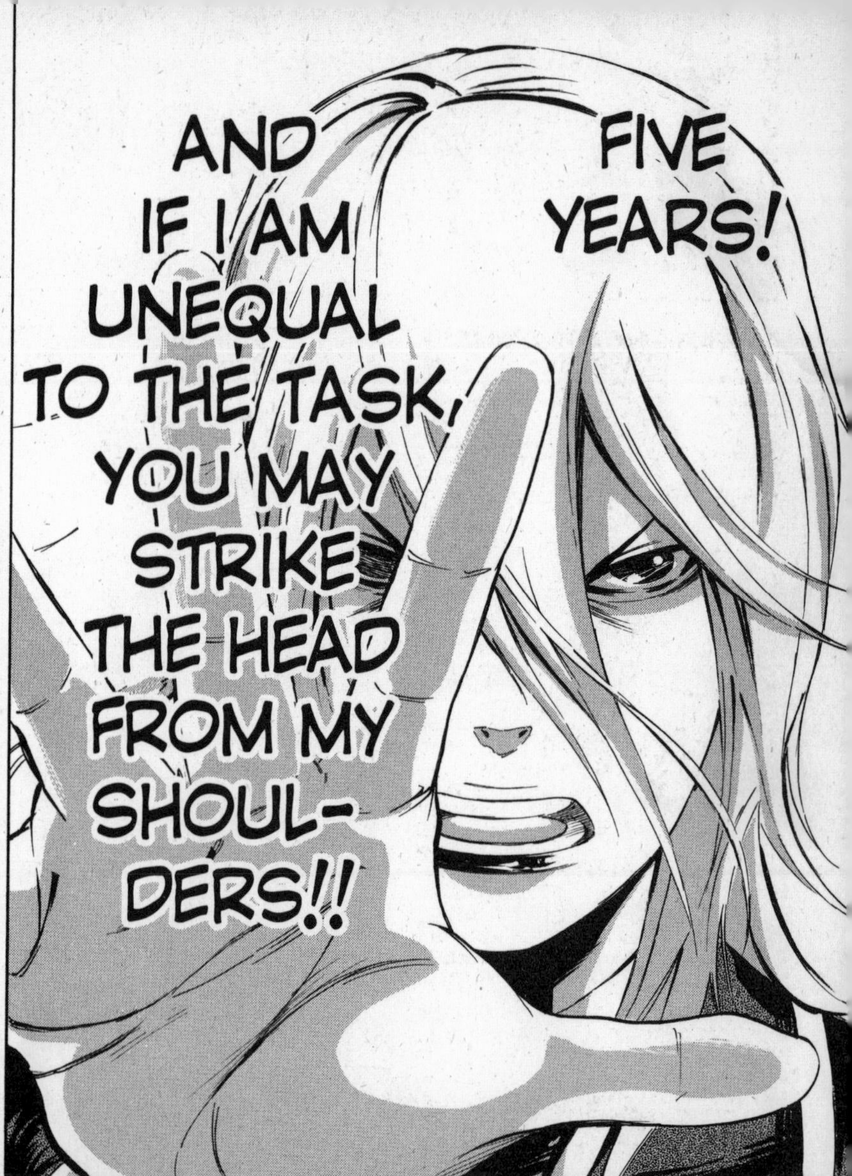
FIVE YEARS!
AND IF I AM UNEQUAL TO THE TASK, YOU MAY STRIKE THE HEAD FROM MY SHOUL-DERS!!

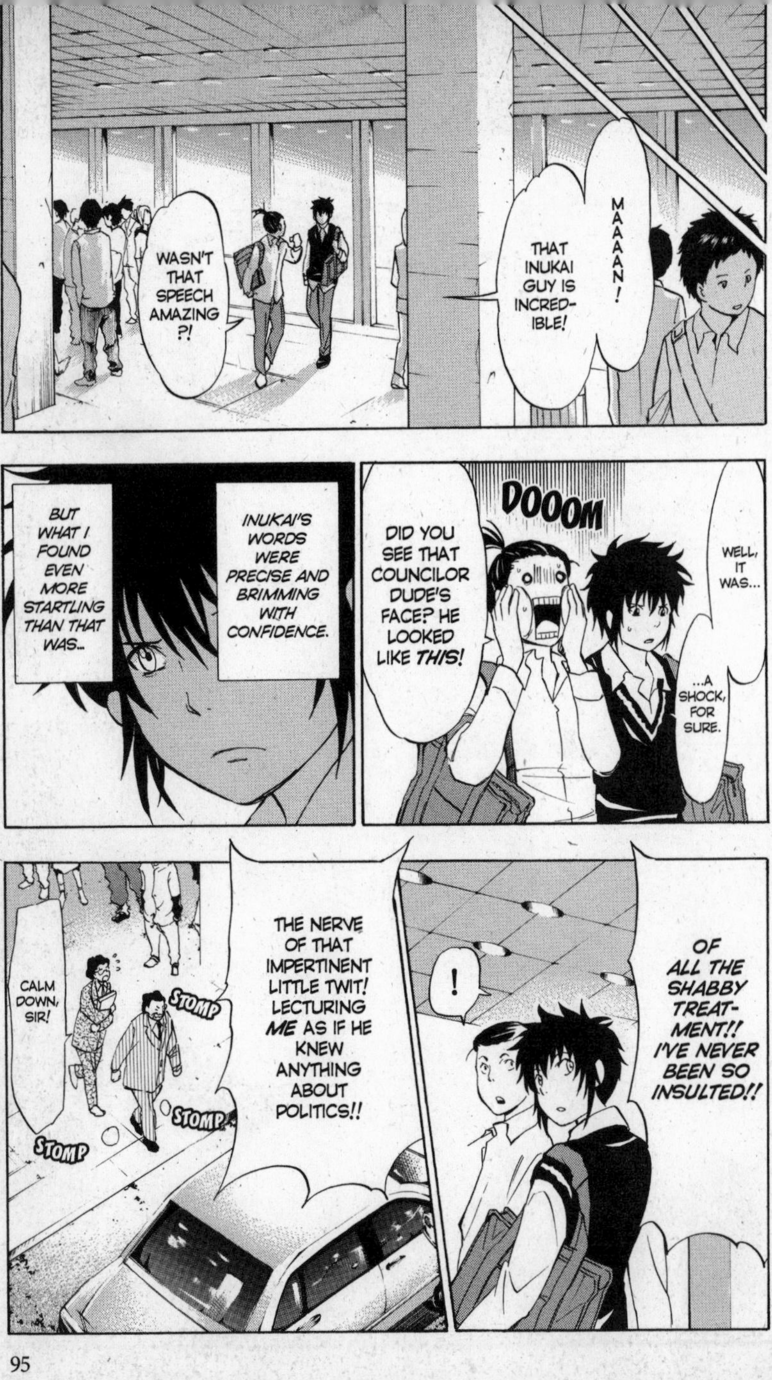
MAAAAN!
THAT INUKAI GUY IS INCRED-IBLE!
WASN'T THAT SPEECH AMAZING?!
DOOOM
DID YOU SEE THAT COUNCILOR DUDE'S FACE? HE LOOKED LIKE *THIS*!
WELL, IT WAS...
...A SHOCK, FOR SURE.
INUKAI'S WORDS WERE PRECISE AND BRIMMING WITH CONFIDENCE.
BUT WHAT I FOUND EVEN MORE STARTLING THAN THAT WAS...
OF ALL THE SHABBY TREAT-MENT!! I'VE NEVER BEEN SO INSULTED!!
!
THE NERVE OF THAT IMPERTINENT LITTLE TWIT! LECTURING *ME* AS IF HE KNEW ANYTHING ABOUT POLITICS!!
STOMP
CALM DOWN, SIR!
STOMP
STOMP

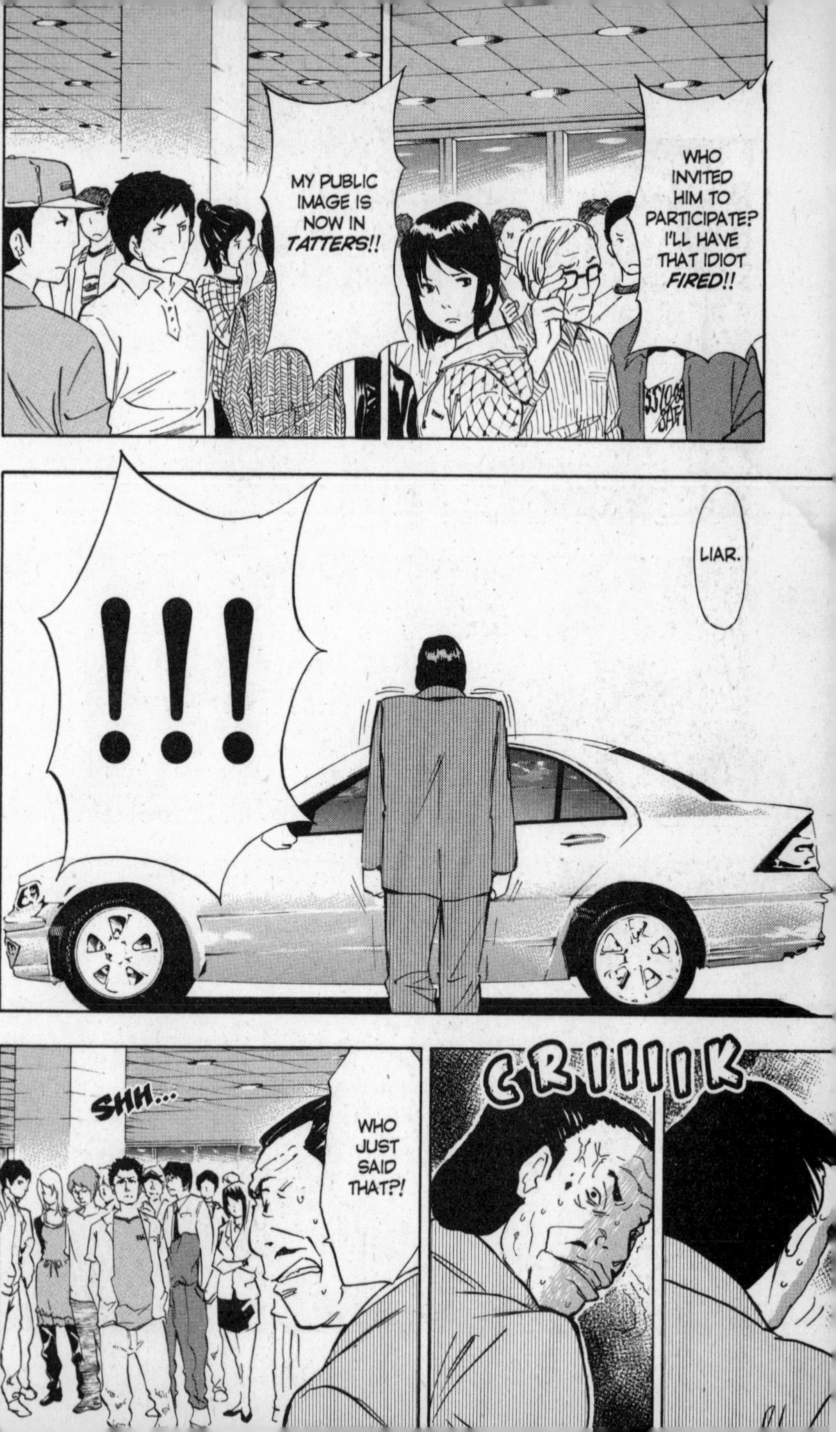
WHO INVITED HIM TO PARTICIPATE? I'LL HAVE THAT IDIOT FIRED!!
MY PUBLIC IMAGE IS NOW IN TATTERS!!
LIAR.
!!!
CRIIIIK
WHO JUST SAID THAT?!
SHH...

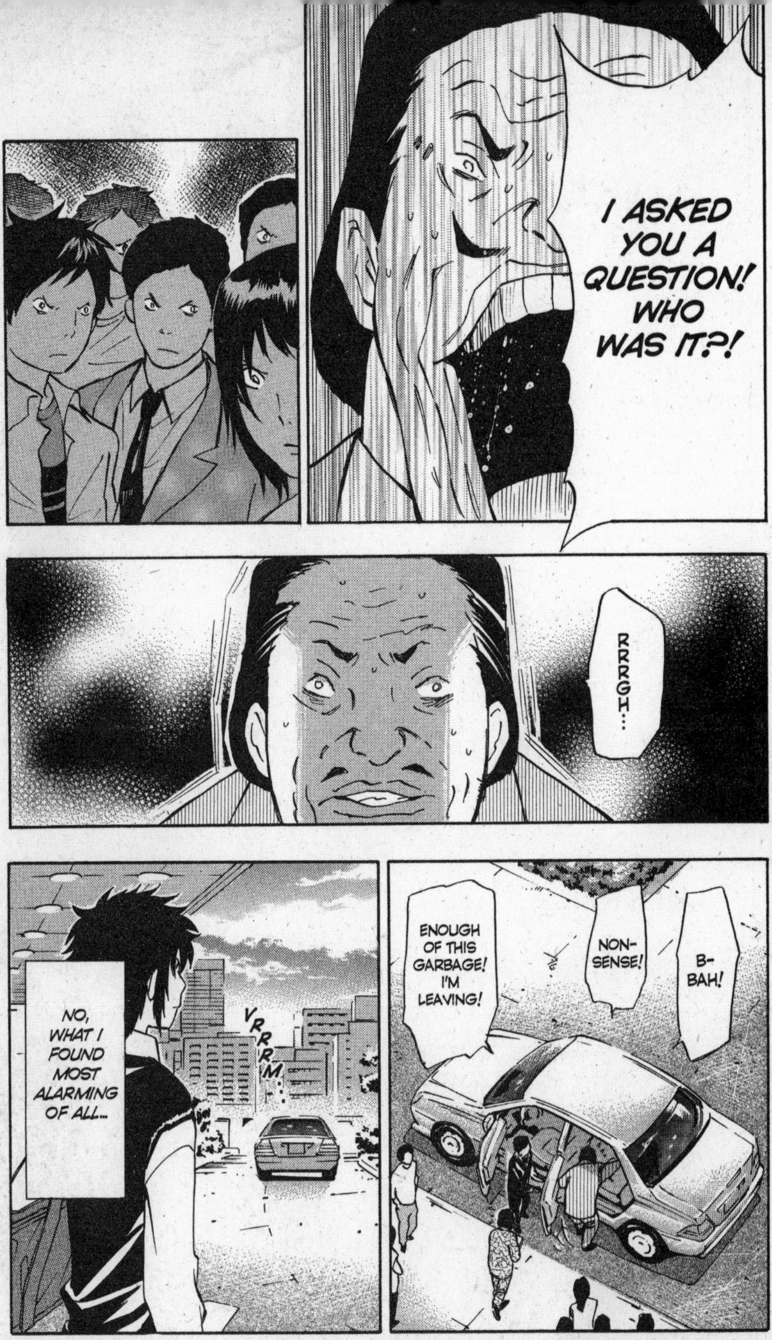
I ASKED YOU A QUESTION! WHO WAS IT?!
RRRGH...
B-BAH!
NON-SENSE!
ENOUGH OF THIS GARBAGE! I'M LEAVING!
VRRRM
NO, WHAT I FOUND MOST ALARMING OF ALL...

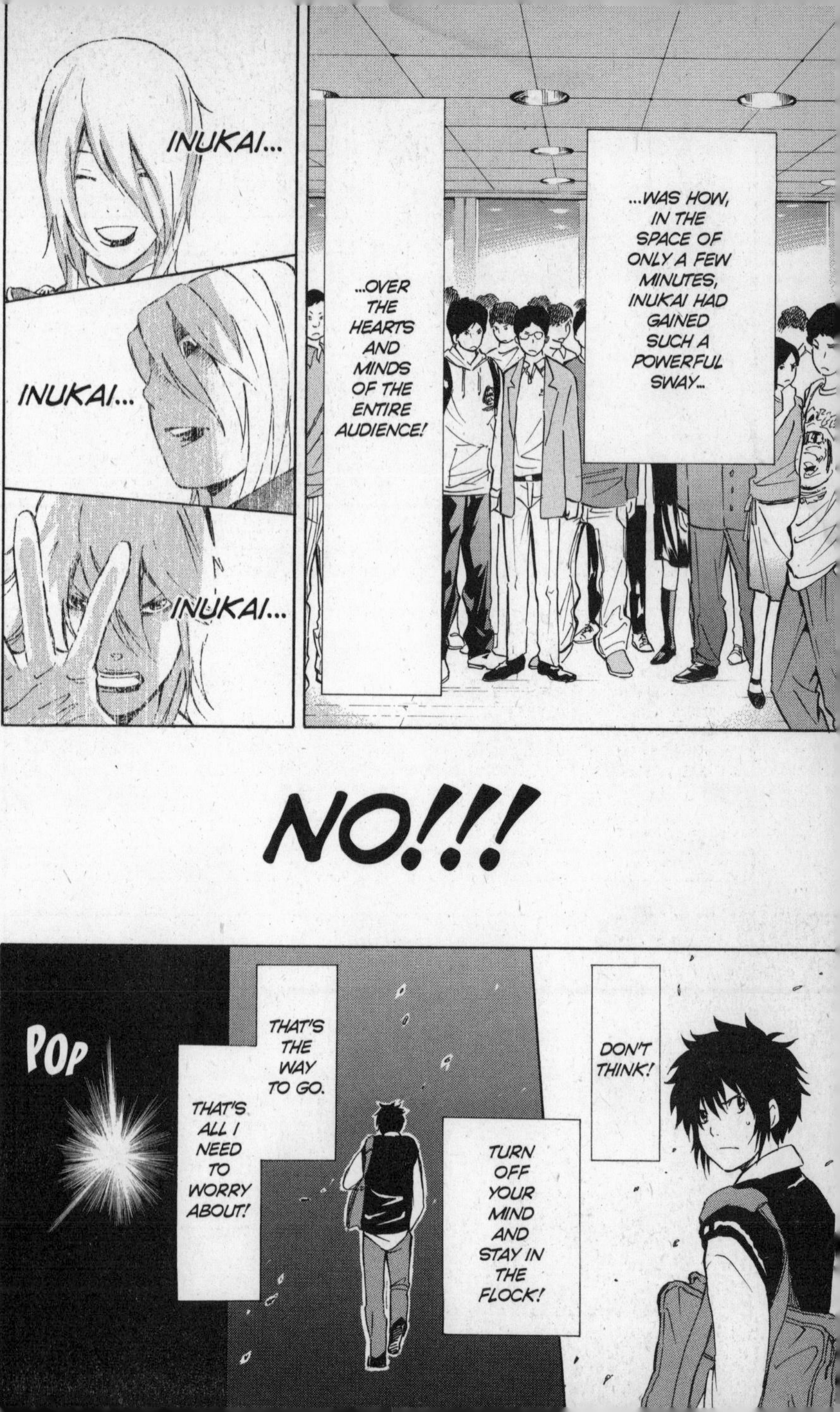
...WAS HOW, IN THE SPACE OF ONLY A FEW MINUTES, INUKAI HAD GAINED SUCH A POWERFUL SWAY...
...OVER THE HEARTS AND MINDS OF THE ENTIRE AUDIENCE!
INUKAI...
INUKAI...
INUKAI...
NO!!!
DON'T THINK!
TURN OFF YOUR MIND AND STAY IN THE FLOCK!
THAT'S THE WAY TO GO.
THAT'S ALL I NEED TO WORRY ABOUT!
POP

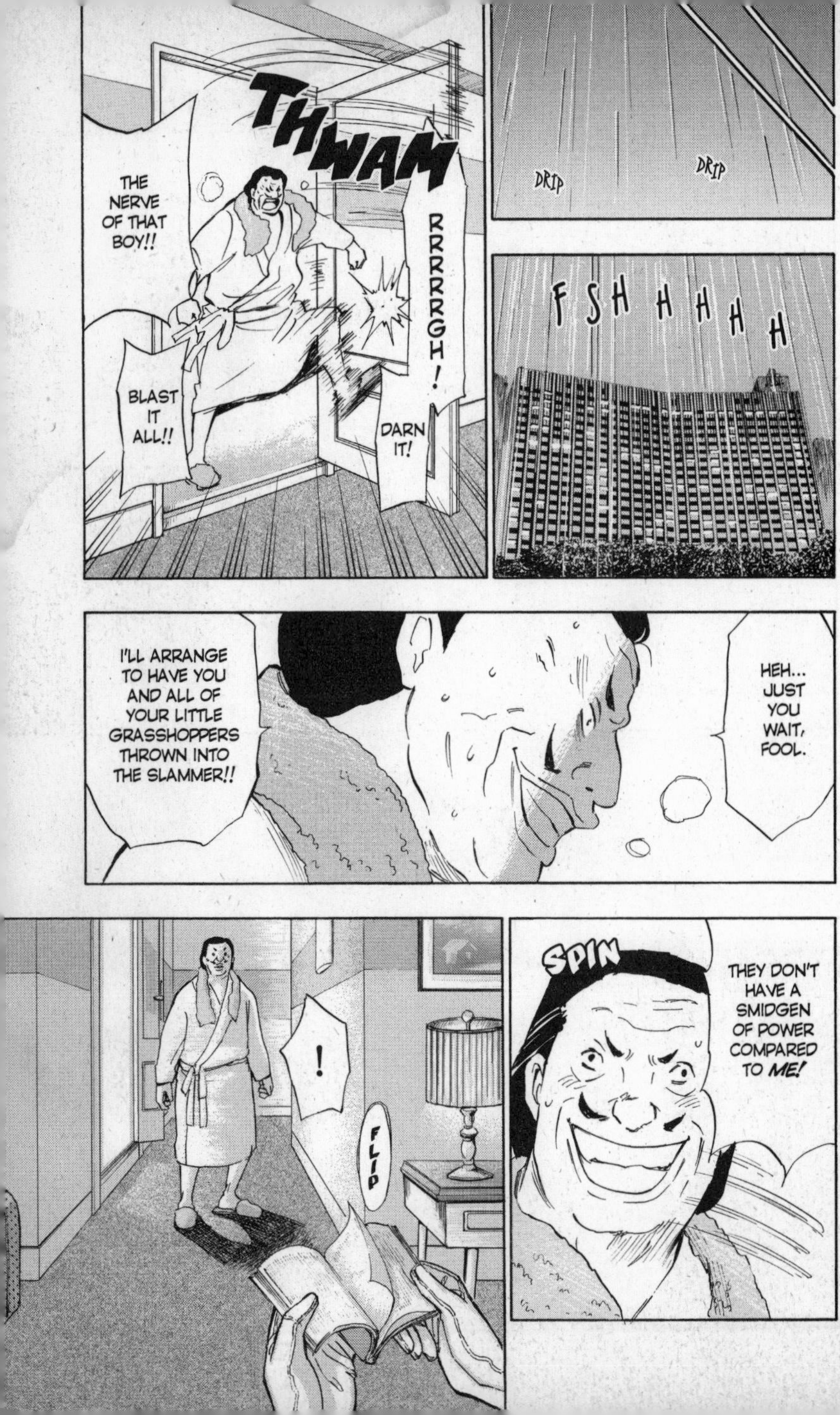
DRIP
DRIP
FSHHHHHH
THWAM
RRRRRGH!
THE NERVE OF THAT BOY!!
DARN IT!
BLAST IT ALL!!
HEH... JUST YOU WAIT, FOOL.
I'LL ARRANGE TO HAVE YOU AND ALL OF YOUR LITTLE GRASSHOPPERS THROWN INTO THE SLAMMER!!
SPIN
THEY DON'T HAVE A SMIDGEN OF POWER COMPARED TO *ME!*
!
FLIP

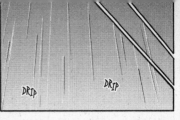

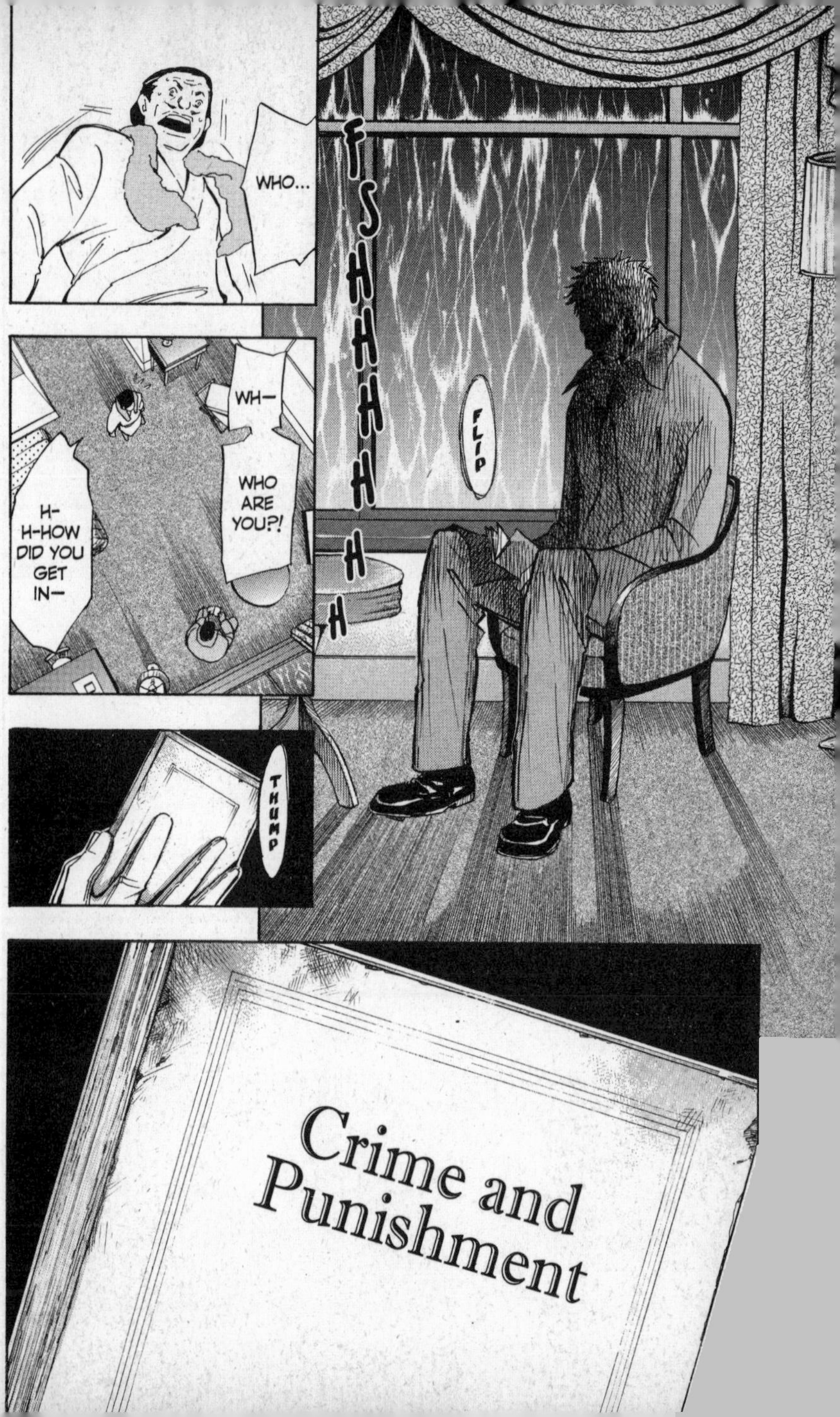
FSHHHHHHH
FLIP
WHO...
WH—
WHO ARE YOU?!
H-H-HOW DID YOU GET IN—
THUMP
Crime and Punishment

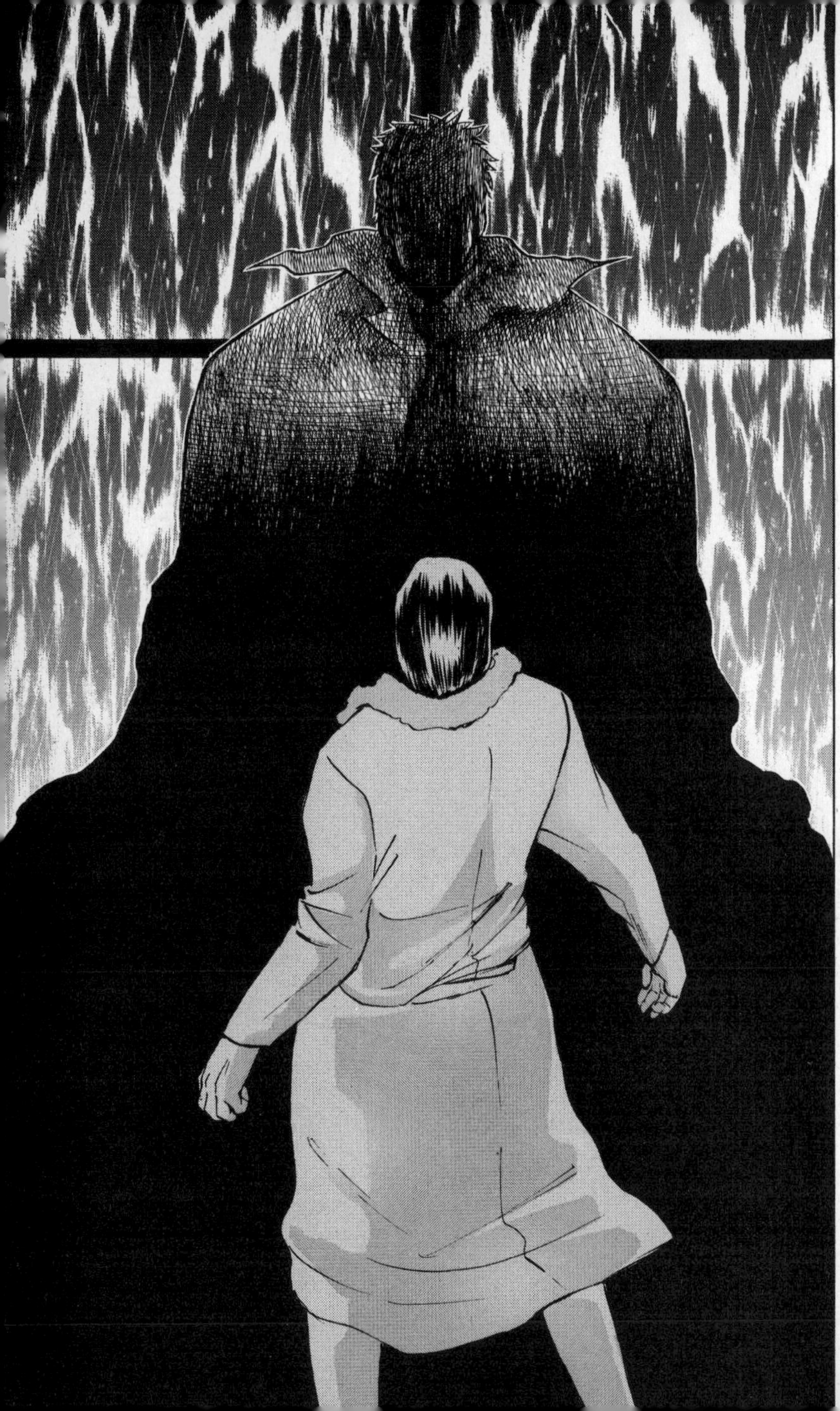

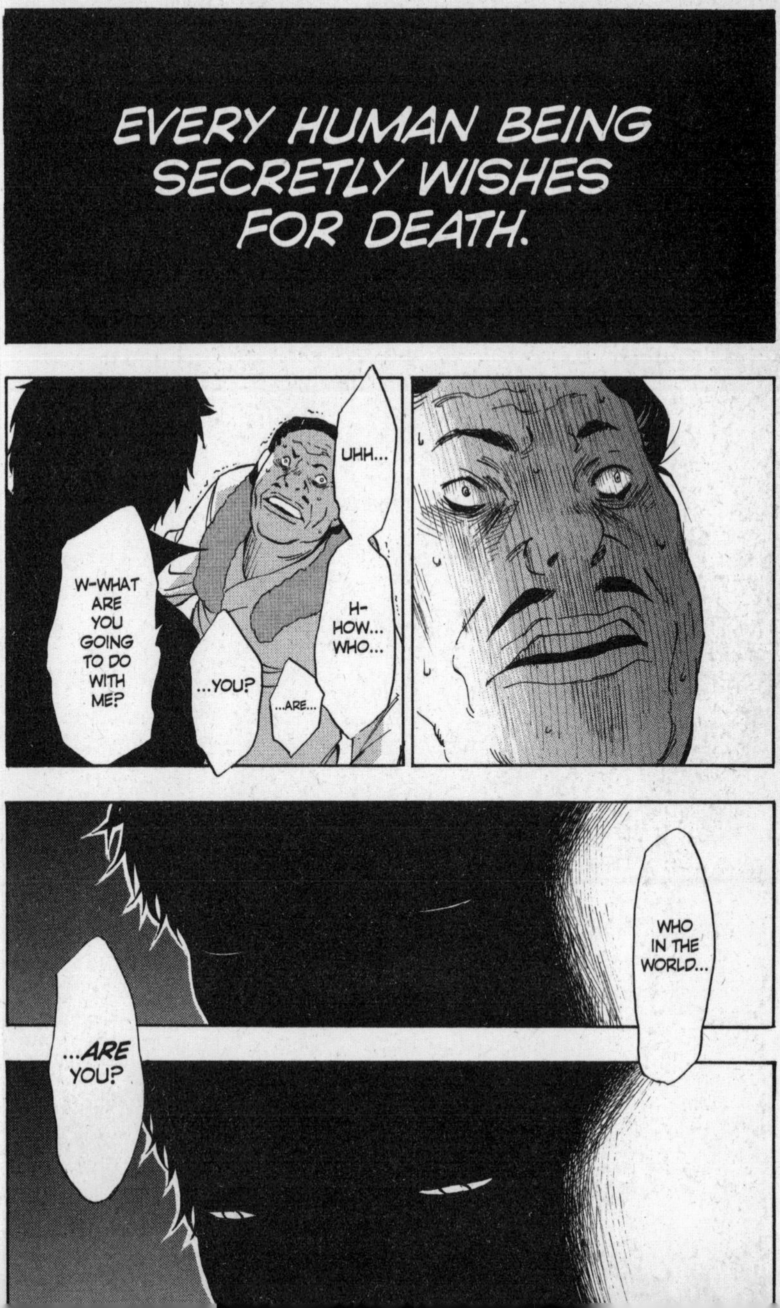
EVERY HUMAN BEING SECRETLY WISHES FOR DEATH.
UHH...
H- HOW... WHO...
...ARE...
...YOU?
W-WHAT ARE YOU GOING TO DO WITH ME?
WHO IN THE WORLD...
...ARE YOU?

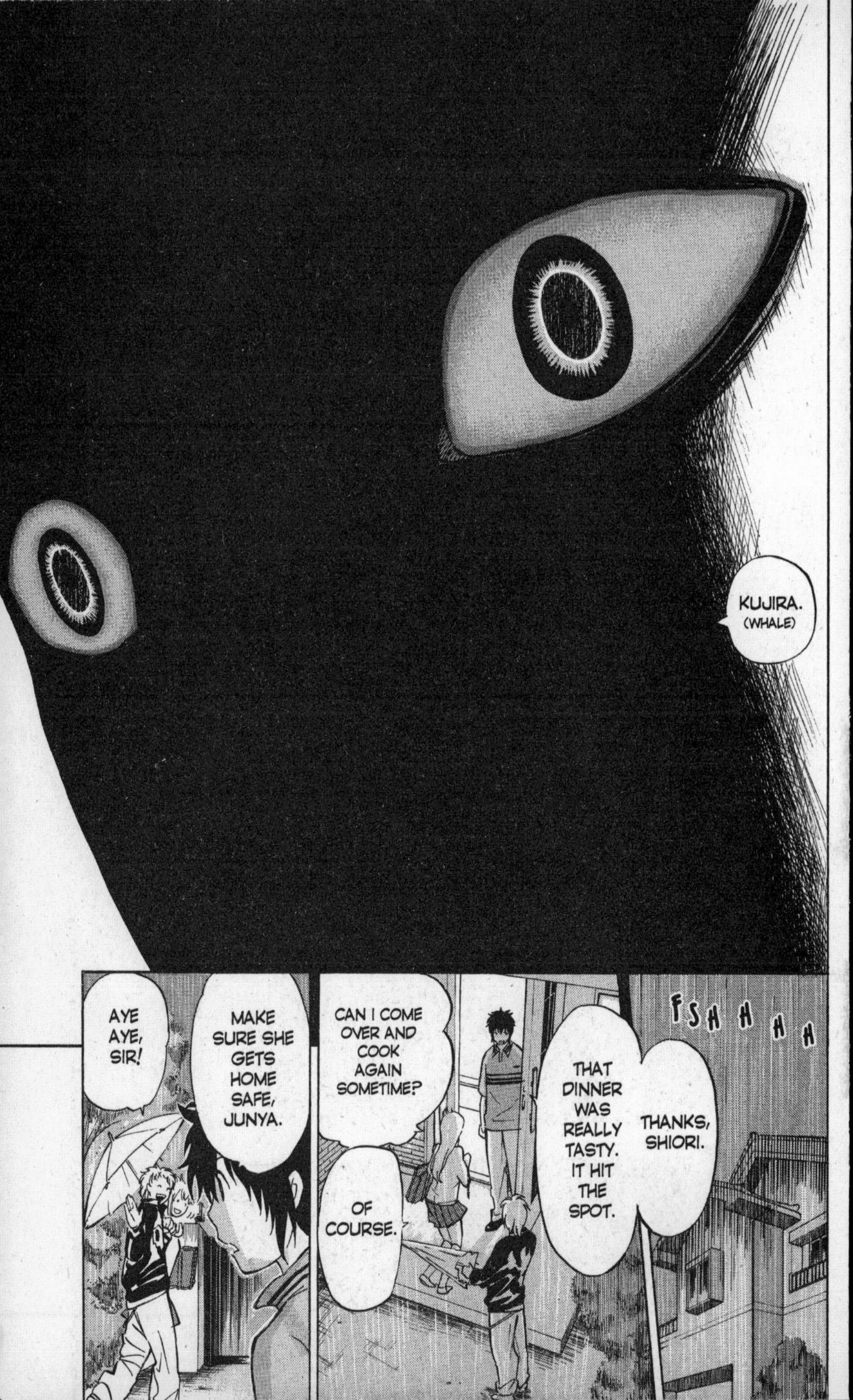
KUJIRA. (WHALE)
FSHHHHH
THANKS, SHIORI.
THAT DINNER WAS REALLY TASTY. IT HIT THE SPOT.
CAN I COME OVER AND COOK AGAIN SOMETIME?
OF COURSE.
MAKE SURE SHE GETS HOME SAFE, JUNYA.
AYE AYE, SIR!

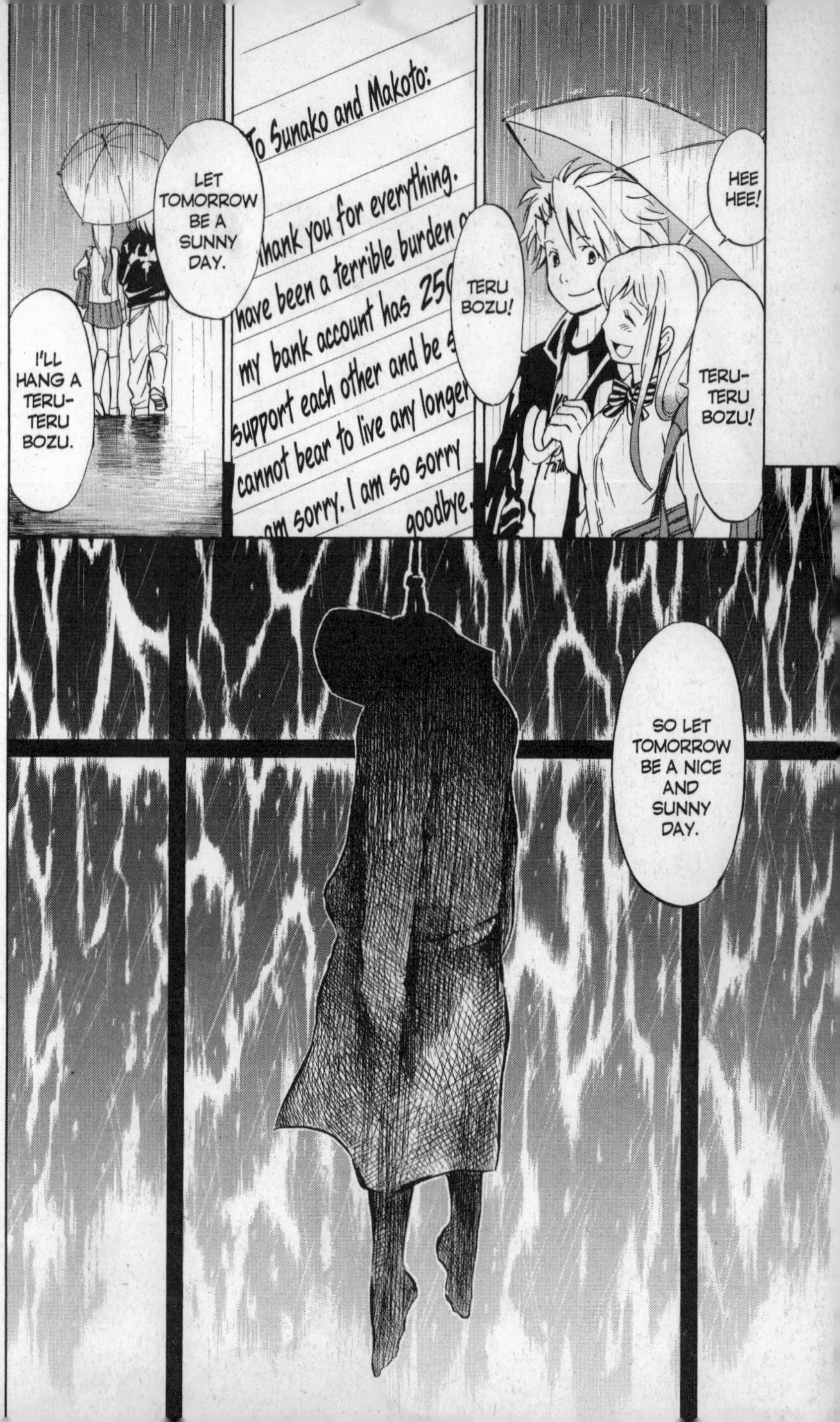
HEE HEE!
TERU-TERU BOZU!
TERU BOZU!
To Sunako and Makoto:
hank you for everything.
have been a terrible burden o
my bank account has 250
support each other and be s
cannot bear to live any longer
am sorry. I am so sorry
goodbye.
LET TOMORROW BE A SUNNY DAY.
I'LL HANG A TERU-TERU BOZU.
SO LET TOMORROW BE A NICE AND SUNNY DAY.

Chapter 3 The Bystander

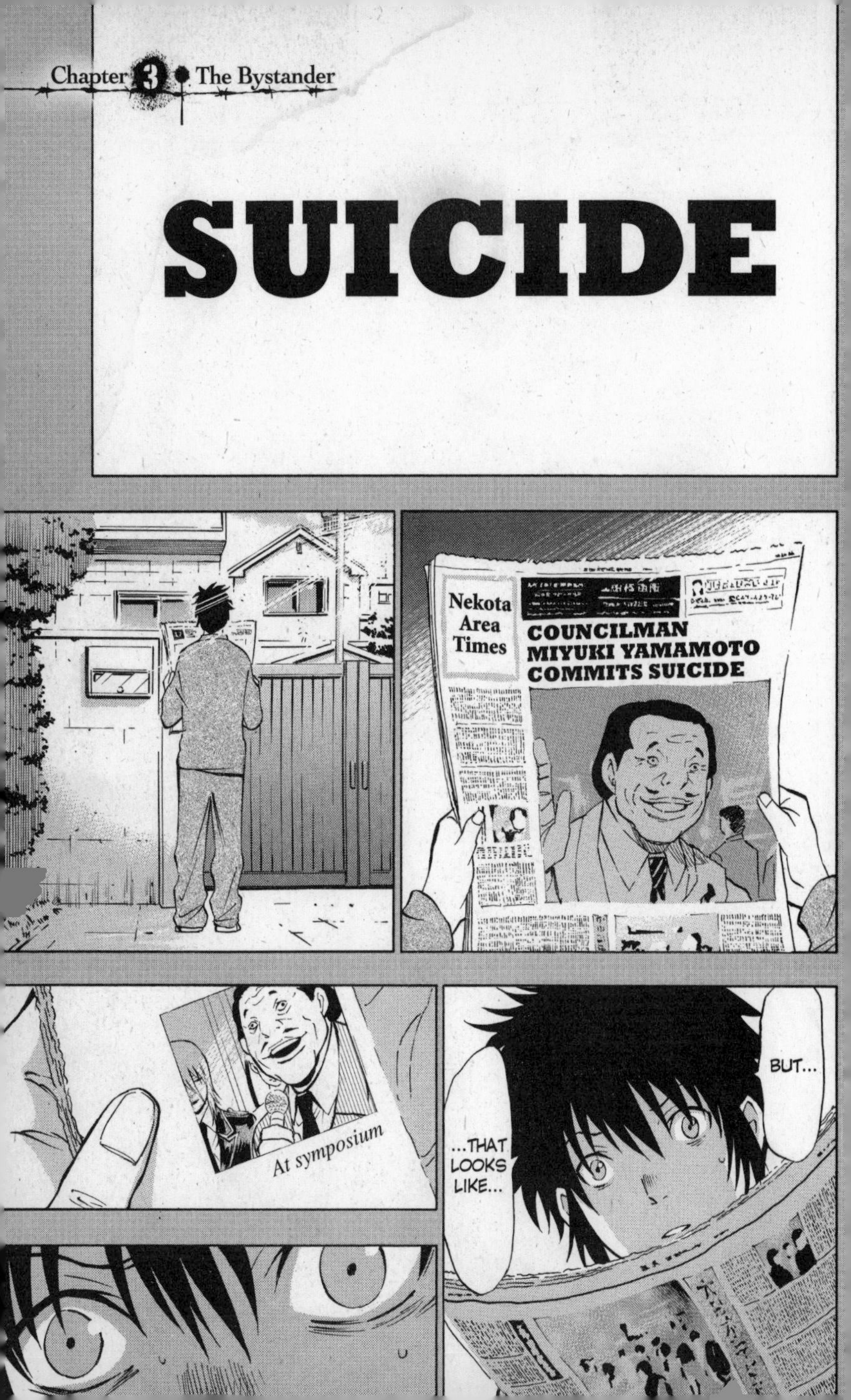
SUICIDE
Nekota Area Times
COUNCILMAN MIYUKI YAMAMOTO COMMITS SUICIDE
BUT...
...THAT LOOKS LIKE...
At symposium

Chapter 3 The Bystander

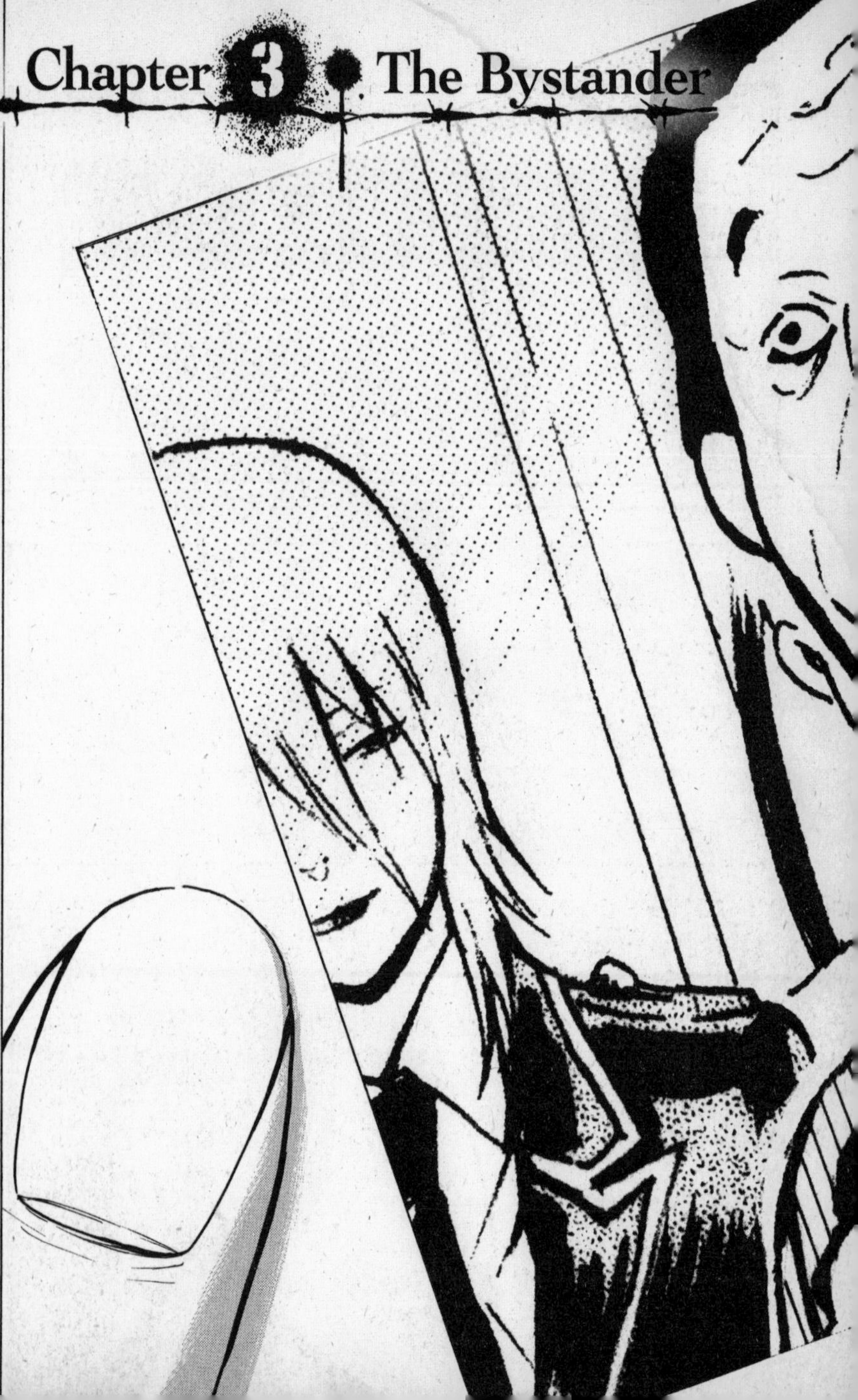

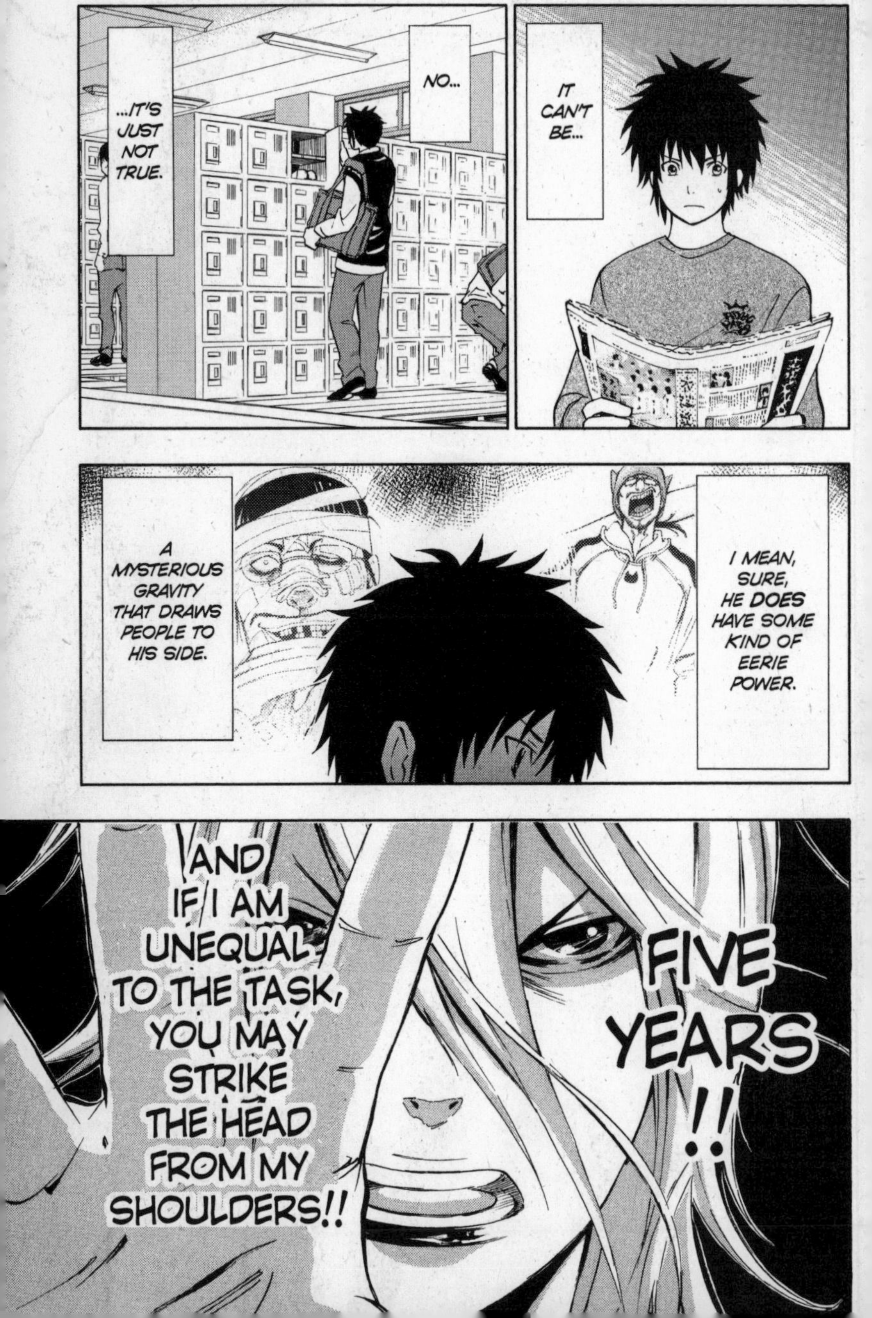
IT CAN'T BE...
NO...
...IT'S JUST NOT TRUE.
I MEAN, SURE, HE DOES HAVE SOME KIND OF EERIE POWER.
A MYSTERIOUS GRAVITY THAT DRAWS PEOPLE TO HIS SIDE.
FIVE YEARS!!
AND IF I AM UNEQUAL TO THE TASK, YOU MAY STRIKE THE HEAD FROM MY SHOULDERS!!

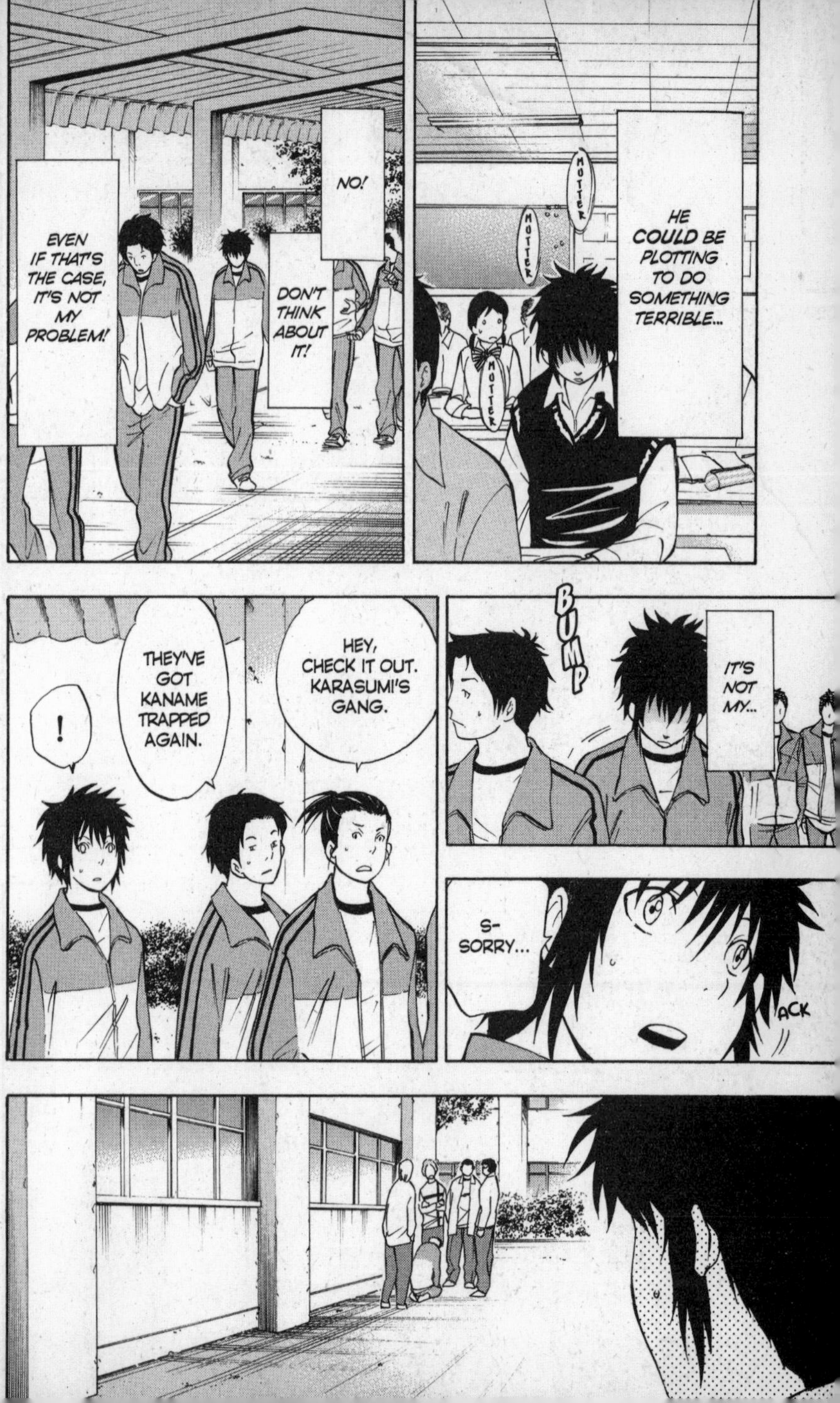
MUTTER
MUTTER
MUTTER
HE COULD BE PLOTTING TO DO SOMETHING TERRIBLE...
NO!
DON'T THINK ABOUT IT!
EVEN IF THAT'S THE CASE, IT'S NOT MY PROBLEM!
BUMP
IT'S NOT MY...
S-SORRY...
ACK
HEY, CHECK IT OUT. KARASUMI'S GANG.
THEY'VE GOT KANAME TRAPPED AGAIN.
!

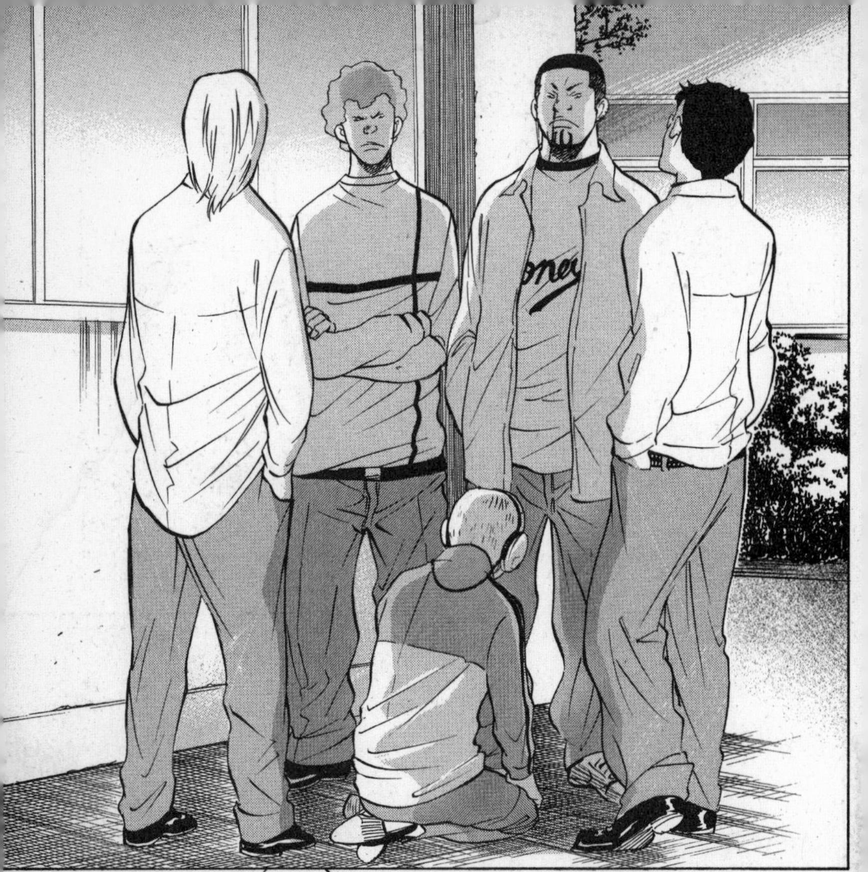

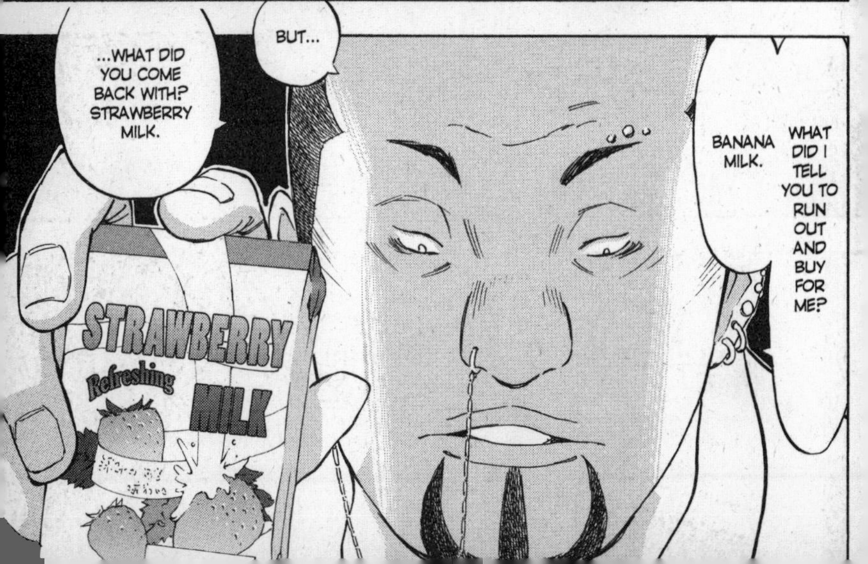
WHAT DID I TELL YOU TO RUN OUT AND BUY FOR ME?
BANANA MILK.
BUT...
...WHAT DID YOU COME BACK WITH? STRAWBERRY MILK.
STRAWBERRY
Refreshing
MILK

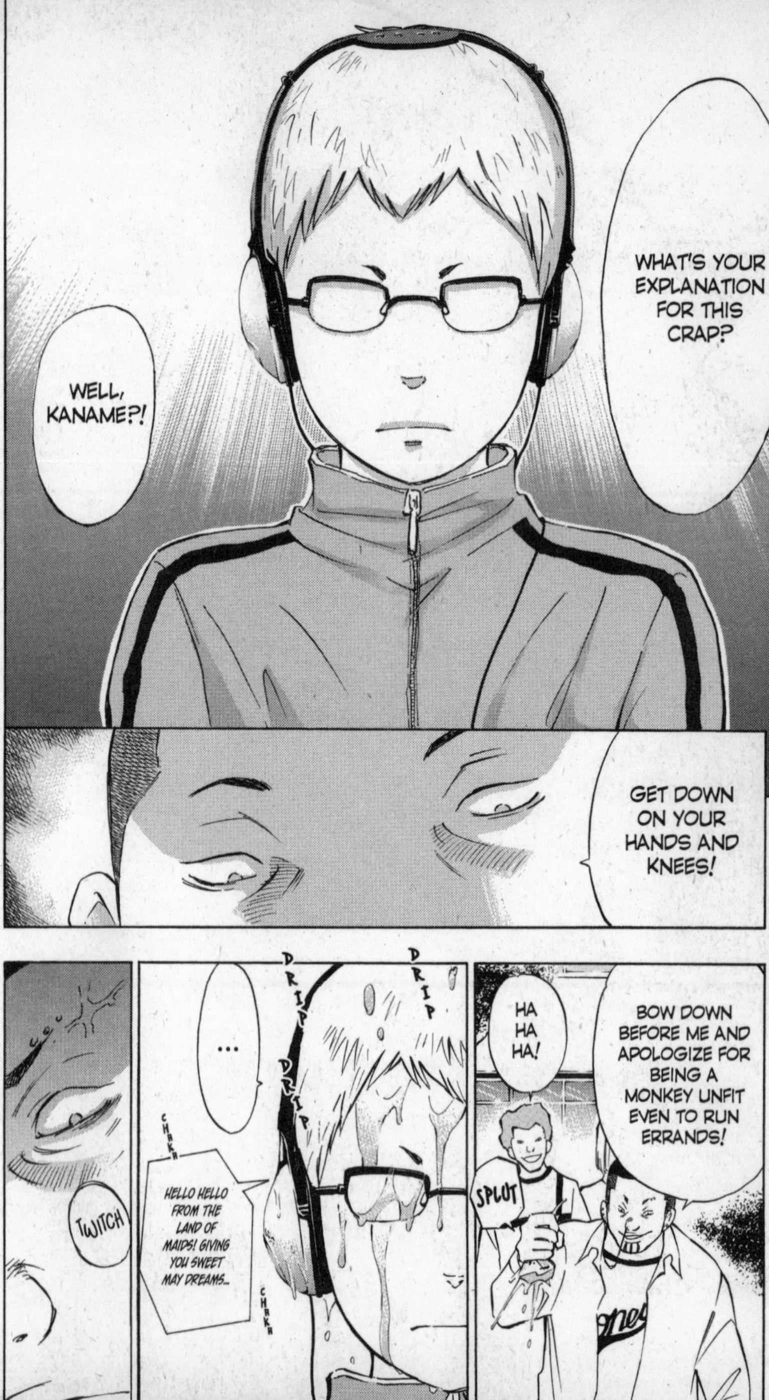
WHAT'S YOUR EXPLANATION FOR THIS CRAP?
WELL, KANAME?!
GET DOWN ON YOUR HANDS AND KNEES!
BOW DOWN BEFORE ME AND APOLOGIZE FOR BEING A MONKEY UNFIT EVEN TO RUN ERRANDS!
HA HA HA!
SPLUT
DRIP
DRIP
DRIP
DRIP
...
HELLO HELLO FROM THE LAND OF MAIDS! GIVING YOU SWEET MAY DREAMS...
TWITCH

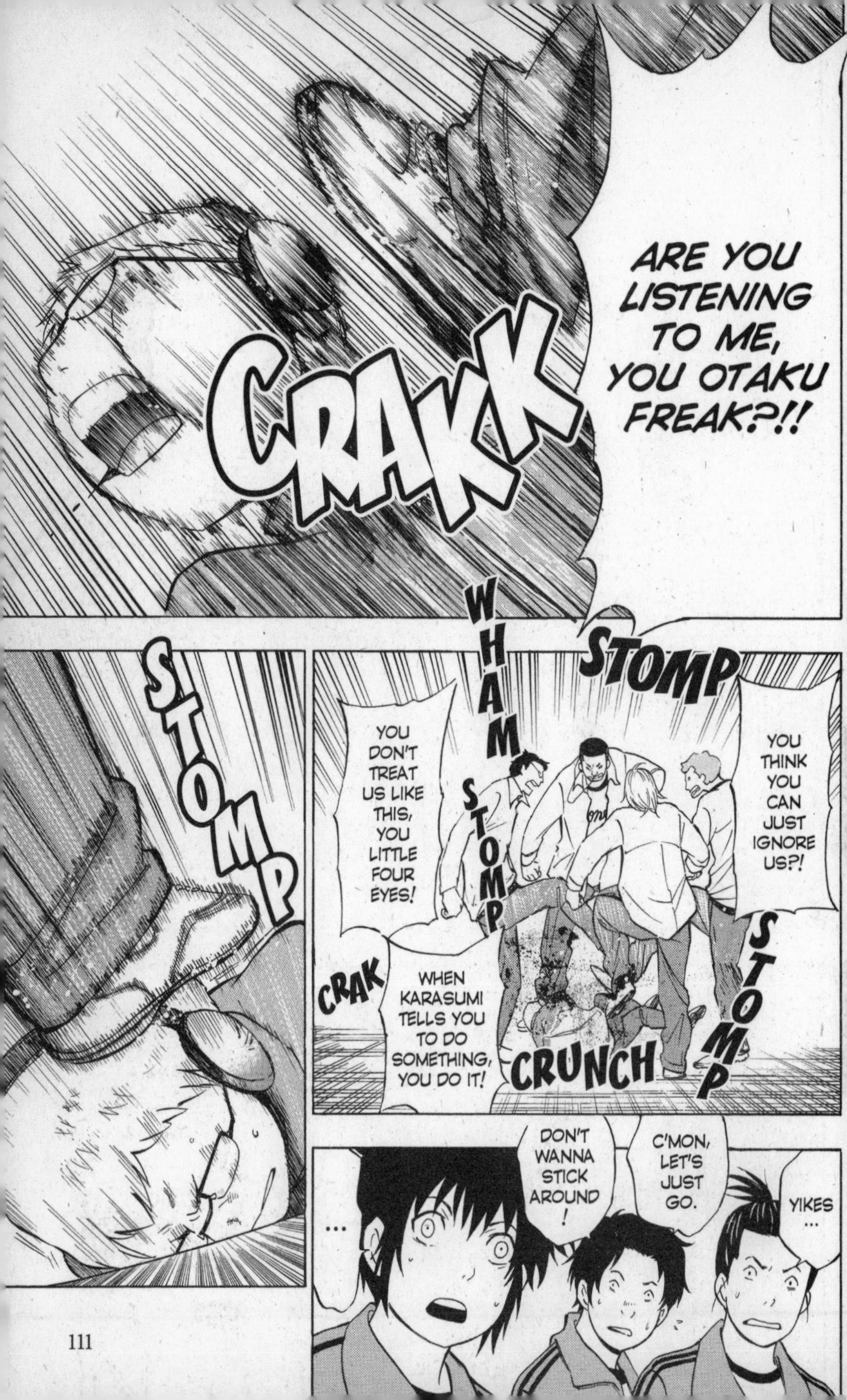
ARE YOU LISTENING TO ME, YOU OTAKU FREAK?!!
CRAKK
STOMP
YOU THINK YOU CAN JUST IGNORE US?!
WHAM
YOU DON'T TREAT US LIKE THIS, YOU LITTLE FOUR EYES!
STOMP
STOMP
CRAK
WHEN KARASUMI TELLS YOU TO DO SOMETHING, YOU DO IT!
CRUNCH
YIKES ...
C'MON, LET'S JUST GO.
DON'T WANNA STICK AROUND!
...
STOMP

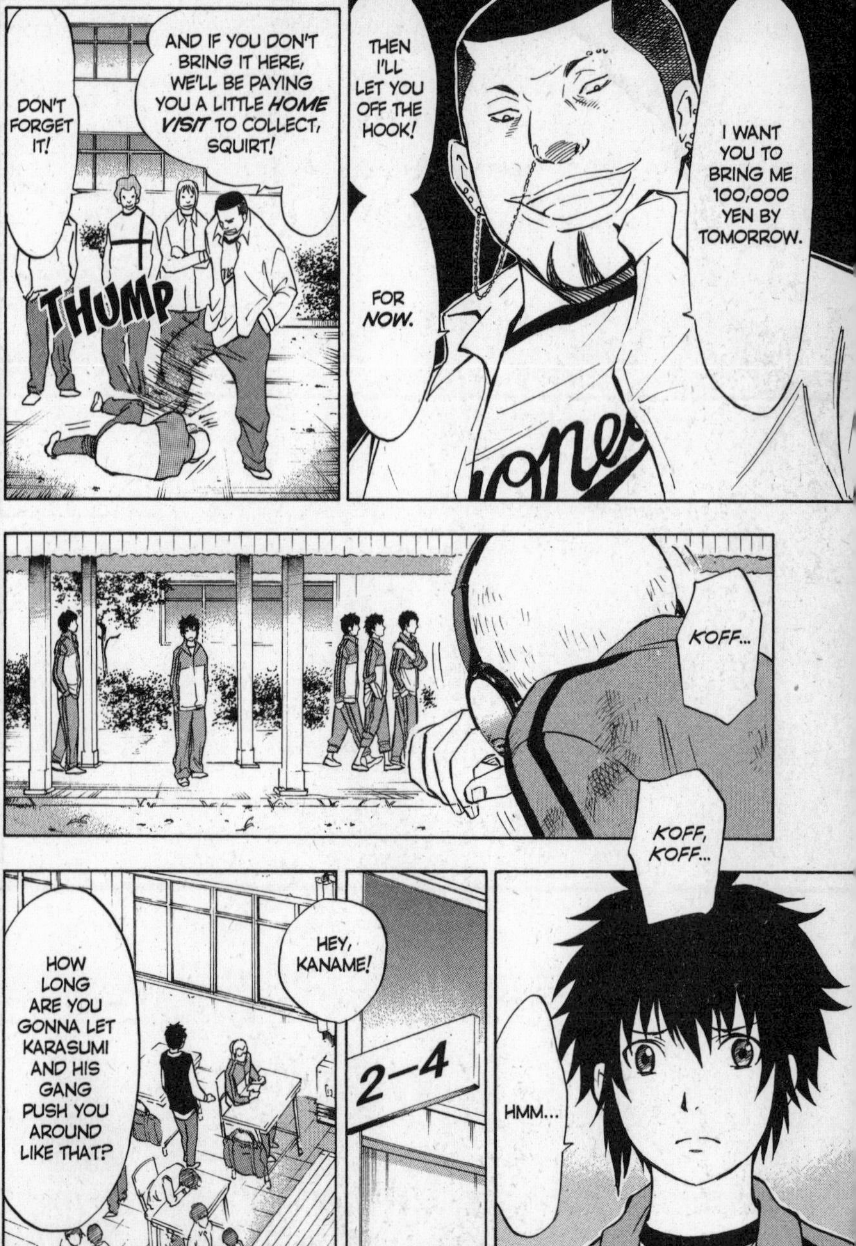
I WANT YOU TO BRING ME 100,000 YEN BY TOMORROW.
THEN I'LL LET YOU OFF THE HOOK!
FOR NOW.
AND IF YOU DON'T BRING IT HERE, WE'LL BE PAYING YOU A LITTLE HOME VISIT TO COLLECT, SQUIRT!
THUMP
DON'T FORGET IT!
KOFF...
KOFF, KOFF...
HMM...
HEY, KANAME!
HOW LONG ARE YOU GONNA LET KARASUMI AND HIS GANG PUSH YOU AROUND LIKE THAT?

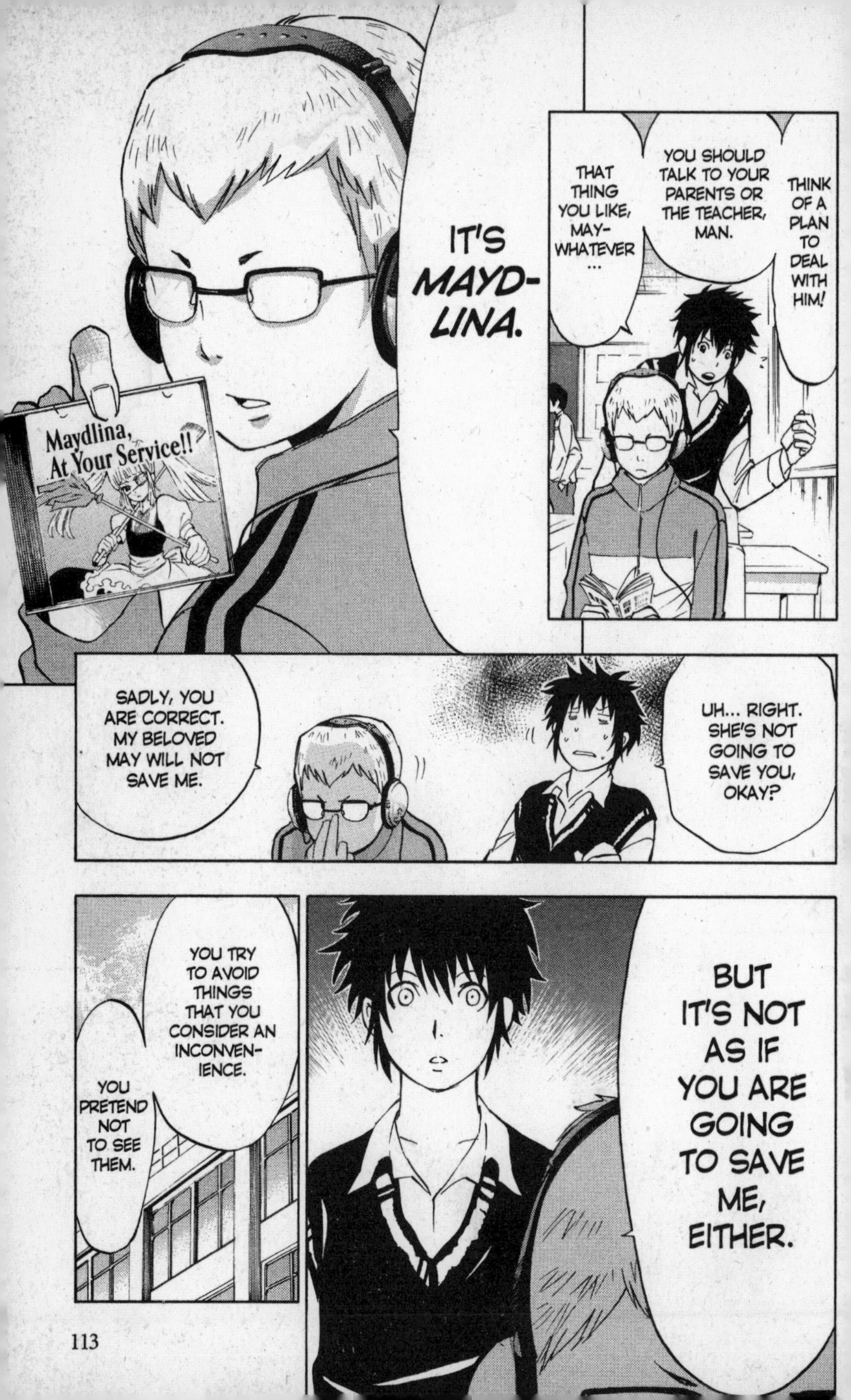
THINK OF A PLAN TO DEAL WITH HIM!
YOU SHOULD TALK TO YOUR PARENTS OR THE TEACHER, MAN.
THAT THING YOU LIKE, MAY-WHATEVER ...
IT'S MAYDLINA.
Maydlina, At Your Service!!
UH... RIGHT. SHE'S NOT GOING TO SAVE YOU, OKAY?
SADLY, YOU ARE CORRECT. MY BELOVED MAY WILL NOT SAVE ME.
BUT IT'S NOT AS IF YOU ARE GOING TO SAVE ME, EITHER.
YOU TRY TO AVOID THINGS THAT YOU CONSIDER AN INCONVENIENCE.
YOU PRETEND NOT TO SEE THEM.

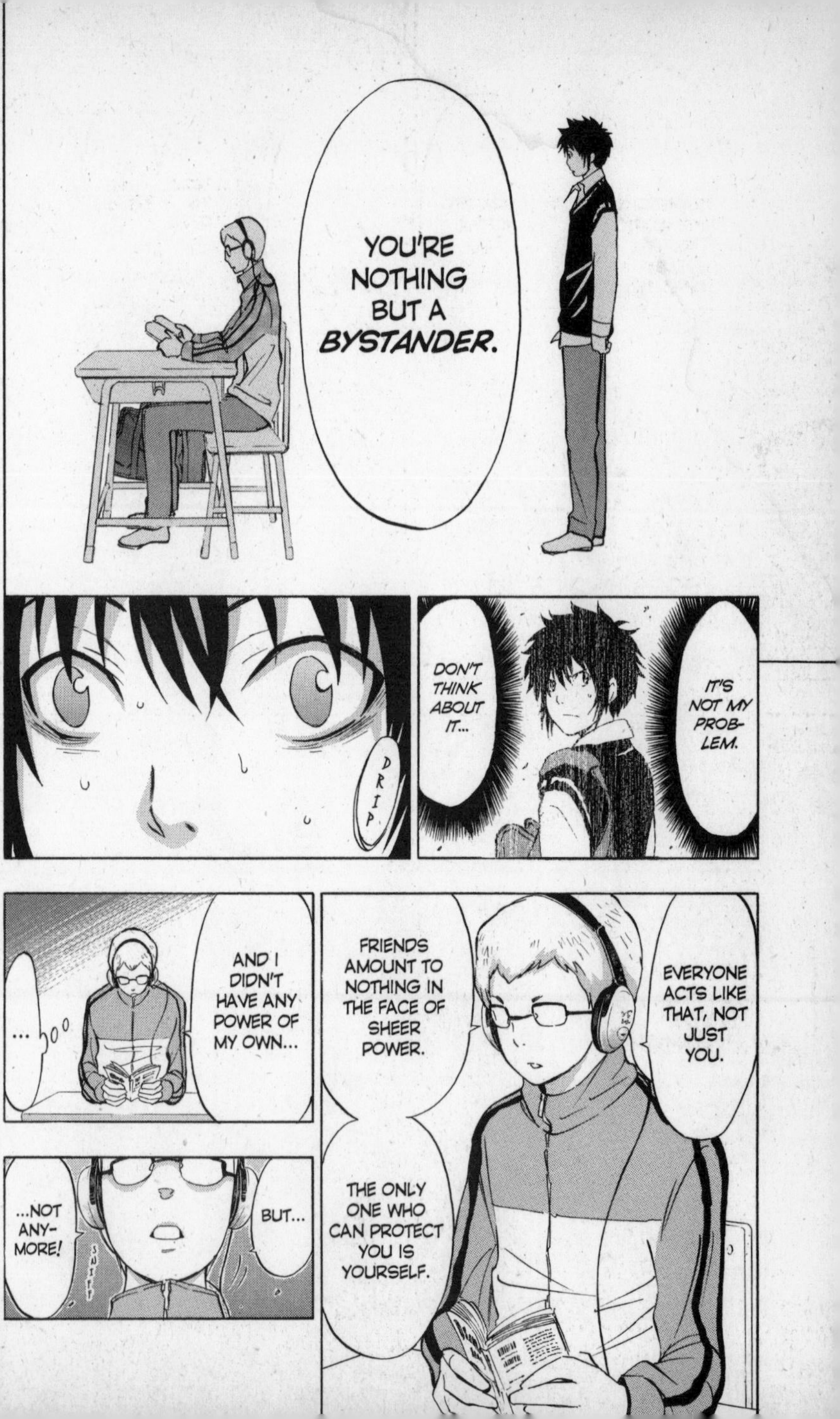
YOU'RE NOTHING BUT A *BYSTANDER.*
IT'S NOT MY PROB-LEM.
DON'T THINK ABOUT IT...
DRIP
EVERYONE ACTS LIKE THAT, NOT JUST YOU.
FRIENDS AMOUNT TO NOTHING IN THE FACE OF SHEER POWER.
THE ONLY ONE WHO CAN PROTECT YOU IS YOURSELF.
AND I DIDN'T HAVE ANY POWER OF MY OWN...
...
BUT...
...NOT ANY-MORE!
SNIFF

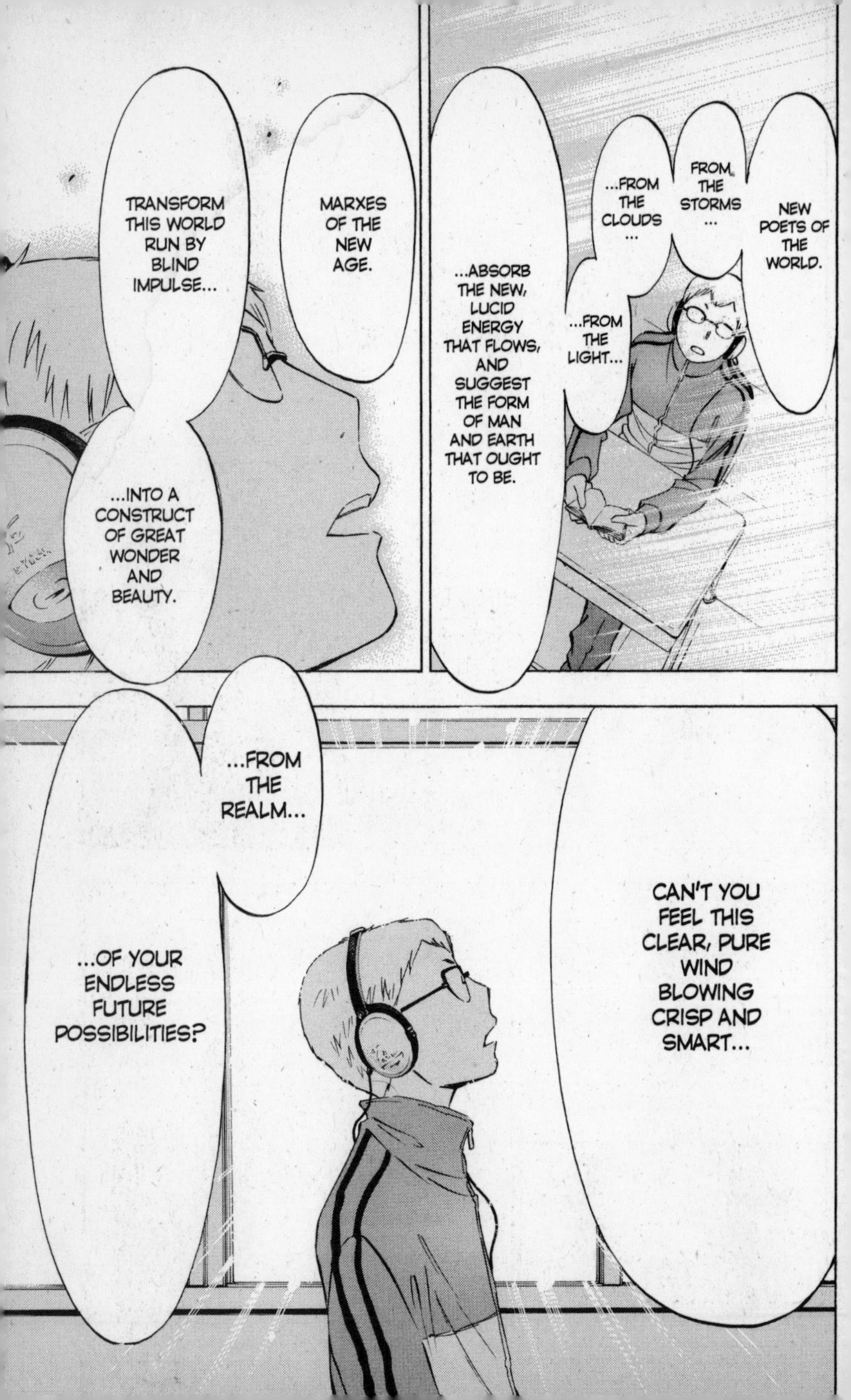
NEW POETS OF THE WORLD.
FROM THE STORMS...
...FROM THE CLOUDS...
...FROM THE LIGHT...
...ABSORB THE NEW, LUCID ENERGY THAT FLOWS, AND SUGGEST THE FORM OF MAN AND EARTH THAT OUGHT TO BE.
MARXES OF THE NEW AGE.
TRANSFORM THIS WORLD RUN BY BLIND IMPULSE...
...INTO A CONSTRUCT OF GREAT WONDER AND BEAUTY.
CAN'T YOU FEEL THIS CLEAR, PURE WIND BLOWING CRISP AND SMART...
...FROM THE REALM...
...OF YOUR ENDLESS FUTURE POSSIBILITIES?

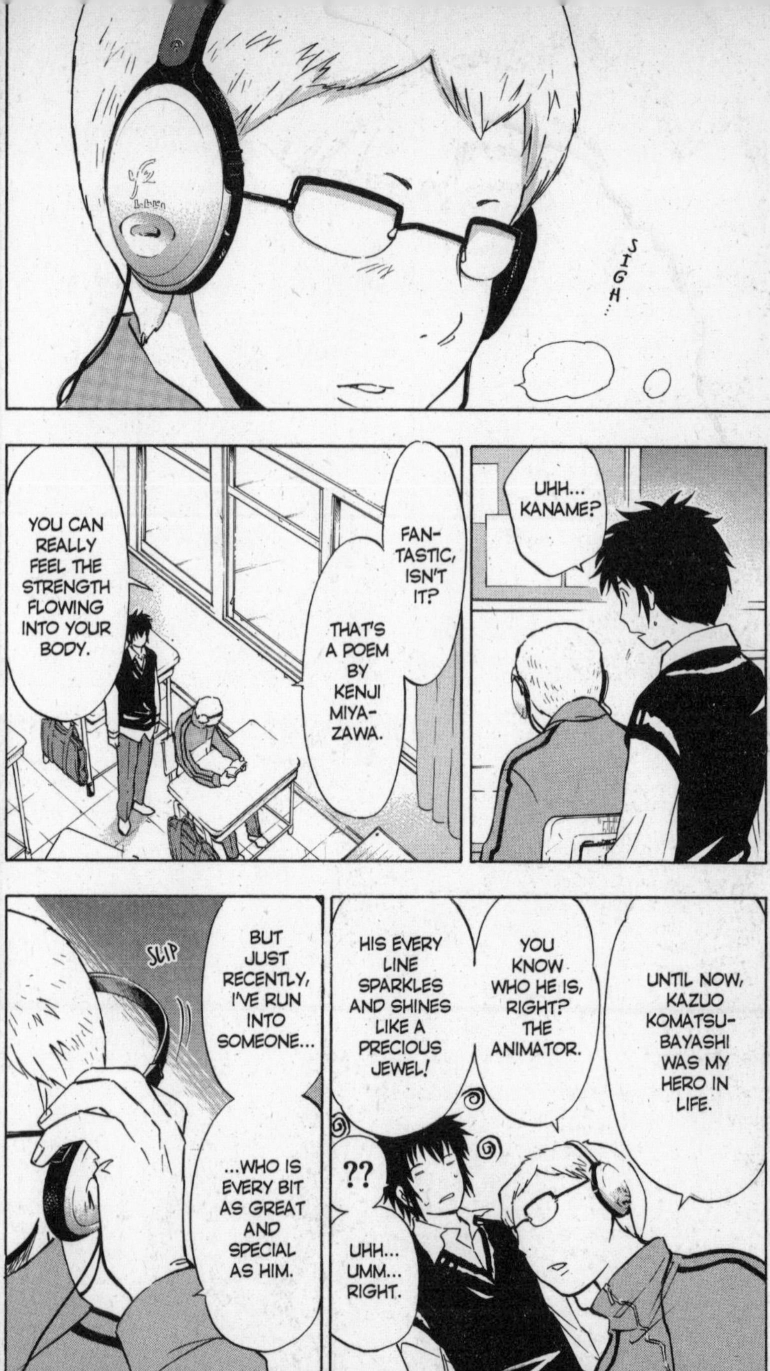
SIGH...
UHH... KANAME?
FAN-TASTIC, ISN'T IT?
THAT'S A POEM BY KENJI MIYA-ZAWA.
YOU CAN REALLY FEEL THE STRENGTH FLOWING INTO YOUR BODY.
UNTIL NOW, KAZUO KOMATSU-BAYASHI WAS MY HERO IN LIFE.
YOU KNOW WHO HE IS, RIGHT? THE ANIMATOR.
HIS EVERY LINE SPARKLES AND SHINES LIKE A PRECIOUS JEWEL!
??
UHH... UMM... RIGHT.
SLIP
BUT JUST RECENTLY, I'VE RUN INTO SOMEONE...
...WHO IS EVERY BIT AS GREAT AND SPECIAL AS HIM.

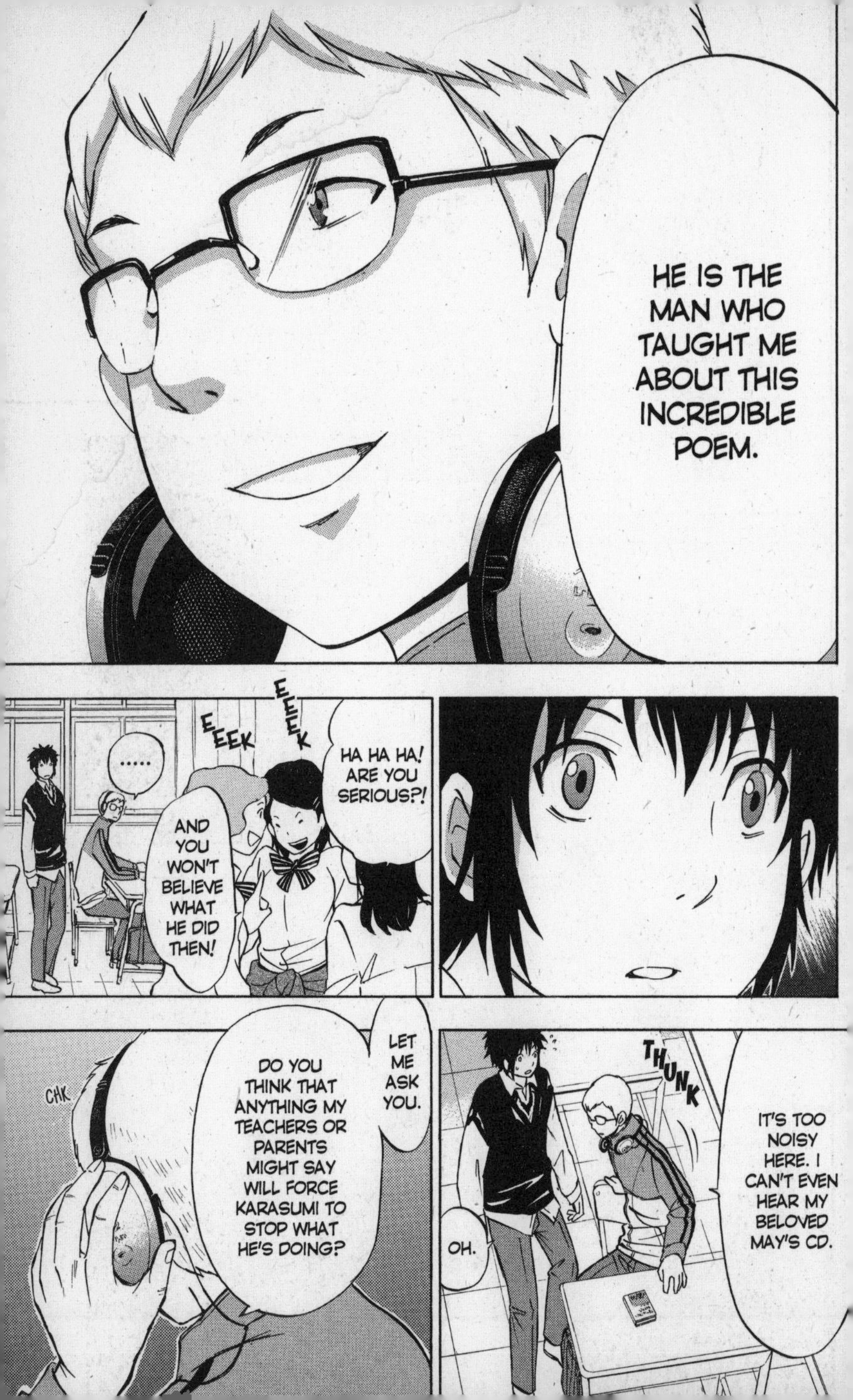
HE IS THE MAN WHO TAUGHT ME ABOUT THIS INCREDIBLE POEM.
HA HA HA! ARE YOU SERIOUS?!
EEEK
EEEK
AND YOU WON'T BELIEVE WHAT HE DID THEN!
......
THUNK
IT'S TOO NOISY HERE. I CAN'T EVEN HEAR MY BELOVED MAY'S CD.
OH.
LET ME ASK YOU.
DO YOU THINK THAT ANYTHING MY TEACHERS OR PARENTS MIGHT SAY WILL FORCE KARASUMI TO STOP WHAT HE'S DOING?
CHK

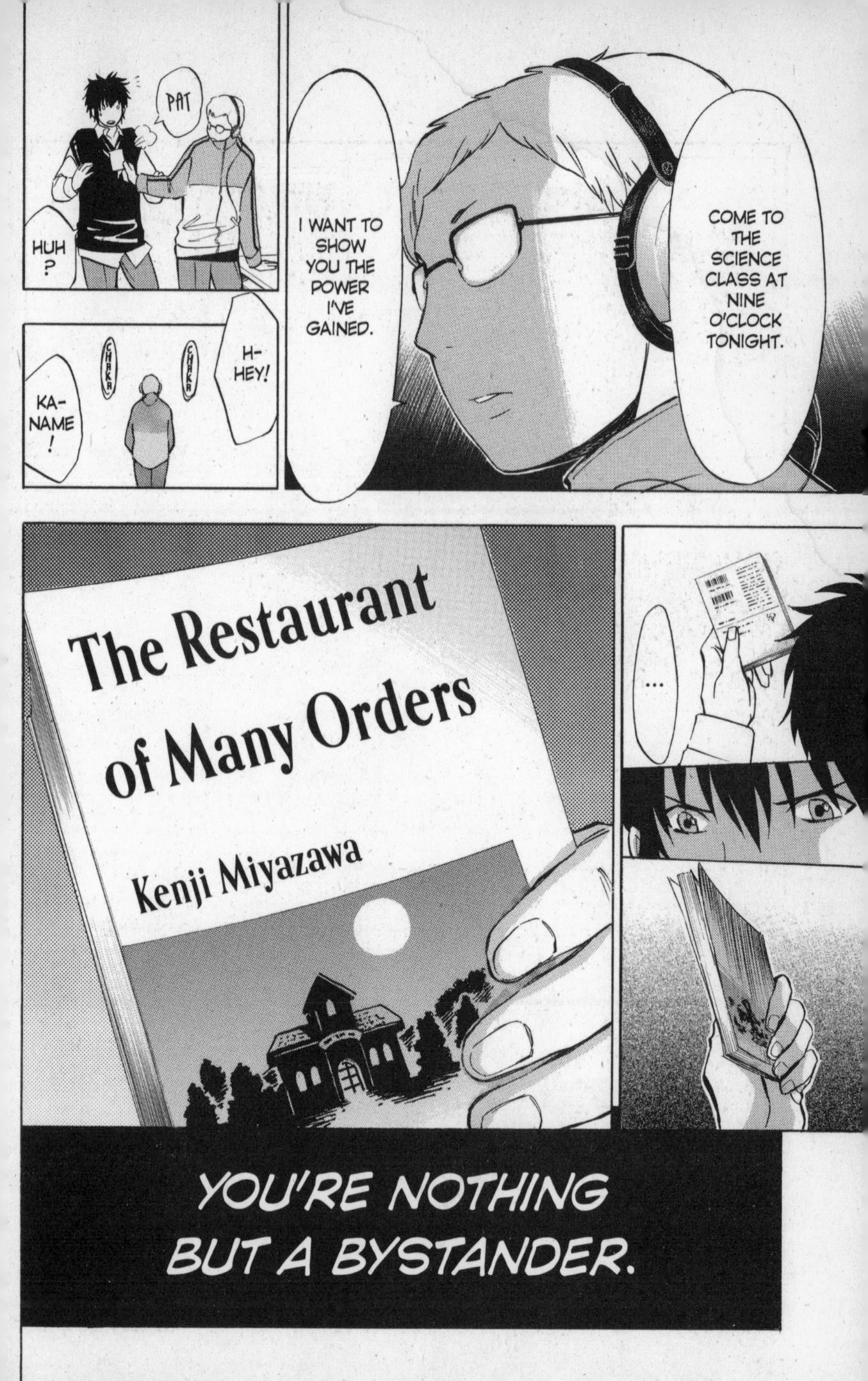
COME TO THE SCIENCE CLASS AT NINE O'CLOCK TONIGHT.
I WANT TO SHOW YOU THE POWER I'VE GAINED.
PAT
HUH?
H-HEY!
CHAKA
CHAKA
KA-NAME!
...
The Restaurant of Many Orders
Kenji Miyazawa
YOU'RE NOTHING BUT A BYSTANDER.

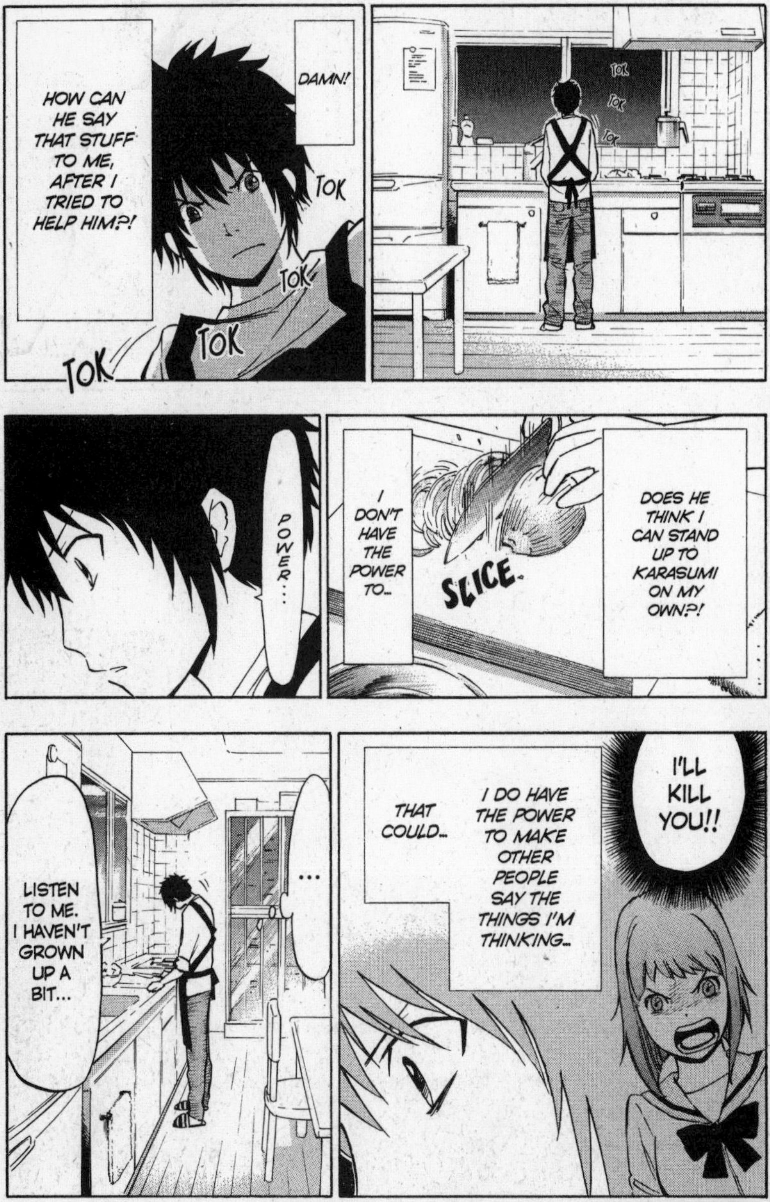
TOK
TOK
TOK
DAMN!
HOW CAN HE SAY THAT STUFF TO ME, AFTER I TRIED TO HELP HIM?!
TOK
TOK
TOK
TOK
DOES HE THINK I CAN STAND UP TO KARASUMI ON MY OWN?!
I DON'T HAVE THE POWER TO...
SLICE
POWER...
I'LL KILL YOU!!
I DO HAVE THE POWER TO MAKE OTHER PEOPLE SAY THE THINGS I'M THINKING...
THAT COULD...
...
LISTEN TO ME. I HAVEN'T GROWN UP A BIT...

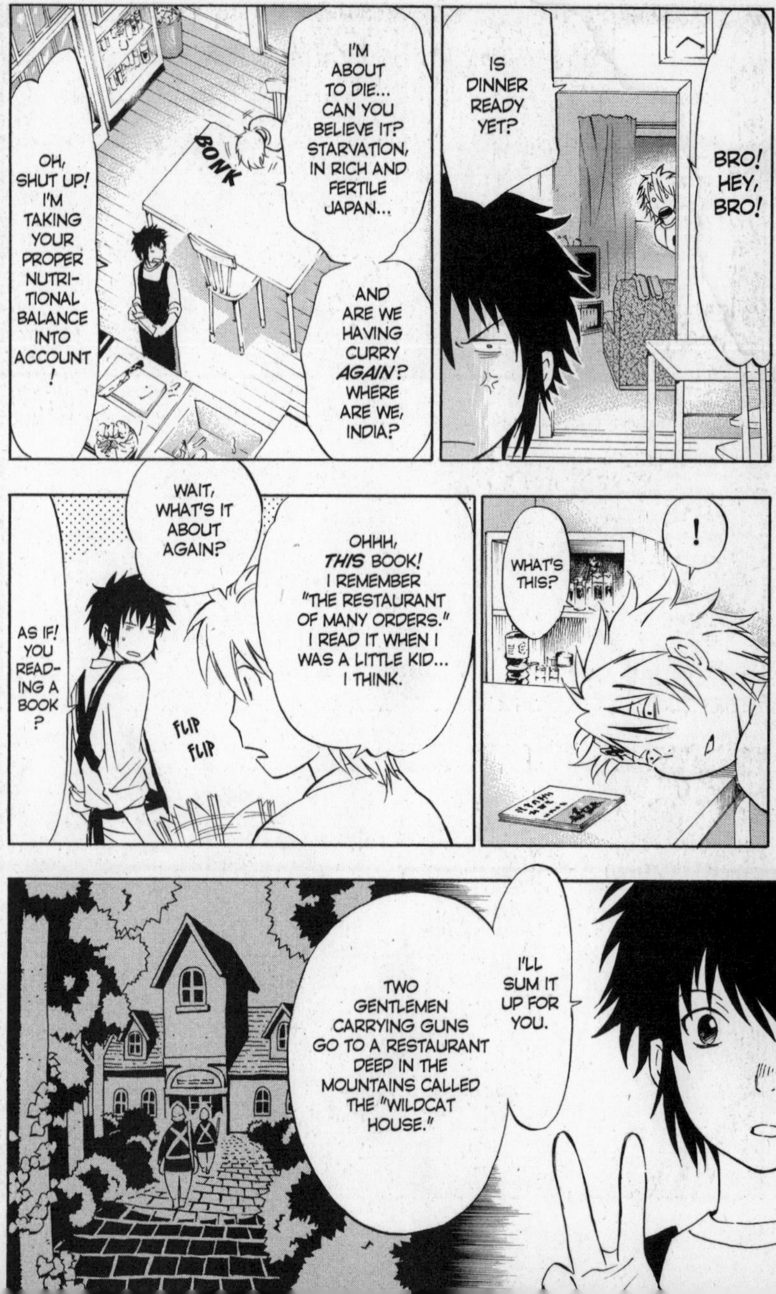
BRO! HEY, BRO!
IS DINNER READY YET?
I'M ABOUT TO DIE... CAN YOU BELIEVE IT? STARVATION, IN RICH AND FERTILE JAPAN...
BONK
AND ARE WE HAVING CURRY AGAIN? WHERE ARE WE, INDIA?
OH, SHUT UP! I'M TAKING YOUR PROPER NUTRITIONAL BALANCE INTO ACCOUNT!
!
WHAT'S THIS?
OHHH, THIS BOOK! I REMEMBER "THE RESTAURANT OF MANY ORDERS." I READ IT WHEN I WAS A LITTLE KID... I THINK.
WAIT, WHAT'S IT ABOUT AGAIN?
FLIP FLIP
AS IF! YOU READING A BOOK?
I'LL SUM IT UP FOR YOU.
TWO GENTLEMEN CARRYING GUNS GO TO A RESTAURANT DEEP IN THE MOUNTAINS CALLED THE "WILDCAT HOUSE."

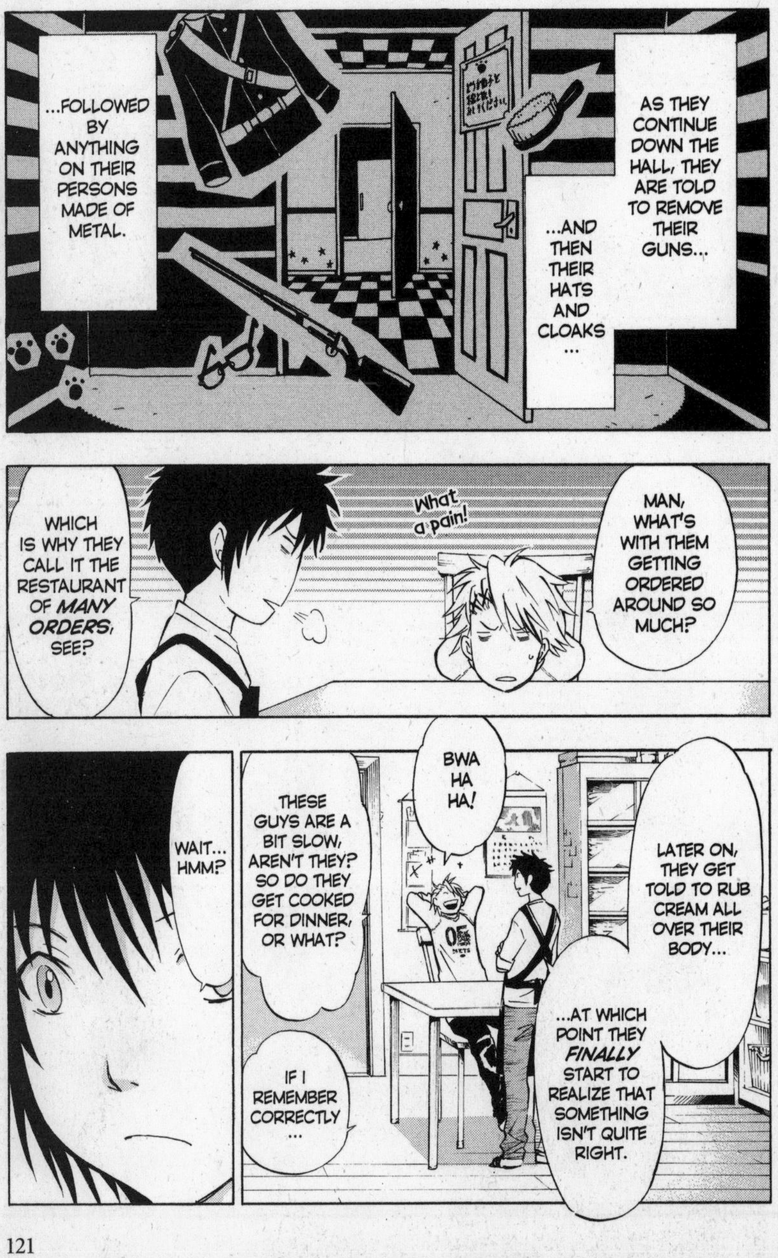
AS THEY CONTINUE DOWN THE HALL, THEY ARE TOLD TO REMOVE THEIR GUNS...
...AND THEN THEIR HATS AND CLOAKS ...
...FOLLOWED BY ANYTHING ON THEIR PERSONS MADE OF METAL.
MAN, WHAT'S WITH THEM GETTING ORDERED AROUND SO MUCH?
What a pain!
WHICH IS WHY THEY CALL IT THE RESTAURANT OF *MANY ORDERS*, SEE?
LATER ON, THEY GET TOLD TO RUB CREAM ALL OVER THEIR BODY...
...AT WHICH POINT THEY *FINALLY* START TO REALIZE THAT SOMETHING ISN'T QUITE RIGHT.
BWA HA HA!
THESE GUYS ARE A BIT SLOW, AREN'T THEY? SO DO THEY GET COOKED FOR DINNER, OR WHAT?
IF I REMEMBER CORRECTLY ...
WAIT... HMM?

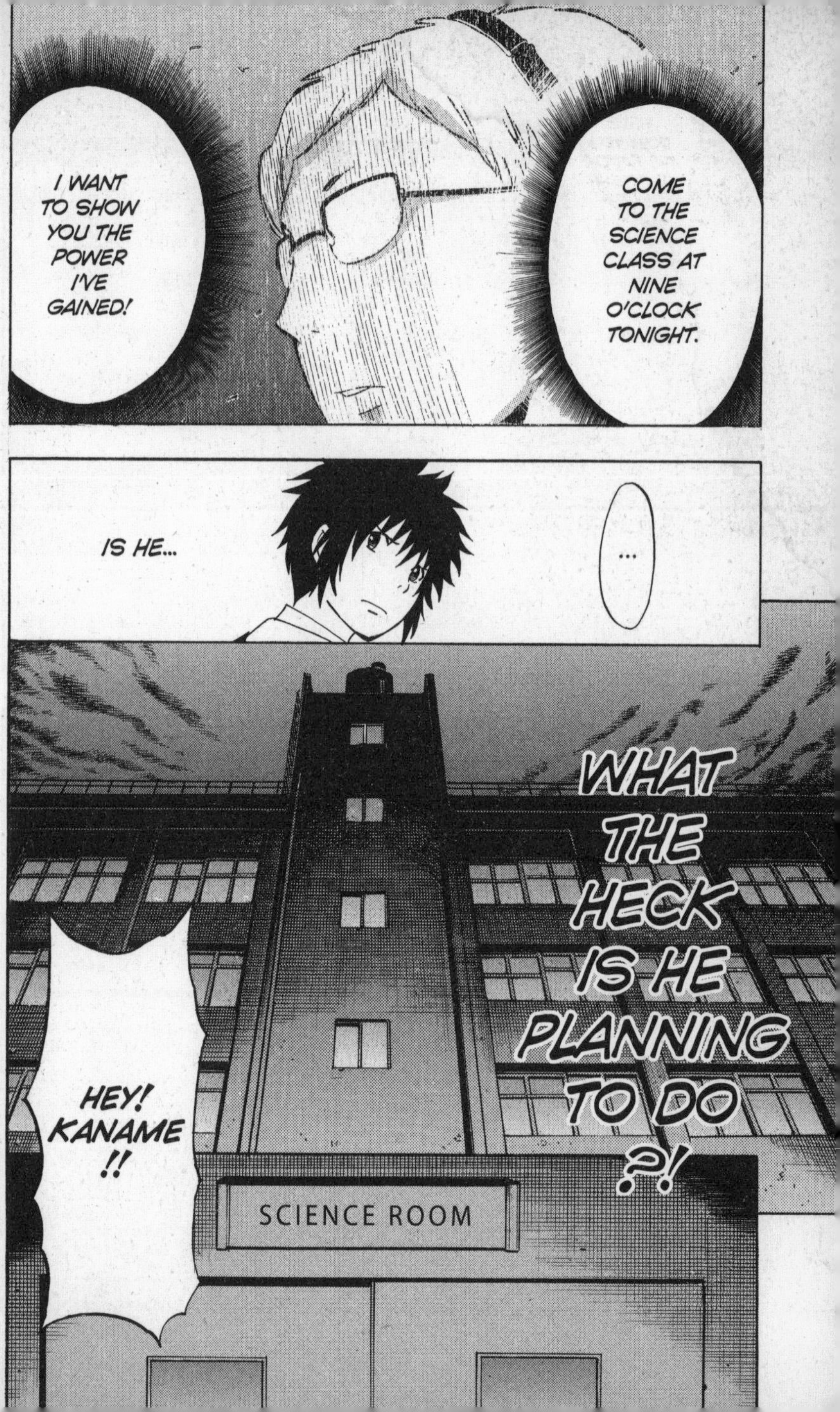
COME TO THE SCIENCE CLASS AT NINE O'CLOCK TONIGHT.
I WANT TO SHOW YOU THE POWER I'VE GAINED!
...
IS HE...
WHAT THE HECK IS HE PLANNING TO DO ?!
HEY! KANAME !!
SCIENCE ROOM

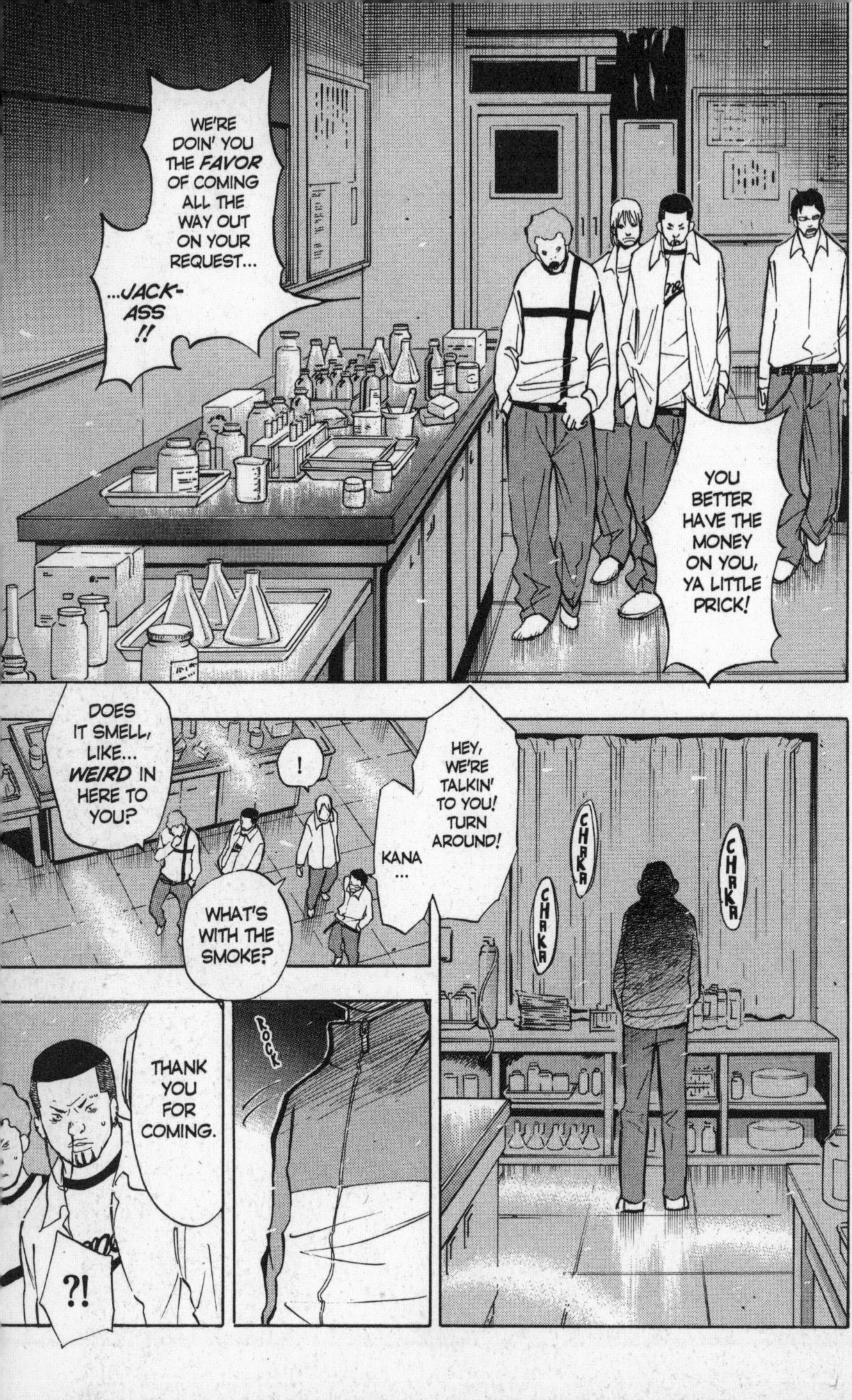
WE'RE DOIN' YOU THE FAVOR OF COMING ALL THE WAY OUT ON YOUR REQUEST... ...JACK-ASS!!
YOU BETTER HAVE THE MONEY ON YOU, YA LITTLE PRICK!
HEY, WE'RE TALKIN' TO YOU! TURN AROUND!
CHAKA
CHAKA
KANA...
CHAKA
DOES IT SMELL, LIKE... WEIRD IN HERE TO YOU?
!
WHAT'S WITH THE SMOKE?
ROCK
THANK YOU FOR COMING.
?!

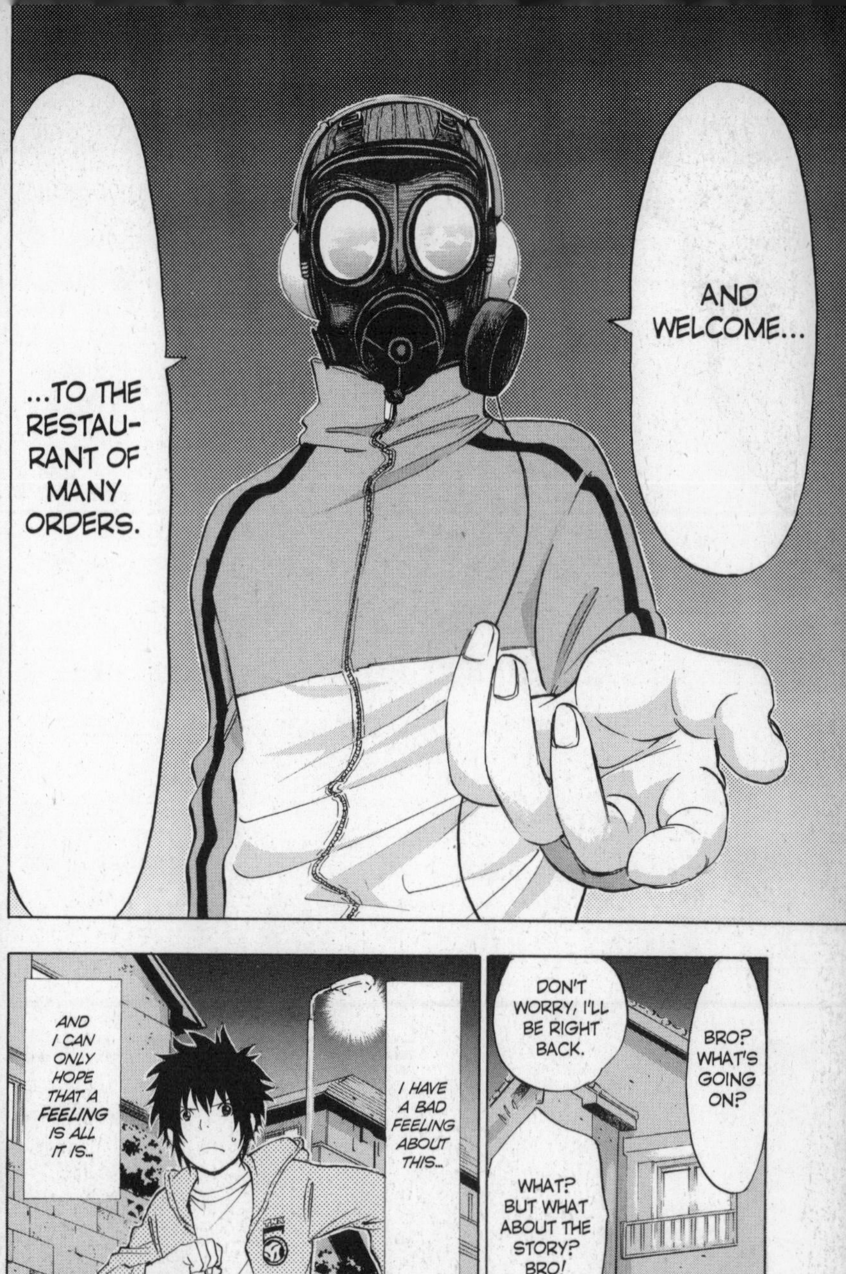
AND WELCOME...
...TO THE RESTAU-RANT OF MANY ORDERS.
BRO? WHAT'S GOING ON?
DON'T WORRY, I'LL BE RIGHT BACK.
WHAT? BUT WHAT ABOUT THE STORY? BRO!
I HAVE A BAD FEELING ABOUT THIS...
AND I CAN ONLY HOPE THAT A FEELING IS ALL IT IS...

Chapter 4 Seeping Discord

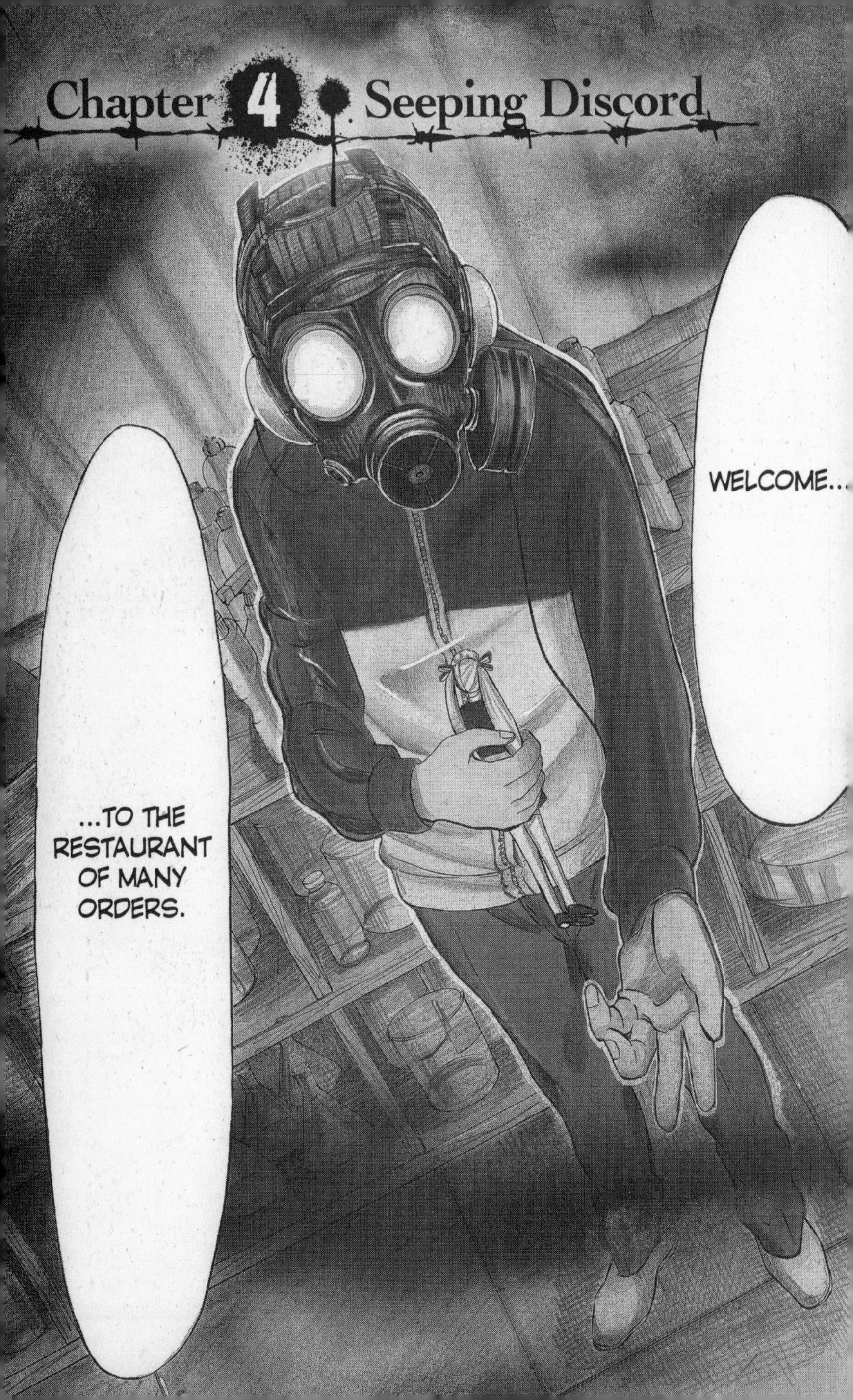
WELCOME...
...TO THE RESTAURANT OF MANY ORDERS.

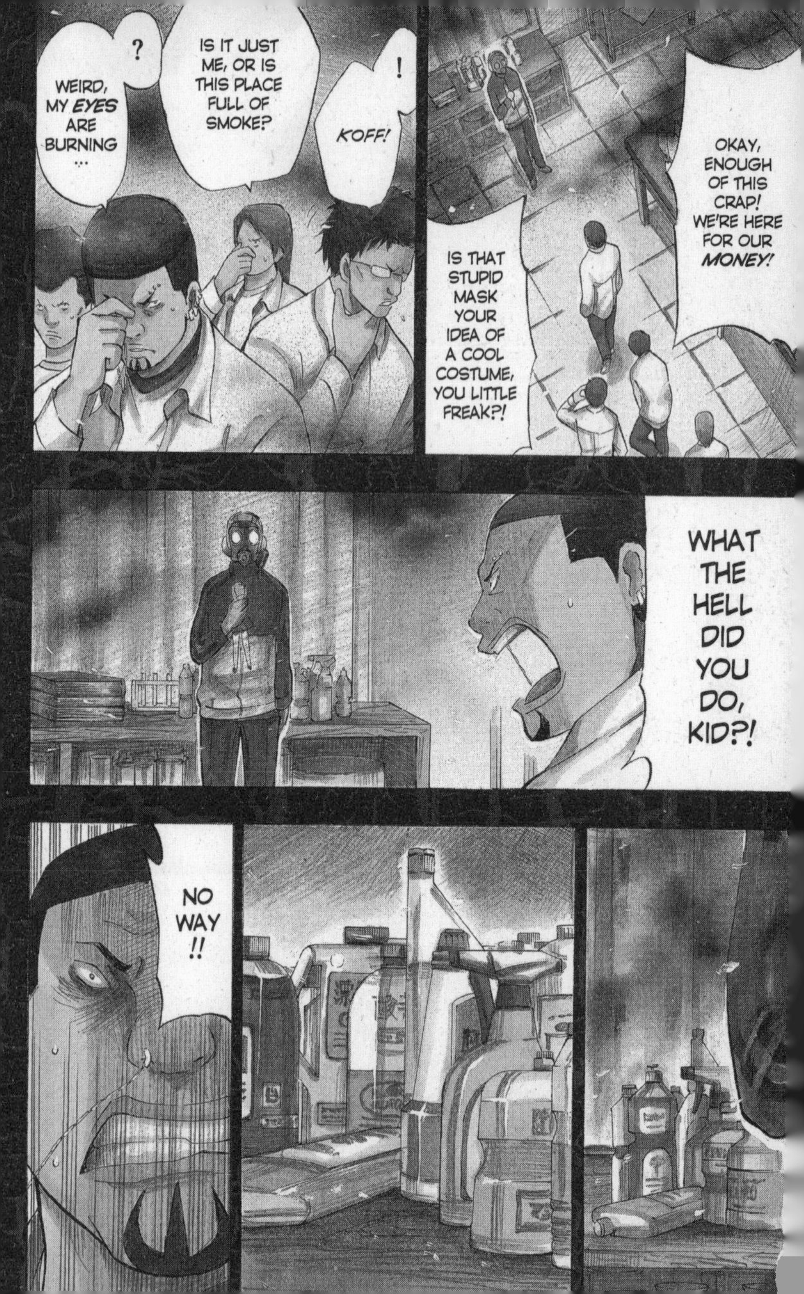
OKAY, ENOUGH OF THIS CRAP! WE'RE HERE FOR OUR *MONEY!*
IS THAT STUPID MASK YOUR IDEA OF A COOL COSTUME, YOU LITTLE FREAK?!
!
KOFF!
IS IT JUST ME, OR IS THIS PLACE FULL OF SMOKE?
?
WEIRD, MY *EYES* ARE BURNING ...
WHAT THE HELL DID YOU DO, KID?!
NO WAY !!

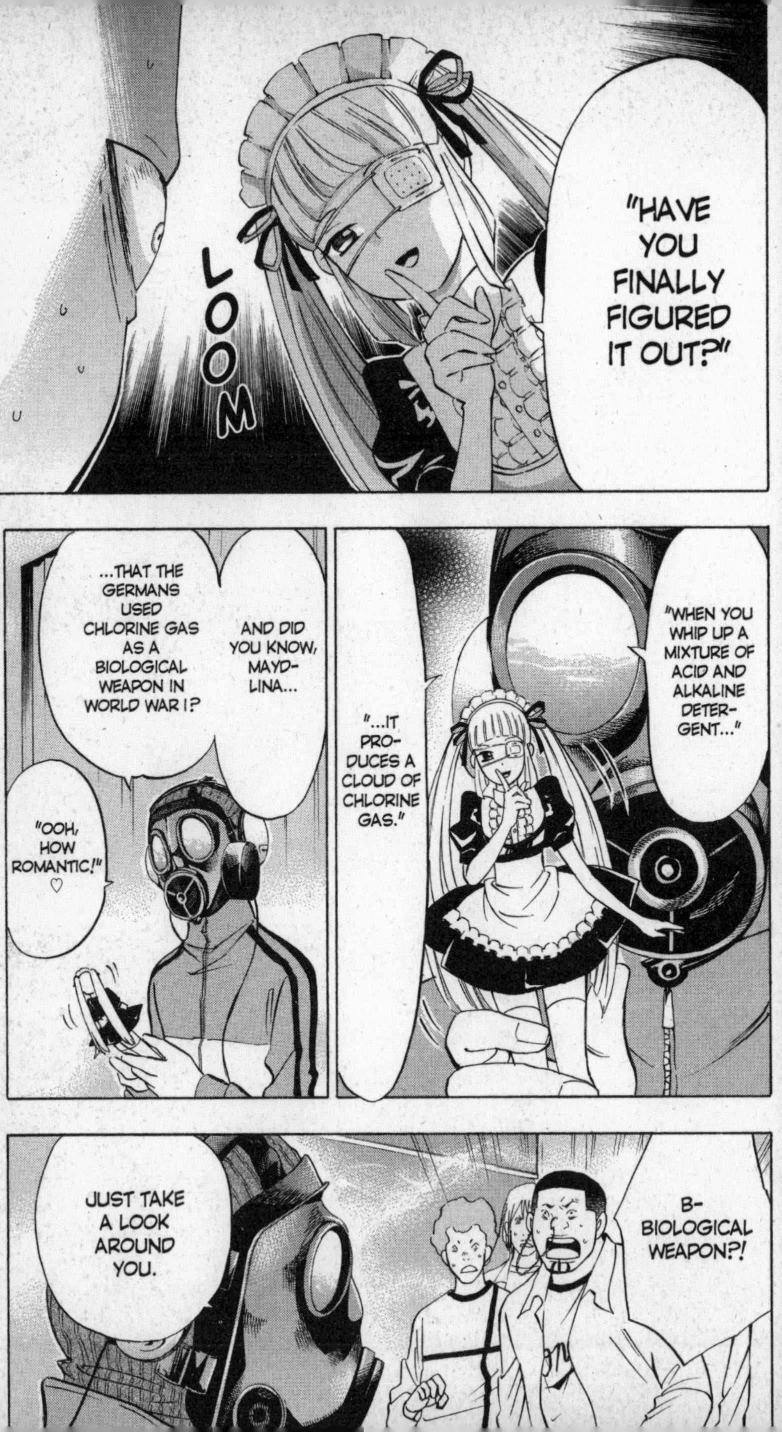
"HAVE YOU FINALLY FIGURED IT OUT?"
LOOM
"WHEN YOU WHIP UP A MIXTURE OF ACID AND ALKALINE DETER-GENT..."
"...IT PRO-DUCES A CLOUD OF CHLORINE GAS."
AND DID YOU KNOW, MAYD-LINA...
...THAT THE GERMANS USED CHLORINE GAS AS A BIOLOGICAL WEAPON IN WORLD WAR I?
"OOH, HOW ROMANTIC!" ♡
B-BIOLOGICAL WEAPON?!
JUST TAKE A LOOK AROUND YOU.

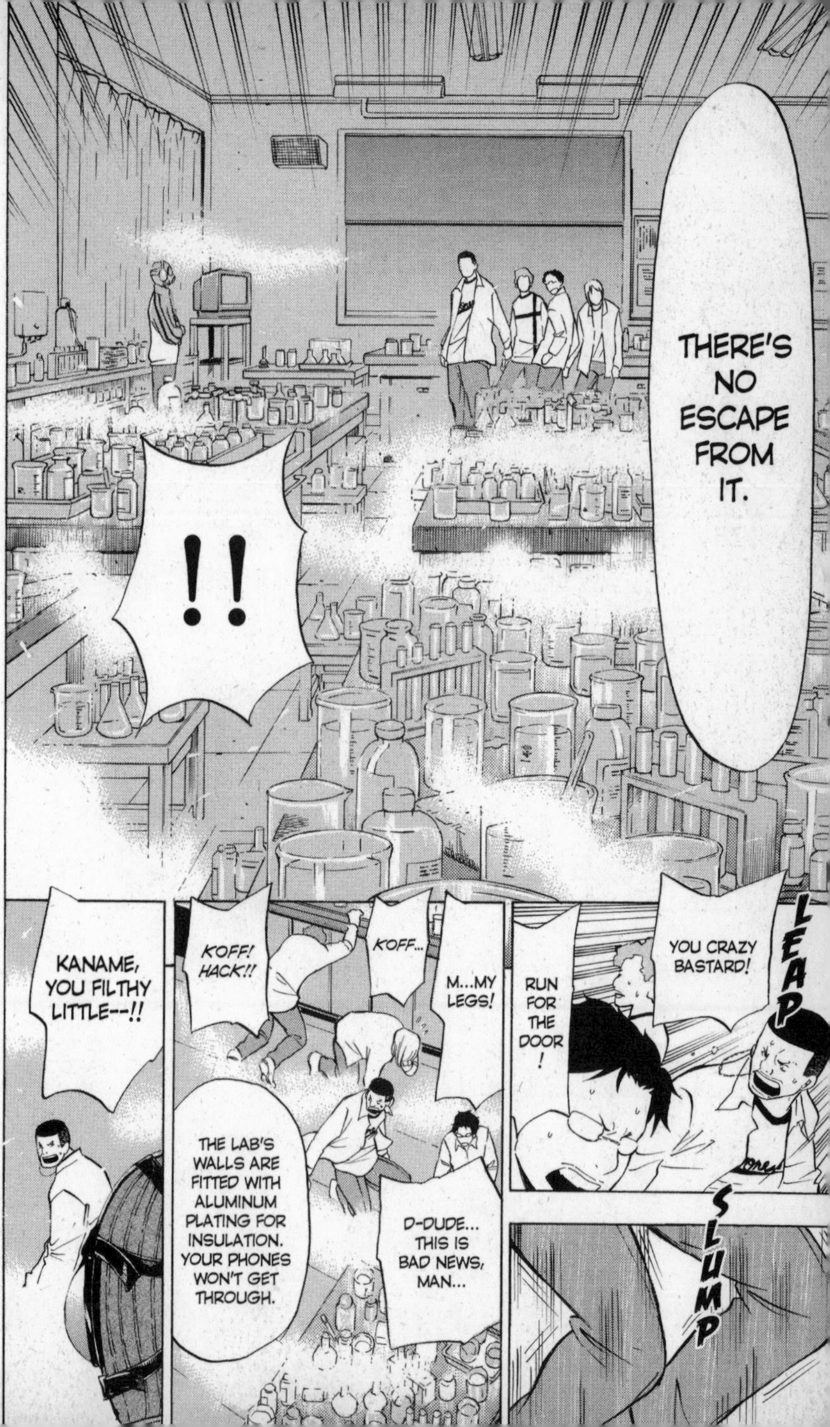

THERE'S NO ESCAPE FROM IT.
!!
LEAP
YOU CRAZY BASTARD!
RUN FOR THE DOOR!
SLUMP
M...MY LEGS!
KOFF...
KOFF! HACK!!
D-DUDE... THIS IS BAD NEWS, MAN...
THE LAB'S WALLS ARE FITTED WITH ALUMINUM PLATING FOR INSULATION. YOUR PHONES WON'T GET THROUGH.
KANAME, YOU FILTHY LITTLE--!!

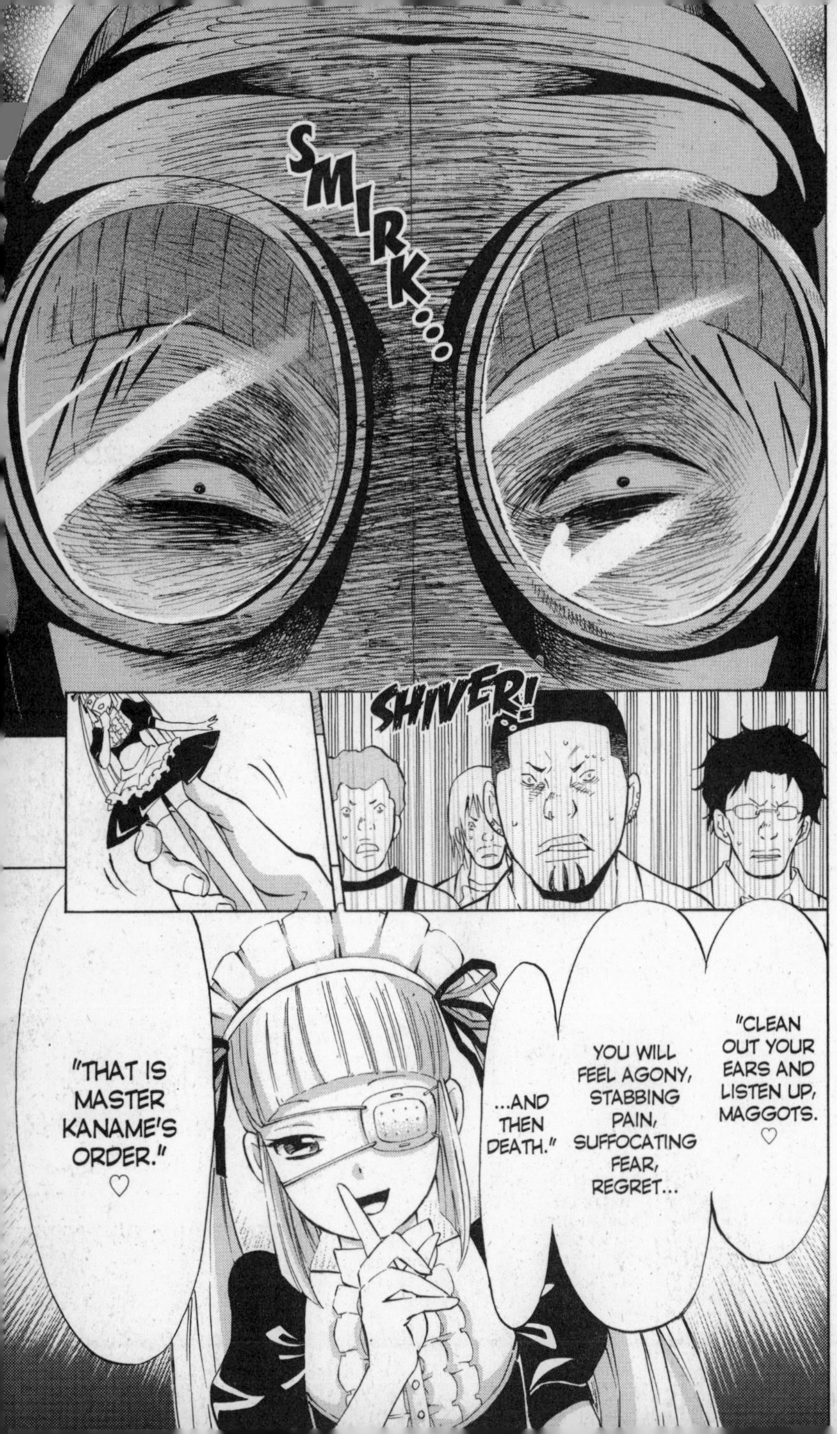
SMIRK...
SHIVER!
"CLEAN OUT YOUR EARS AND LISTEN UP, MAGGOTS. ♡
YOU WILL FEEL AGONY, STABBING PAIN, SUFFOCATING FEAR, REGRET...
...AND THEN DEATH."
"THAT IS MASTER KANAME'S ORDER." ♡

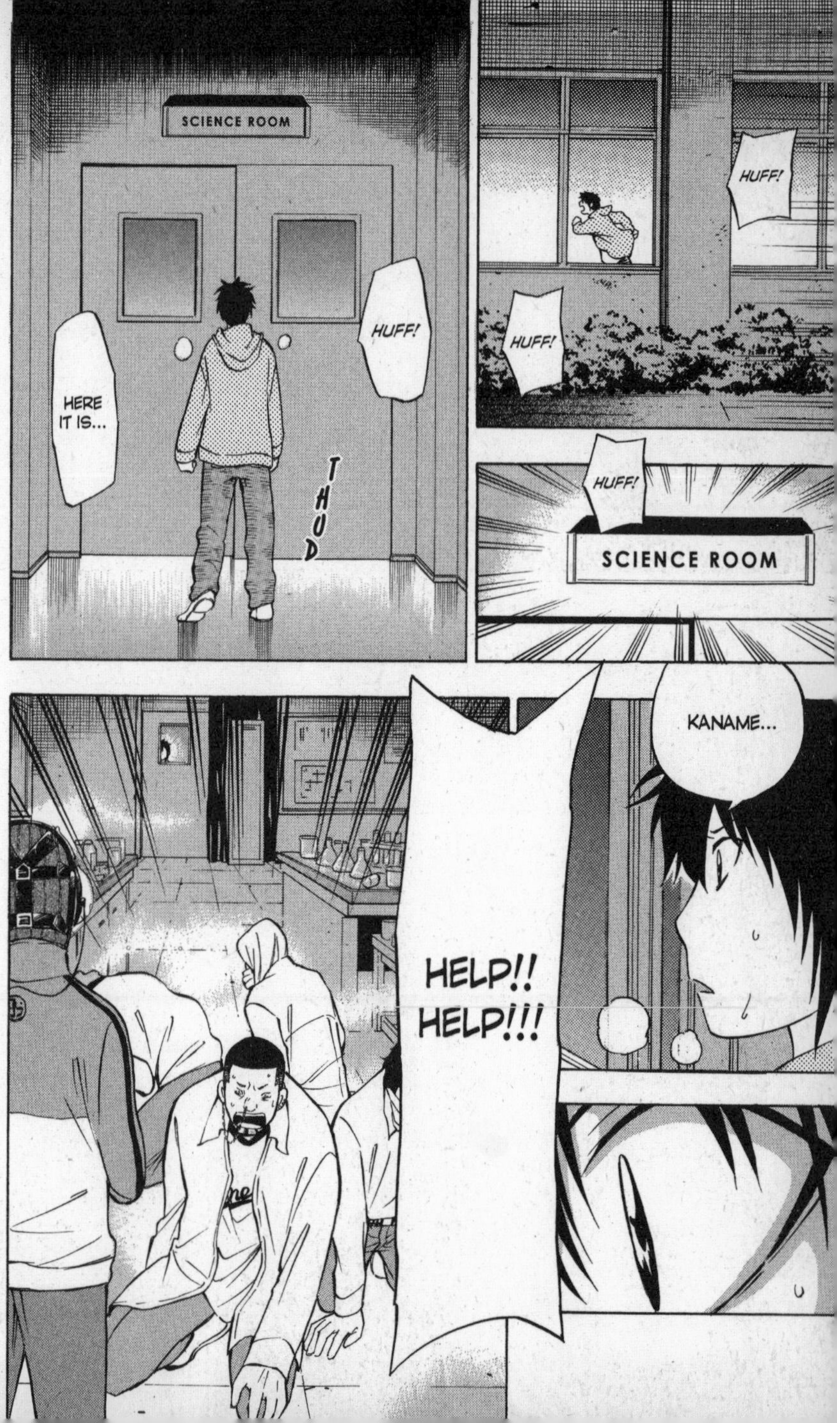
HUFF!
HUFF!
HUFF!
SCIENCE ROOM
SCIENCE ROOM
HUFF!
HERE IT IS...
THUD
KANAME...
HELP!! HELP!!!

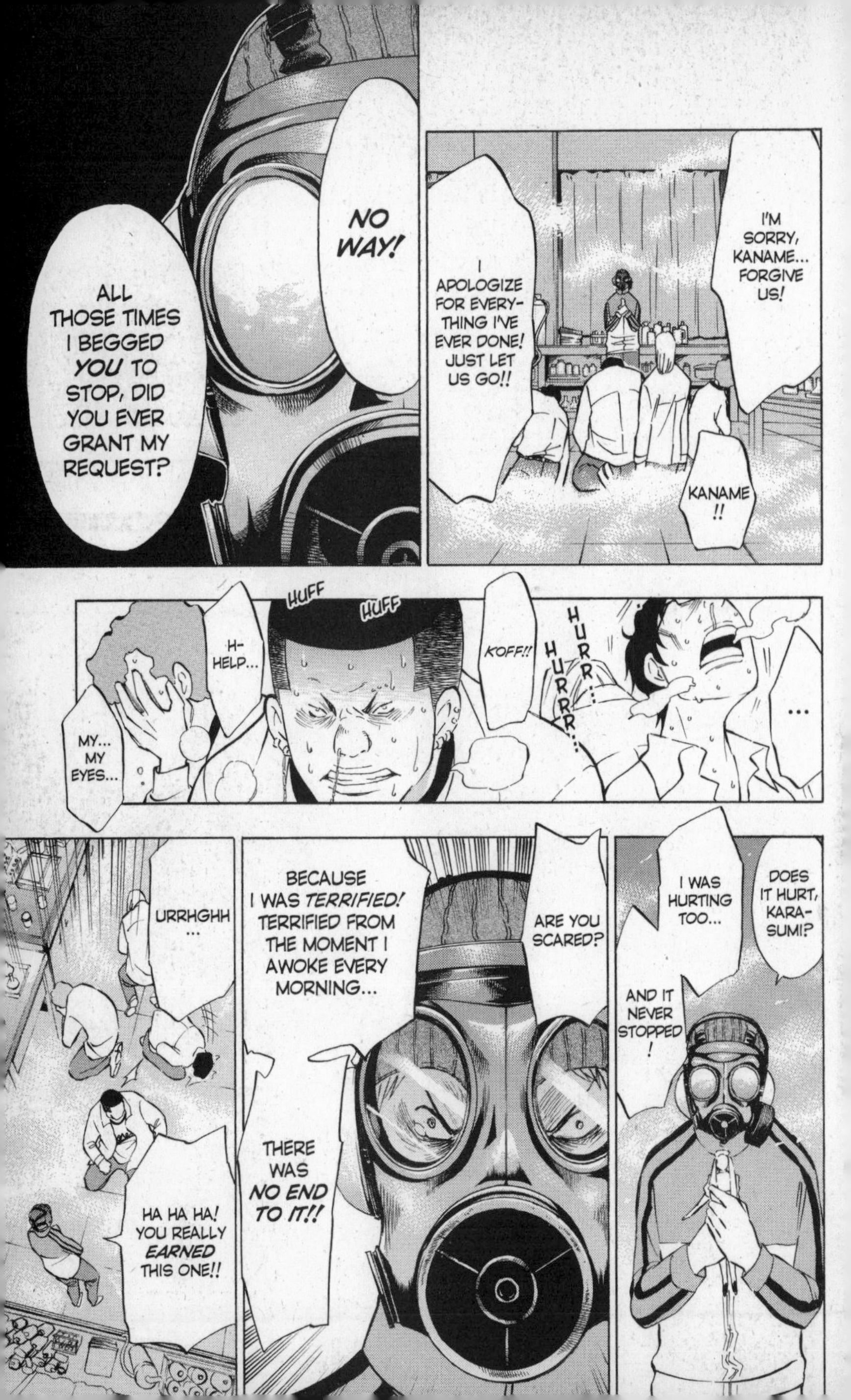
I'M SORRY, KANAME... FORGIVE US!
I APOLOGIZE FOR EVERY-THING I'VE EVER DONE! JUST LET US GO!!
KANAME!!
NO WAY!
ALL THOSE TIMES I BEGGED YOU TO STOP, DID YOU EVER GRANT MY REQUEST?
...
HURR... HURRR...
KOFF!!
HUFF HUFF
H-HELP...
MY... MY EYES...
DOES IT HURT, KARA-SUMI?
I WAS HURTING TOO...
AND IT NEVER STOPPED!
ARE YOU SCARED?
BECAUSE I WAS TERRIFIED! TERRIFIED FROM THE MOMENT I AWOKE EVERY MORNING...
THERE WAS NO END TO IT!!
URRHGHH...
HA HA HA! YOU REALLY EARNED THIS ONE!!

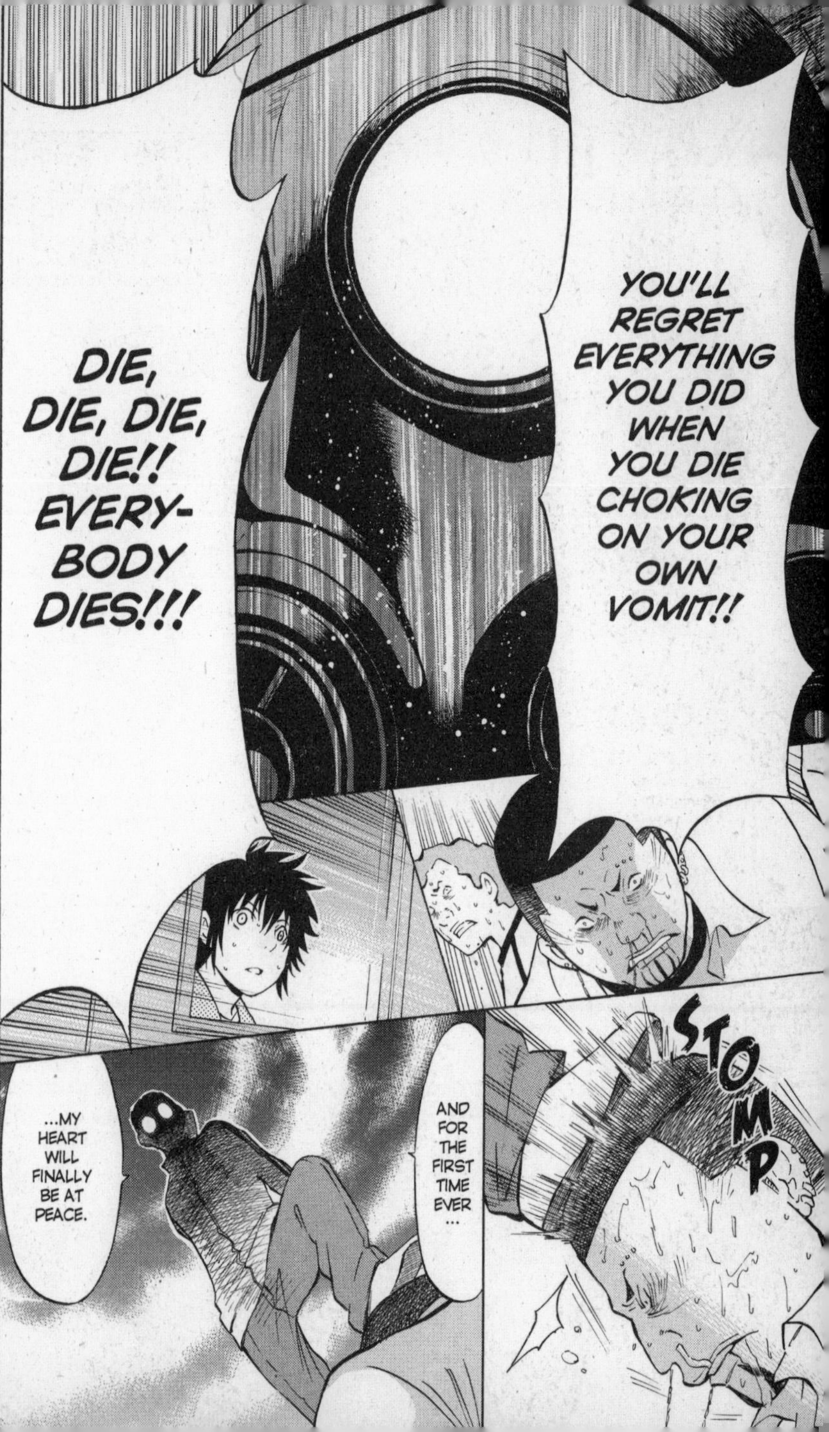
YOU'LL REGRET EVERYTHING YOU DID WHEN YOU DIE CHOKING ON YOUR OWN VOMIT!!
DIE, DIE, DIE, DIE!! EVERY-BODY DIES!!!
STOMP
AND FOR THE FIRST TIME EVER...
...MY HEART WILL FINALLY BE AT PEACE.

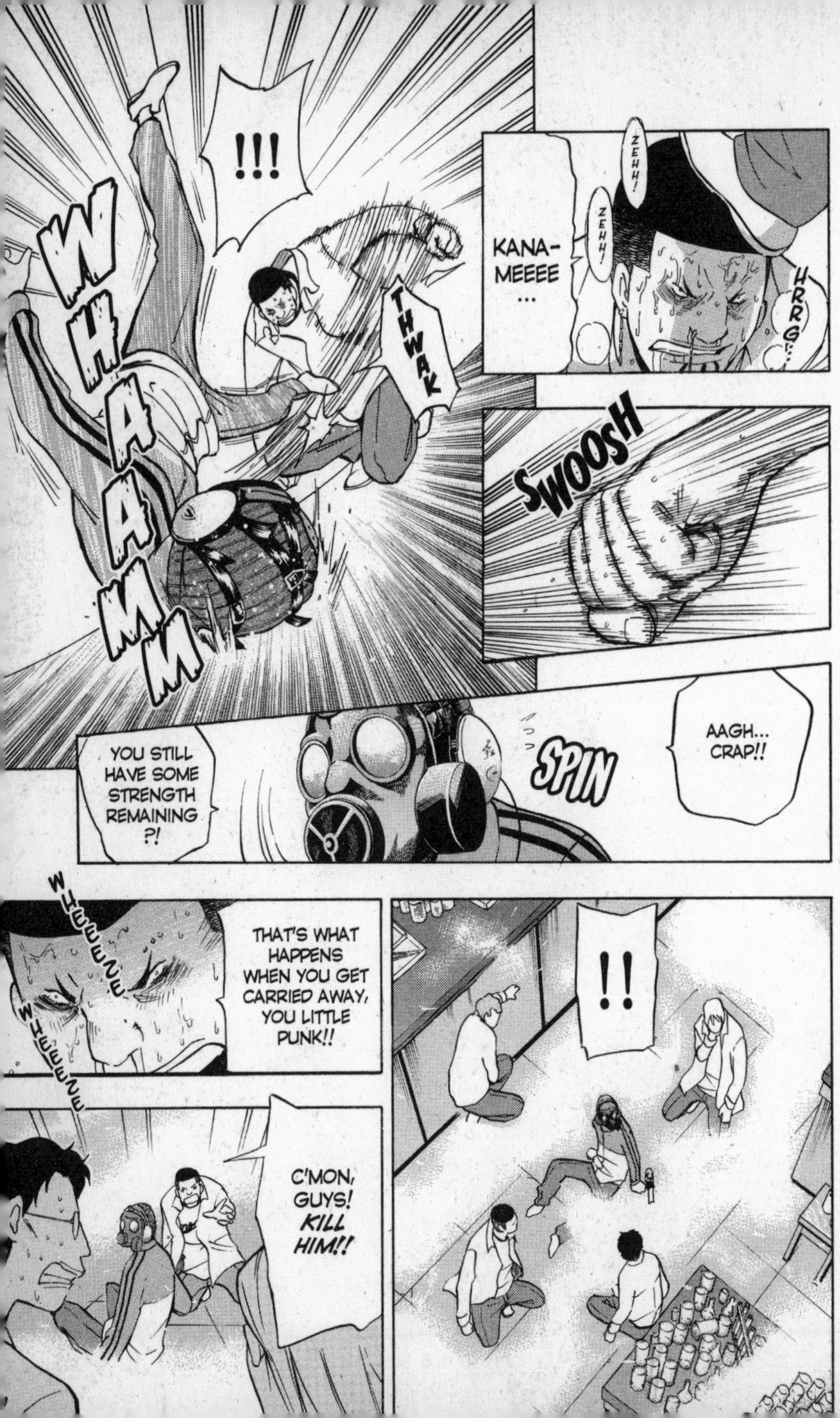
ZEHH!
ZEHH!
KANA-MEEEE...
HRRG!!
SWOOSH
!!!
THWAK
WHAMM
AAGH... CRAP!!
SPIN
YOU STILL HAVE SOME STRENGTH REMAINING?!
!!
THAT'S WHAT HAPPENS WHEN YOU GET CARRIED AWAY, YOU LITTLE PUNK!!
WHEEEZE
WHEEEZE
C'MON, GUYS! KILL HIM!!

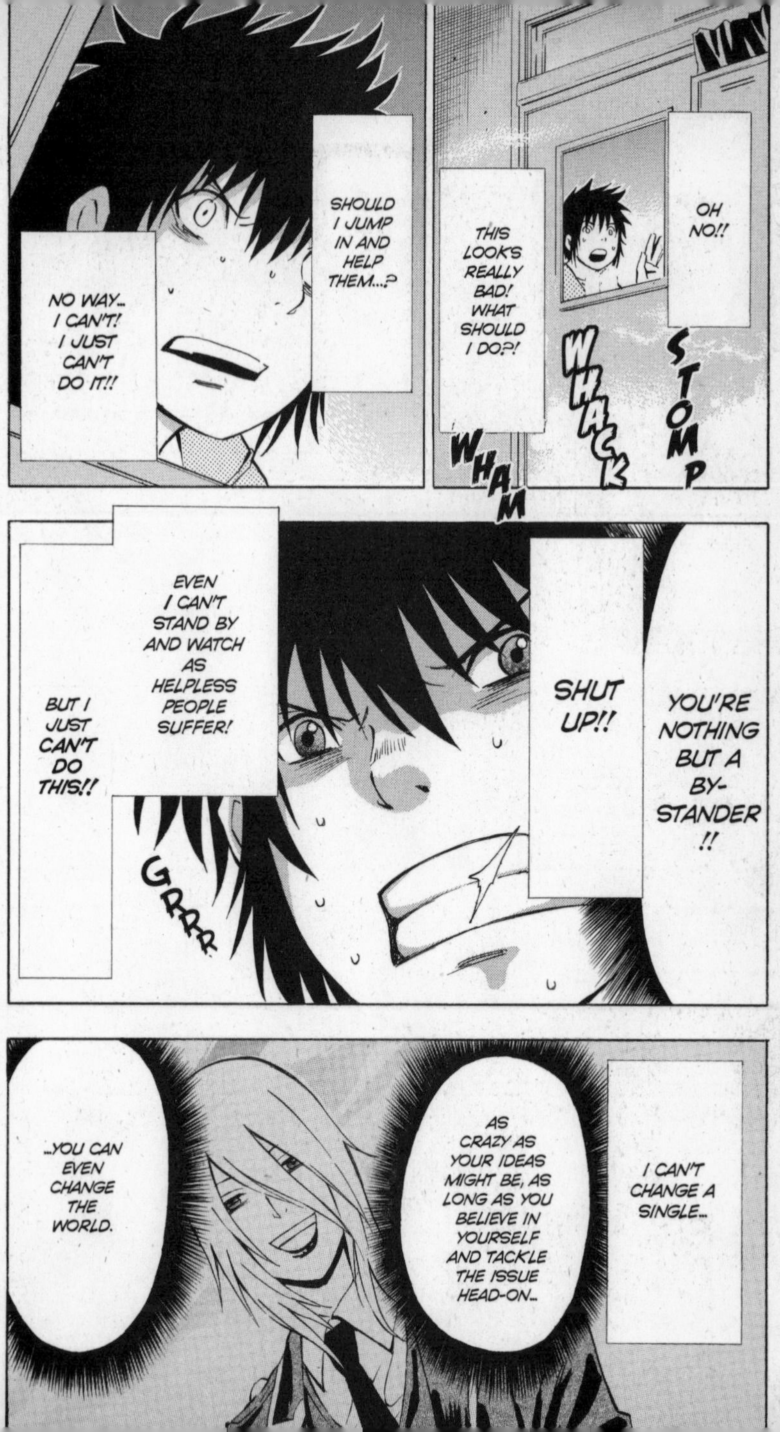
OH NO!!
THIS LOOKS REALLY BAD! WHAT SHOULD I DO?!
STOMP
WHACK
WHAM
SHOULD I JUMP IN AND HELP THEM...?
NO WAY... I CAN'T! I JUST CAN'T DO IT!!
YOU'RE NOTHING BUT A BY-STANDER!!
SHUT UP!!
EVEN I CAN'T STAND BY AND WATCH AS HELPLESS PEOPLE SUFFER!
BUT I JUST CAN'T DO THIS!!
GRRRR
I CAN'T CHANGE A SINGLE...
AS CRAZY AS YOUR IDEAS MIGHT BE, AS LONG AS YOU BELIEVE IN YOURSELF AND TACKLE THE ISSUE HEAD-ON...
...YOU CAN EVEN CHANGE THE WORLD.

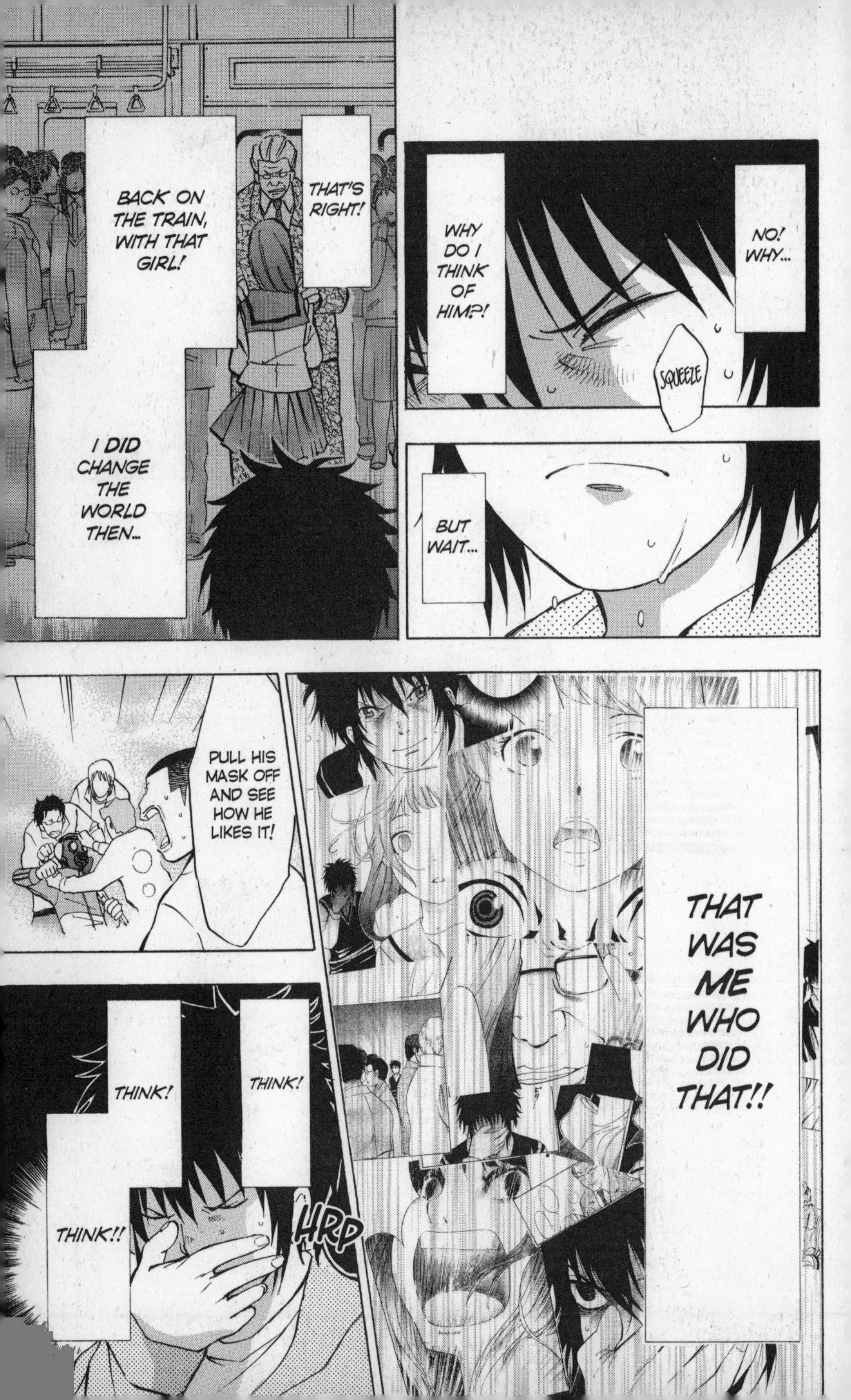
NO! WHY...
WHY DO I THINK OF HIM?!
SQUEEZE
BUT WAIT...
THAT'S RIGHT!
BACK ON THE TRAIN, WITH THAT GIRL!
I DID CHANGE THE WORLD THEN...
THAT WAS ME WHO DID THAT!!
PULL HIS MASK OFF AND SEE HOW HE LIKES IT!
THINK!
THINK!
THINK!!
HRP

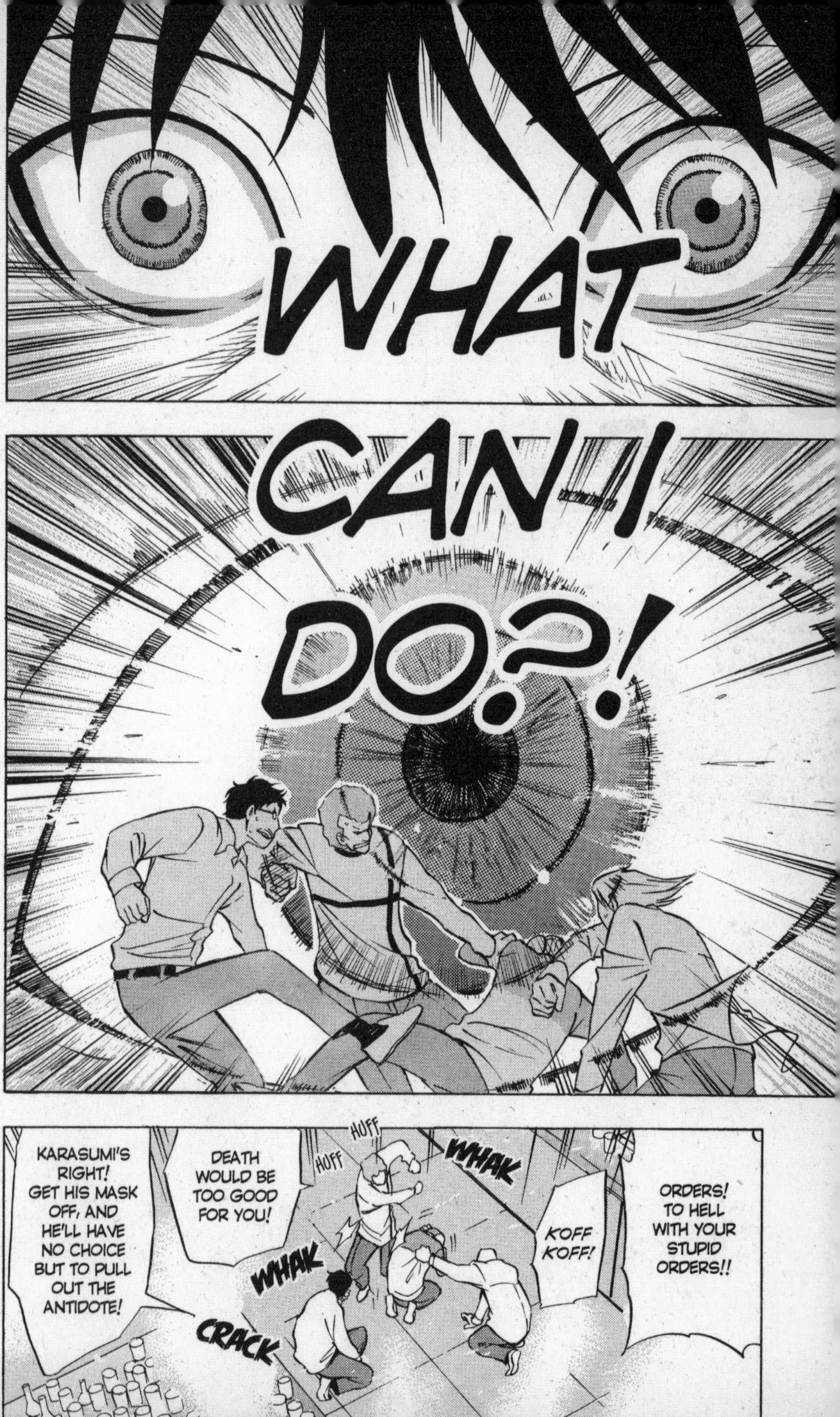
WHAT
CAN I
DO?!
ORDERS! TO HELL WITH YOUR STUPID ORDERS!!
KOFF KOFF!
WHAK
HUFF
HUFF
DEATH WOULD BE TOO GOOD FOR YOU!
KARASUMI'S RIGHT! GET HIS MASK OFF, AND HE'LL HAVE NO CHOICE BUT TO PULL OUT THE ANTIDOTE!
WHAK
CRACK

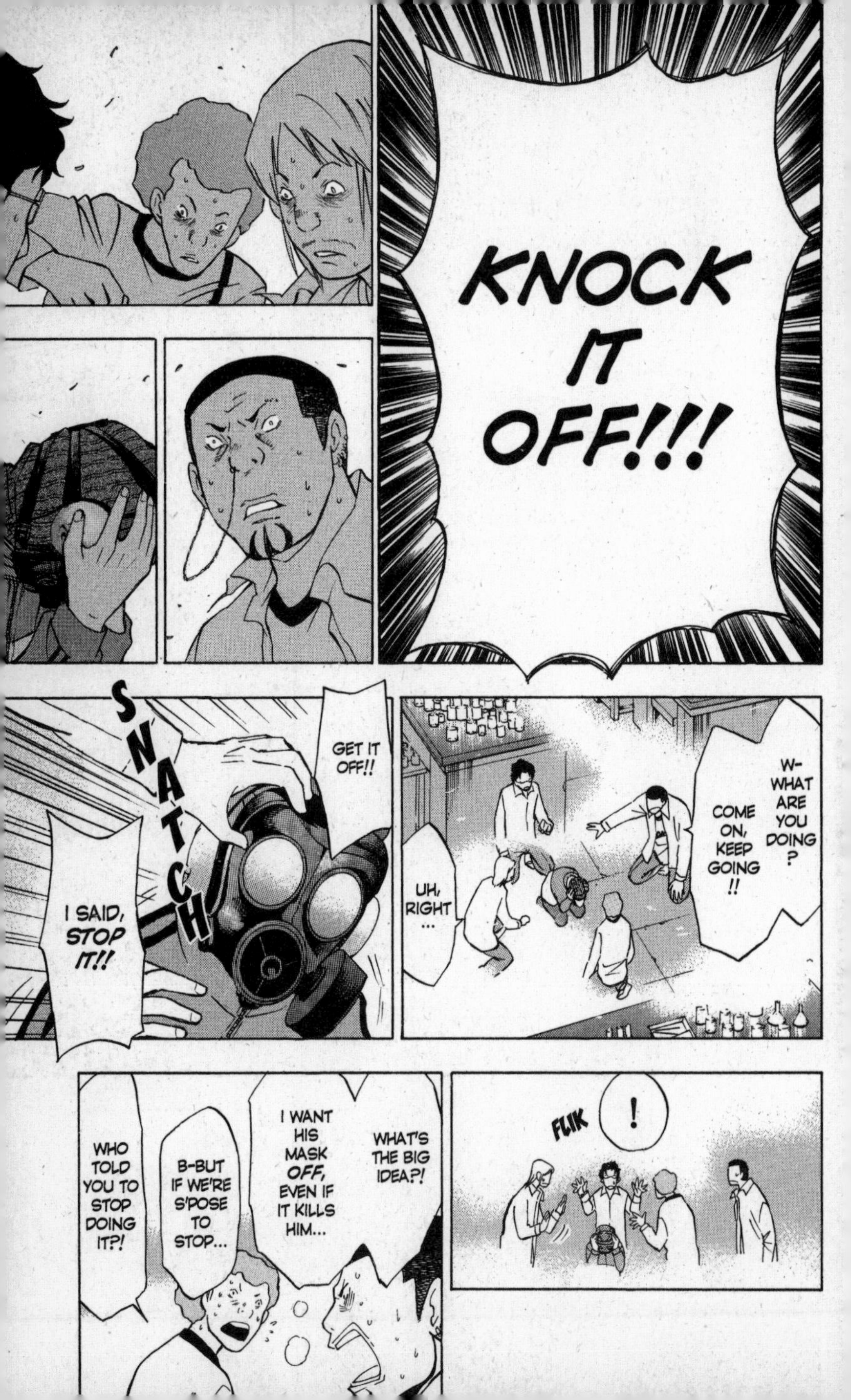
KNOCK IT OFF!!!
W-WHAT ARE YOU DOING?
COME ON, KEEP GOING!!
UH, RIGHT...
GET IT OFF!!
SNATCH
I SAID, STOP IT!!
FLIK
!
WHAT'S THE BIG IDEA?!
I WANT HIS MASK OFF, EVEN IF IT KILLS HIM...
B-BUT IF WE'RE S'POSE TO STOP...
WHO TOLD YOU TO STOP DOING IT?!

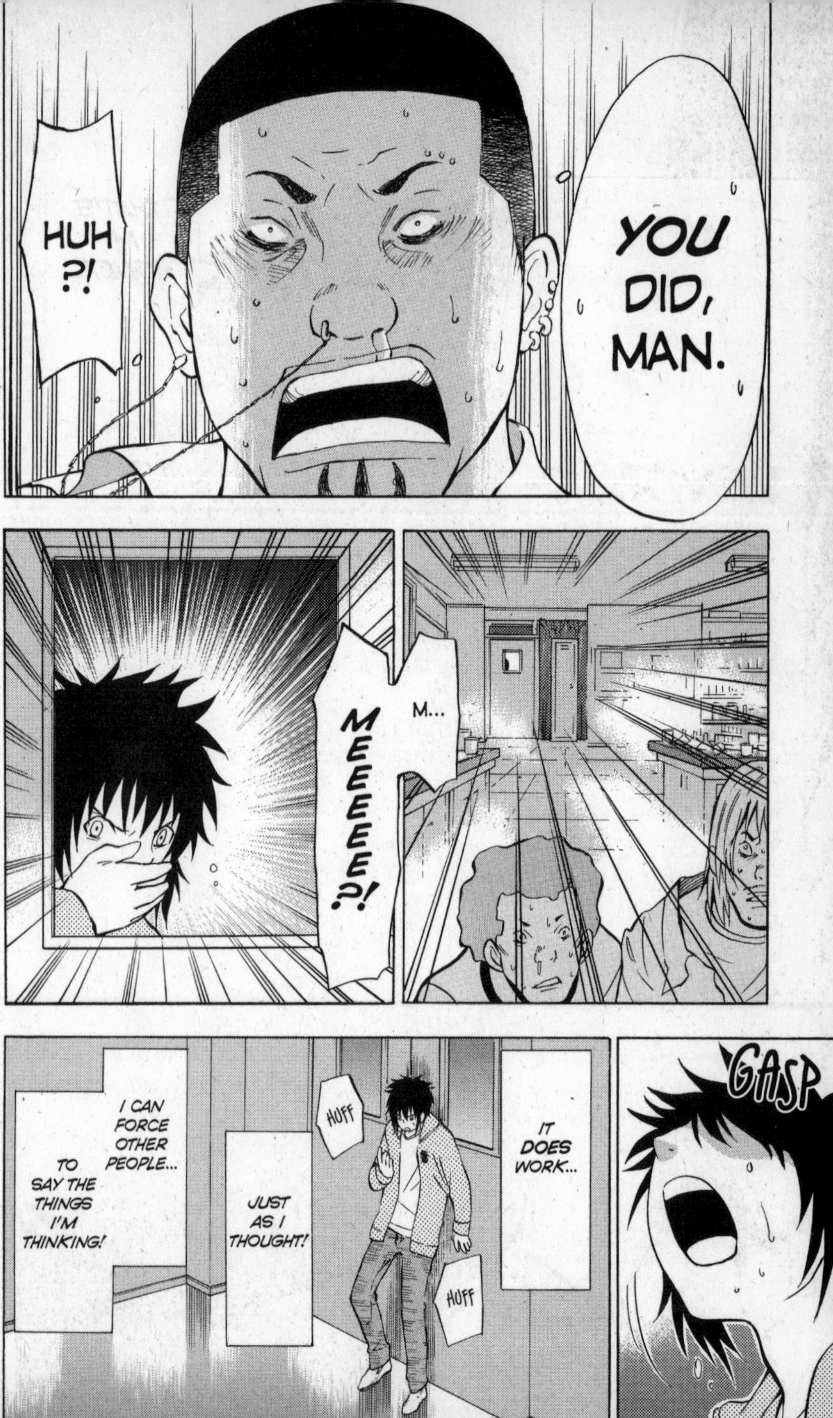
YOU DID, MAN.
HUH ?!
M...
MEEEEEE?!
GASP
IT DOES WORK...
HUFF
HUFF
JUST AS I THOUGHT!
I CAN FORCE OTHER PEOPLE...
TO SAY THE THINGS I'M THINKING!

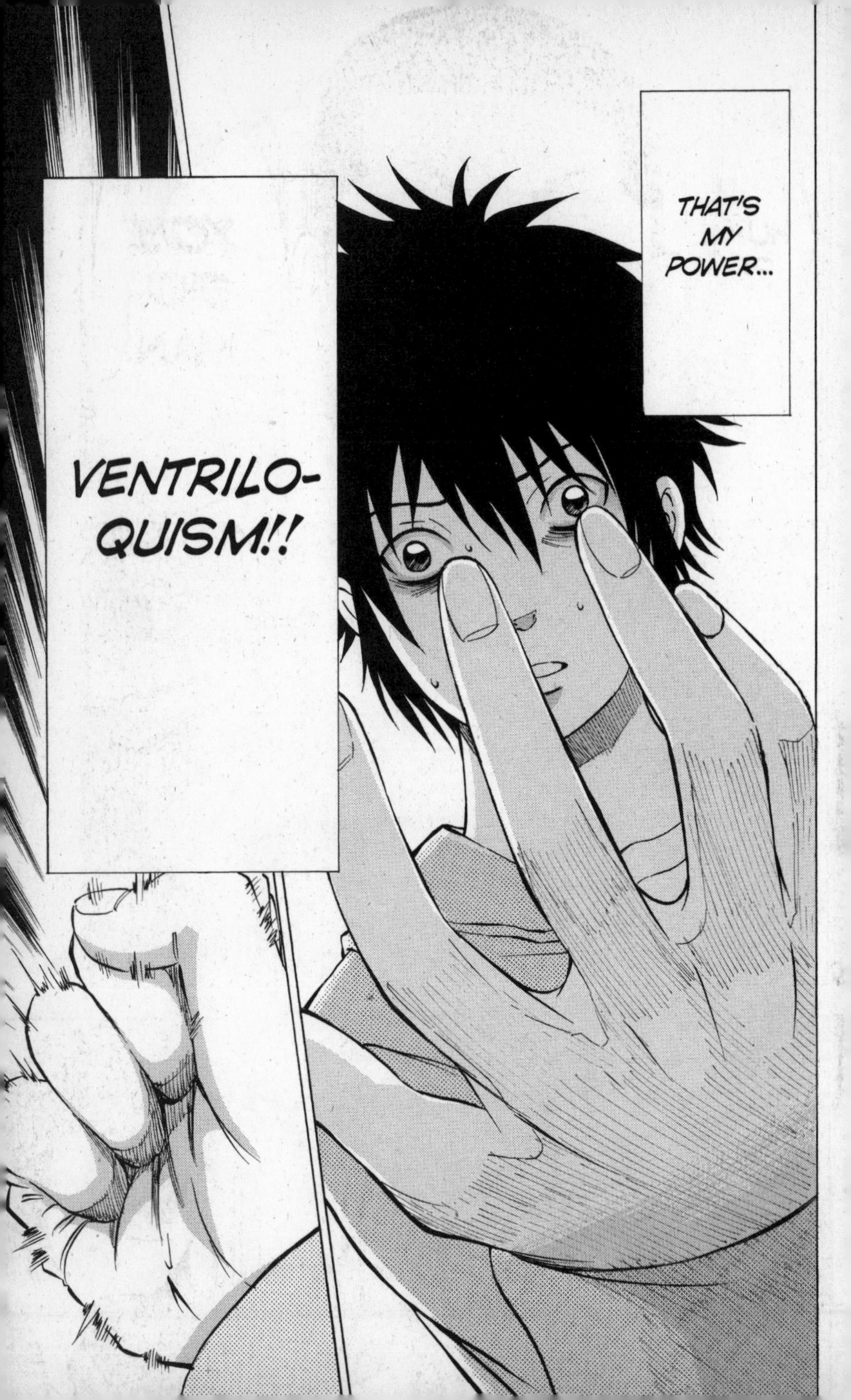
THAT'S MY POWER...
VENTRILO-QUISM!!

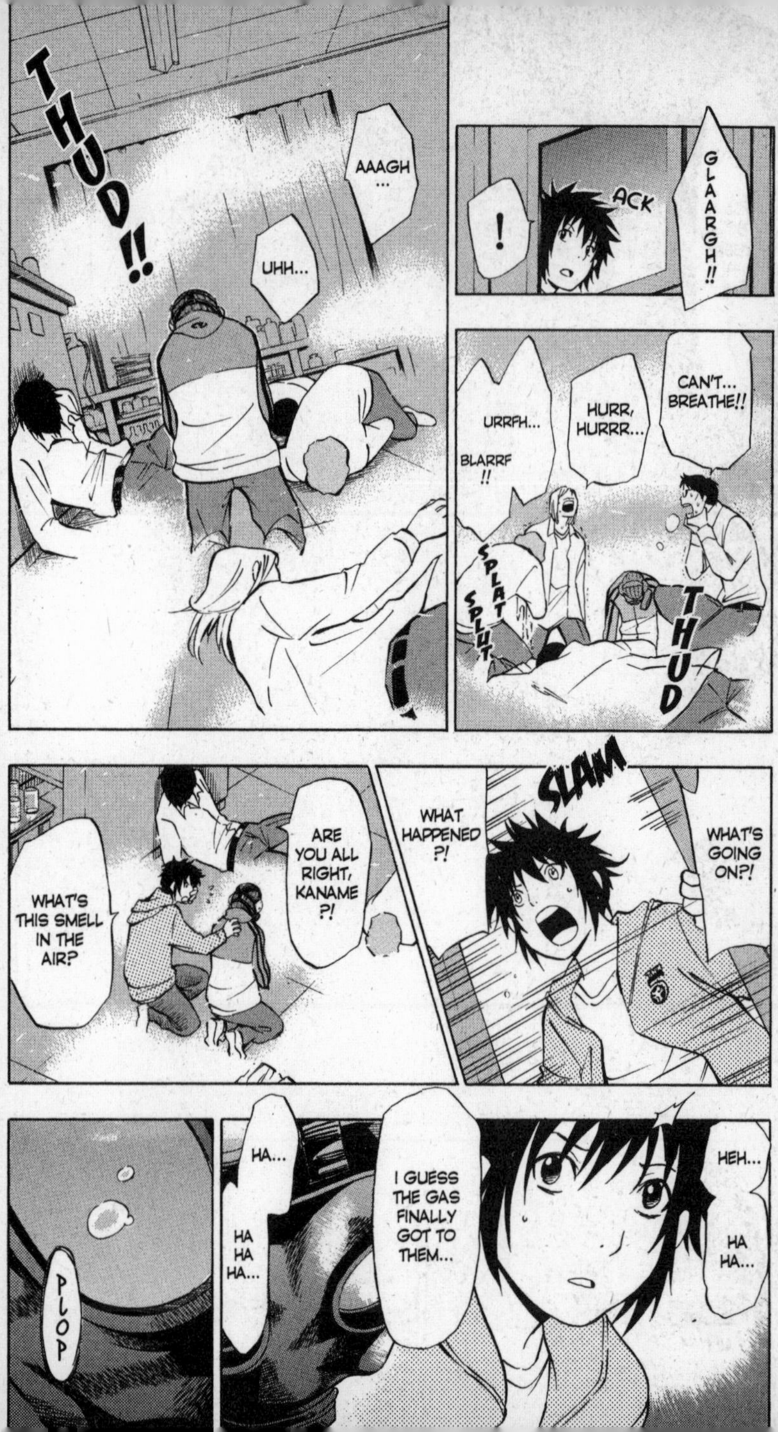
GLAARGH!!
ACK
!
CAN'T... BREATHE!!
HURR, HURRR...
URRFH...
BLARRF!!
THUD
SPLAT
SPLUT
AAAGH...
UHH...
THUD!!
WHAT'S GOING ON?!
SLAM
WHAT HAPPENED?!
ARE YOU ALL RIGHT, KANAME?!
WHAT'S THIS SMELL IN THE AIR?
HEH...
HA HA...
I GUESS THE GAS FINALLY GOT TO THEM...
HA...
HA HA HA...
PLOP

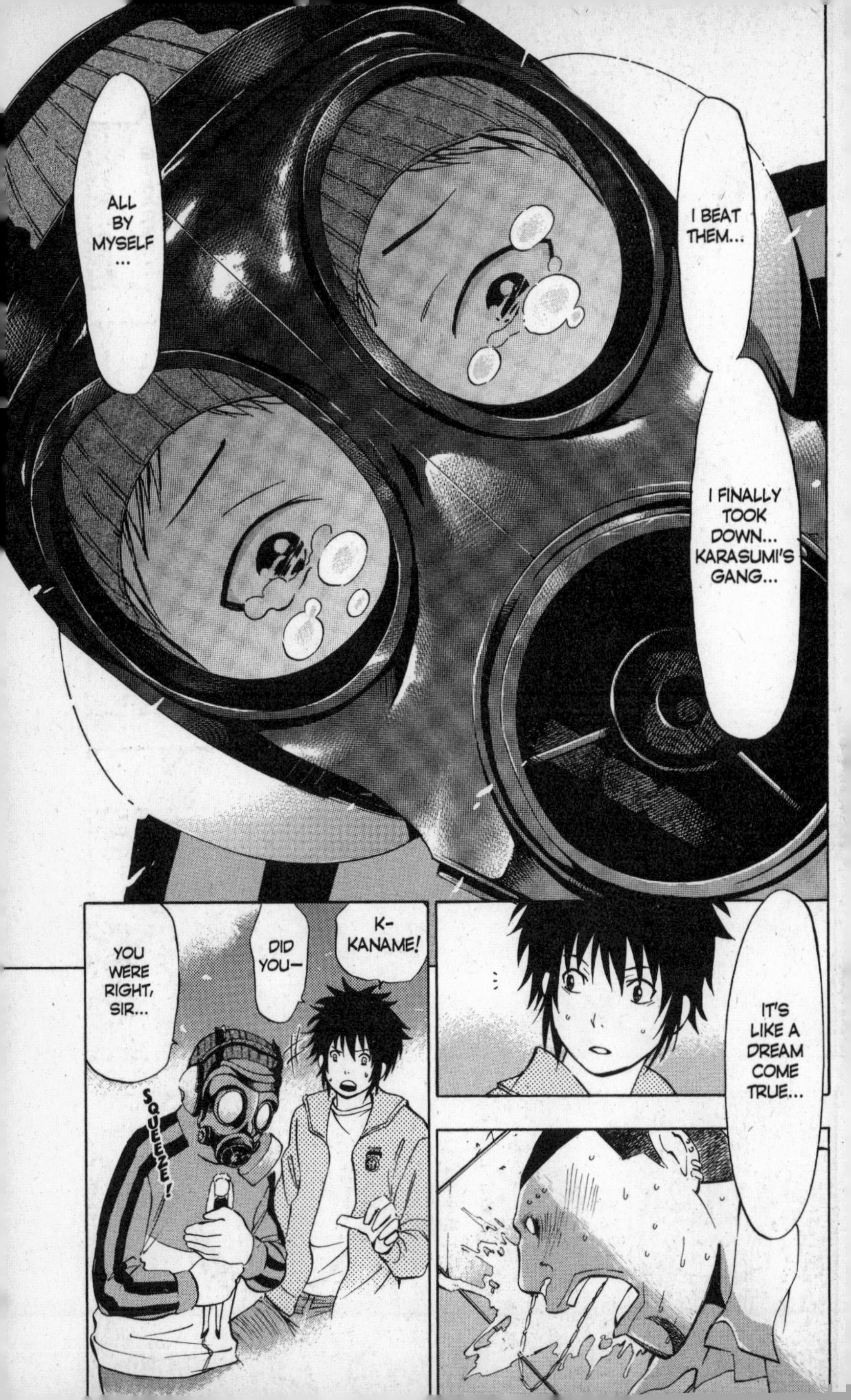
I BEAT THEM...
I FINALLY TOOK DOWN... KARASUMI'S GANG...
ALL BY MYSELF...
IT'S LIKE A DREAM COME TRUE...
K-KANAME!
DID YOU—
YOU WERE RIGHT, SIR...
SQUEEZE!

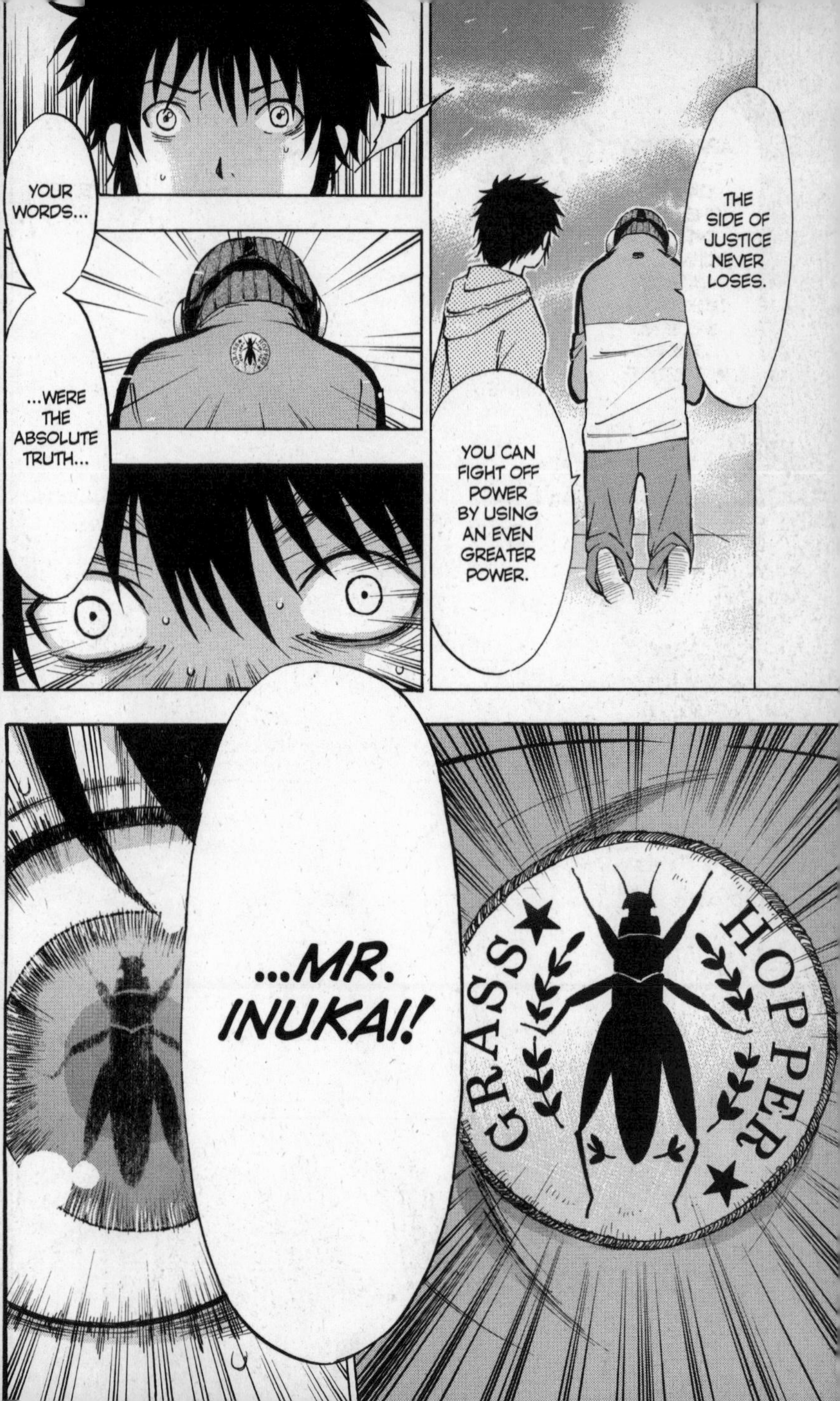
THE SIDE OF JUSTICE NEVER LOSES.
YOU CAN FIGHT OFF POWER BY USING AN EVEN GREATER POWER.
YOUR WORDS...
...WERE THE ABSOLUTE TRUTH...
...MR. INUKAI!
GRASS HOPPER

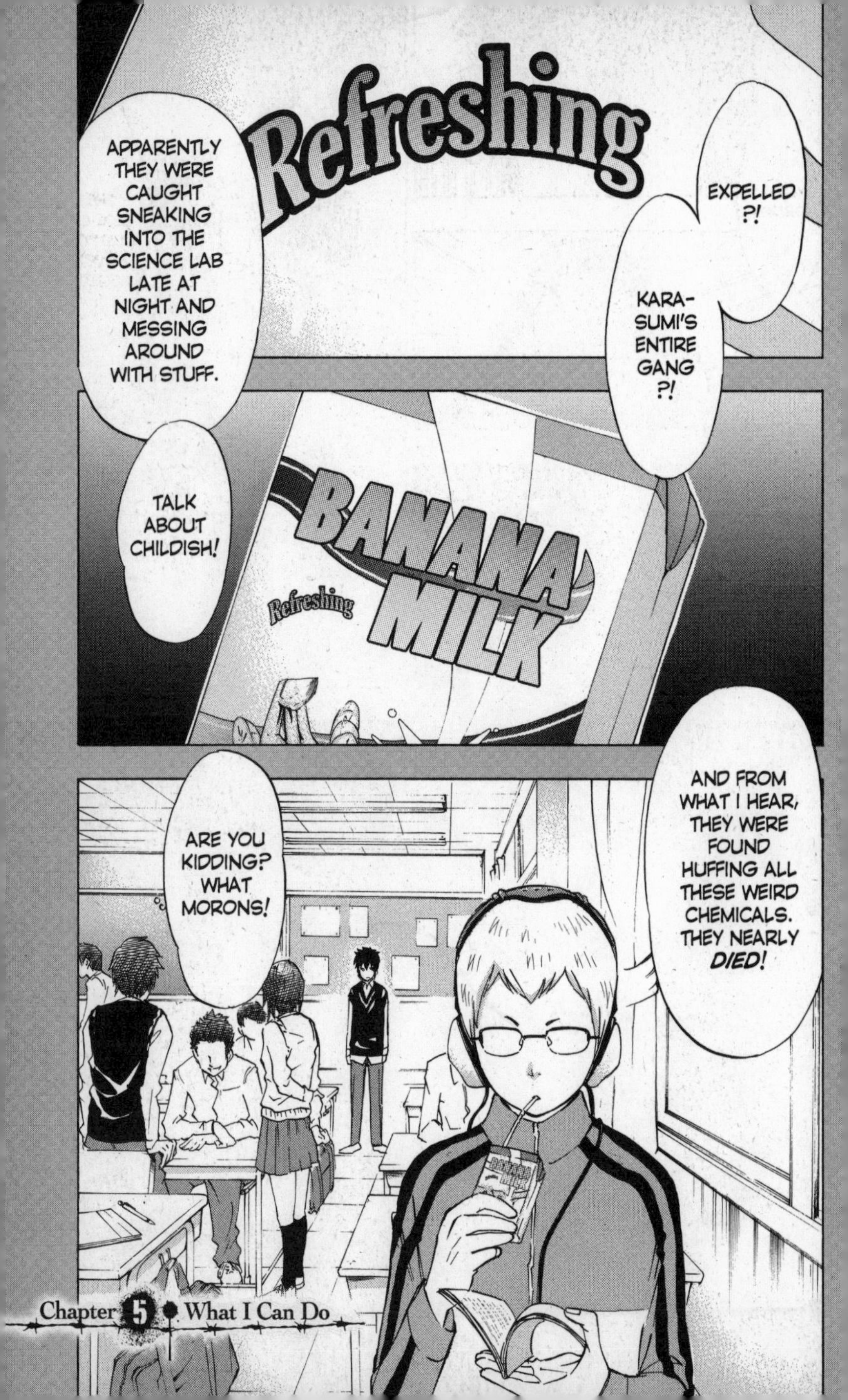
Refreshing
EXPELLED ?!
KARA-SUMI'S ENTIRE GANG ?!
APPARENTLY THEY WERE CAUGHT SNEAKING INTO THE SCIENCE LAB LATE AT NIGHT AND MESSING AROUND WITH STUFF.
TALK ABOUT CHILDISH!
BANANA MILK
Refreshing
AND FROM WHAT I HEAR, THEY WERE FOUND HUFFING ALL THESE WEIRD CHEMICALS. THEY NEARLY *DIED*!
ARE YOU KIDDING? WHAT MORONS!
Chapter 5 What I Can Do

Chapter 5 ● What I Can Do

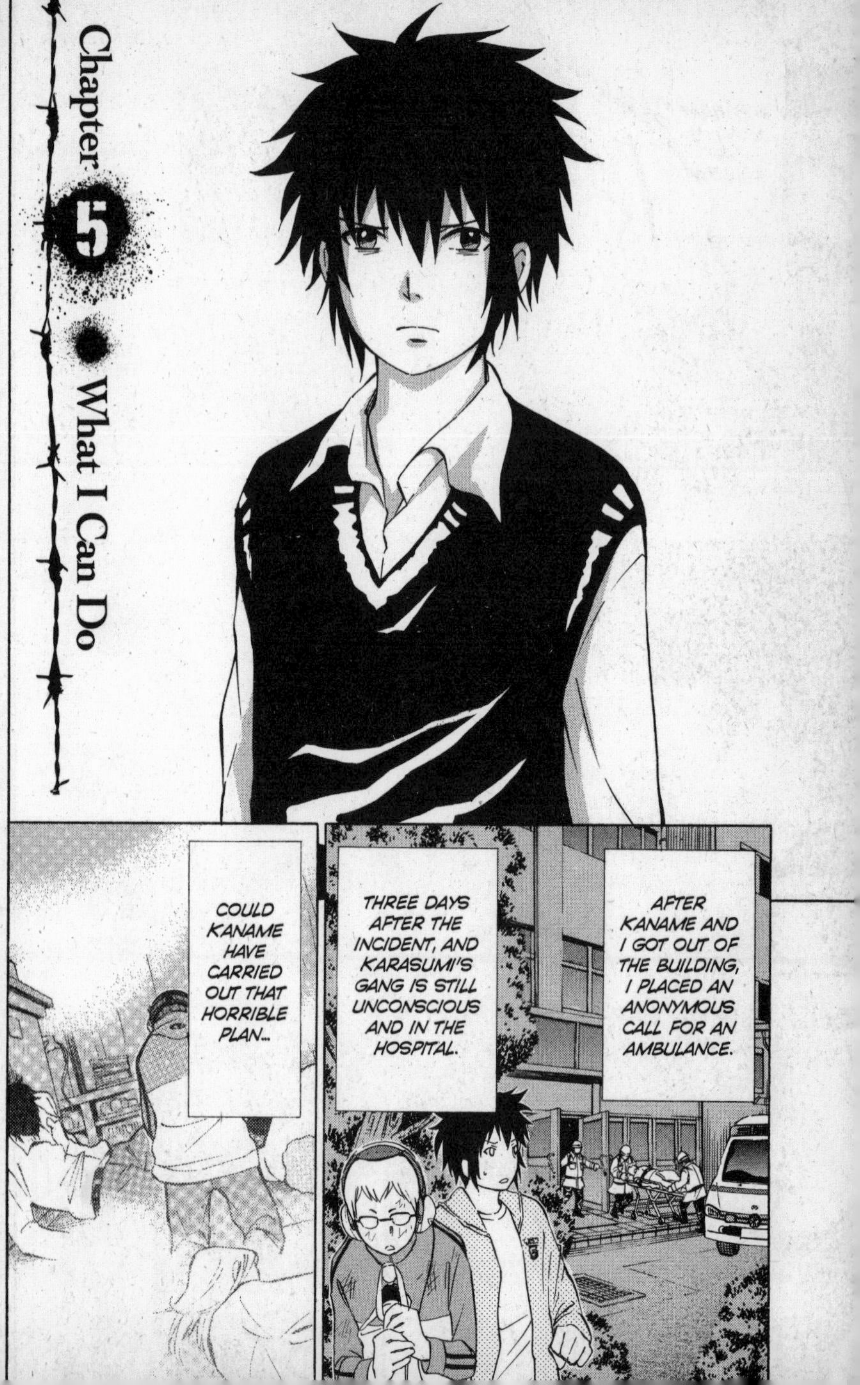
AFTER KANAME AND I GOT OUT OF THE BUILDING, I PLACED AN ANONYMOUS CALL FOR AN AMBULANCE.
THREE DAYS AFTER THE INCIDENT, AND KARASUMI'S GANG IS STILL UNCONSCIOUS AND IN THE HOSPITAL.
COULD KANAME HAVE CARRIED OUT THAT HORRIBLE PLAN...

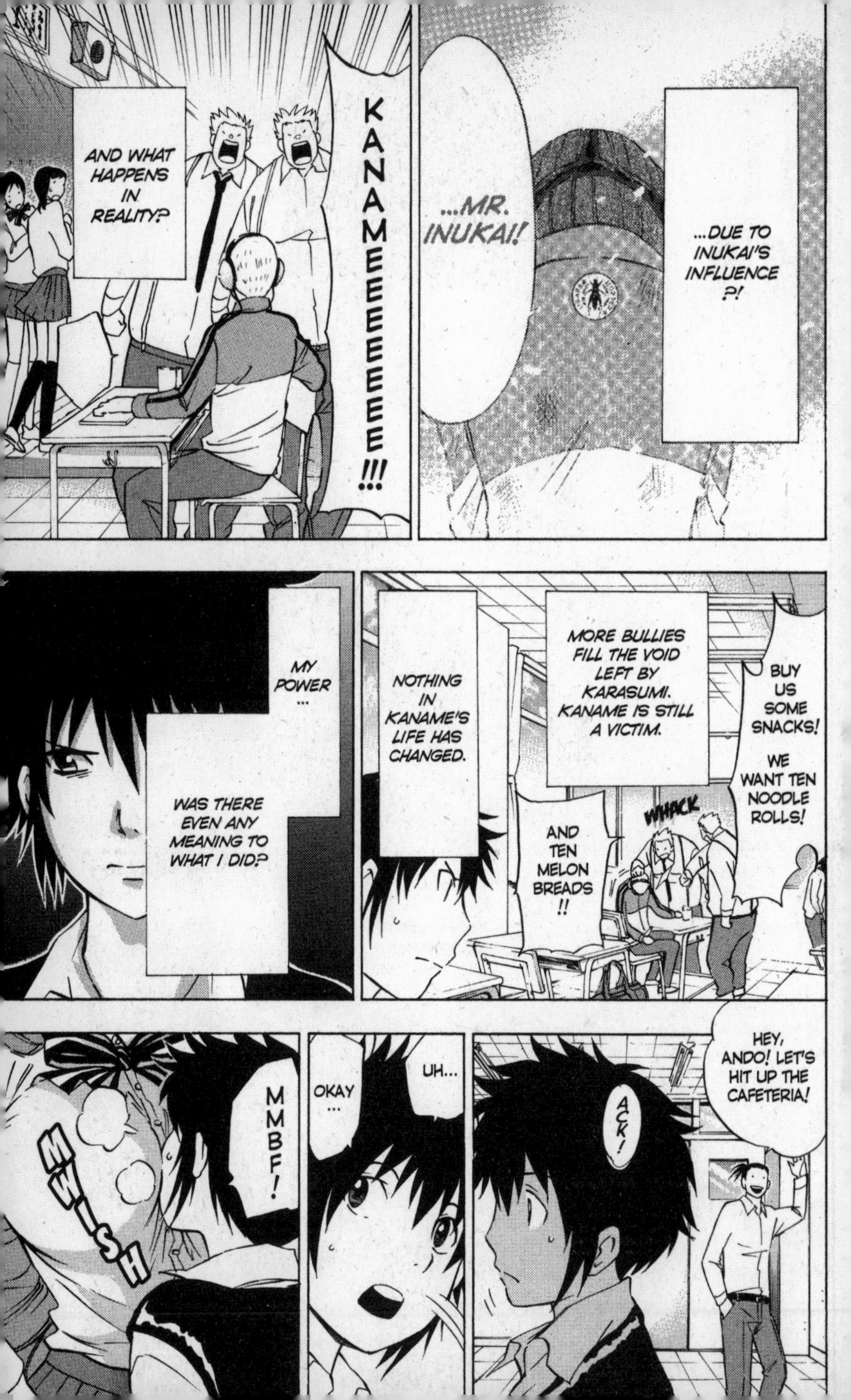
...DUE TO INUKAI'S INFLUENCE ?!
...MR. INUKAI!
KANAMEEEEEEE!!!
AND WHAT HAPPENS IN REALITY?
BUY US SOME SNACKS!
WE WANT TEN NOODLE ROLLS!
MORE BULLIES FILL THE VOID LEFT BY KARASUMI. KANAME IS STILL A VICTIM.
NOTHING IN KANAME'S LIFE HAS CHANGED.
WHACK
AND TEN MELON BREADS!!
MY POWER...
WAS THERE EVEN ANY MEANING TO WHAT I DID?
HEY, ANDO! LET'S HIT UP THE CAFETERIA!
ACK!
UH...
OKAY...
MMBF!
MWISH

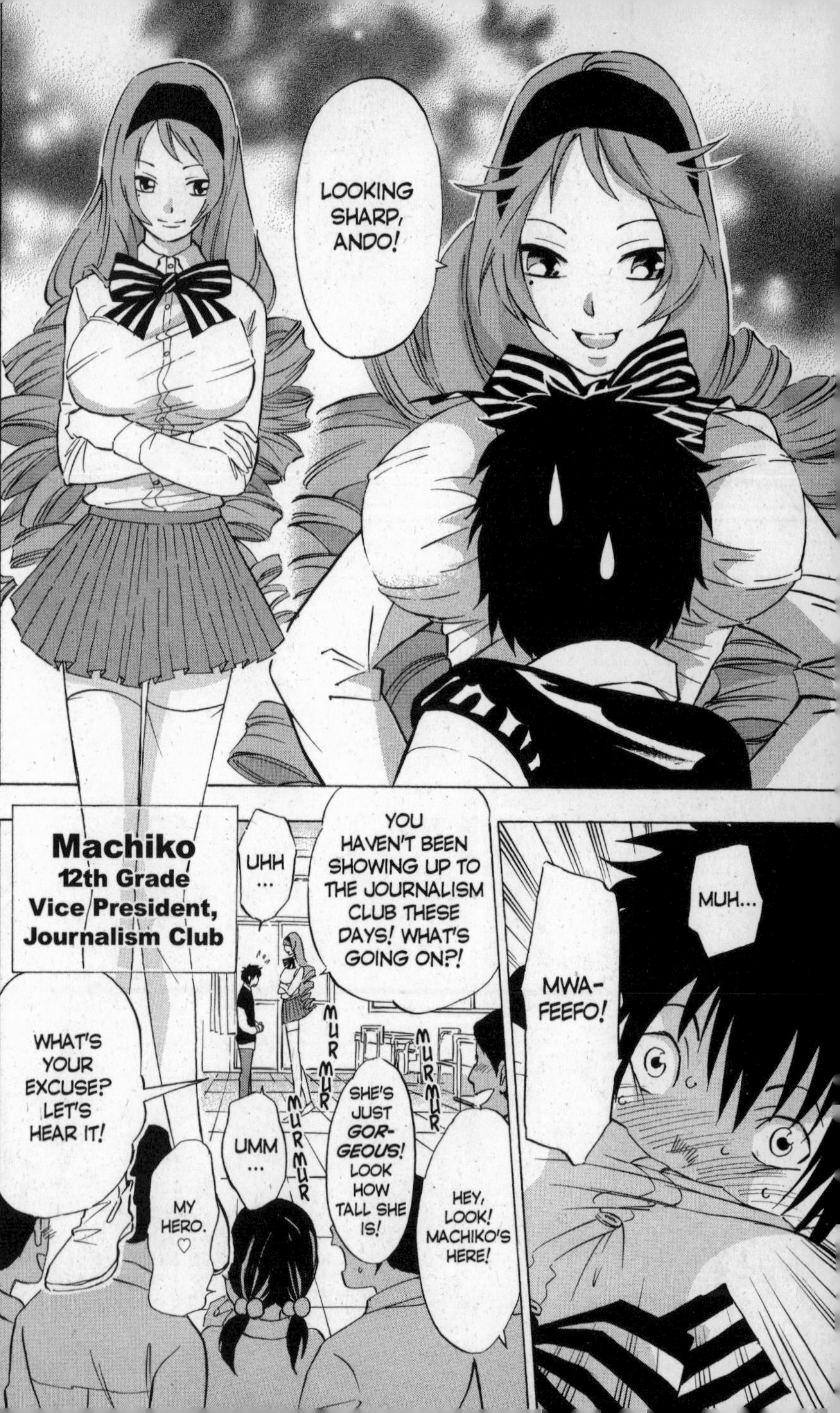
LOOKING SHARP, ANDO!
MUH...
MWA-FEEFO!
YOU HAVEN'T BEEN SHOWING UP TO THE JOURNALISM CLUB THESE DAYS! WHAT'S GOING ON?!
UHH ...
Machiko
12th Grade
Vice President, Journalism Club
MURMUR
MURMUR
HEY, LOOK! MACHIKO'S HERE!
SHE'S JUST GORGEOUS! LOOK HOW TALL SHE IS!
MURMUR
MURMUR
UMM ...
WHAT'S YOUR EXCUSE? LET'S HEAR IT!
MY HERO. ♡

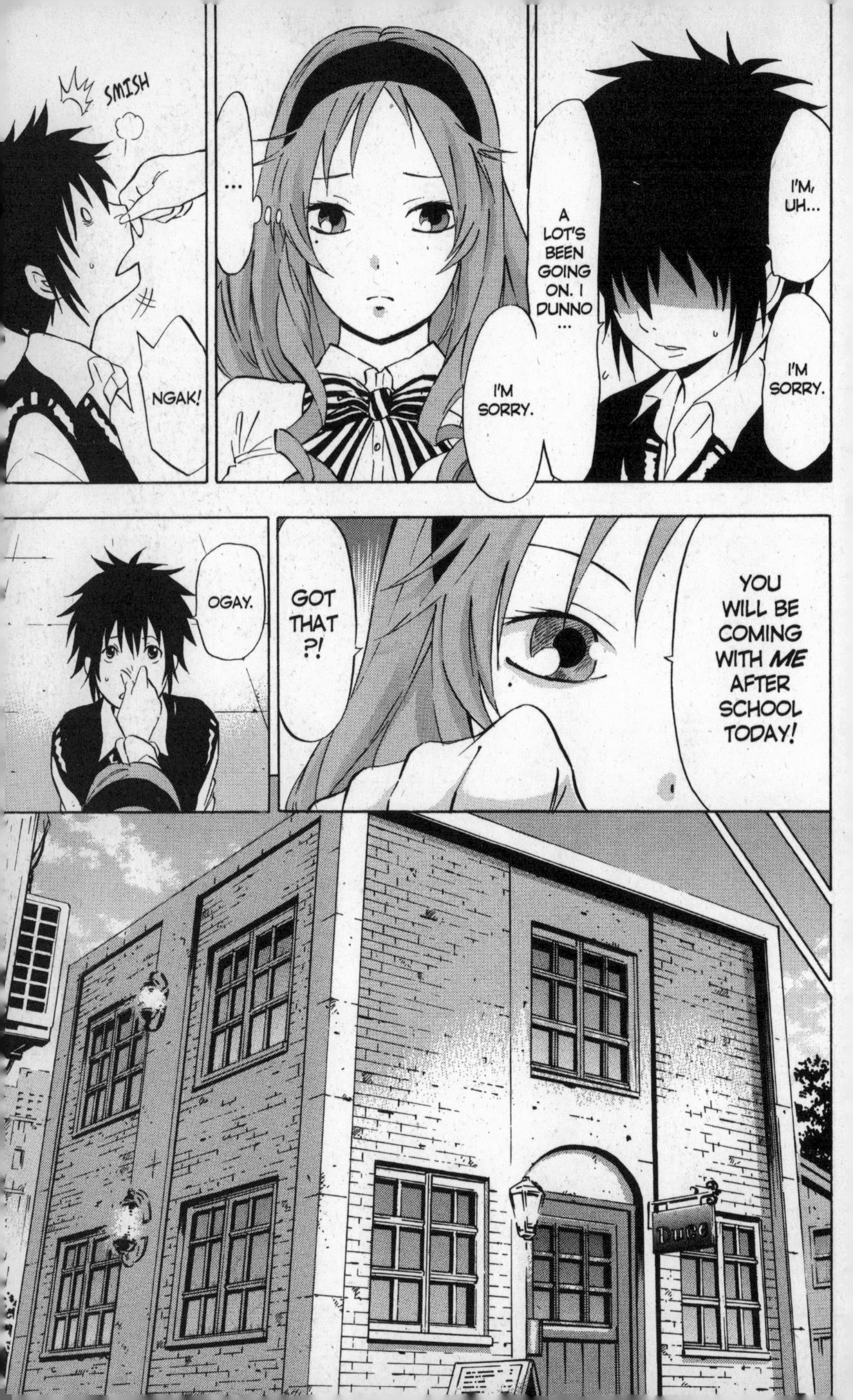
I'M, UH...
A LOT'S BEEN GOING ON. I DUNNO...
I'M SORRY.
I'M SORRY.
...
SMISH
NGAK!
YOU WILL BE COMING WITH *ME* AFTER SCHOOL TODAY!
GOT THAT?!
OGAY.

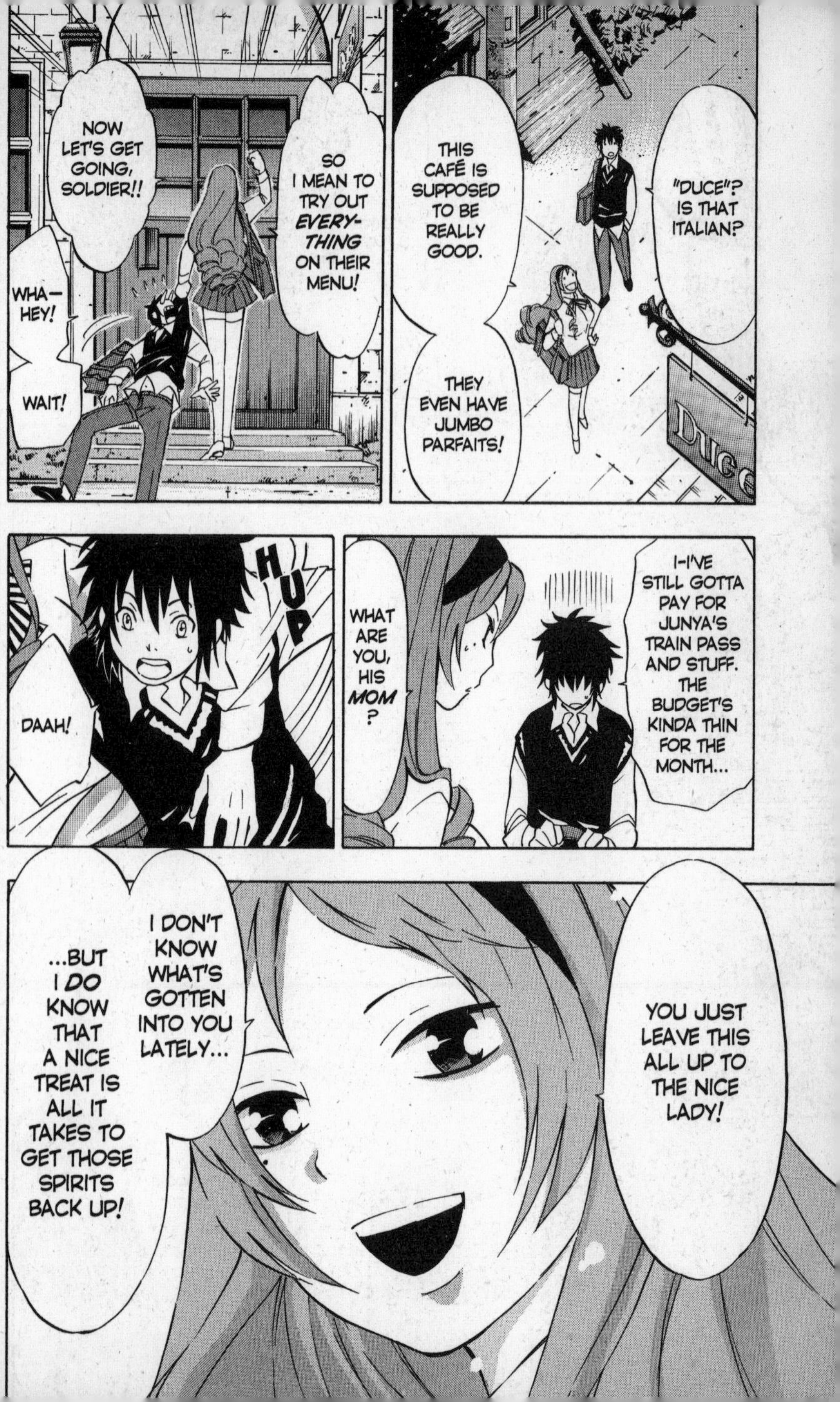
"DUCE"? IS THAT ITALIAN?
THIS CAFÉ IS SUPPOSED TO BE REALLY GOOD.
THEY EVEN HAVE JUMBO PARFAITS!
SO I MEAN TO TRY OUT *EVERYTHING* ON THEIR MENU!
NOW LET'S GET GOING, SOLDIER!!
WHA—HEY!
WAIT!
I-I'VE STILL GOTTA PAY FOR JUNYA'S TRAIN PASS AND STUFF. THE BUDGET'S KINDA THIN FOR THE MONTH...
WHAT ARE YOU, HIS *MOM*?
HUP
DAAH!
YOU JUST LEAVE THIS ALL UP TO THE NICE LADY!
I DON'T KNOW WHAT'S GOTTEN INTO YOU LATELY...
...BUT I *DO* KNOW THAT A NICE TREAT IS ALL IT TAKES TO GET THOSE SPIRITS BACK UP!

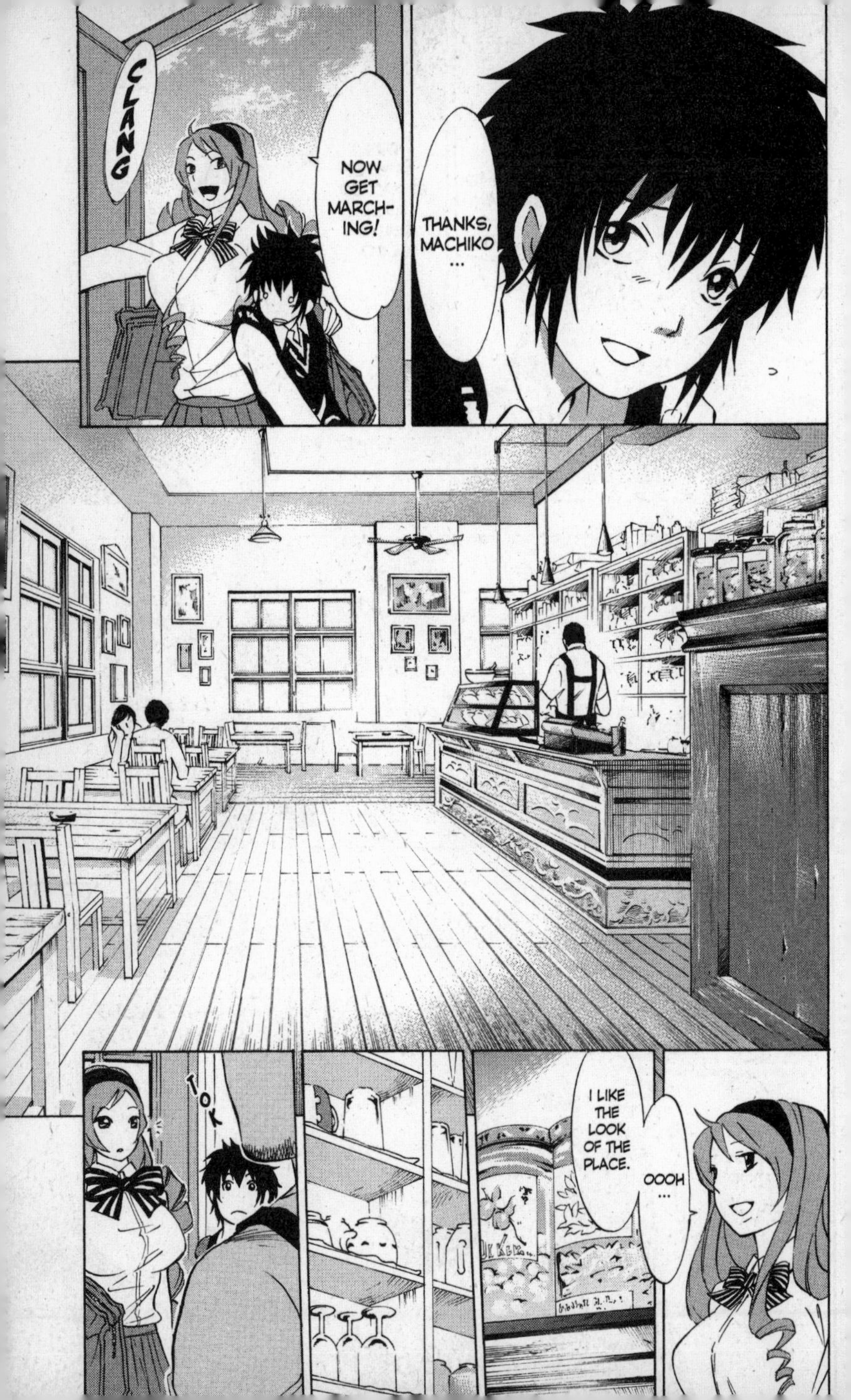
THANKS, MACHIKO ...
NOW GET MARCHING!
CLANG
I LIKE THE LOOK OF THE PLACE.
OOOH ...
TOK

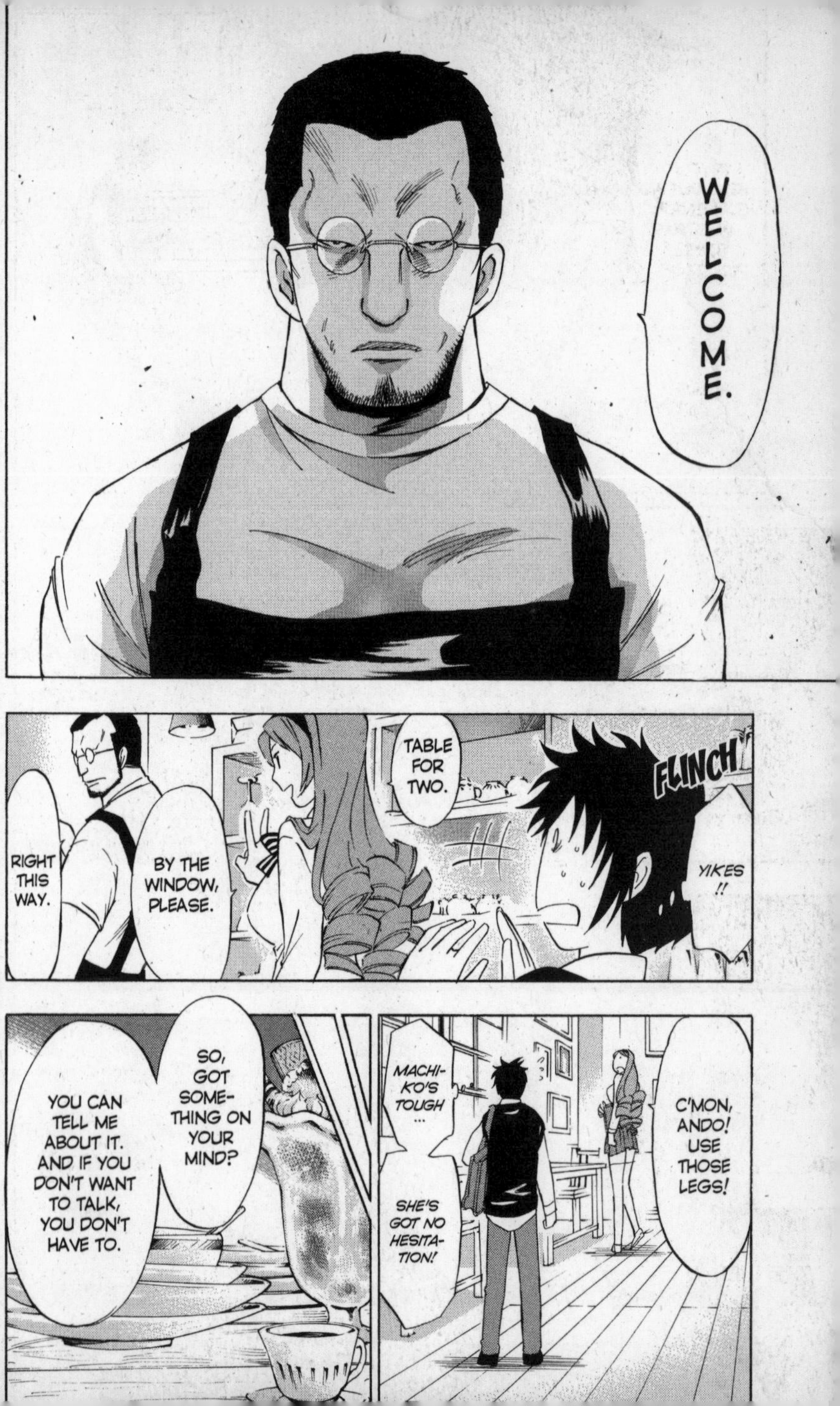
WELCOME.
FLINCH
TABLE FOR TWO.
YIKES!!
BY THE WINDOW, PLEASE.
RIGHT THIS WAY.
C'MON, ANDO! USE THOSE LEGS!
MACHIKO'S TOUGH...
SHE'S GOT NO HESITATION!
SO, GOT SOMETHING ON YOUR MIND?
YOU CAN TELL ME ABOUT IT. AND IF YOU DON'T WANT TO TALK, YOU DON'T HAVE TO.

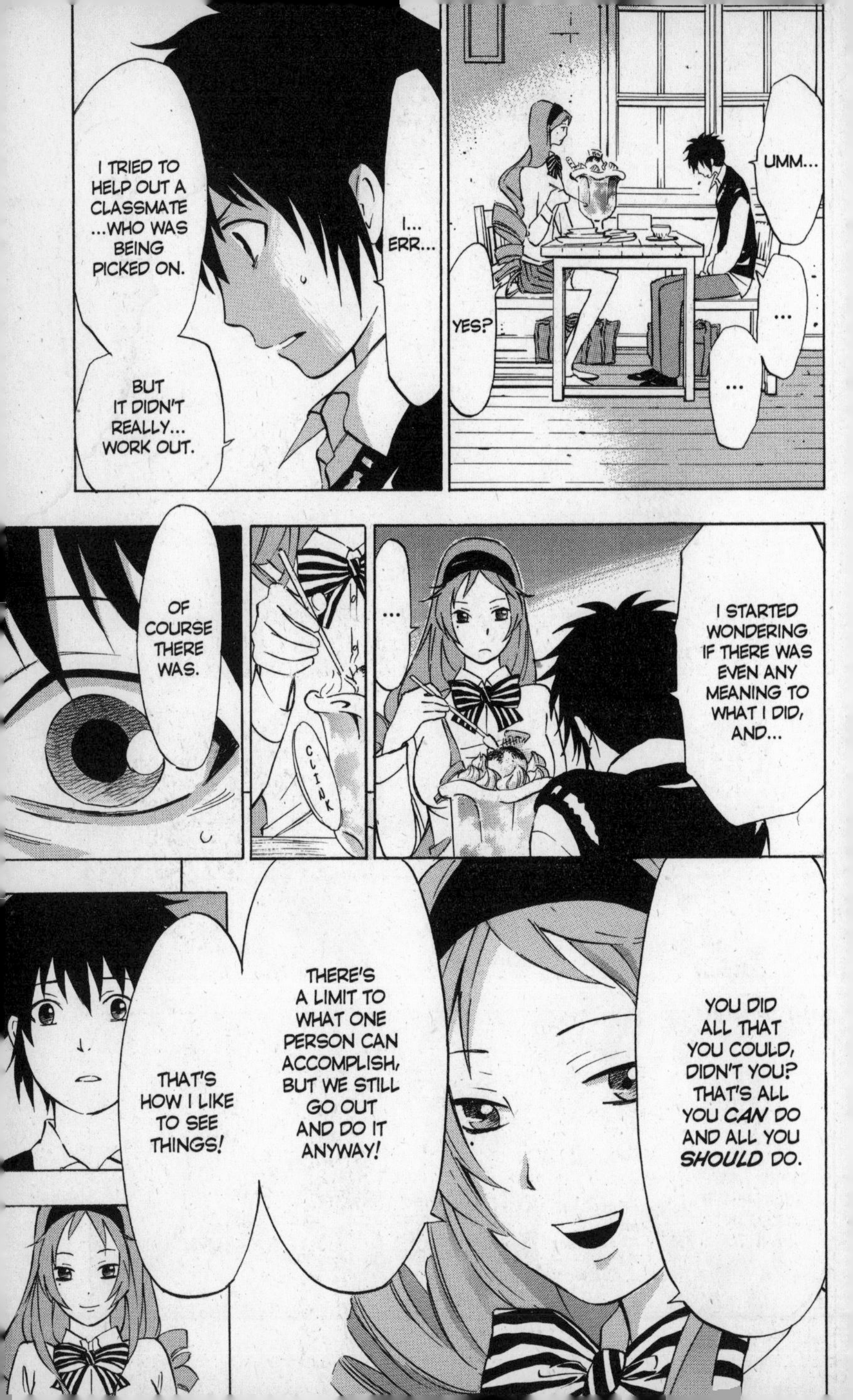
UMM...
YES?
...
...
I... ERR...
I TRIED TO HELP OUT A CLASSMATE ...WHO WAS BEING PICKED ON.
BUT IT DIDN'T REALLY... WORK OUT.
I STARTED WONDERING IF THERE WAS EVEN ANY MEANING TO WHAT I DID, AND...
...
CLINK
OF COURSE THERE WAS.
YOU DID ALL THAT YOU COULD, DIDN'T YOU? THAT'S ALL YOU *CAN* DO AND ALL YOU ***SHOULD*** DO.
THERE'S A LIMIT TO WHAT ONE PERSON CAN ACCOMPLISH, BUT WE STILL GO OUT AND DO IT ANYWAY!
THAT'S HOW I LIKE TO SEE THINGS!

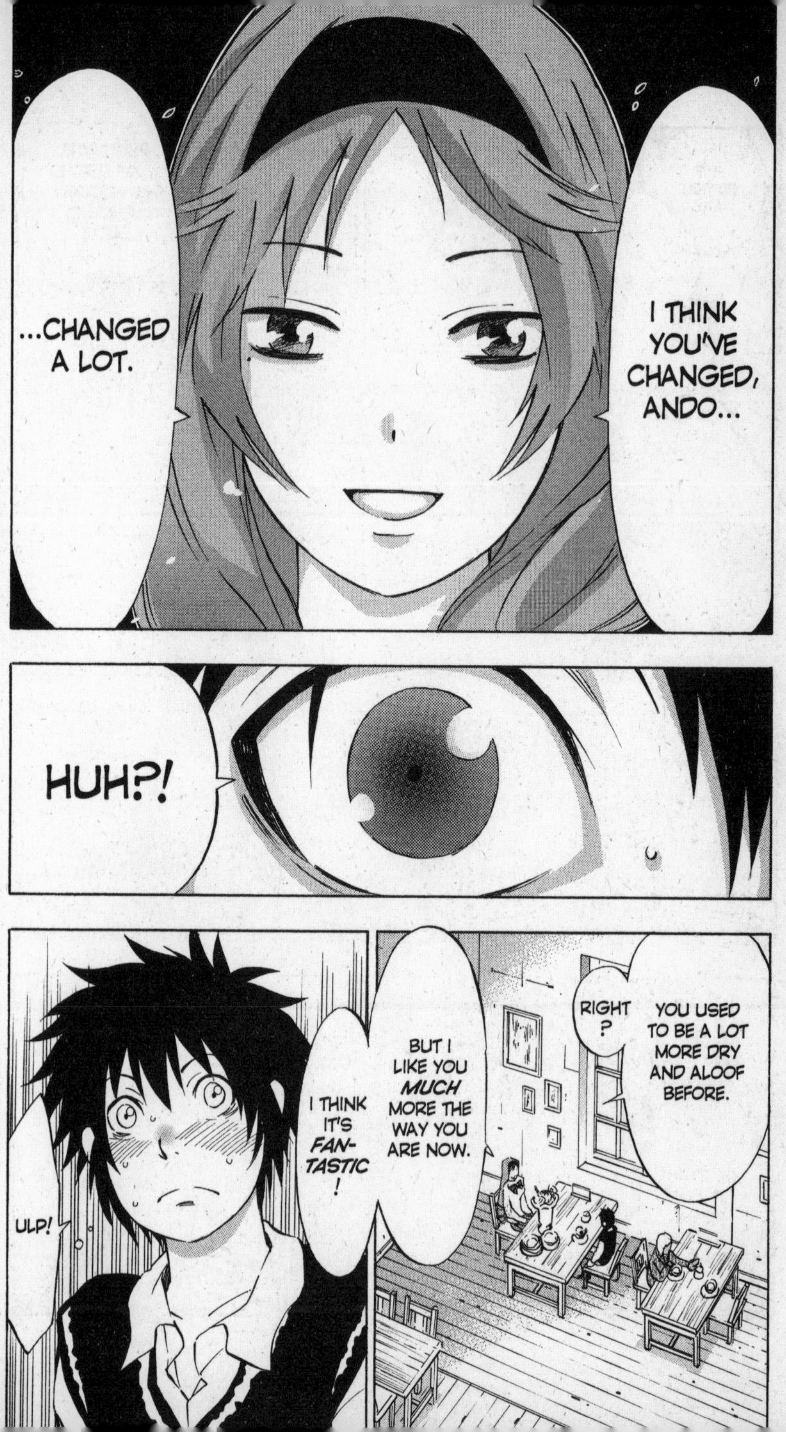
I THINK YOU'VE CHANGED, ANDO...
...CHANGED A LOT.
HUH?!
YOU USED TO BE A LOT MORE DRY AND ALOOF BEFORE.
RIGHT?
BUT I LIKE YOU *MUCH* MORE THE WAY YOU ARE NOW.
I THINK IT'S *FANTASTIC*!
ULP!

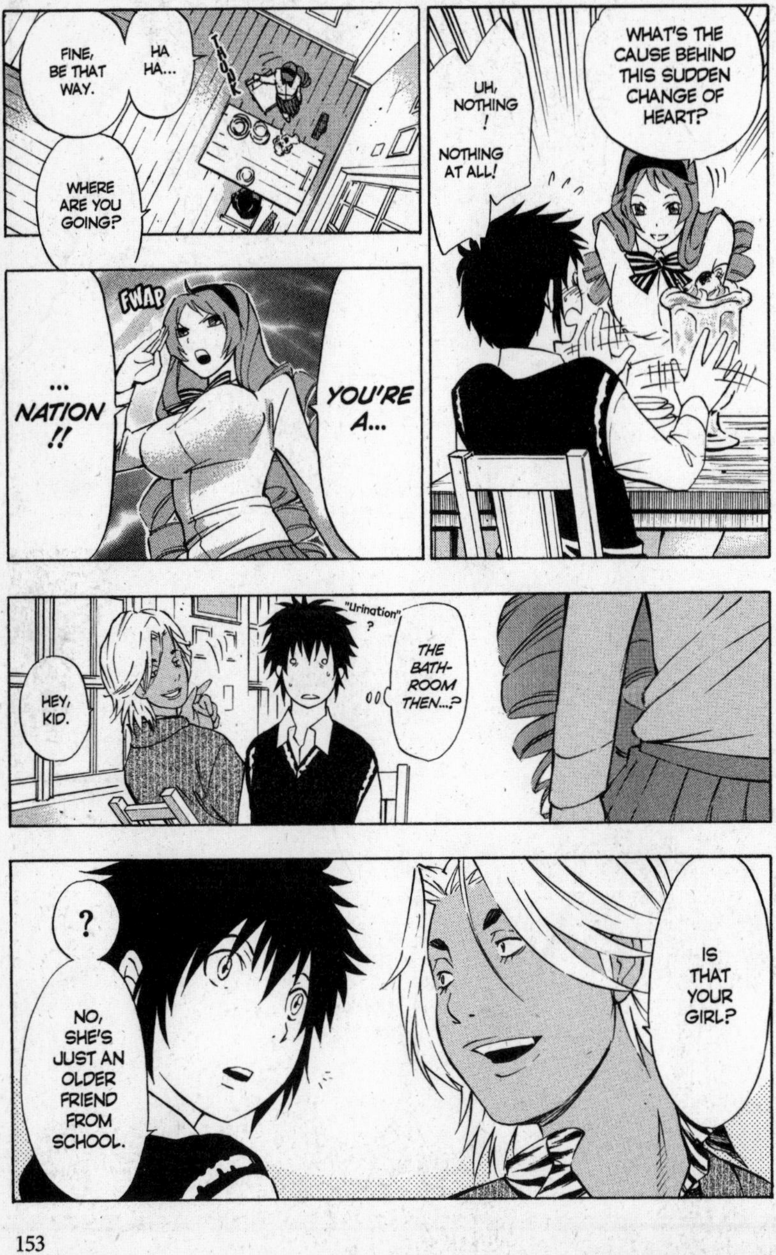
WHAT'S THE CAUSE BEHIND THIS SUDDEN CHANGE OF HEART?
UH, NOTHING!
NOTHING AT ALL!
HA HA...
FINE, BE THAT WAY.
THUNK
WHERE ARE YOU GOING?
YOU'RE A...
FWAP
...NATION!!
"Urination"?
THE BATH-ROOM THEN...?
HEY, KID.
IS THAT YOUR GIRL?
?
NO, SHE'S JUST AN OLDER FRIEND FROM SCHOOL.

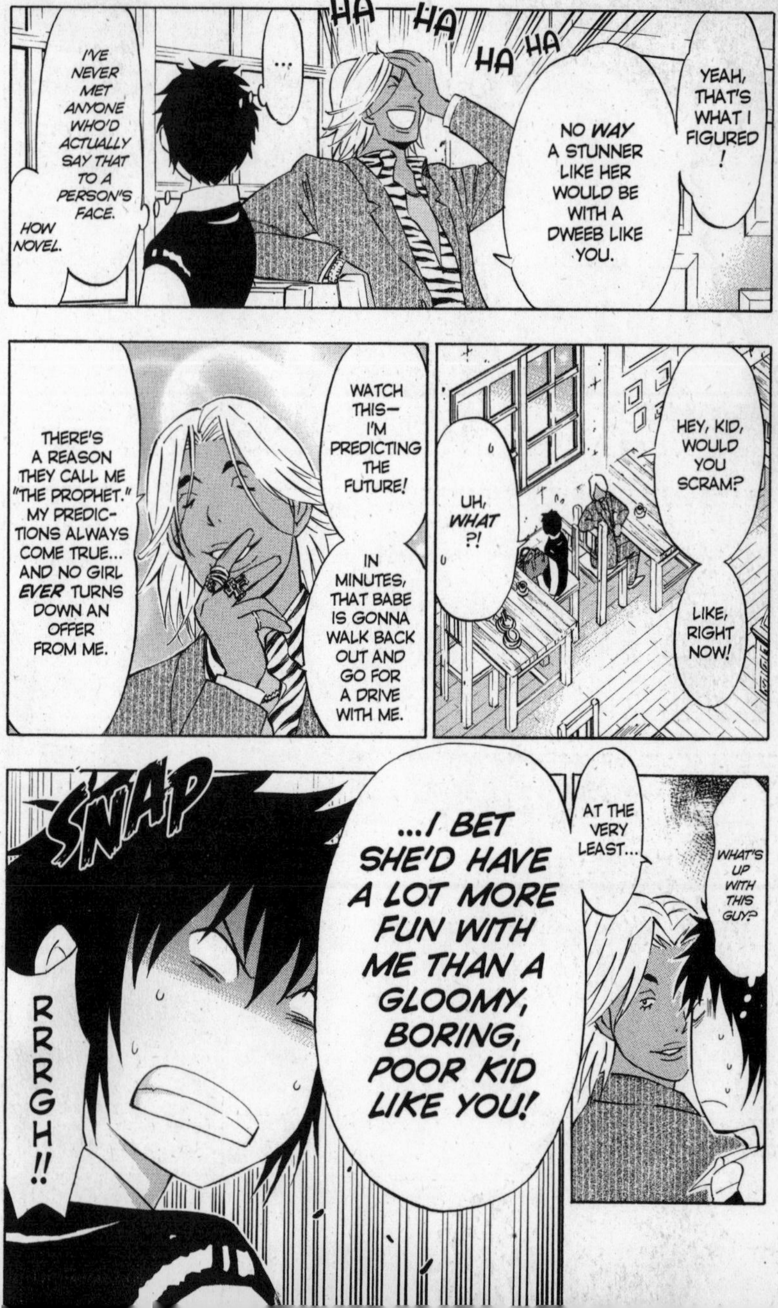
YEAH, THAT'S WHAT I FIGURED!
HA HA HA HA
NO WAY A STUNNER LIKE HER WOULD BE WITH A DWEEB LIKE YOU.
...
I'VE NEVER MET ANYONE WHO'D ACTUALLY SAY THAT TO A PERSON'S FACE.
HOW NOVEL.
HEY, KID, WOULD YOU SCRAM?
LIKE, RIGHT NOW!
UH, WHAT?!
WATCH THIS— I'M PREDICTING THE FUTURE!
IN MINUTES, THAT BABE IS GONNA WALK BACK OUT AND GO FOR A DRIVE WITH ME.
THERE'S A REASON THEY CALL ME "THE PROPHET." MY PREDICTIONS ALWAYS COME TRUE... AND NO GIRL EVER TURNS DOWN AN OFFER FROM ME.
WHAT'S UP WITH THIS GUY?
AT THE VERY LEAST...
...I BET SHE'D HAVE A LOT MORE FUN WITH ME THAN A GLOOMY, BORING, POOR KID LIKE YOU!
SNAP
RRRGH!!

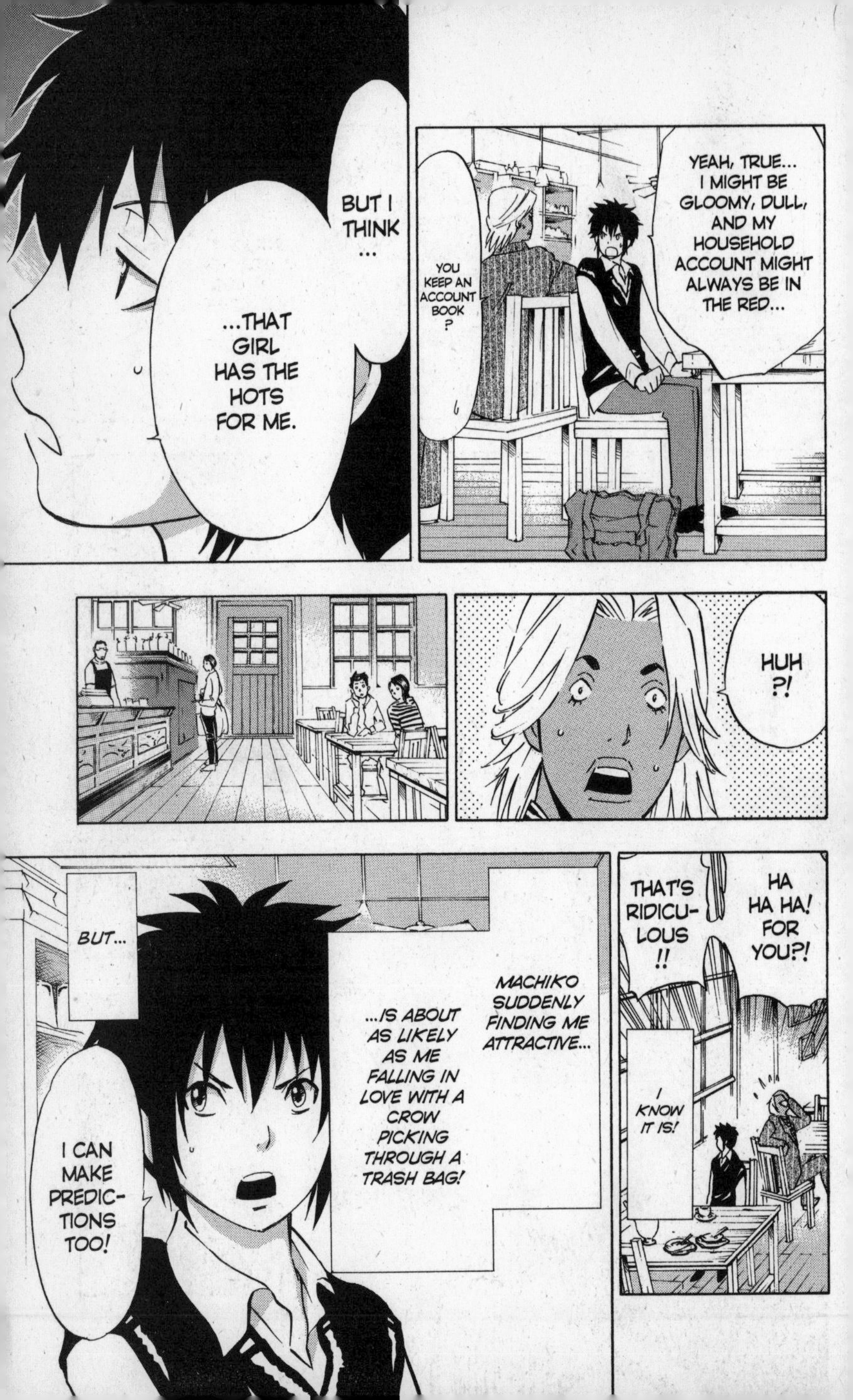
YEAH, TRUE... I MIGHT BE GLOOMY, DULL, AND MY HOUSEHOLD ACCOUNT MIGHT ALWAYS BE IN THE RED...
YOU KEEP AN ACCOUNT BOOK?
BUT I THINK...
...THAT GIRL HAS THE HOTS FOR ME.
HUH?!
HA HA HA! FOR YOU?!
THAT'S RIDICULOUS!!
I KNOW IT IS!
BUT...
MACHIKO SUDDENLY FINDING ME ATTRACTIVE...
...IS ABOUT AS LIKELY AS ME FALLING IN LOVE WITH A CROW PICKING THROUGH A TRASH BAG!
I CAN MAKE PREDICTIONS TOO!

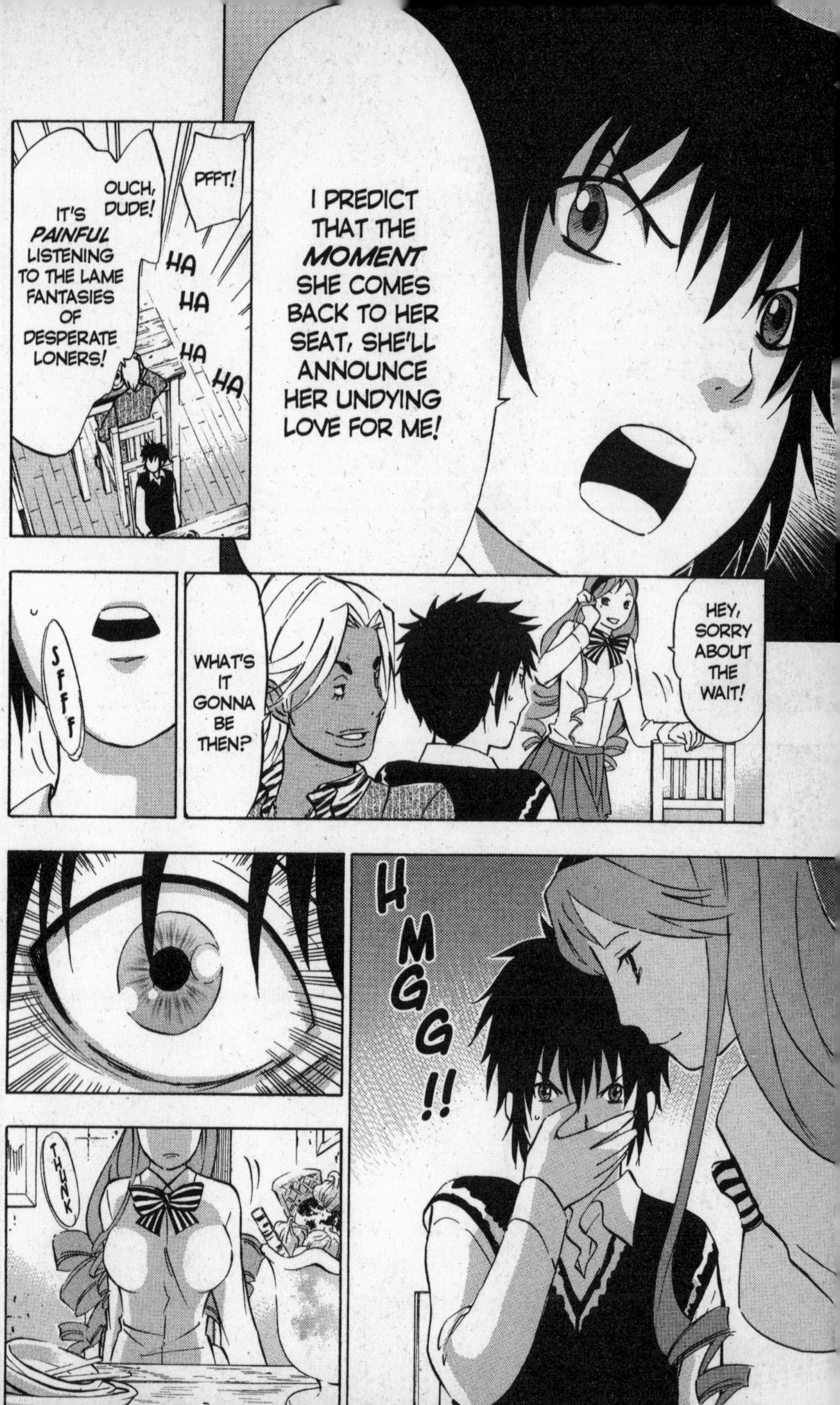
I PREDICT THAT THE *MOMENT* SHE COMES BACK TO HER SEAT, SHE'LL ANNOUNCE HER UNDYING LOVE FOR ME!
PFFT!
OUCH, DUDE!
IT'S *PAINFUL* LISTENING TO THE LAME FANTASIES OF DESPERATE LONERS!
HA HA HA HA
HEY, SORRY ABOUT THE WAIT!
WHAT'S IT GONNA BE THEN?
SFFF
HMGG!!
THUNK

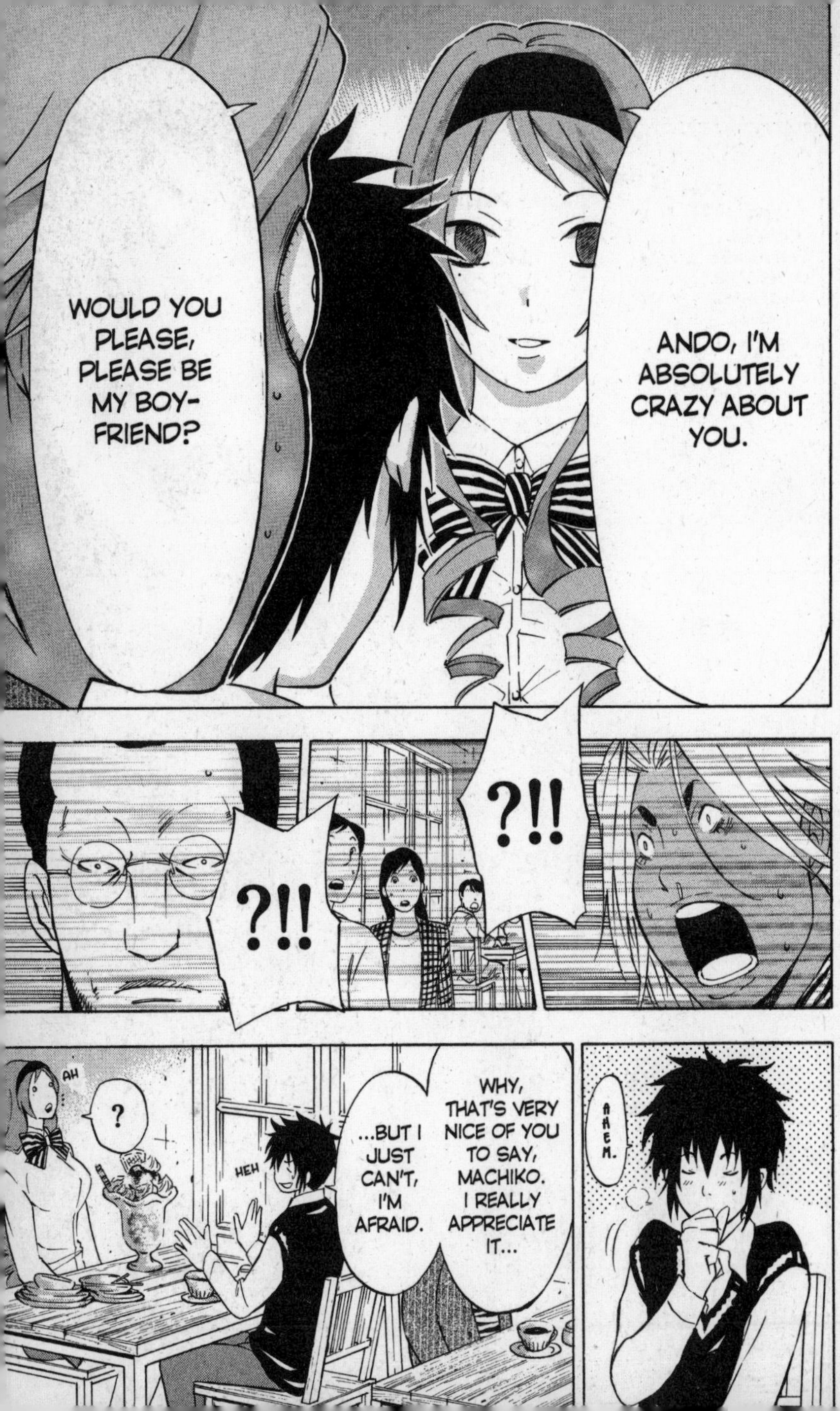
ANDO, I'M ABSOLUTELY CRAZY ABOUT YOU.
WOULD YOU PLEASE, PLEASE BE MY BOY-FRIEND?
?!!
?!!
AHEM.
WHY, THAT'S VERY NICE OF YOU TO SAY, MACHIKO. I REALLY APPRECIATE IT...
...BUT I JUST CAN'T, I'M AFRAID.
AH
?
HEH

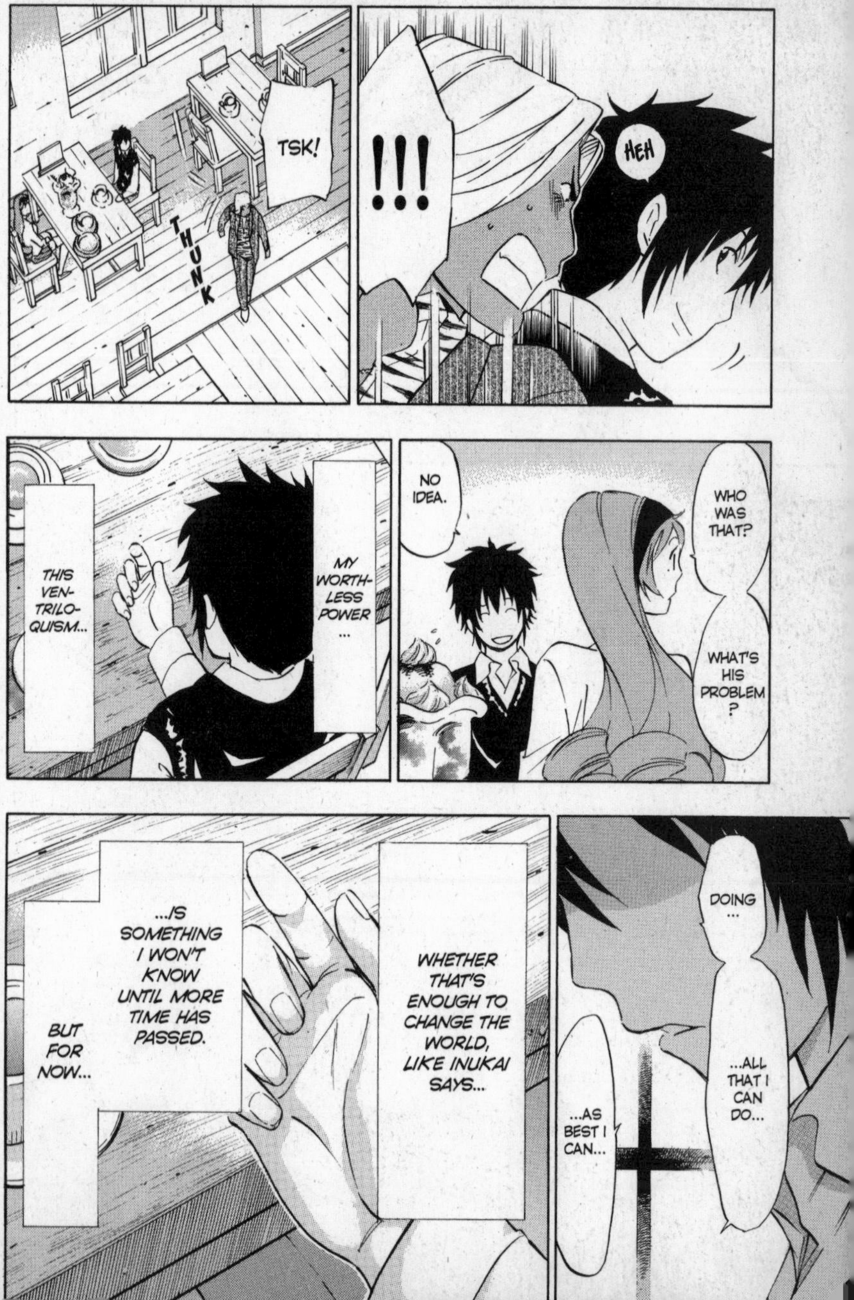
HEH
!!!
TSK!
THUNK
WHO WAS THAT?
WHAT'S HIS PROBLEM?
NO IDEA.
MY WORTHLESS POWER...
THIS VENTRILOQUISM...
DOING...
...ALL THAT I CAN DO...
...AS BEST I CAN...
WHETHER THAT'S ENOUGH TO CHANGE THE WORLD, LIKE INUKAI SAYS...
...IS SOMETHING I WON'T KNOW UNTIL MORE TIME HAS PASSED.
BUT FOR NOW...

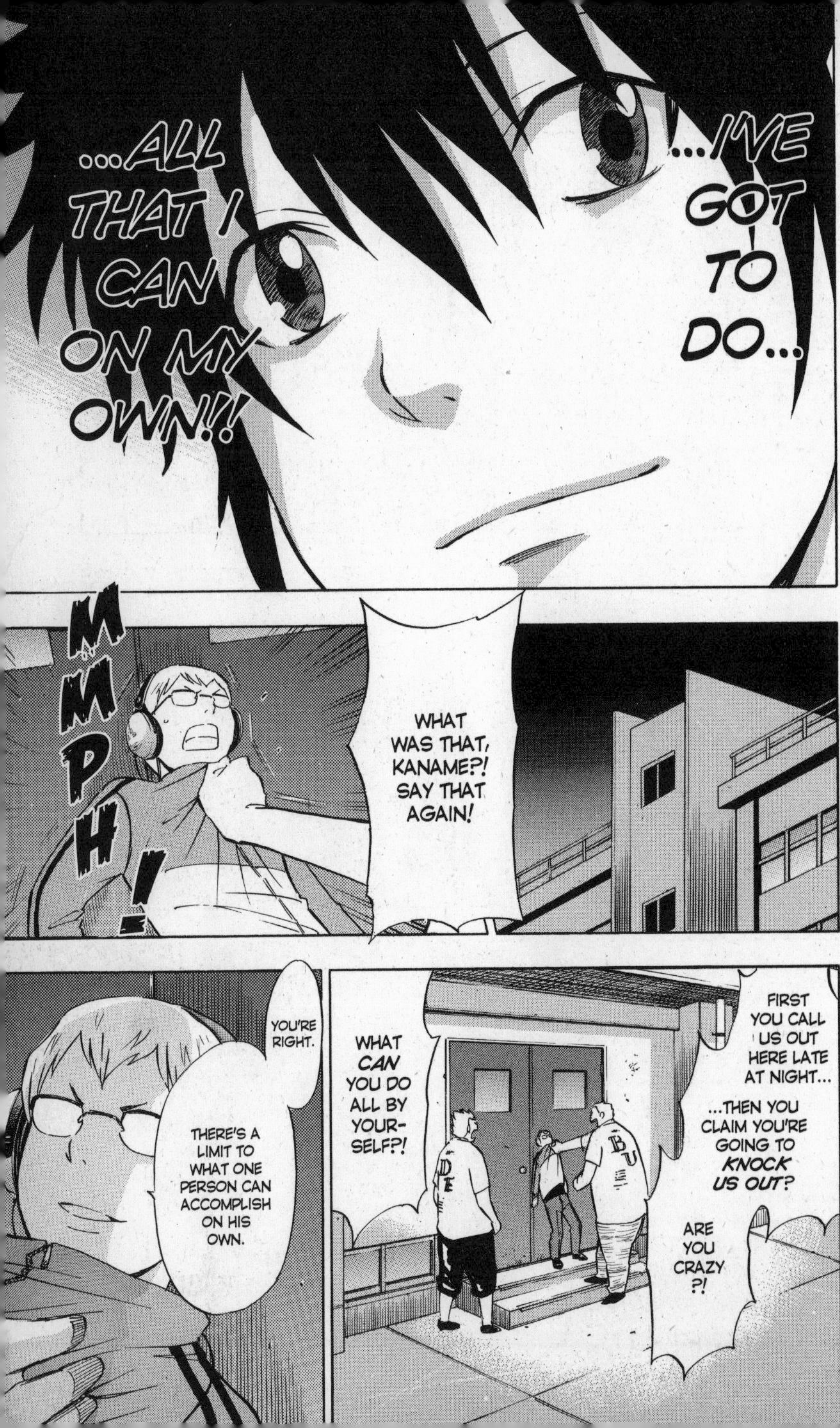

...I'VE GOT TO DO...
...ALL THAT I CAN ON MY OWN!!
WHAT WAS THAT, KANAME?! SAY THAT AGAIN!
MMMPH!
FIRST YOU CALL US OUT HERE LATE AT NIGHT...
...THEN YOU CLAIM YOU'RE GOING TO *KNOCK US OUT*?
ARE YOU CRAZY?!
WHAT *CAN* YOU DO ALL BY YOUR-SELF?!
YOU'RE RIGHT.
THERE'S A LIMIT TO WHAT ONE PERSON CAN ACCOMPLISH ON HIS OWN.

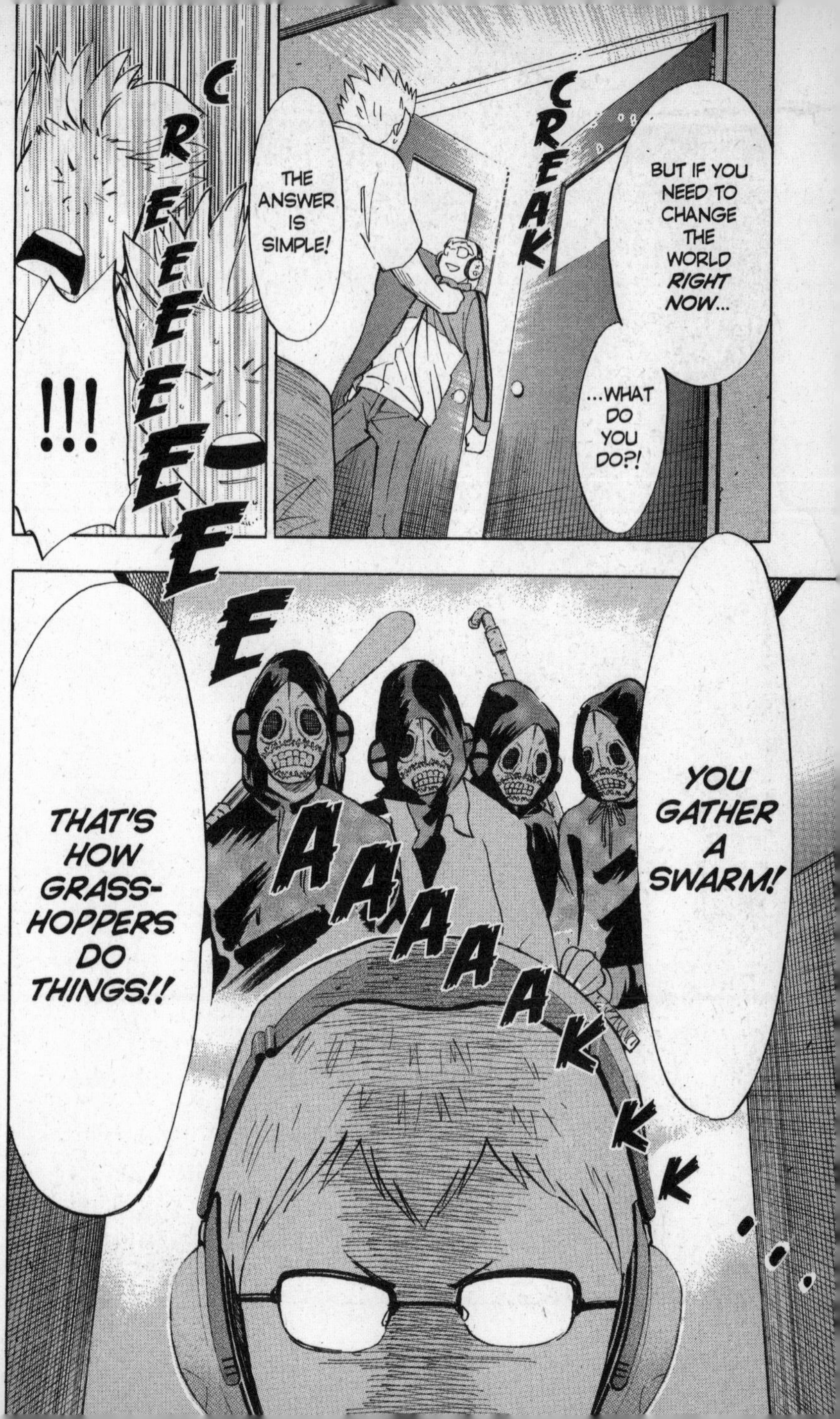
BUT IF YOU NEED TO CHANGE THE WORLD RIGHT NOW...
...WHAT DO YOU DO?!
CREAK
THE ANSWER IS SIMPLE!
CREEEEEEEEE
!!!
YOU GATHER A SWARM!
AAAAAKKK...
THAT'S HOW GRASS-HOPPERS DO THINGS!!

Chapter 6 The Book of Everyone's Death

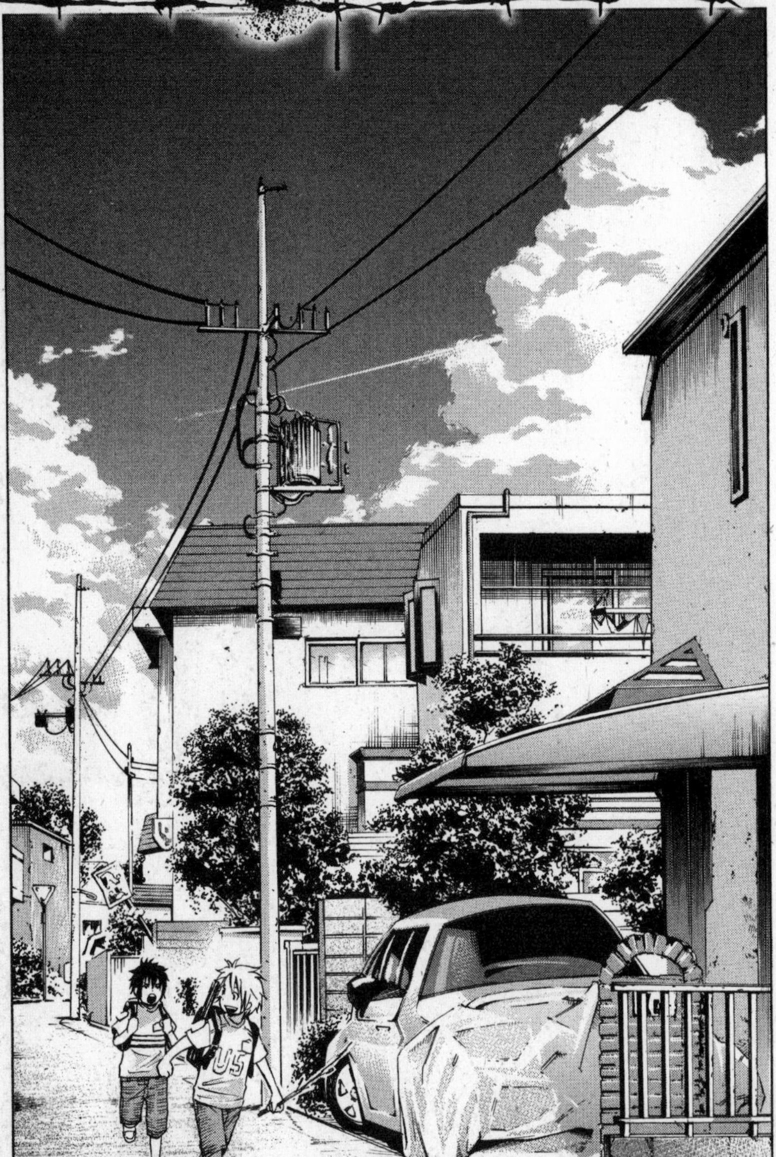

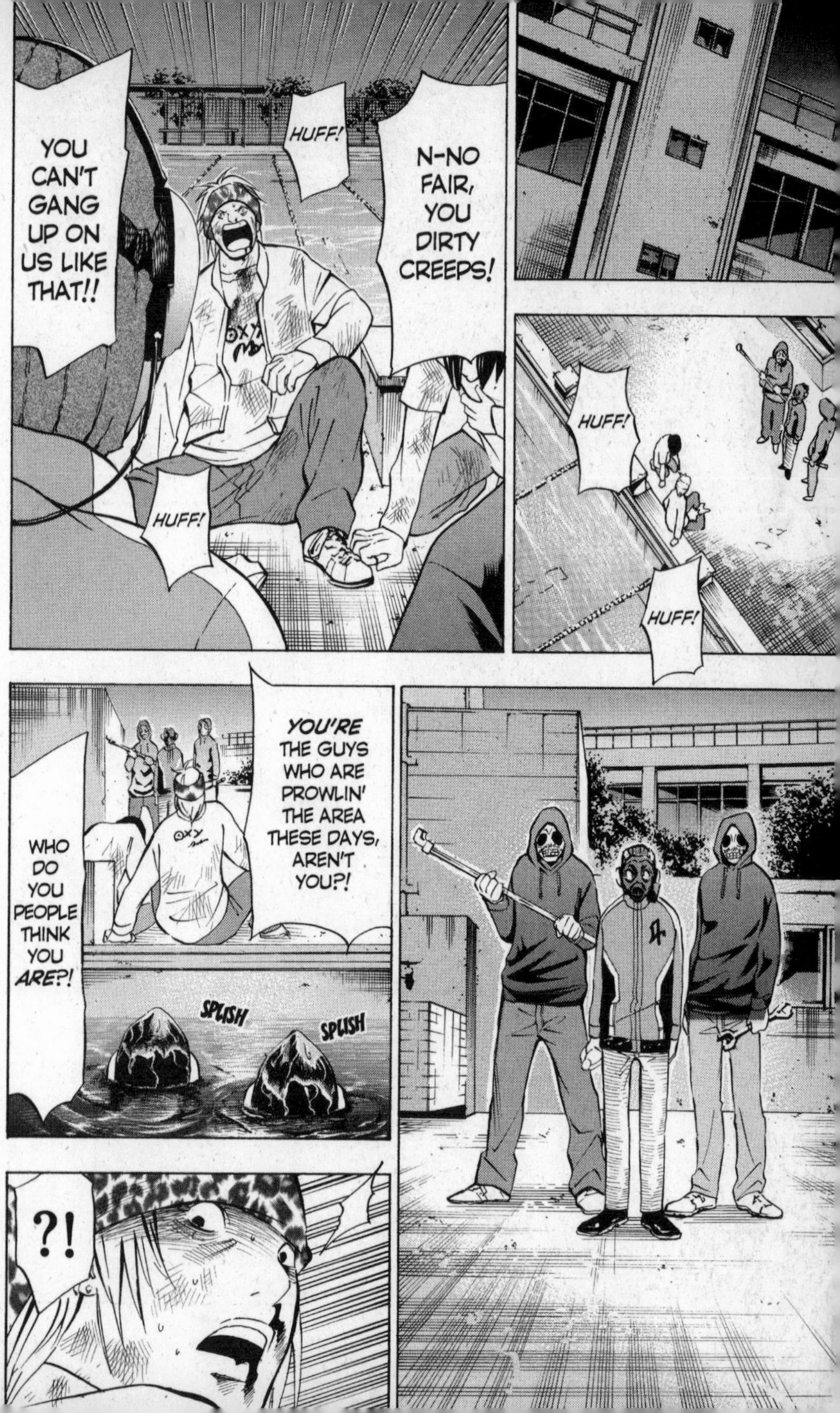
HUFF!
HUFF!
N-NO FAIR, YOU DIRTY CREEPS!
HUFF!
YOU CAN'T GANG UP ON US LIKE THAT!!
HUFF!
YOU'RE THE GUYS WHO ARE PROWLIN' THE AREA THESE DAYS, AREN'T YOU?!
WHO DO YOU PEOPLE THINK YOU *ARE*?!
SPLISH
SPLISH
?!

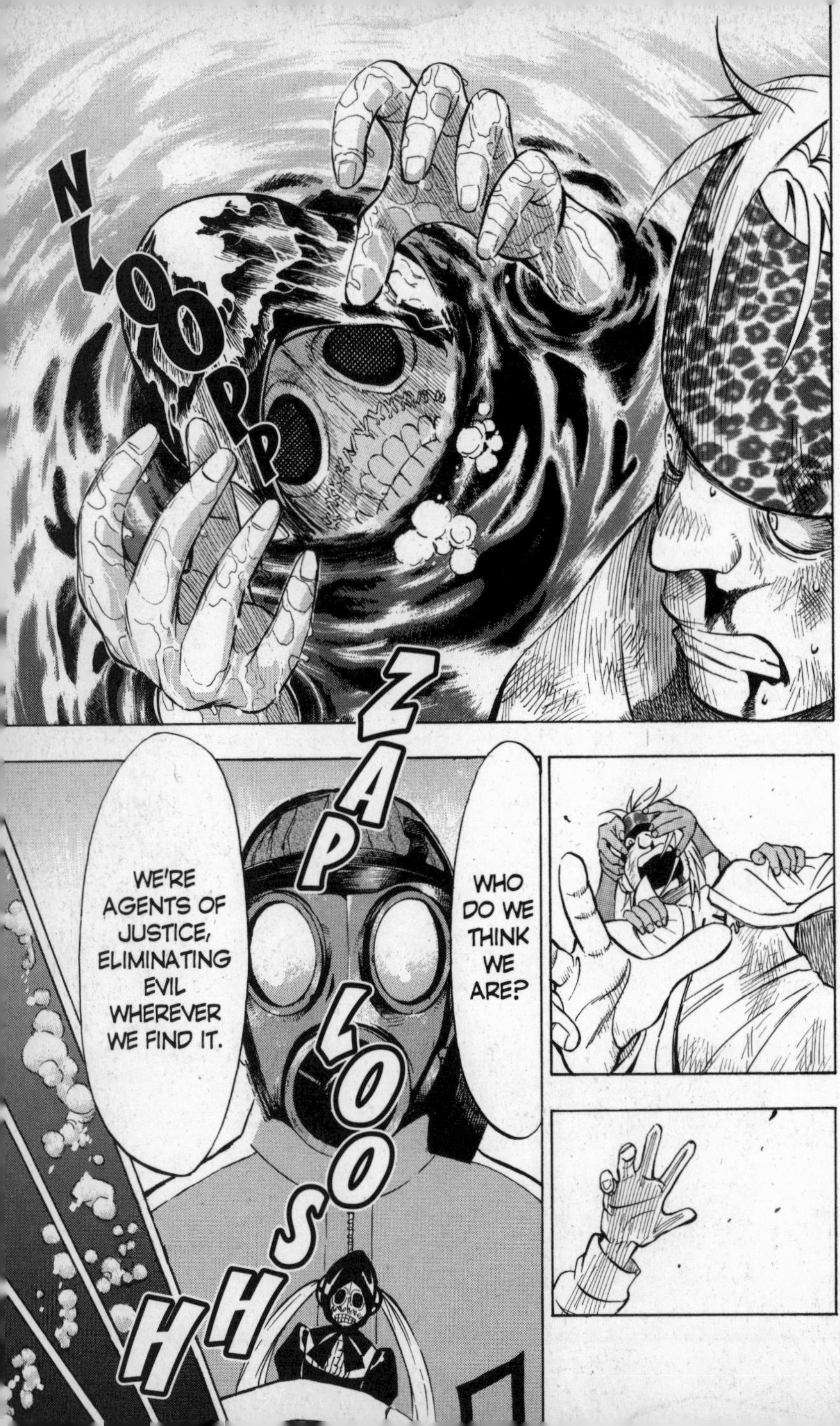
NLOOPP
WHO DO WE THINK WE ARE?
WE'RE AGENTS OF JUSTICE, ELIMINATING EVIL WHEREVER WE FIND IT.
ZAPLOOOSHHH

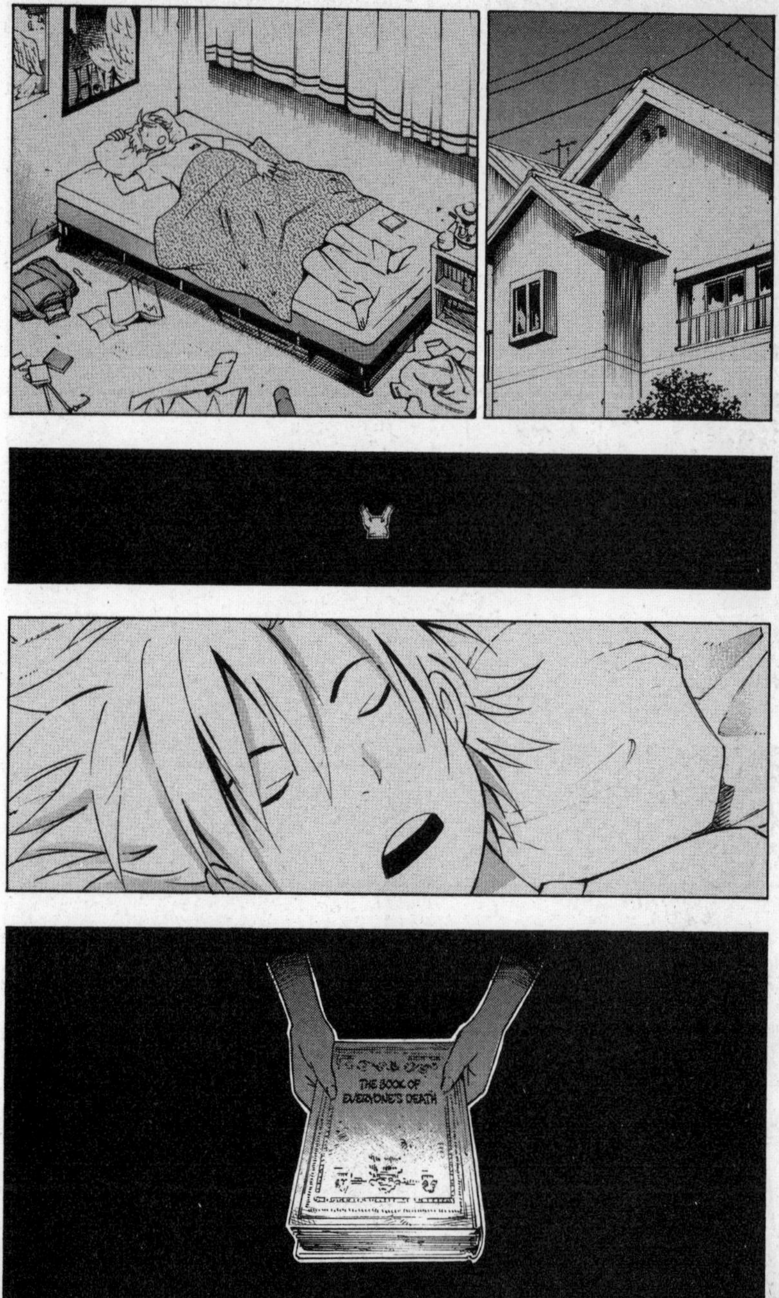
THE BOOK OF
EVERYONE'S DEATH

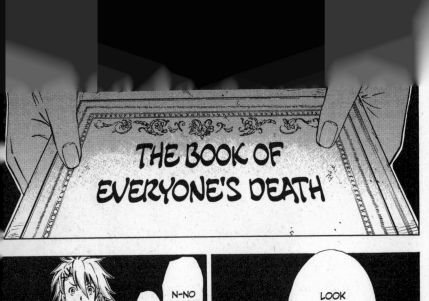

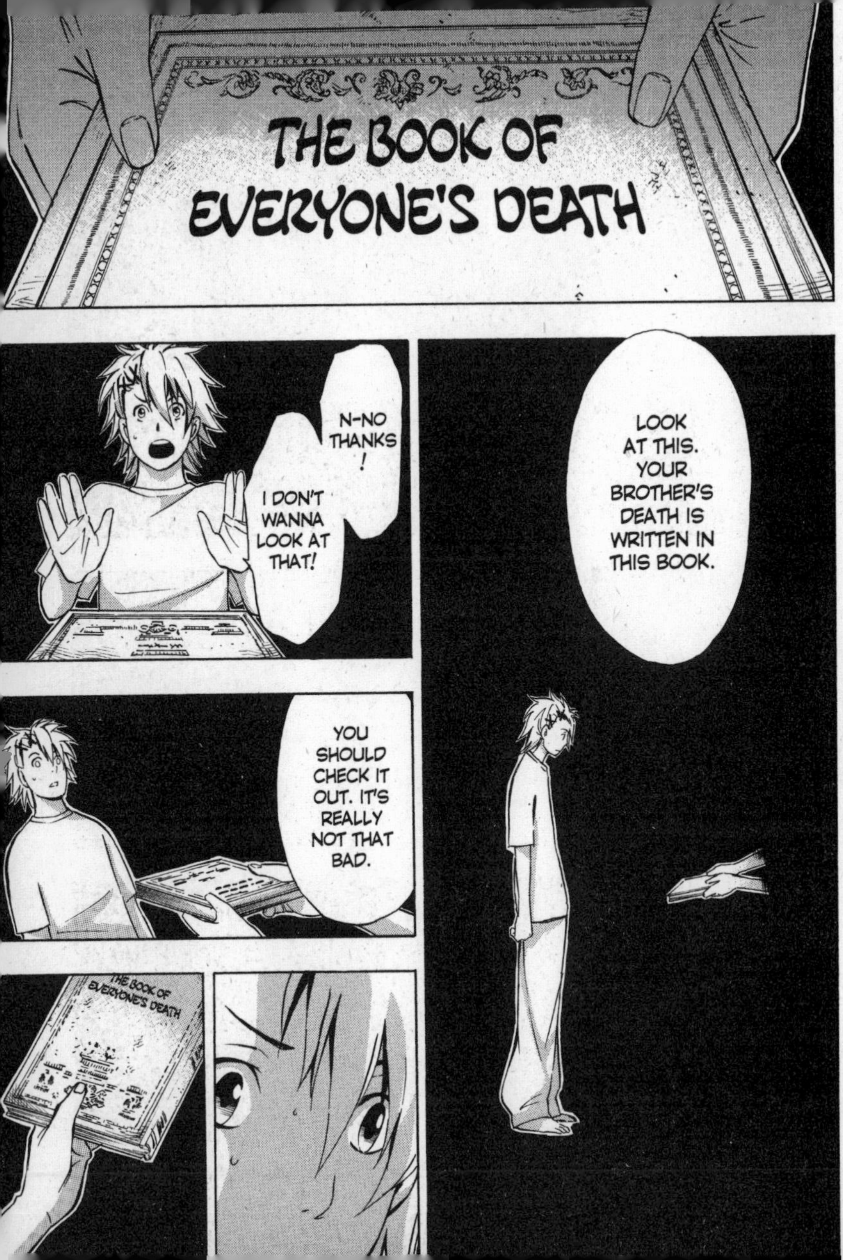
THE BOOK OF EVERYONE'S DEATH
LOOK AT THIS. YOUR BROTHER'S DEATH IS WRITTEN IN THIS BOOK.
N-NO THANKS!
I DON'T WANNA LOOK AT THAT!
YOU SHOULD CHECK IT OUT. IT'S REALLY NOT THAT BAD.
THE BOOK OF EVERYONE'S DEATH

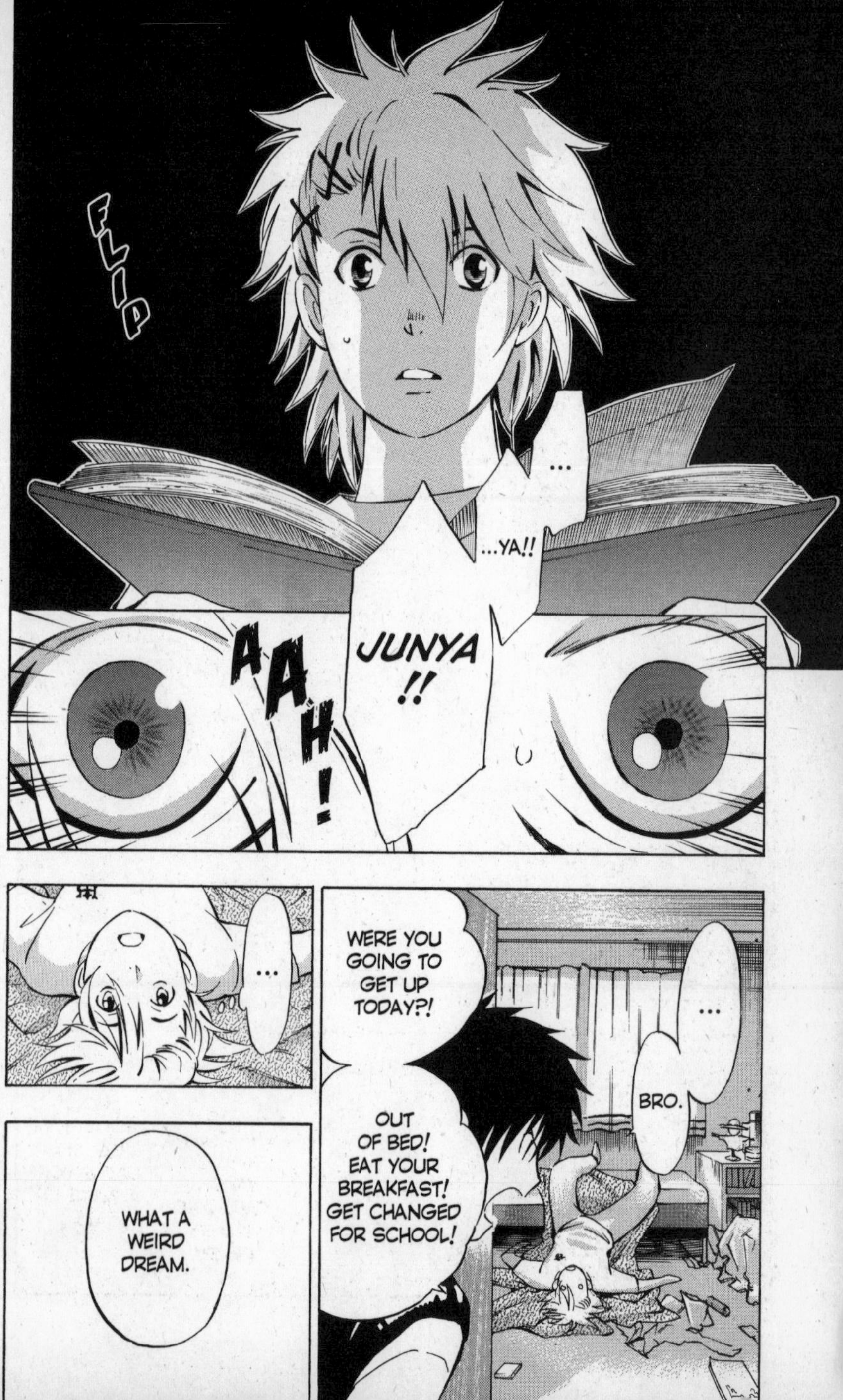
FLIP
...
...YA!!
JUNYA !!
AAH!
...
BRO.
WERE YOU GOING TO GET UP TODAY?!
OUT OF BED! EAT YOUR BREAKFAST! GET CHANGED FOR SCHOOL!
...
WHAT A WEIRD DREAM.

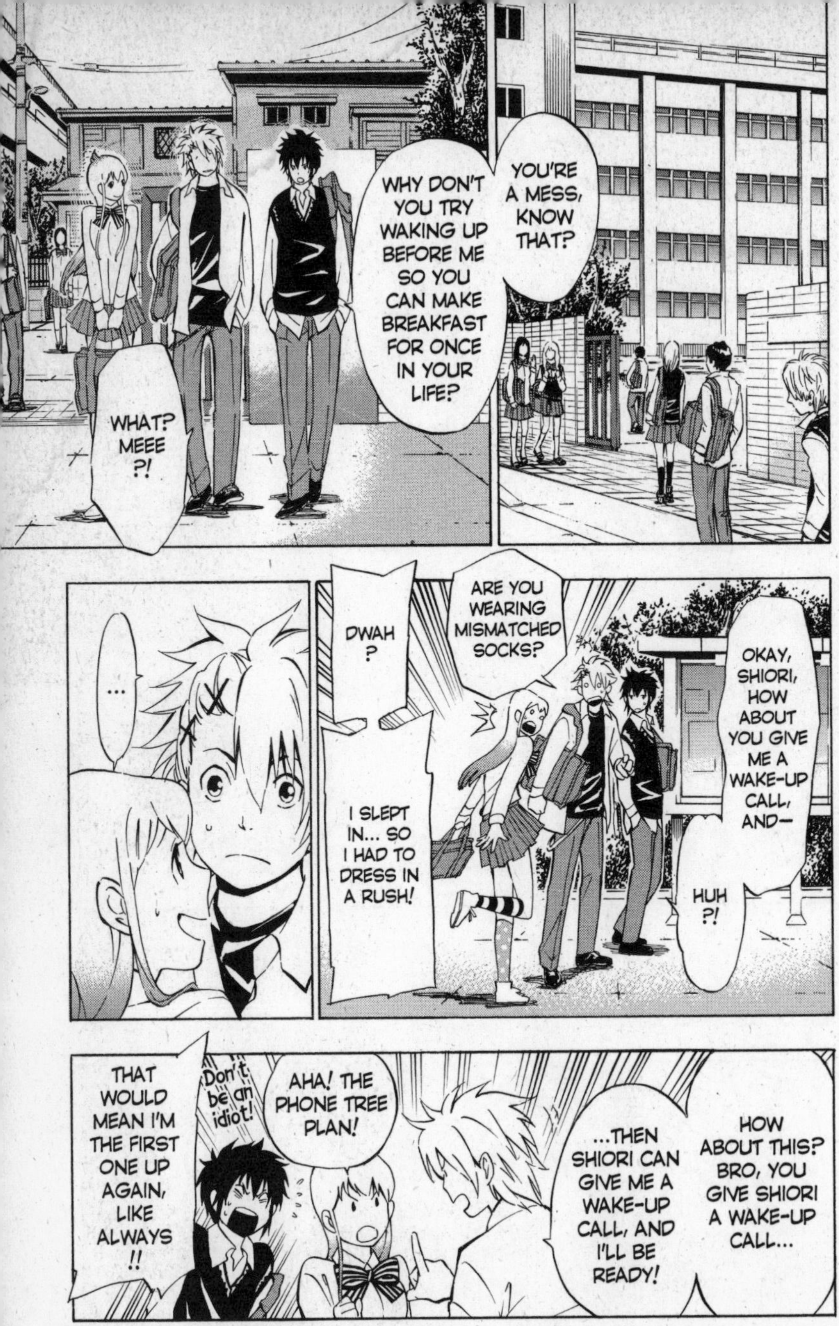
YOU'RE A MESS, KNOW THAT?
WHY DON'T YOU TRY WAKING UP BEFORE ME SO YOU CAN MAKE BREAKFAST FOR ONCE IN YOUR LIFE?
WHAT? MEEE ?!
OKAY, SHIORI, HOW ABOUT YOU GIVE ME A WAKE-UP CALL, AND—
HUH ?!
ARE YOU WEARING MISMATCHED SOCKS?
DWAH ?
I SLEPT IN... SO I HAD TO DRESS IN A RUSH!
...
HOW ABOUT THIS? BRO, YOU GIVE SHIORI A WAKE-UP CALL...
...THEN SHIORI CAN GIVE ME A WAKE-UP CALL, AND I'LL BE READY!
AHA! THE PHONE TREE PLAN!
Don't be an idiot!
THAT WOULD MEAN I'M THE FIRST ONE UP AGAIN, LIKE ALWAYS !!

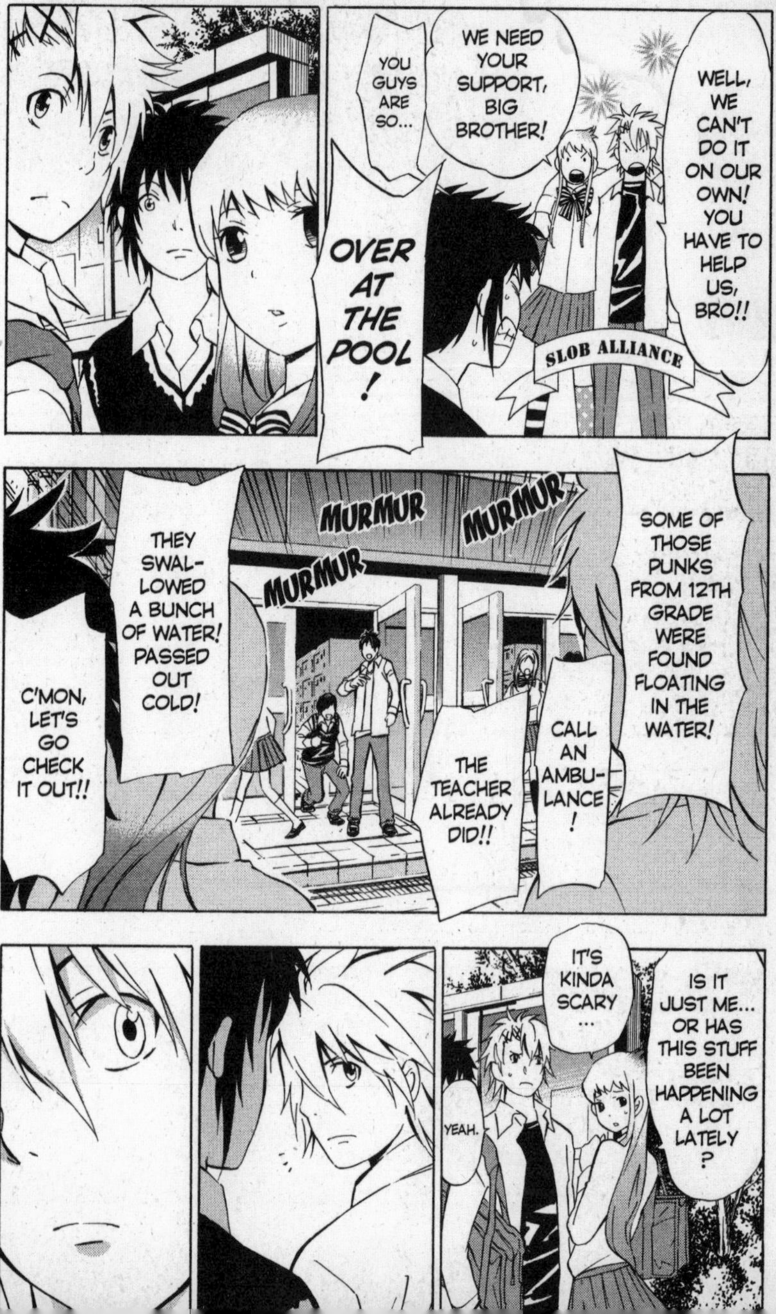
WELL, WE CAN'T DO IT ON OUR OWN! YOU HAVE TO HELP US, BRO!!
SLOB ALLIANCE
WE NEED YOUR SUPPORT, BIG BROTHER!
YOU GUYS ARE SO...
OVER AT THE POOL!
MURMUR
MURMUR
MURMUR
SOME OF THOSE PUNKS FROM 12TH GRADE WERE FOUND FLOATING IN THE WATER!
CALL AN AMBULANCE!
THE TEACHER ALREADY DID!!
THEY SWALLOWED A BUNCH OF WATER! PASSED OUT COLD!
C'MON, LET'S GO CHECK IT OUT!!
IS IT JUST ME... OR HAS THIS STUFF BEEN HAPPENING A LOT LATELY?
IT'S KINDA SCARY...
YEAH.

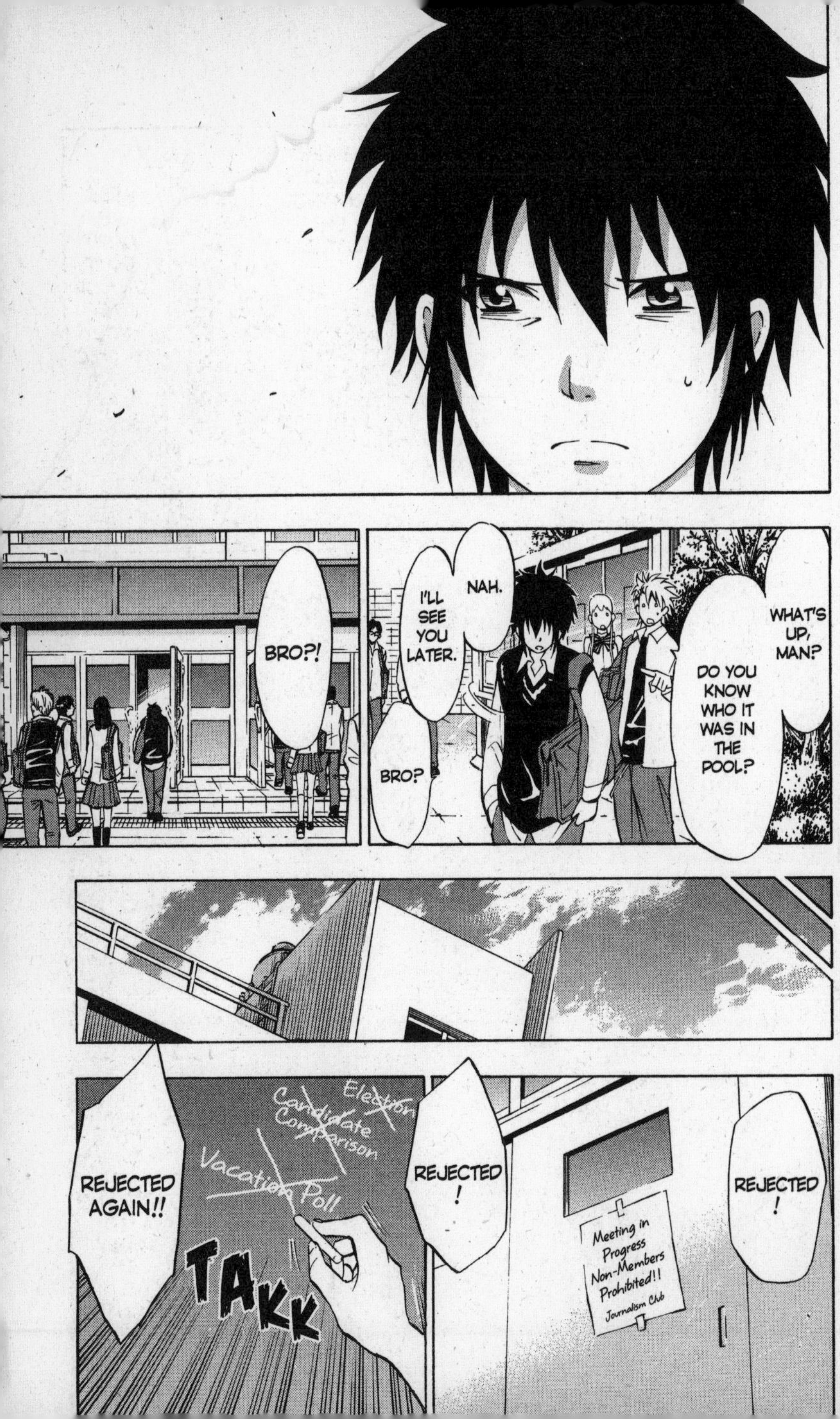
WHAT'S UP, MAN?
DO YOU KNOW WHO IT WAS IN THE POOL?
NAH.
I'LL SEE YOU LATER.
BRO?
BRO?!
REJECTED!
Meeting in Progress Non-Members Prohibited!! Journalism Club
REJECTED!
Election Candidate Comparison
Vacation Poll
REJECTED AGAIN!!
TAKK

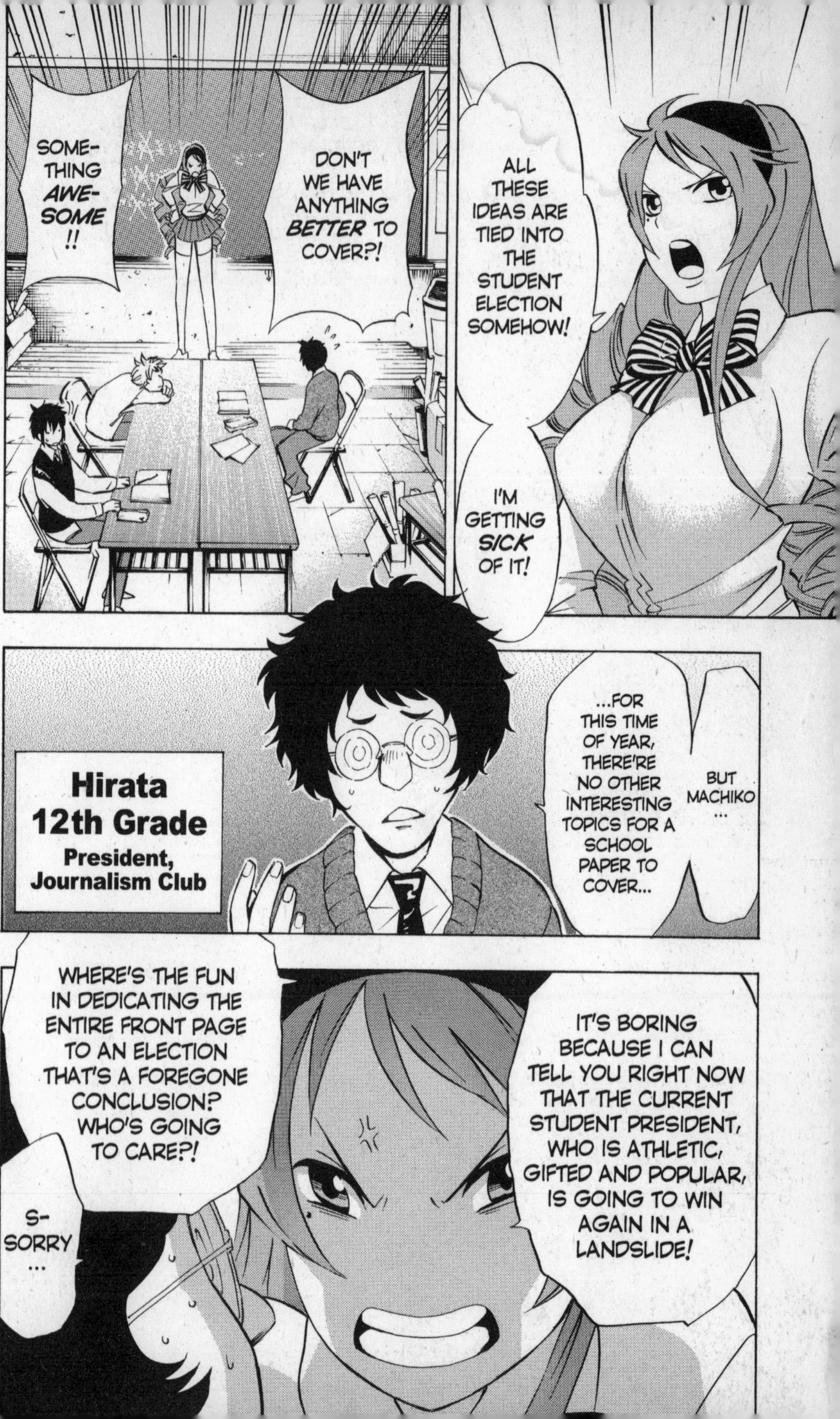
ALL THESE IDEAS ARE TIED INTO THE STUDENT ELECTION SOMEHOW!
I'M GETTING *SICK* OF IT!
DON'T WE HAVE ANYTHING *BETTER* TO COVER?!
SOME-THING *AWE-SOME* !!
BUT MACHIKO...
...FOR THIS TIME OF YEAR, THERE'RE NO OTHER INTERESTING TOPICS FOR A SCHOOL PAPER TO COVER...
Hirata
12th Grade
President, Journalism Club
IT'S BORING BECAUSE I CAN TELL YOU RIGHT NOW THAT THE CURRENT STUDENT PRESIDENT, WHO IS ATHLETIC, GIFTED AND POPULAR, IS GOING TO WIN AGAIN IN A LANDSLIDE!
WHERE'S THE FUN IN DEDICATING THE ENTIRE FRONT PAGE TO AN ELECTION THAT'S A FOREGONE CONCLUSION? WHO'S GOING TO CARE?!
S-SORRY...

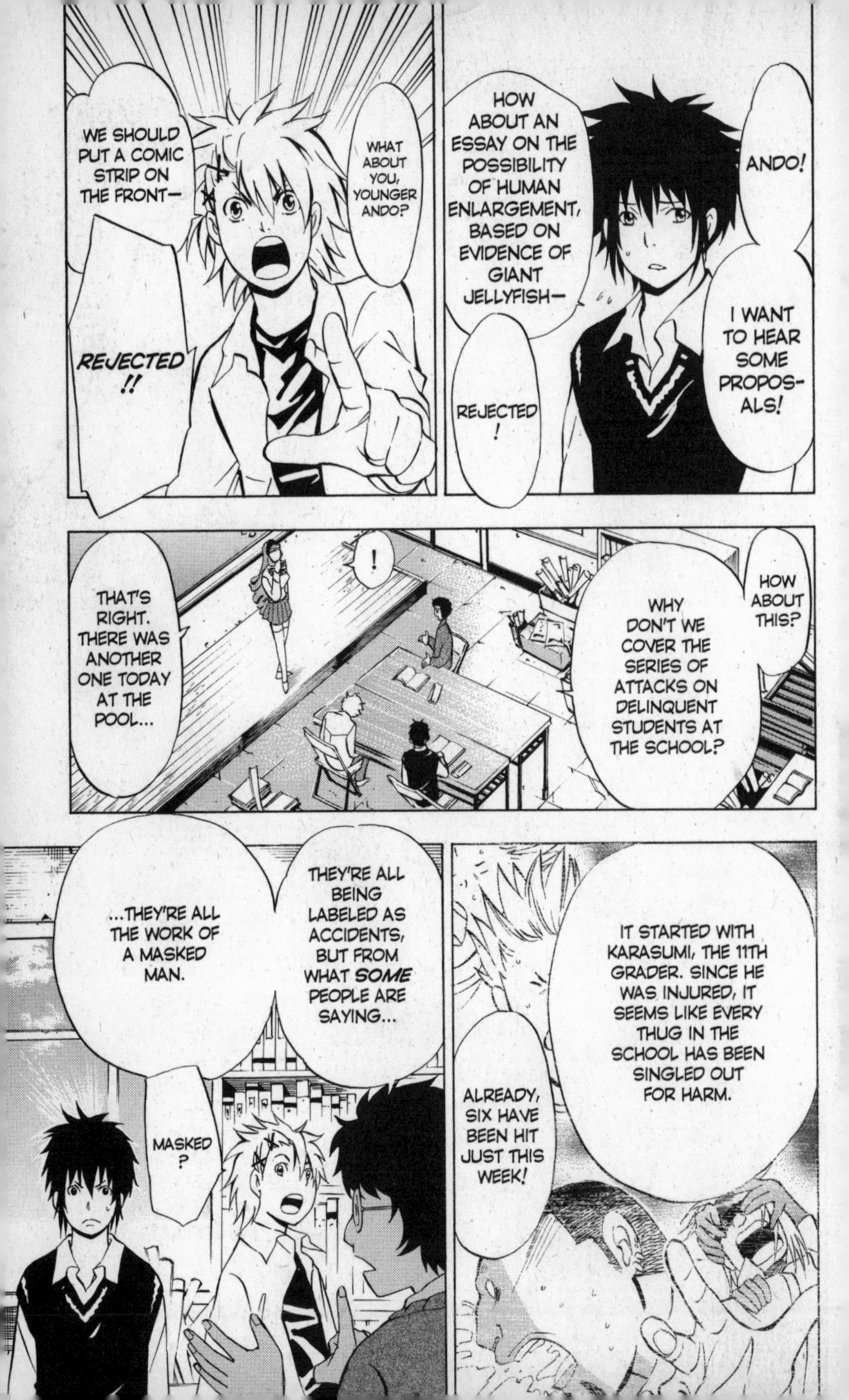
ANDO!
I WANT TO HEAR SOME PROPOSALS!
HOW ABOUT AN ESSAY ON THE POSSIBILITY OF HUMAN ENLARGEMENT, BASED ON EVIDENCE OF GIANT JELLYFISH—
REJECTED!
WHAT ABOUT YOU, YOUNGER ANDO?
WE SHOULD PUT A COMIC STRIP ON THE FRONT—
REJECTED!!
HOW ABOUT THIS?
WHY DON'T WE COVER THE SERIES OF ATTACKS ON DELINQUENT STUDENTS AT THE SCHOOL?
!
THAT'S RIGHT. THERE WAS ANOTHER ONE TODAY AT THE POOL...
IT STARTED WITH KARASUMI, THE 11TH GRADER. SINCE HE WAS INJURED, IT SEEMS LIKE EVERY THUG IN THE SCHOOL HAS BEEN SINGLED OUT FOR HARM.
ALREADY, SIX HAVE BEEN HIT JUST THIS WEEK!
THEY'RE ALL BEING LABELED AS ACCIDENTS, BUT FROM WHAT *SOME* PEOPLE ARE SAYING...
...THEY'RE ALL THE WORK OF A MASKED MAN.
MASKED?

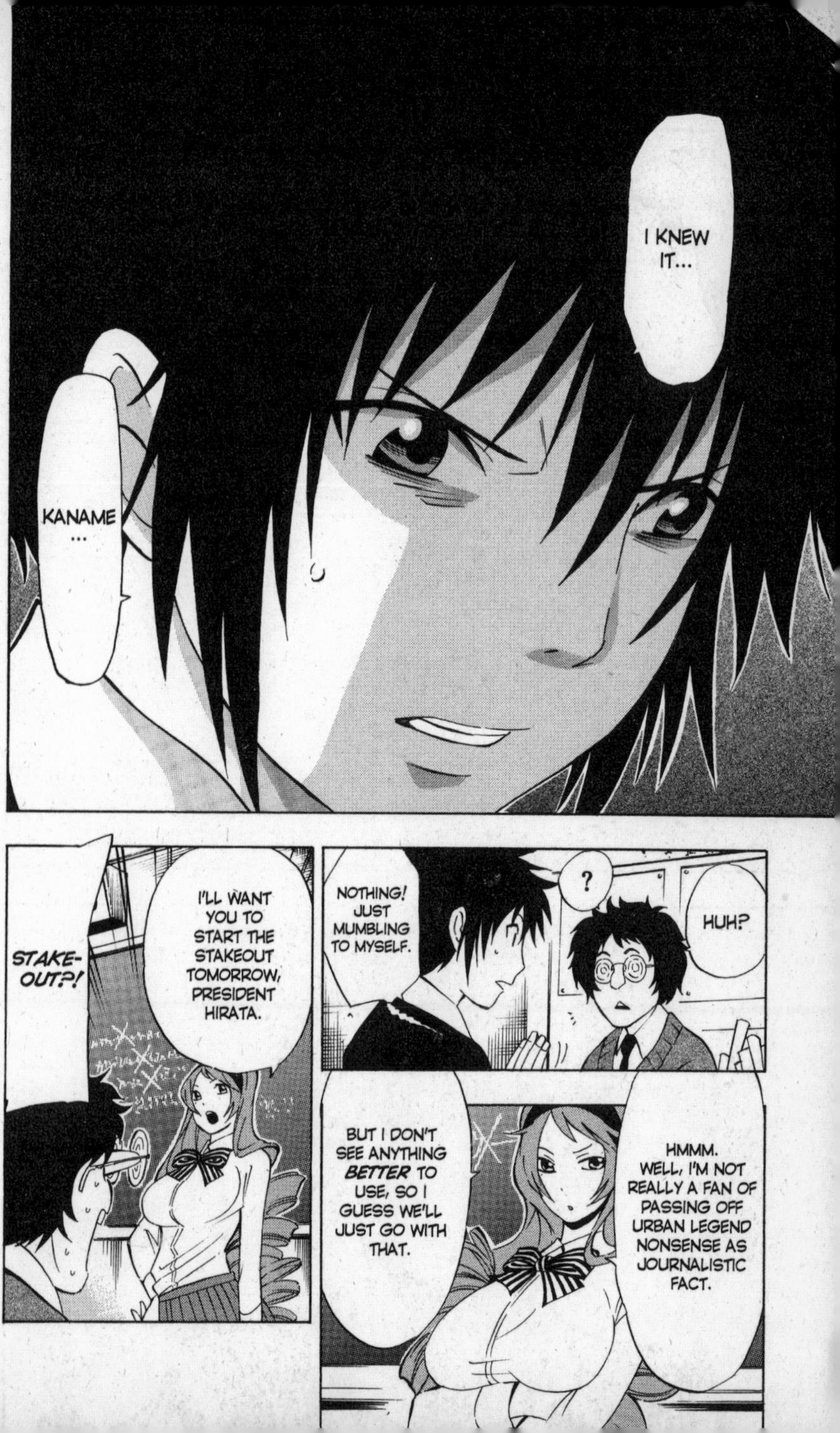
I KNEW IT...
KANAME ...
HUH?
?
NOTHING! JUST MUMBLING TO MYSELF.
HMMM. WELL, I'M NOT REALLY A FAN OF PASSING OFF URBAN LEGEND NONSENSE AS JOURNALISTIC FACT.
BUT I DON'T SEE ANYTHING *BETTER* TO USE, SO I GUESS WE'LL JUST GO WITH THAT.
I'LL WANT YOU TO START THE STAKEOUT TOMORROW, PRESIDENT HIRATA.
STAKE-OUT?!

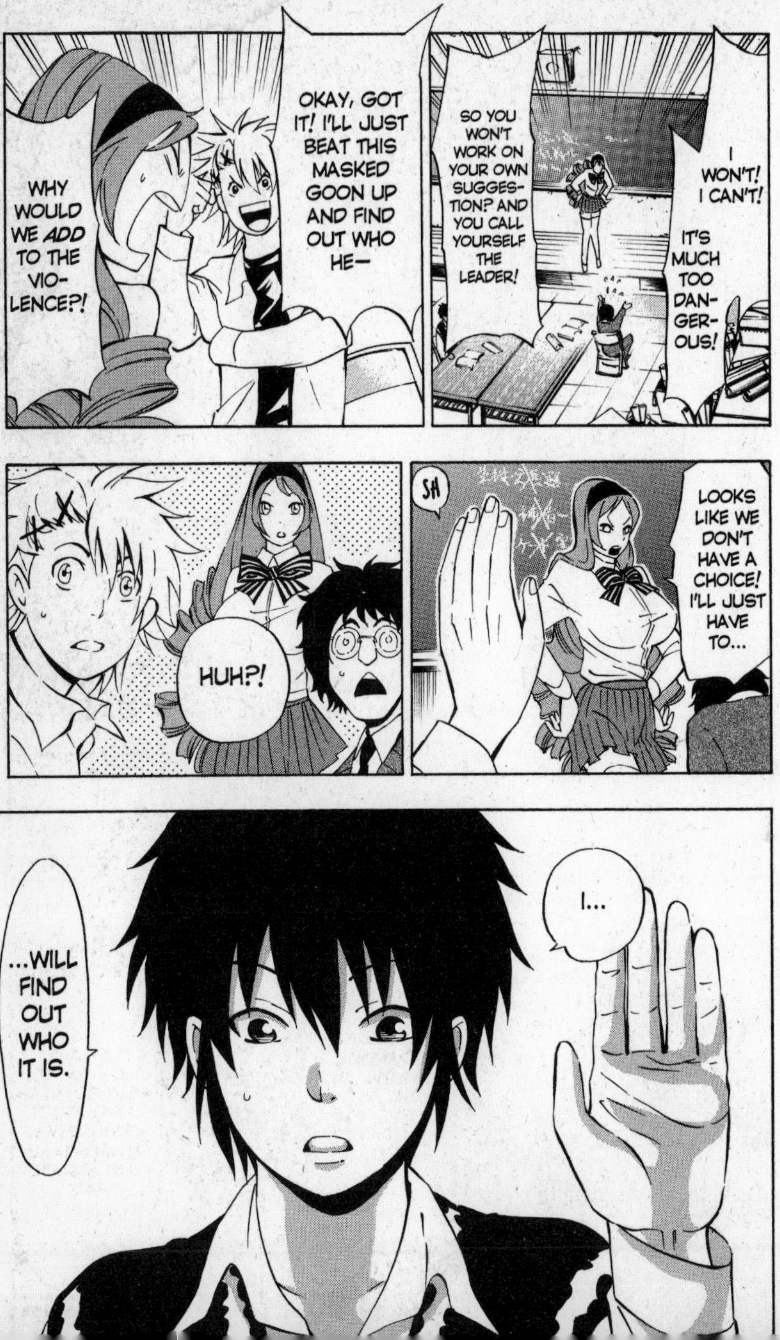
SO YOU WON'T WORK ON YOUR OWN SUGGESTION? AND YOU CALL YOURSELF THE LEADER!
I WON'T! I CAN'T!
IT'S MUCH TOO DANGEROUS!
OKAY, GOT IT! I'LL JUST BEAT THIS MASKED GOON UP AND FIND OUT WHO HE—
WHY WOULD WE ADD TO THE VIOLENCE?!
LOOKS LIKE WE DON'T HAVE A CHOICE! I'LL JUST HAVE TO...
SH
HUH?!
I...
...WILL FIND OUT WHO IT IS.

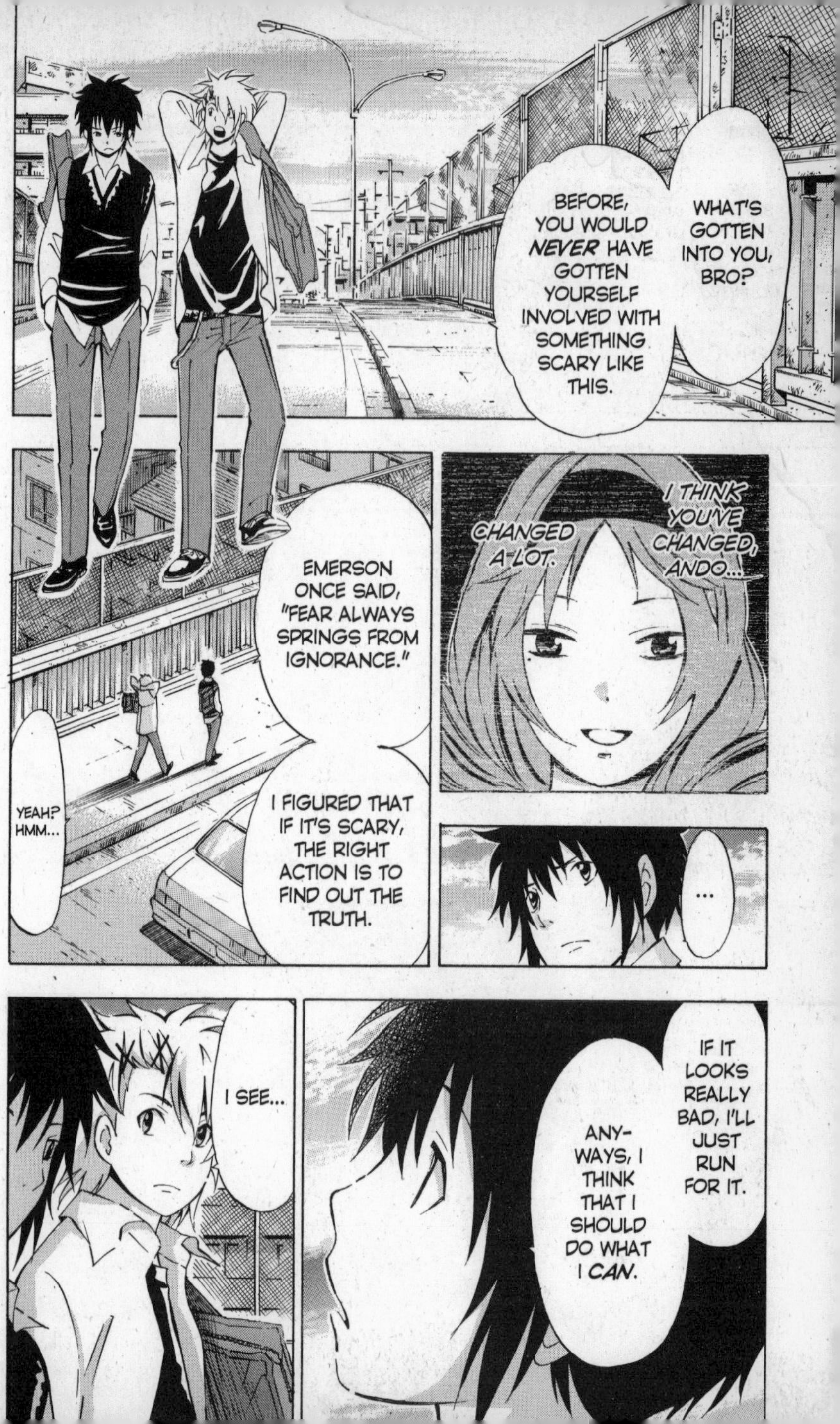
WHAT'S GOTTEN INTO YOU, BRO?
BEFORE, YOU WOULD *NEVER* HAVE GOTTEN YOURSELF INVOLVED WITH SOMETHING SCARY LIKE THIS.
I THINK YOU'VE CHANGED, ANDO...
CHANGED A LOT.
...
EMERSON ONCE SAID, "FEAR ALWAYS SPRINGS FROM IGNORANCE."
I FIGURED THAT IF IT'S SCARY, THE RIGHT ACTION IS TO FIND OUT THE TRUTH.
YEAH? HMM...
IF IT LOOKS REALLY BAD, I'LL JUST RUN FOR IT.
ANY-WAYS, I THINK THAT I SHOULD DO WHAT I *CAN*.
I SEE...

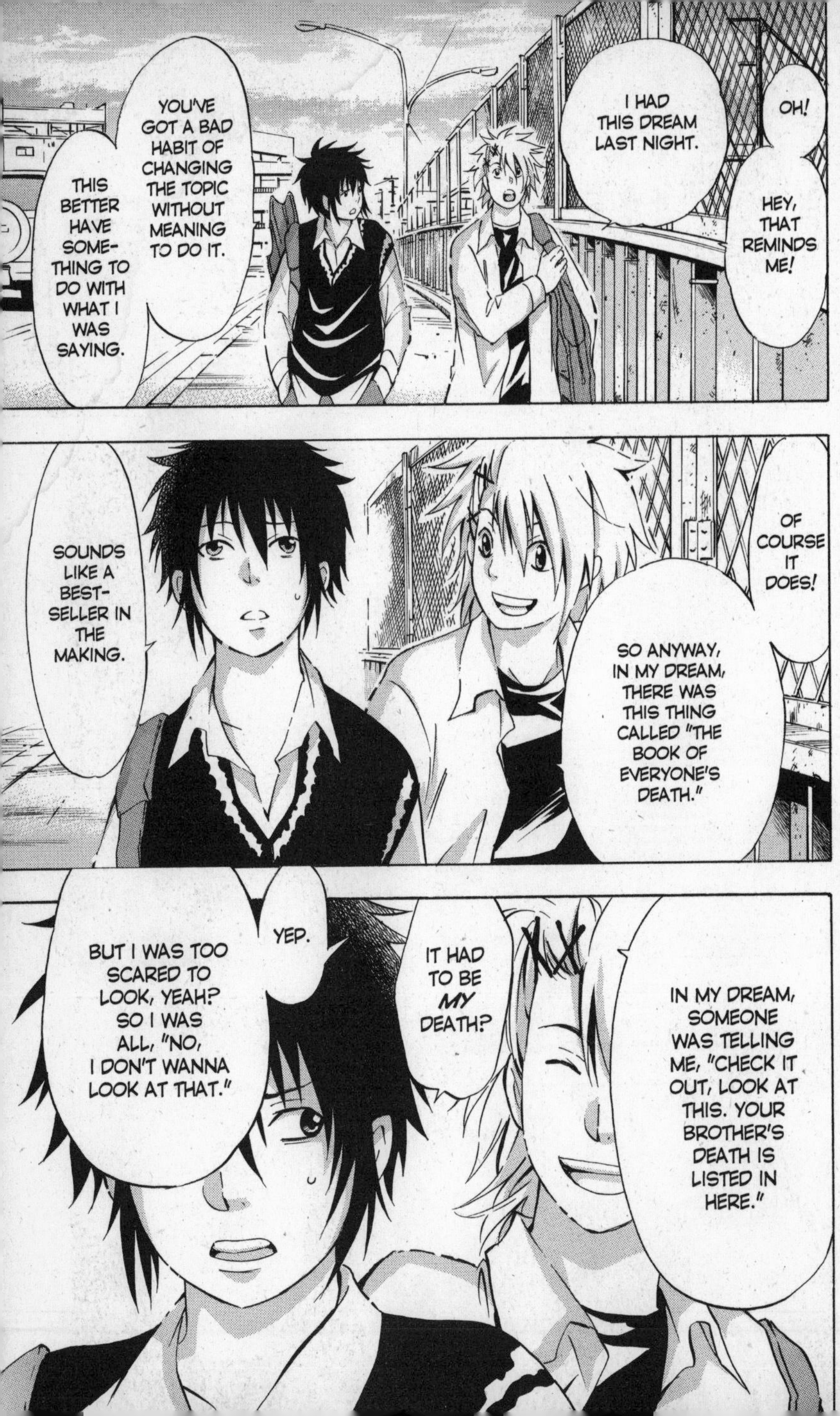
OH!
HEY, THAT REMINDS ME!
I HAD THIS DREAM LAST NIGHT.
YOU'VE GOT A BAD HABIT OF CHANGING THE TOPIC WITHOUT MEANING TO DO IT.
THIS BETTER HAVE SOME-THING TO DO WITH WHAT I WAS SAYING.
OF COURSE IT DOES!
SO ANYWAY, IN MY DREAM, THERE WAS THIS THING CALLED "THE BOOK OF EVERYONE'S DEATH."
SOUNDS LIKE A BEST-SELLER IN THE MAKING.
IN MY DREAM, SOMEONE WAS TELLING ME, "CHECK IT OUT, LOOK AT THIS. YOUR BROTHER'S DEATH IS LISTED IN HERE."
IT HAD TO BE *MY* DEATH?
YEP.
BUT I WAS TOO SCARED TO LOOK, YEAH? SO I WAS ALL, "NO, I DON'T WANNA LOOK AT THAT."

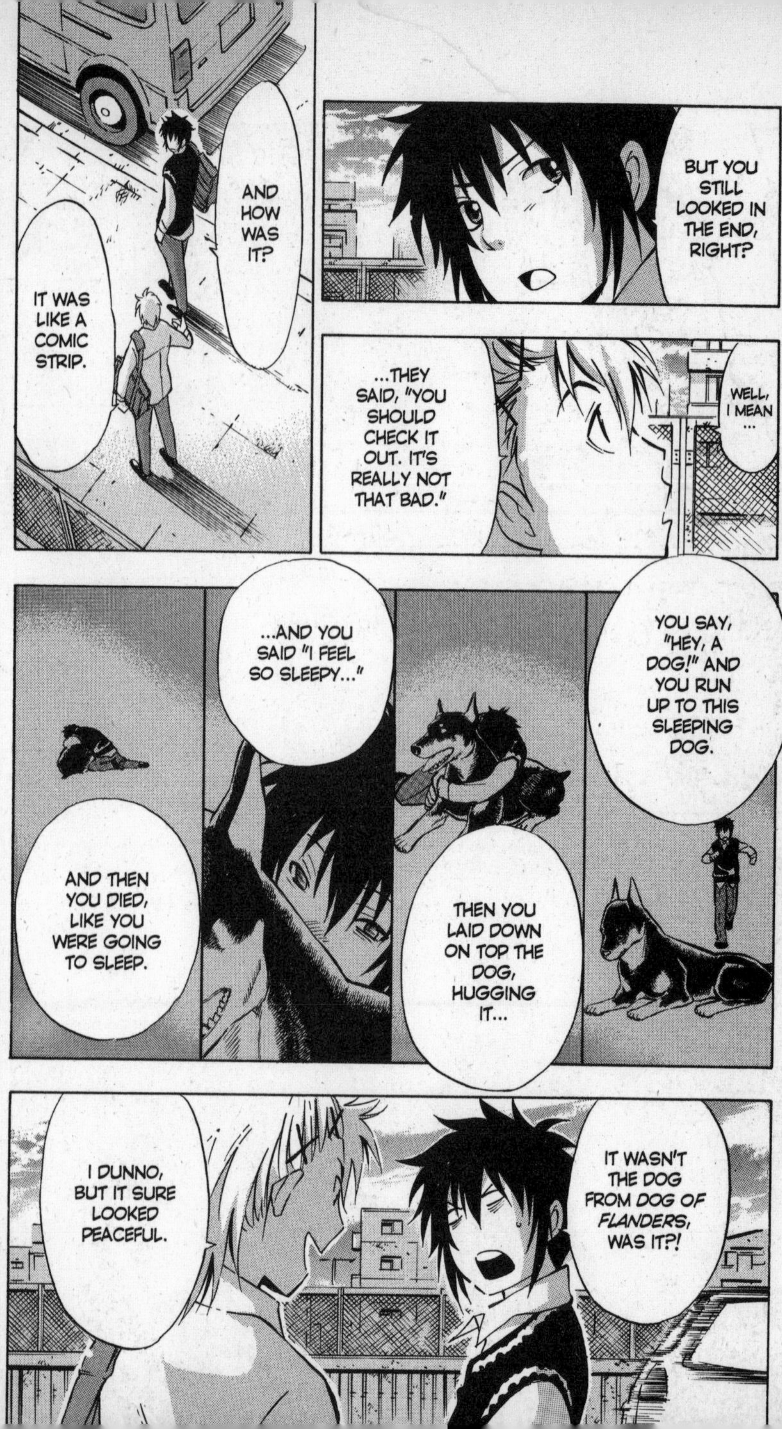
BUT YOU STILL LOOKED IN THE END, RIGHT?
WELL, I MEAN ...
...THEY SAID, "YOU SHOULD CHECK IT OUT. IT'S REALLY NOT THAT BAD."
AND HOW WAS IT?
IT WAS LIKE A COMIC STRIP.
YOU SAY, "HEY, A DOG!" AND YOU RUN UP TO THIS SLEEPING DOG.
THEN YOU LAID DOWN ON TOP THE DOG, HUGGING IT...
...AND YOU SAID "I FEEL SO SLEEPY..."
AND THEN YOU DIED, LIKE YOU WERE GOING TO SLEEP.
IT WASN'T THE DOG FROM *DOG OF FLANDERS*, WAS IT?!
I DUNNO, BUT IT SURE LOOKED PEACEFUL.

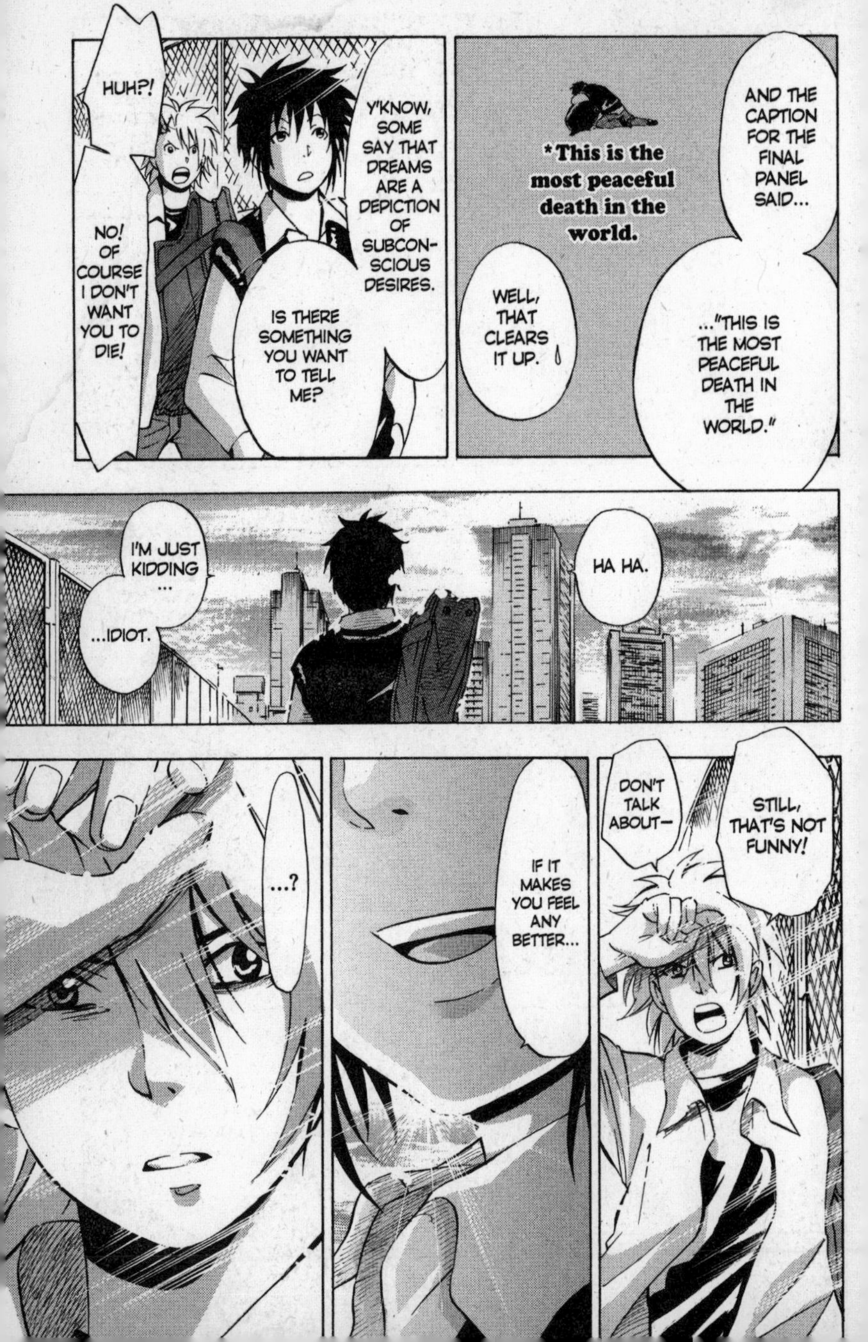
AND THE CAPTION FOR THE FINAL PANEL SAID...
*This is the most peaceful death in the world.
..."THIS IS THE MOST PEACEFUL DEATH IN THE WORLD."
WELL, THAT CLEARS IT UP.
Y'KNOW, SOME SAY THAT DREAMS ARE A DEPICTION OF SUBCON-SCIOUS DESIRES.
HUH?!
IS THERE SOMETHING YOU WANT TO TELL ME?
NO! OF COURSE I DON'T WANT YOU TO DIE!
HA HA.
I'M JUST KIDDING ...
...IDIOT.
STILL, THAT'S NOT FUNNY!
DON'T TALK ABOUT—
IF IT MAKES YOU FEEL ANY BETTER...
...?

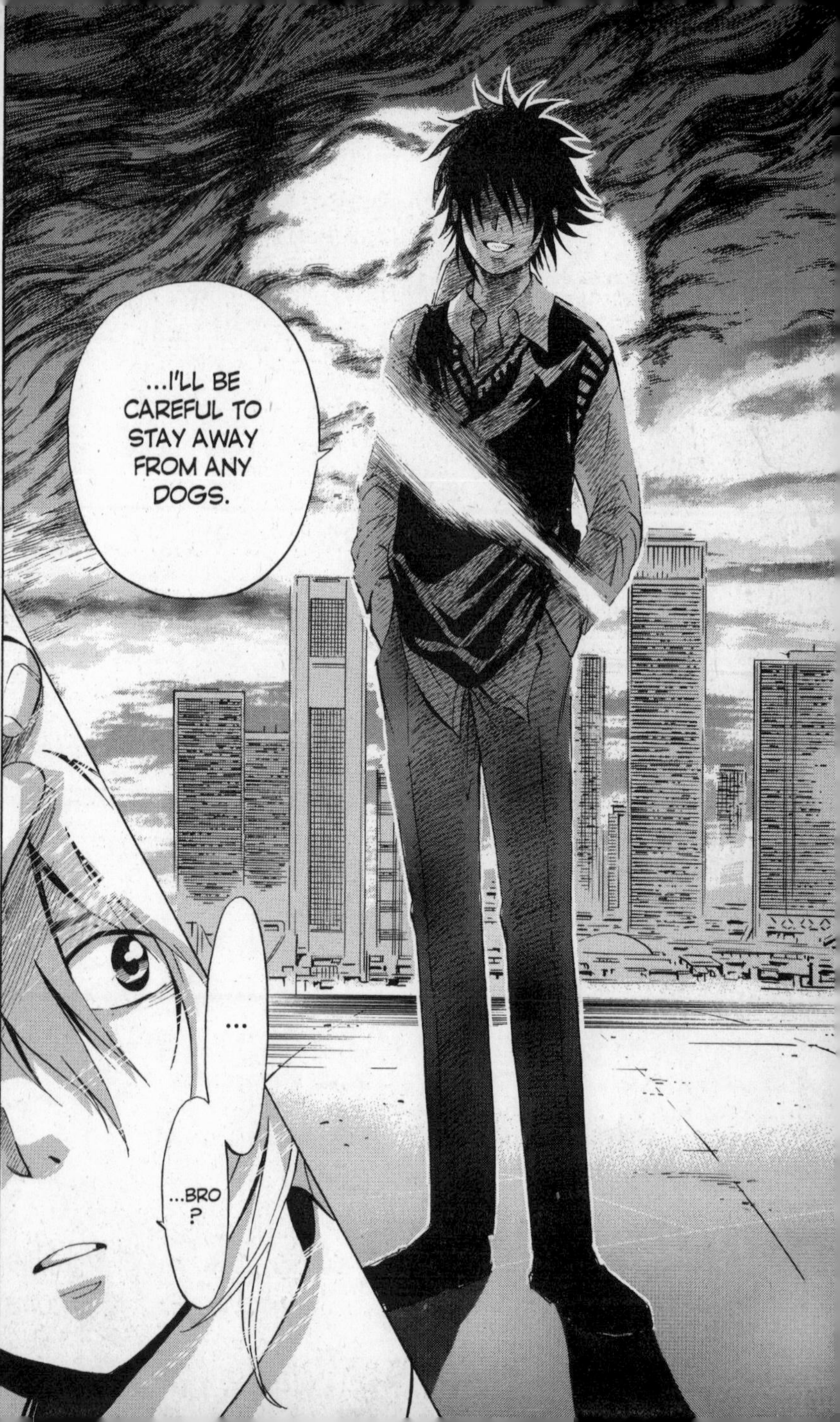
...I'LL BE CAREFUL TO STAY AWAY FROM ANY DOGS.
...
...BRO ?

Chapter 7 The Word That Changes the World

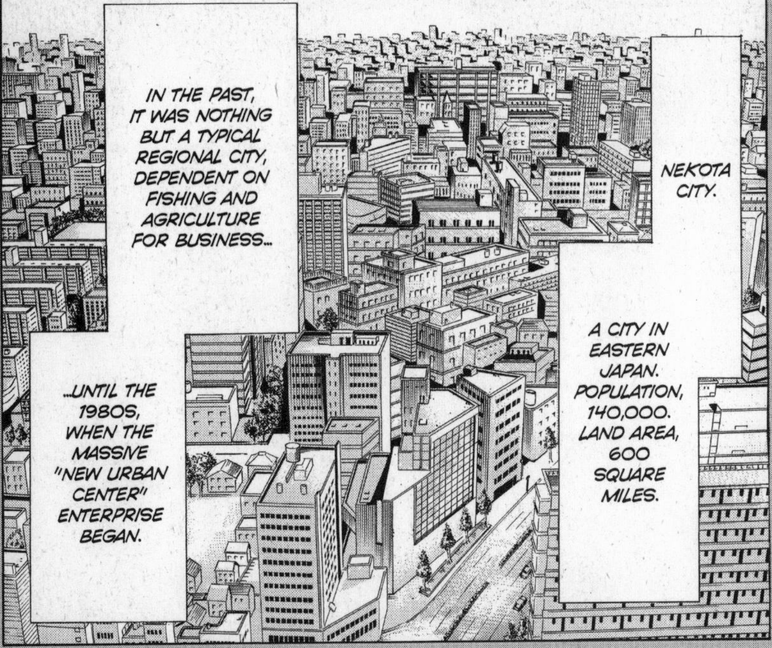
NEKOTA CITY.
A CITY IN EASTERN JAPAN. POPULATION, 140,000. LAND AREA, 600 SQUARE MILES.
IN THE PAST, IT WAS NOTHING BUT A TYPICAL REGIONAL CITY, DEPENDENT ON FISHING AND AGRICULTURE FOR BUSINESS...
...UNTIL THE 1980S, WHEN THE MASSIVE "NEW URBAN CENTER" ENTERPRISE BEGAN.

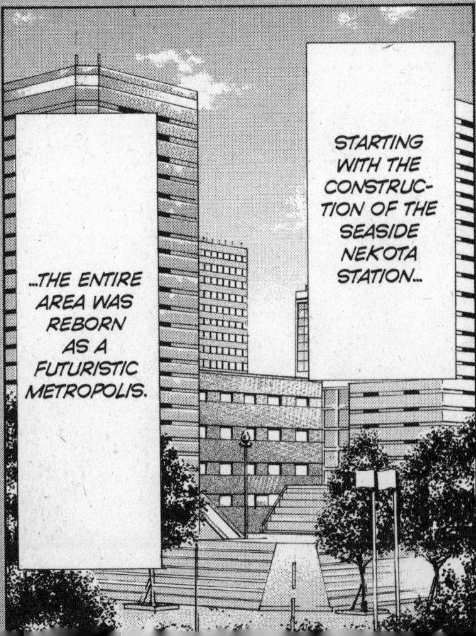
STARTING WITH THE CONSTRUC-TION OF THE SEASIDE NEKOTA STATION...
...THE ENTIRE AREA WAS REBORN AS A FUTURISTIC METROPOLIS.

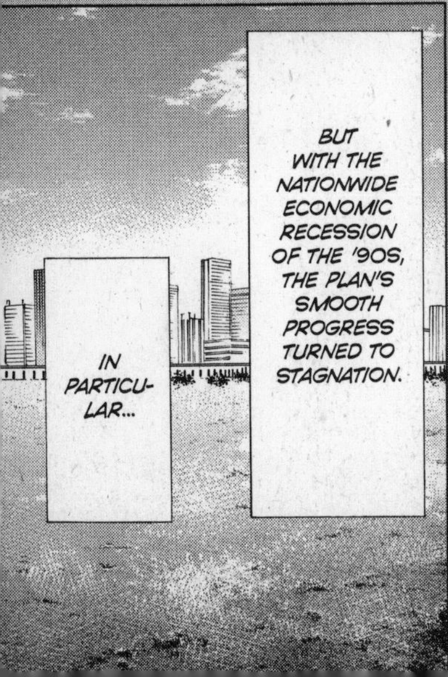
BUT WITH THE NATIONWIDE ECONOMIC RECESSION OF THE '90S, THE PLAN'S SMOOTH PROGRESS TURNED TO STAGNATION.
IN PARTICU-LAR...

Chapter 7 The Word That Changes the World

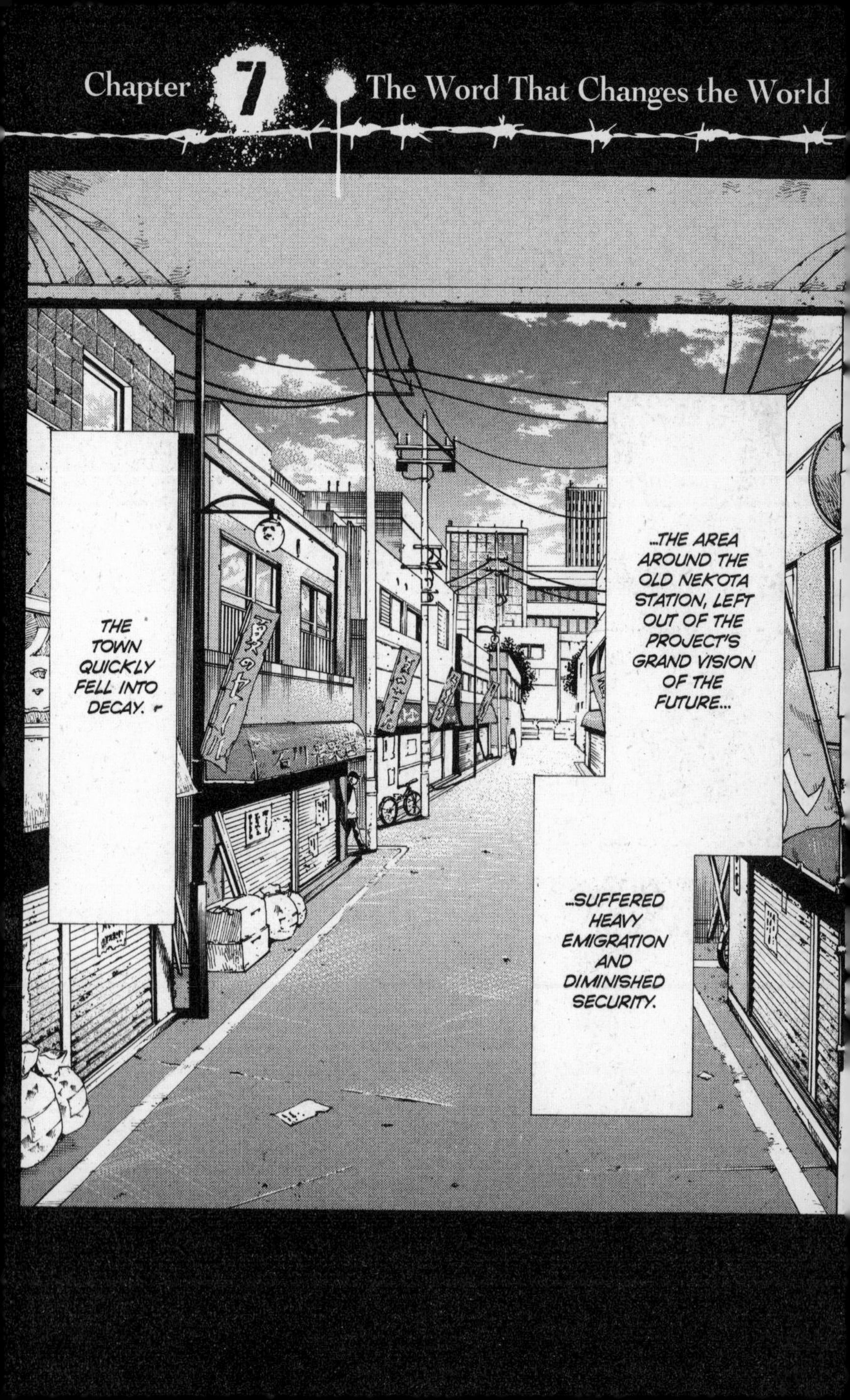
...THE AREA AROUND THE OLD NEKOTA STATION, LEFT OUT OF THE PROJECT'S GRAND VISION OF THE FUTURE...
...SUFFERED HEAVY EMIGRATION AND DIMINISHED SECURITY.
THE TOWN QUICKLY FELL INTO DECAY.

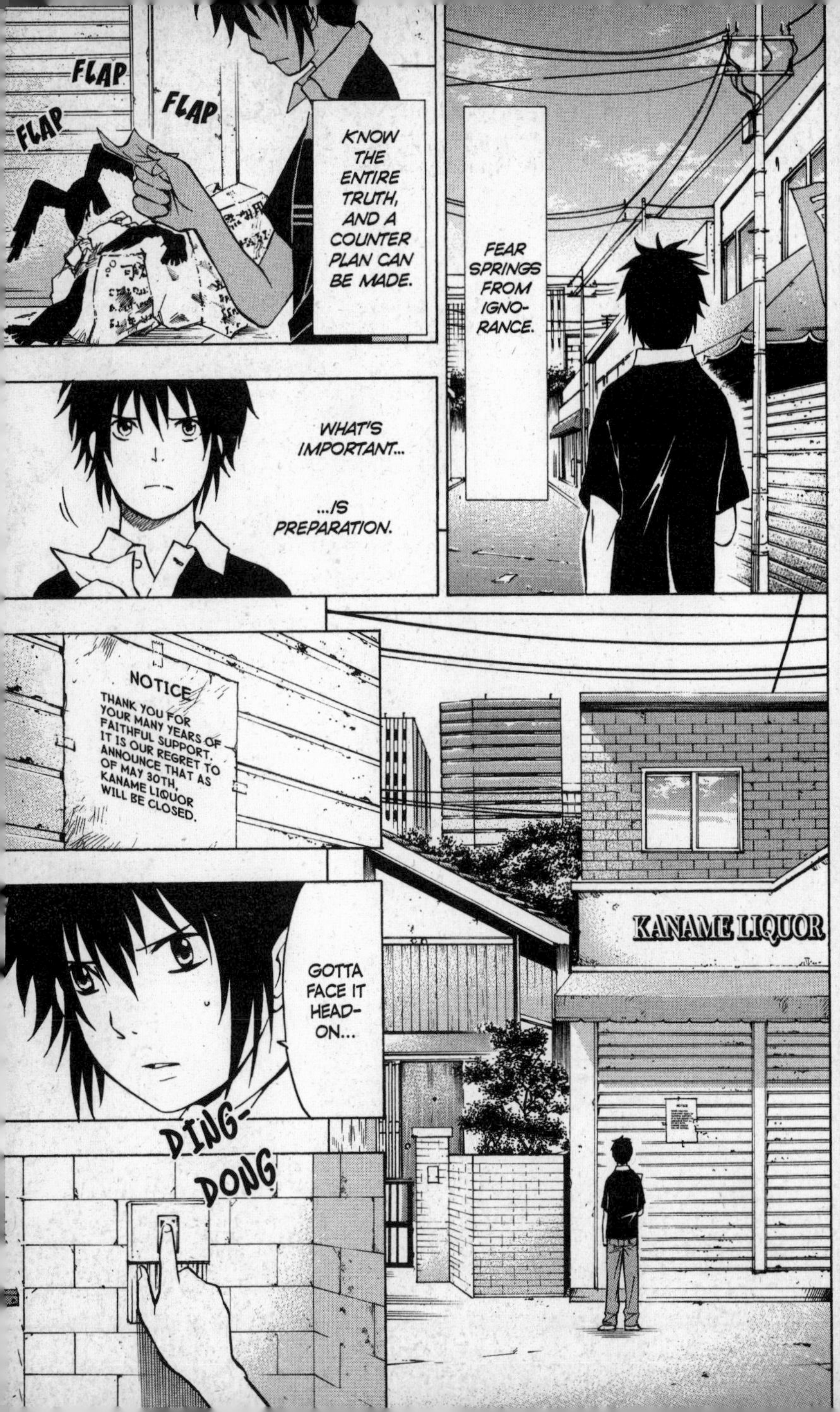
FEAR SPRINGS FROM IGNO-RANCE.
FLAP
FLAP
FLAP
KNOW THE ENTIRE TRUTH, AND A COUNTER PLAN CAN BE MADE.
WHAT'S IMPORTANT...
...IS PREPARATION.
KANAME LIQUOR
NOTICE
THANK YOU FOR YOUR MANY YEARS OF FAITHFUL SUPPORT. IT IS OUR REGRET TO ANNOUNCE THAT AS OF MAY 30TH, KANAME LIQUOR WILL BE CLOSED.
GOTTA FACE IT HEAD-ON...
DING-DONG

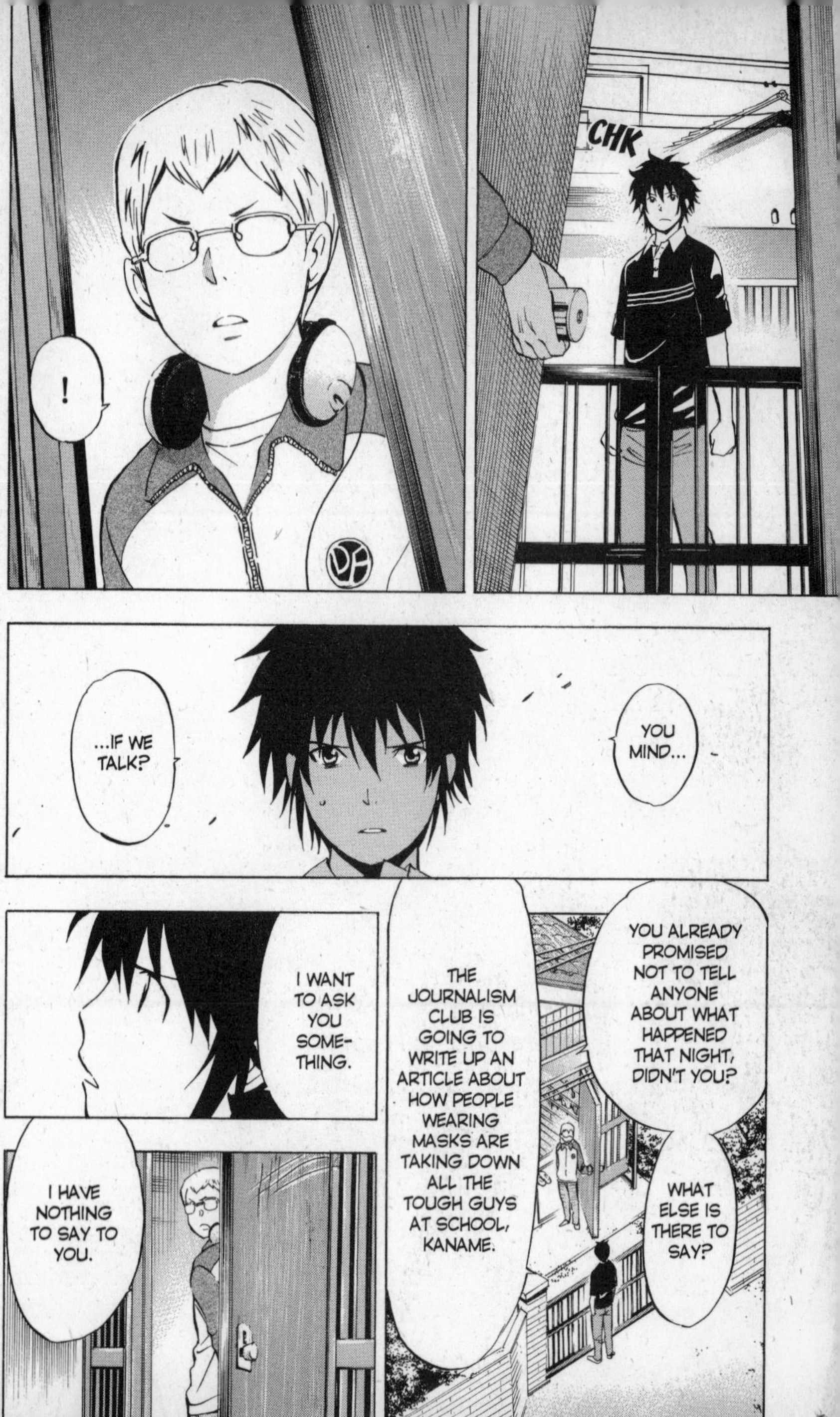

CHK
!
YOU MIND...
...IF WE TALK?
YOU ALREADY PROMISED NOT TO TELL ANYONE ABOUT WHAT HAPPENED THAT NIGHT, DIDN'T YOU?
THE JOURNALISM CLUB IS GOING TO WRITE UP AN ARTICLE ABOUT HOW PEOPLE WEARING MASKS ARE TAKING DOWN ALL THE TOUGH GUYS AT SCHOOL, KANAME.
WHAT ELSE IS THERE TO SAY?
I WANT TO ASK YOU SOME-THING.
I HAVE NOTHING TO SAY TO YOU.

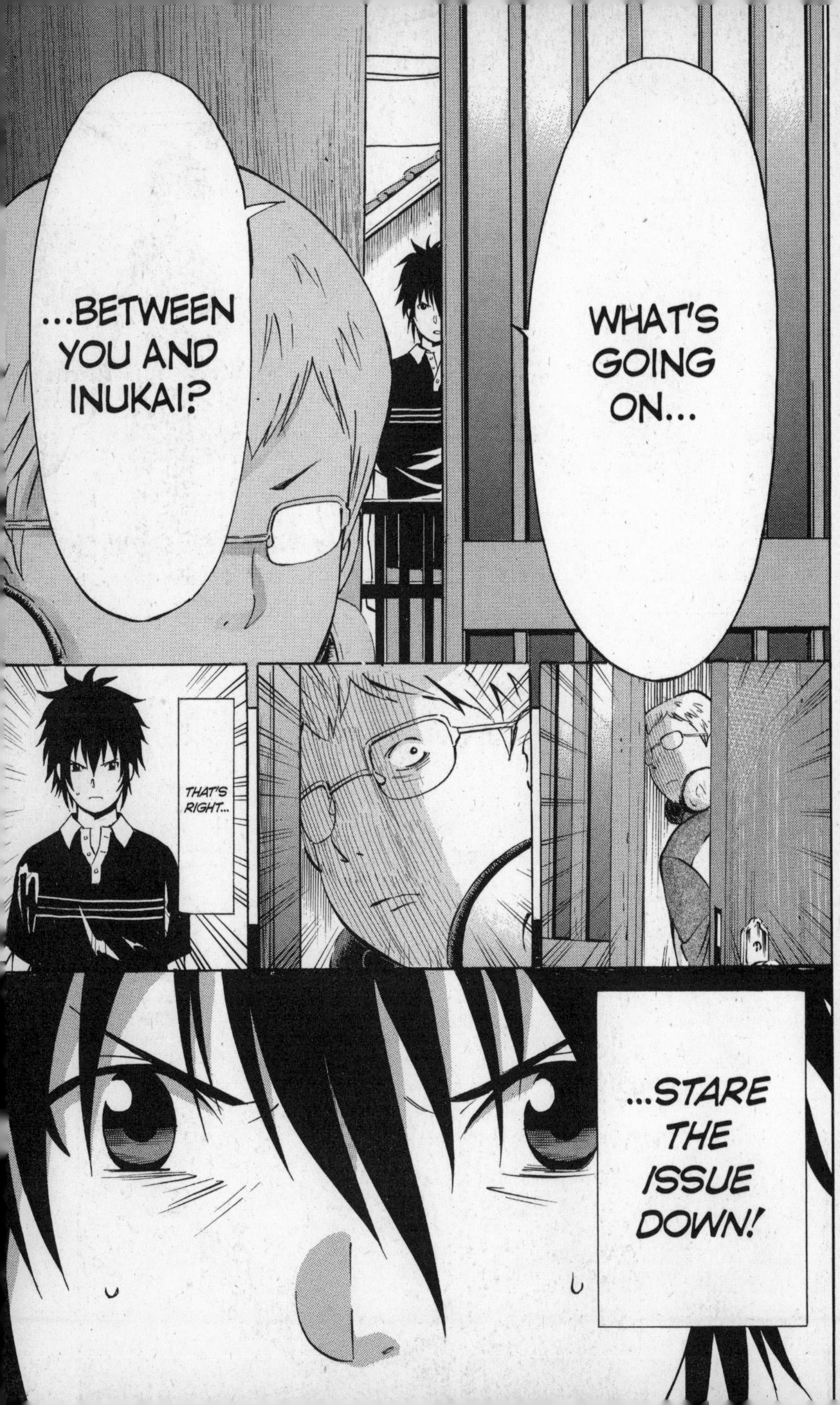
WHAT'S GOING ON...
...BETWEEN YOU AND INUKAI?
THAT'S RIGHT...
...STARE THE ISSUE DOWN!

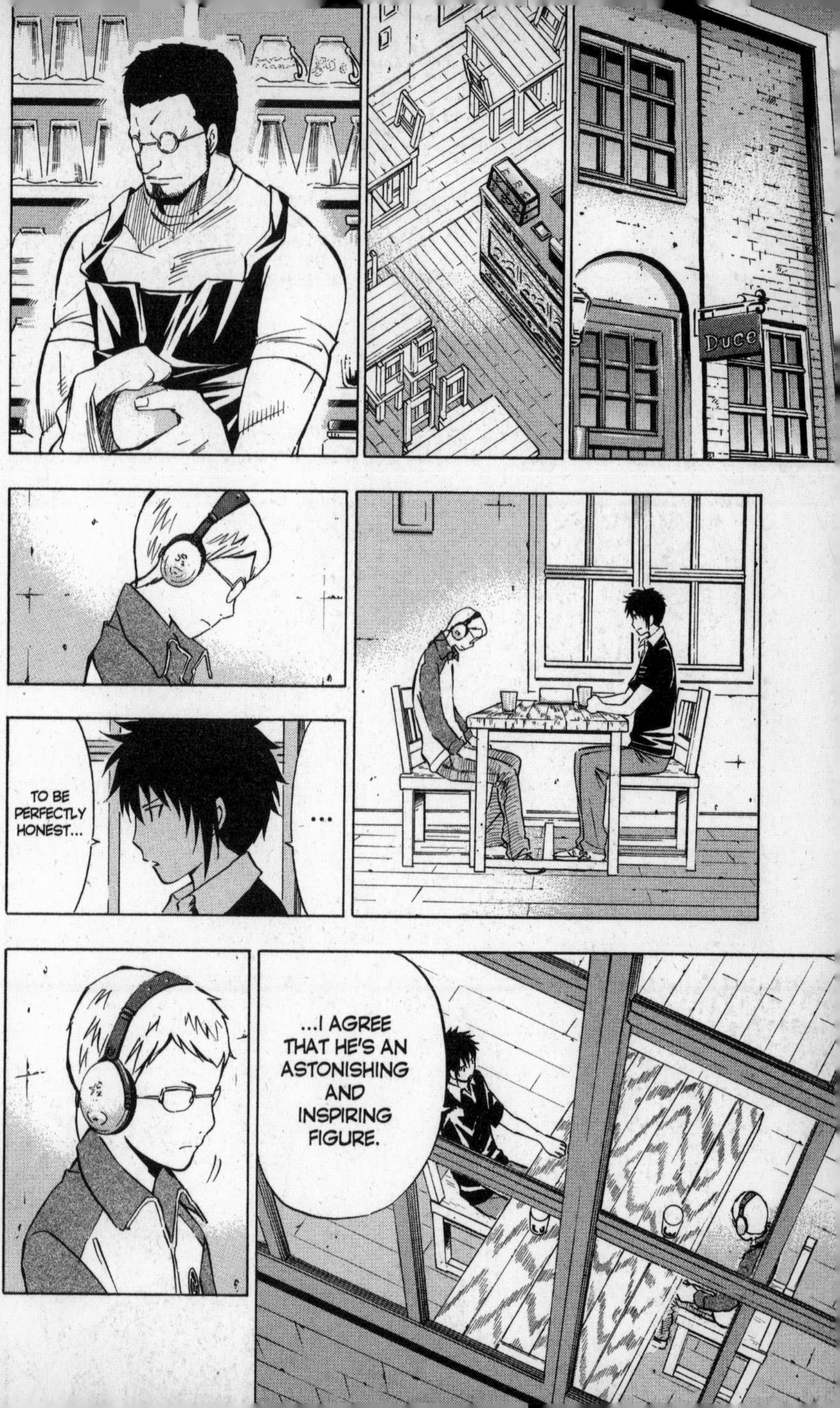
Duce
...
TO BE PERFECTLY HONEST...
...I AGREE THAT HE'S AN ASTONISHING AND INSPIRING FIGURE.

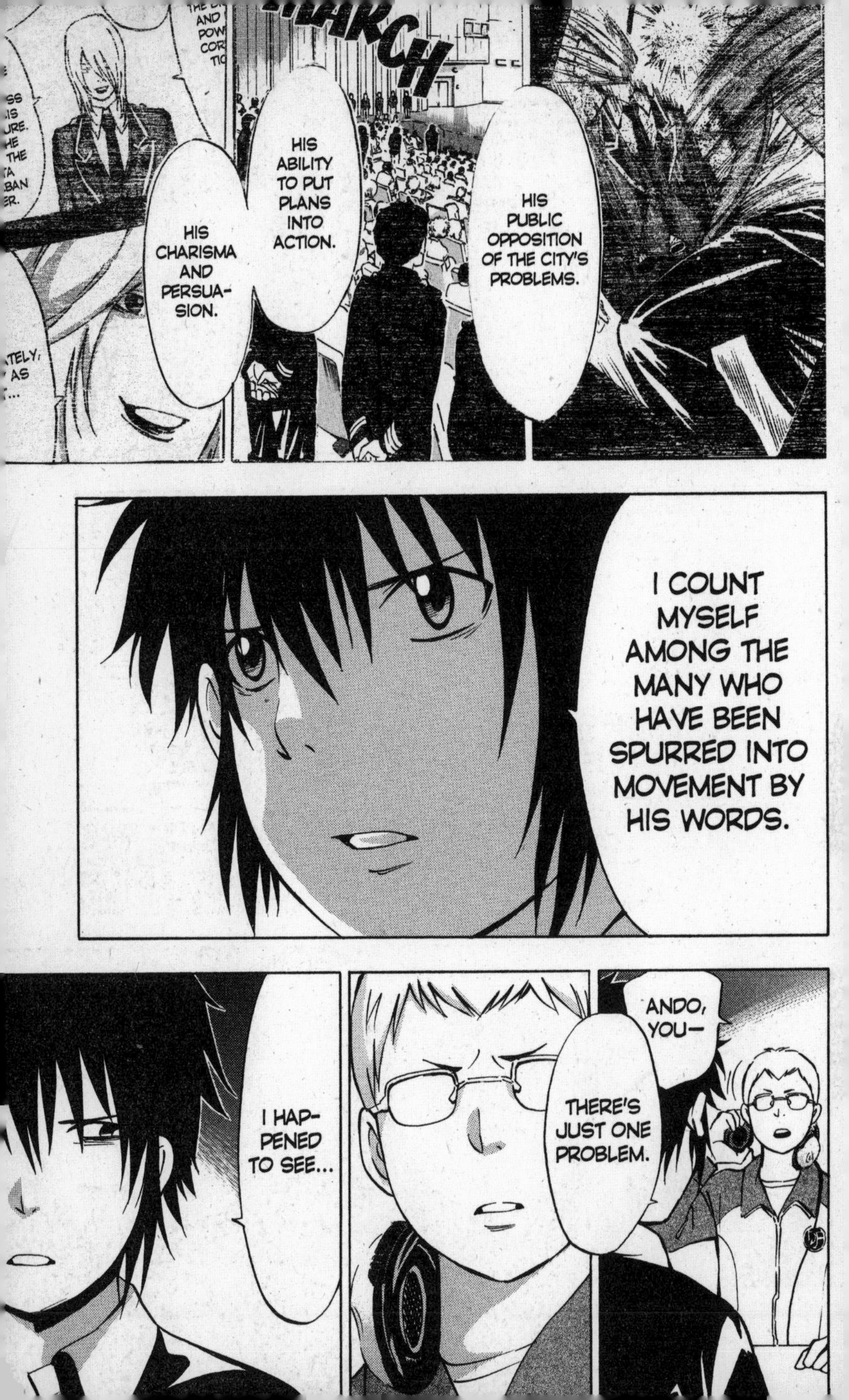
HIS PUBLIC OPPOSITION OF THE CITY'S PROBLEMS.
HIS ABILITY TO PUT PLANS INTO ACTION.
HIS CHARISMA AND PERSUASION.
I COUNT MYSELF AMONG THE MANY WHO HAVE BEEN SPURRED INTO MOVEMENT BY HIS WORDS.
ANDO, YOU—
THERE'S JUST ONE PROBLEM.
I HAPPENED TO SEE...

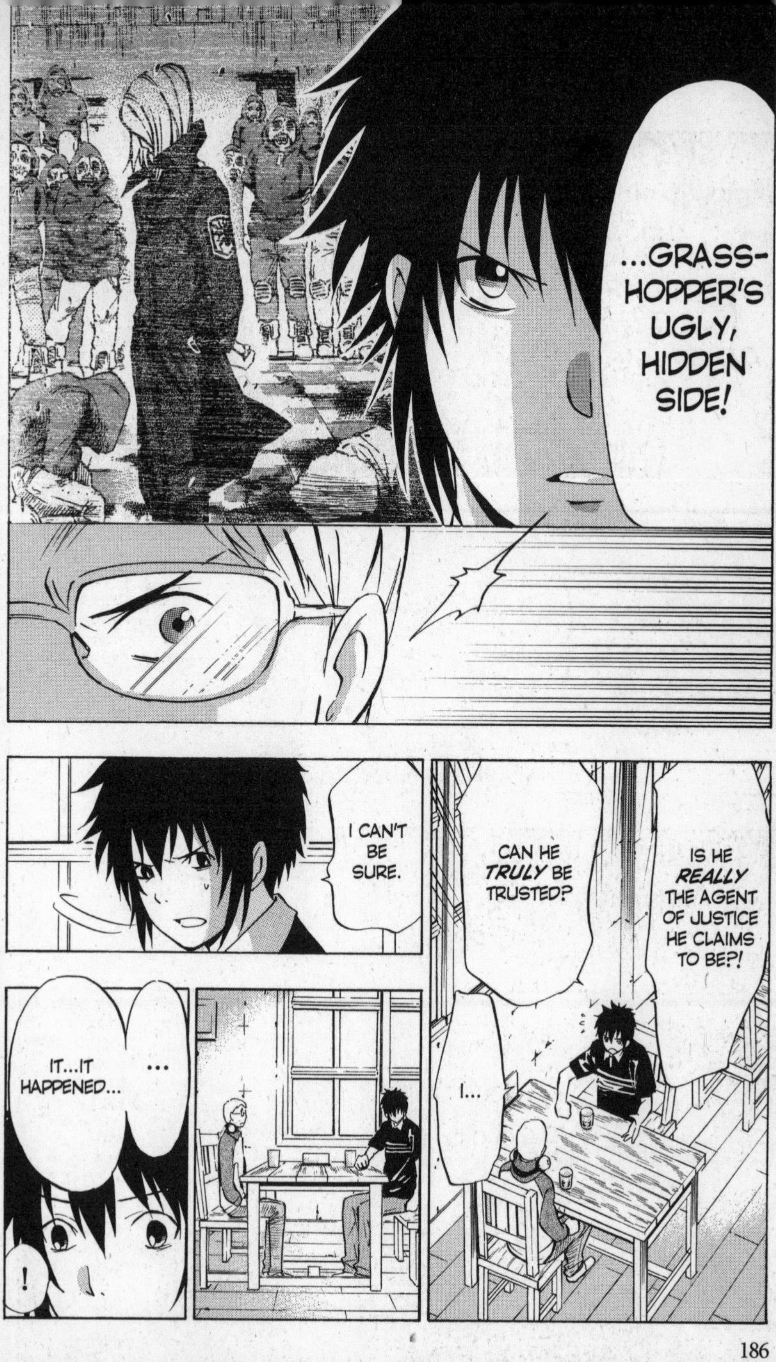
...GRASS-HOPPER'S UGLY, HIDDEN SIDE!
IS HE *REALLY* THE AGENT OF JUSTICE HE CLAIMS TO BE?!
CAN HE *TRULY* BE TRUSTED?
I...
I CAN'T BE SURE.
...
IT...IT HAPPENED...
!

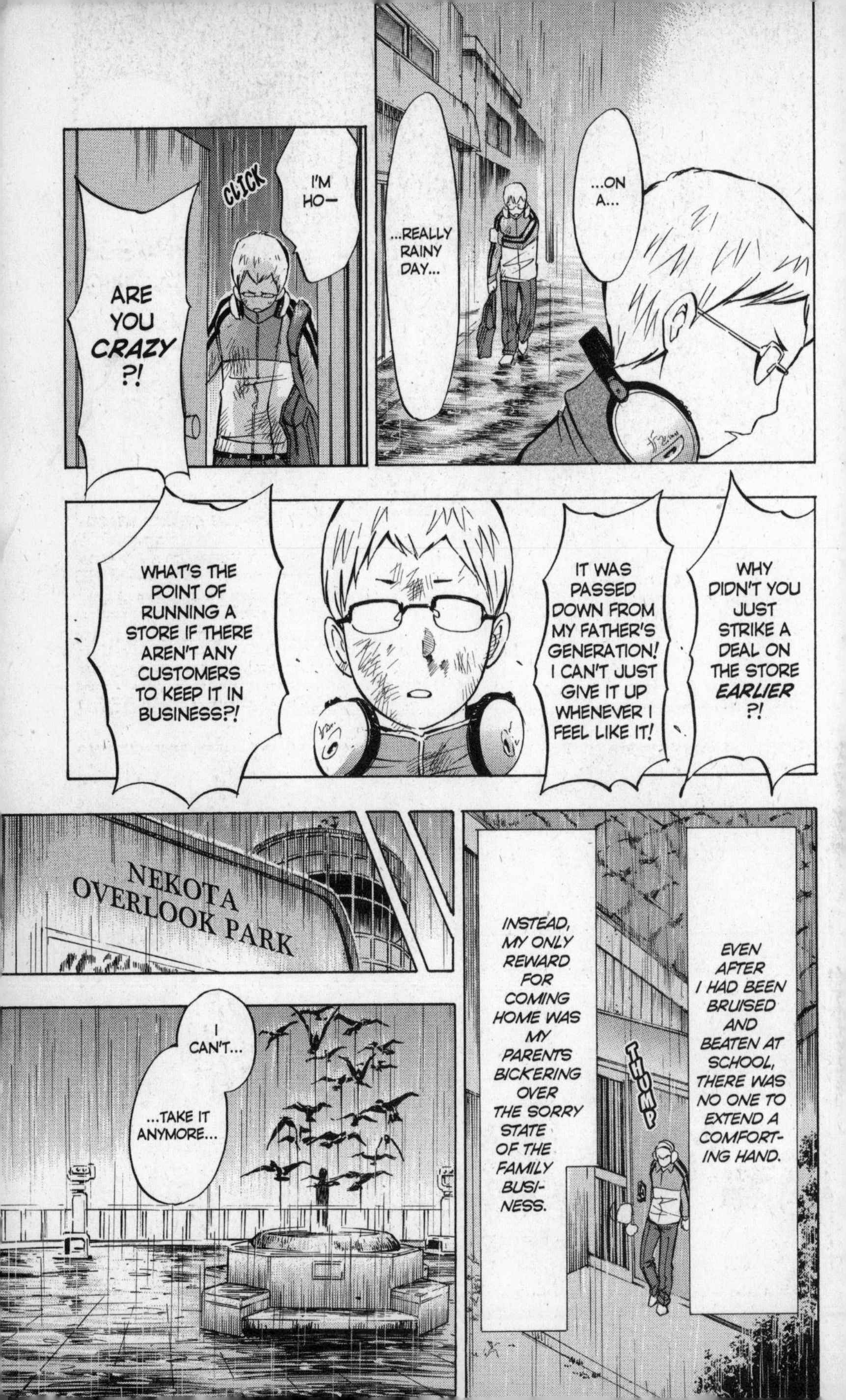

...ON A...
...REALLY RAINY DAY...
CLICK
I'M HO—
ARE YOU CRAZY?!
WHY DIDN'T YOU JUST STRIKE A DEAL ON THE STORE EARLIER?!
IT WAS PASSED DOWN FROM MY FATHER'S GENERATION! I CAN'T JUST GIVE IT UP WHENEVER I FEEL LIKE IT!
WHAT'S THE POINT OF RUNNING A STORE IF THERE AREN'T ANY CUSTOMERS TO KEEP IT IN BUSINESS?!
EVEN AFTER I HAD BEEN BRUISED AND BEATEN AT SCHOOL, THERE WAS NO ONE TO EXTEND A COMFORTING HAND.
THUMP
INSTEAD, MY ONLY REWARD FOR COMING HOME WAS MY PARENTS BICKERING OVER THE SORRY STATE OF THE FAMILY BUSINESS.
NEKOTA OVERLOOK PARK
I CAN'T...
...TAKE IT ANYMORE...

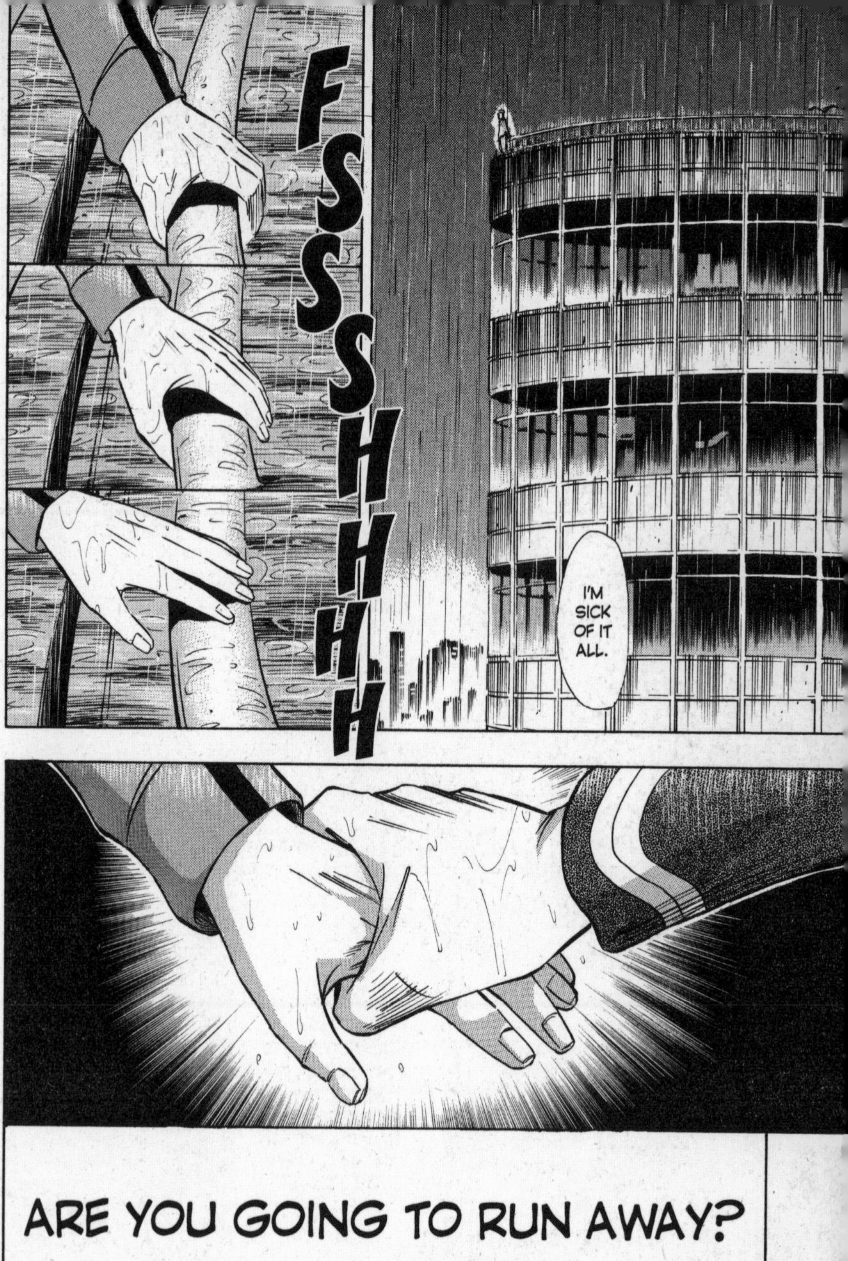
I'M SICK OF IT ALL.
FSSSHHHH
ARE YOU GOING TO RUN AWAY?

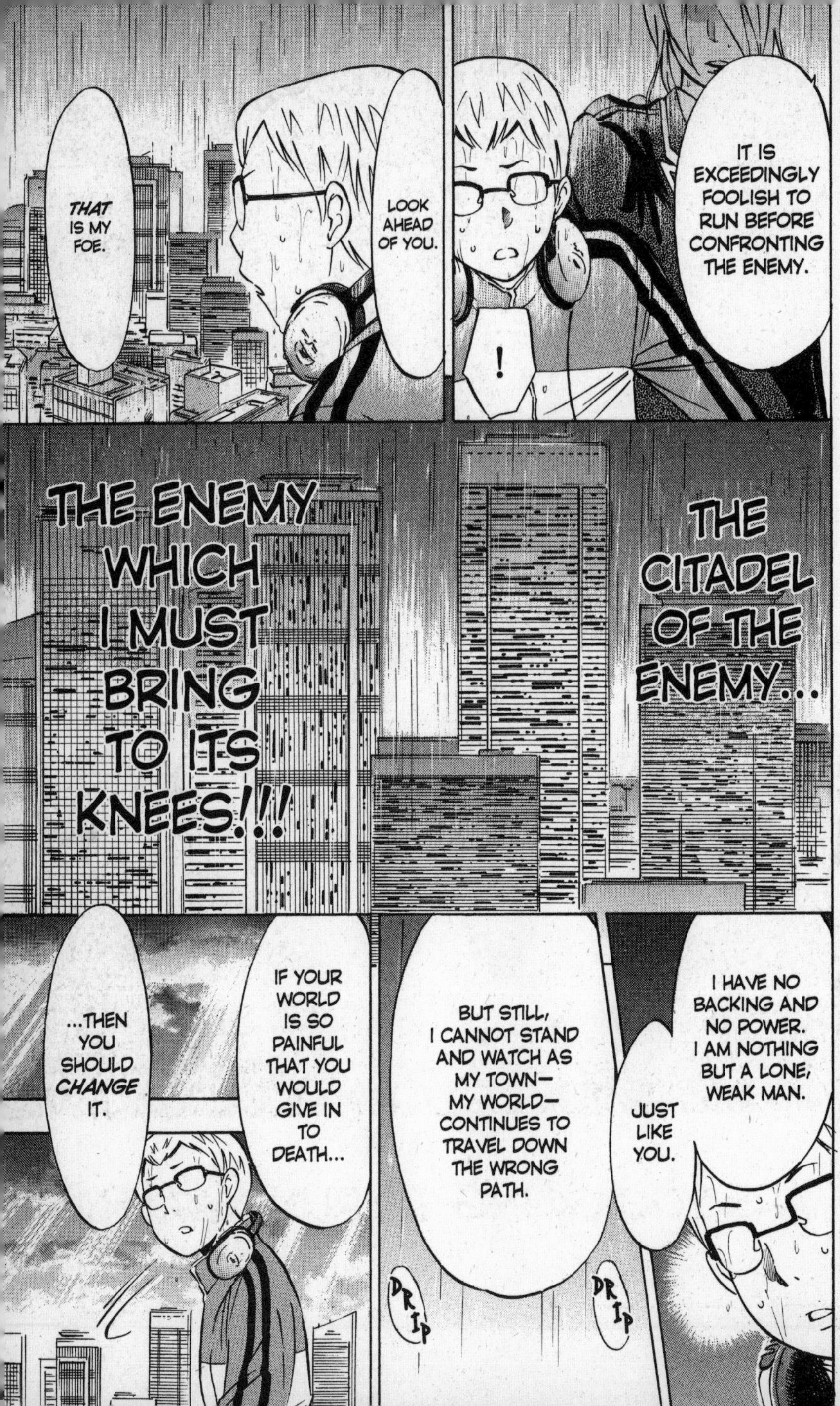
IT IS EXCEEDINGLY FOOLISH TO RUN BEFORE CONFRONTING THE ENEMY.
!
LOOK AHEAD OF YOU.
THAT IS MY FOE.
THE CITADEL OF THE ENEMY...
THE ENEMY WHICH I MUST BRING TO ITS KNEES!!!
I HAVE NO BACKING AND NO POWER. I AM NOTHING BUT A LONE, WEAK MAN.
JUST LIKE YOU.
BUT STILL, I CANNOT STAND AND WATCH AS MY TOWN— MY WORLD— CONTINUES TO TRAVEL DOWN THE WRONG PATH.
DRIP
DRIP
IF YOUR WORLD IS SO PAINFUL THAT YOU WOULD GIVE IN TO DEATH...
...THEN YOU SHOULD CHANGE IT.

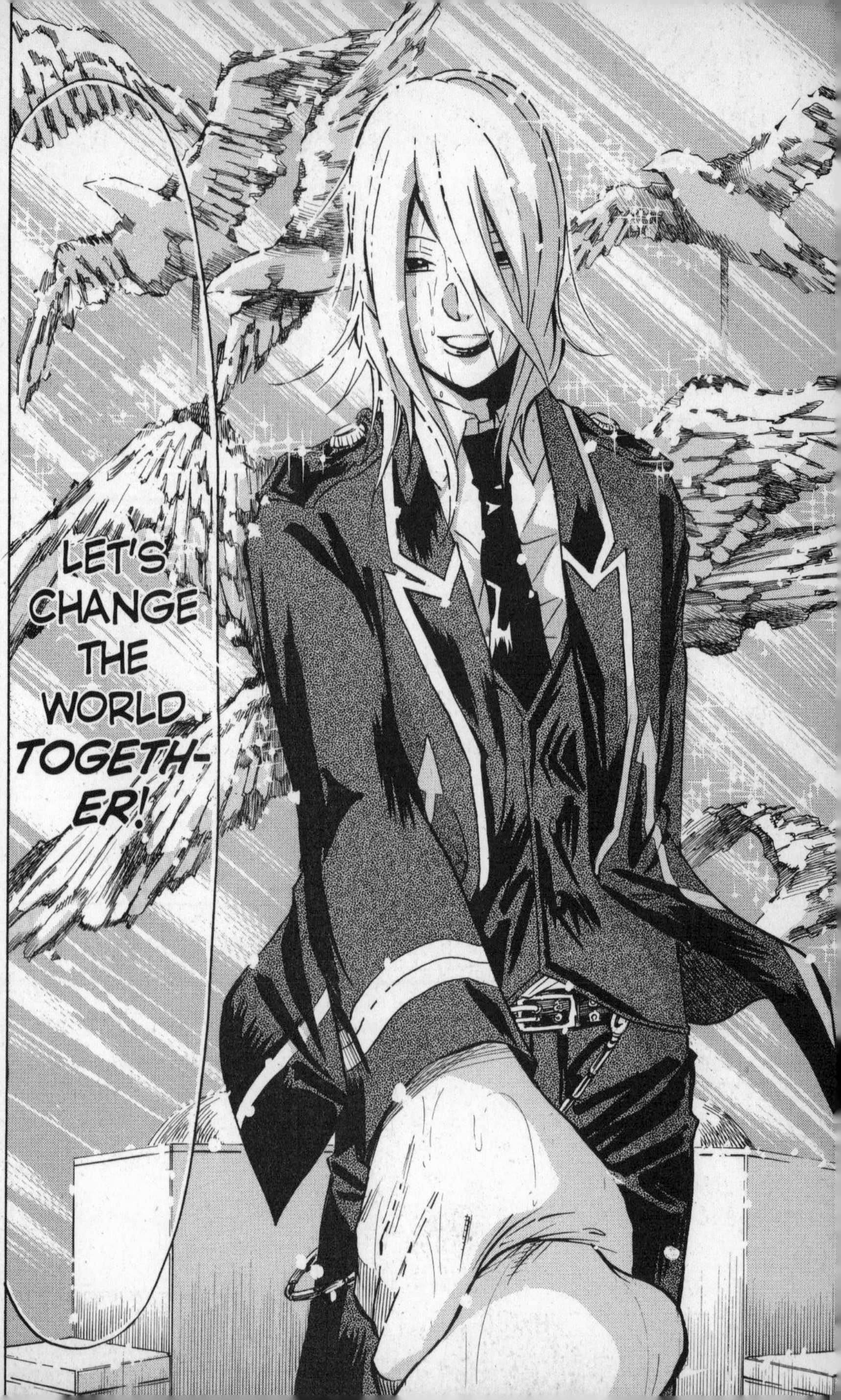
LET'S CHANGE THE WORLD TOGETH-ER!

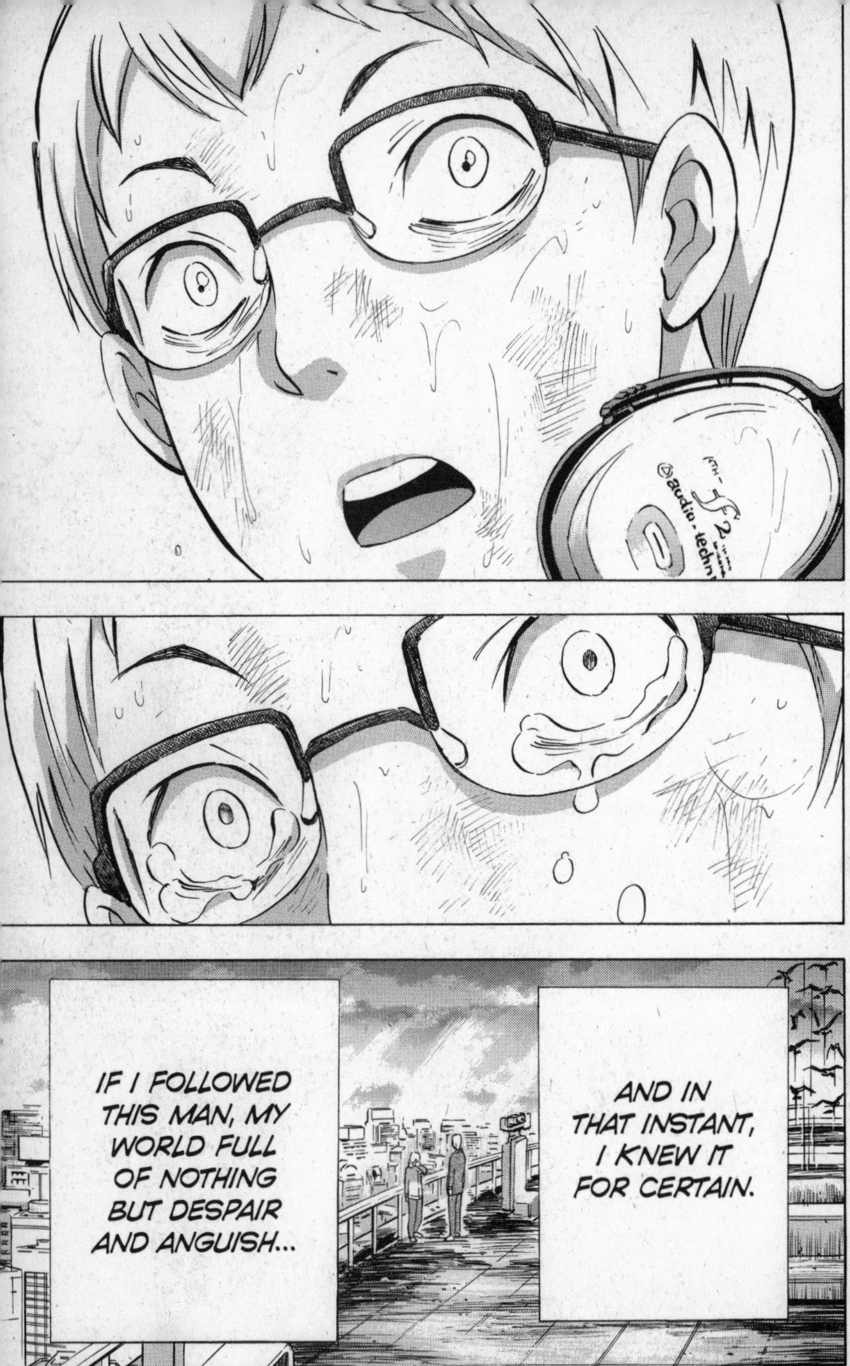
AND IN THAT INSTANT, I KNEW IT FOR CERTAIN.
IF I FOLLOWED THIS MAN, MY WORLD FULL OF NOTHING BUT DESPAIR AND ANGUISH...

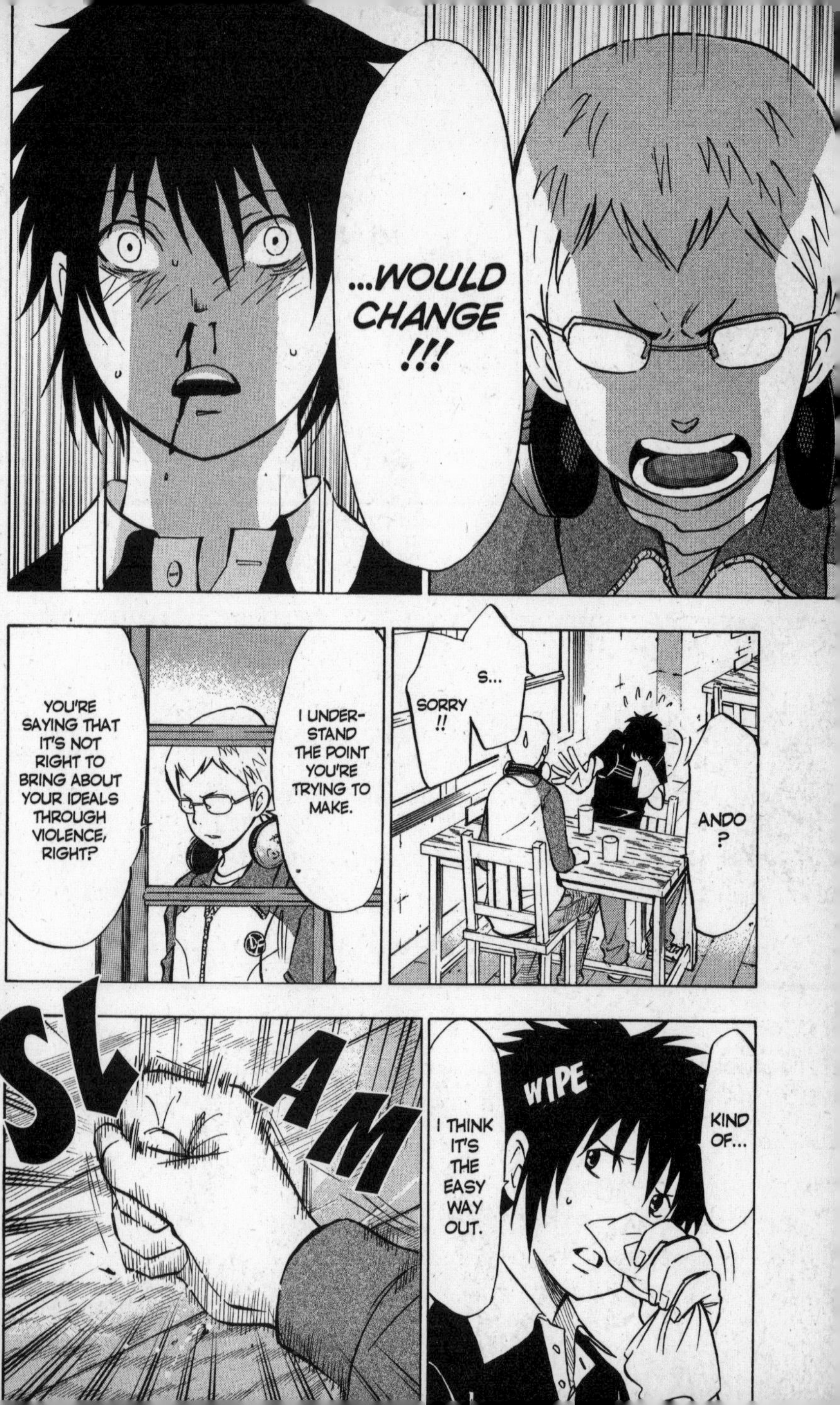

...WOULD CHANGE !!!
S... SORRY !!
ANDO ?
I UNDER-STAND THE POINT YOU'RE TRYING TO MAKE.
YOU'RE SAYING THAT IT'S NOT RIGHT TO BRING ABOUT YOUR IDEALS THROUGH VIOLENCE, RIGHT?
KIND OF...
WIPE
I THINK IT'S THE EASY WAY OUT.
SLAM

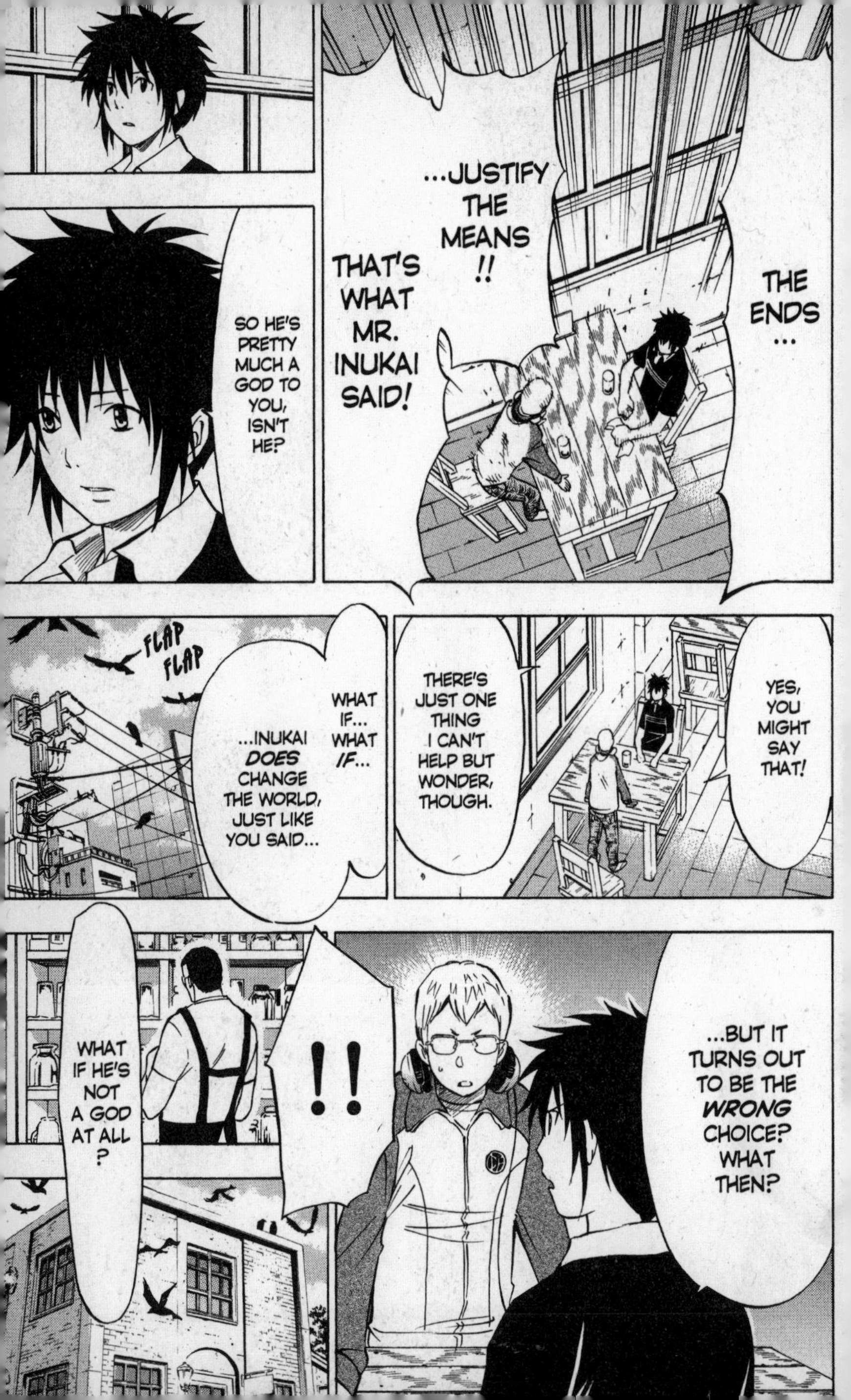
THE ENDS...
...JUSTIFY THE MEANS!!
THAT'S WHAT MR. INUKAI SAID!
SO HE'S PRETTY MUCH A GOD TO YOU, ISN'T HE?
YES, YOU MIGHT SAY THAT!
THERE'S JUST ONE THING I CAN'T HELP BUT WONDER, THOUGH.
WHAT IF... WHAT IF...
...INUKAI DOES CHANGE THE WORLD, JUST LIKE YOU SAID...
FLAP FLAP
...BUT IT TURNS OUT TO BE THE WRONG CHOICE? WHAT THEN?
!!
WHAT IF HE'S NOT A GOD AT ALL?

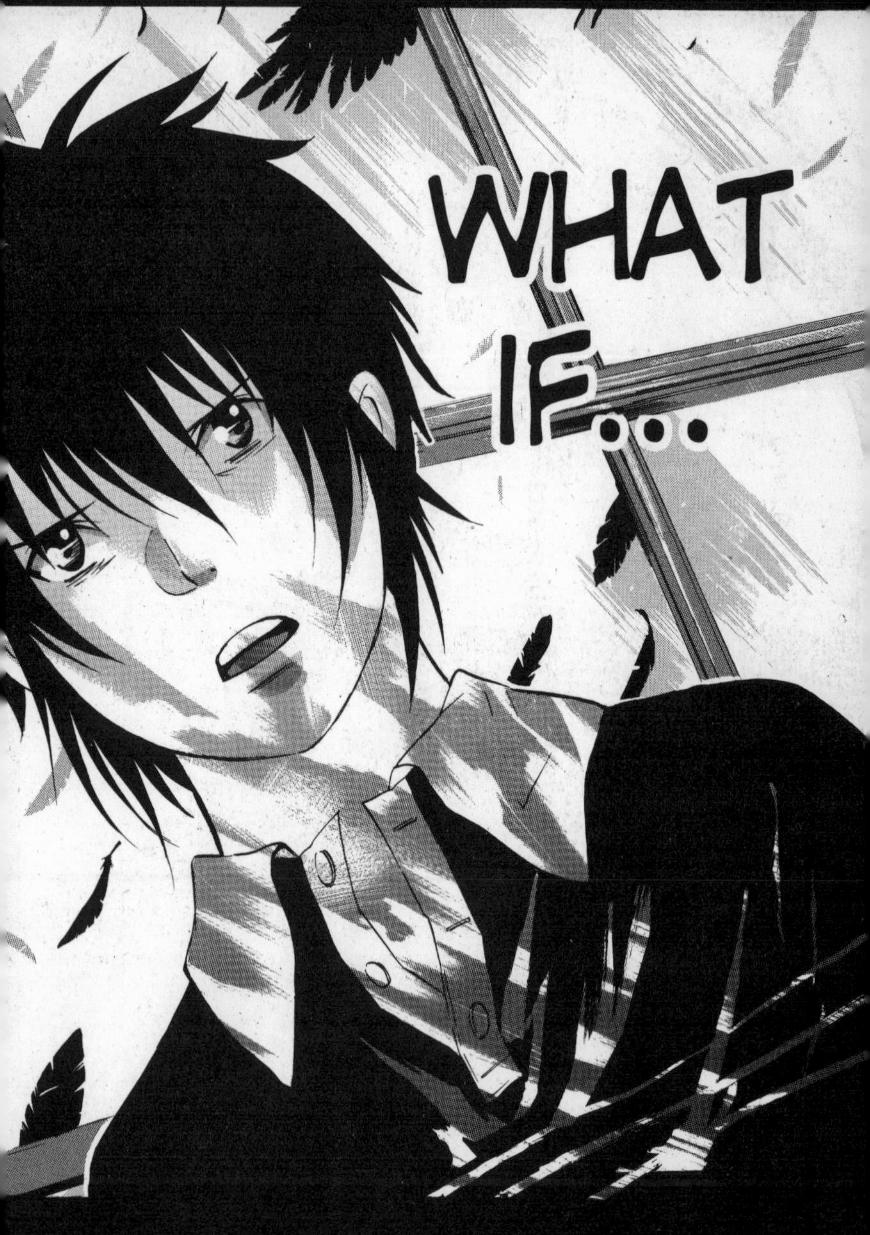
WHAT IF...

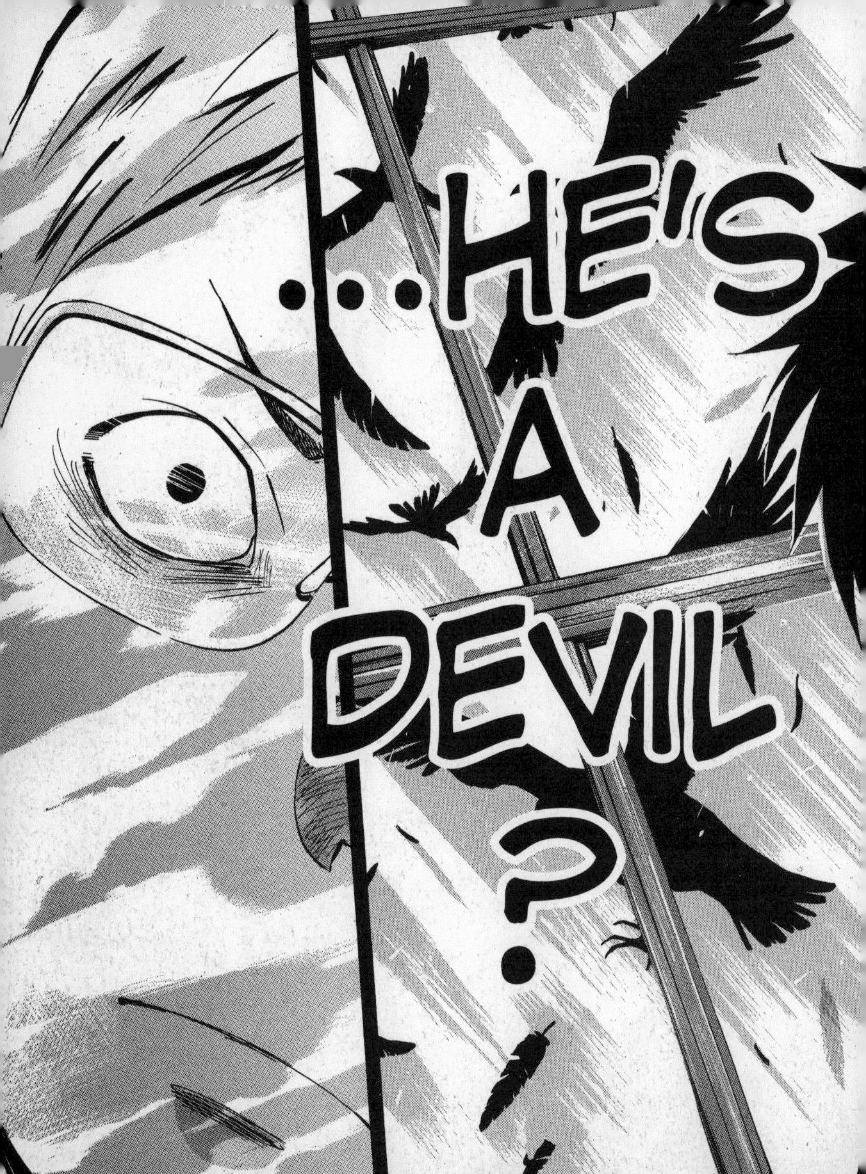
...HE'S A DEVIL?

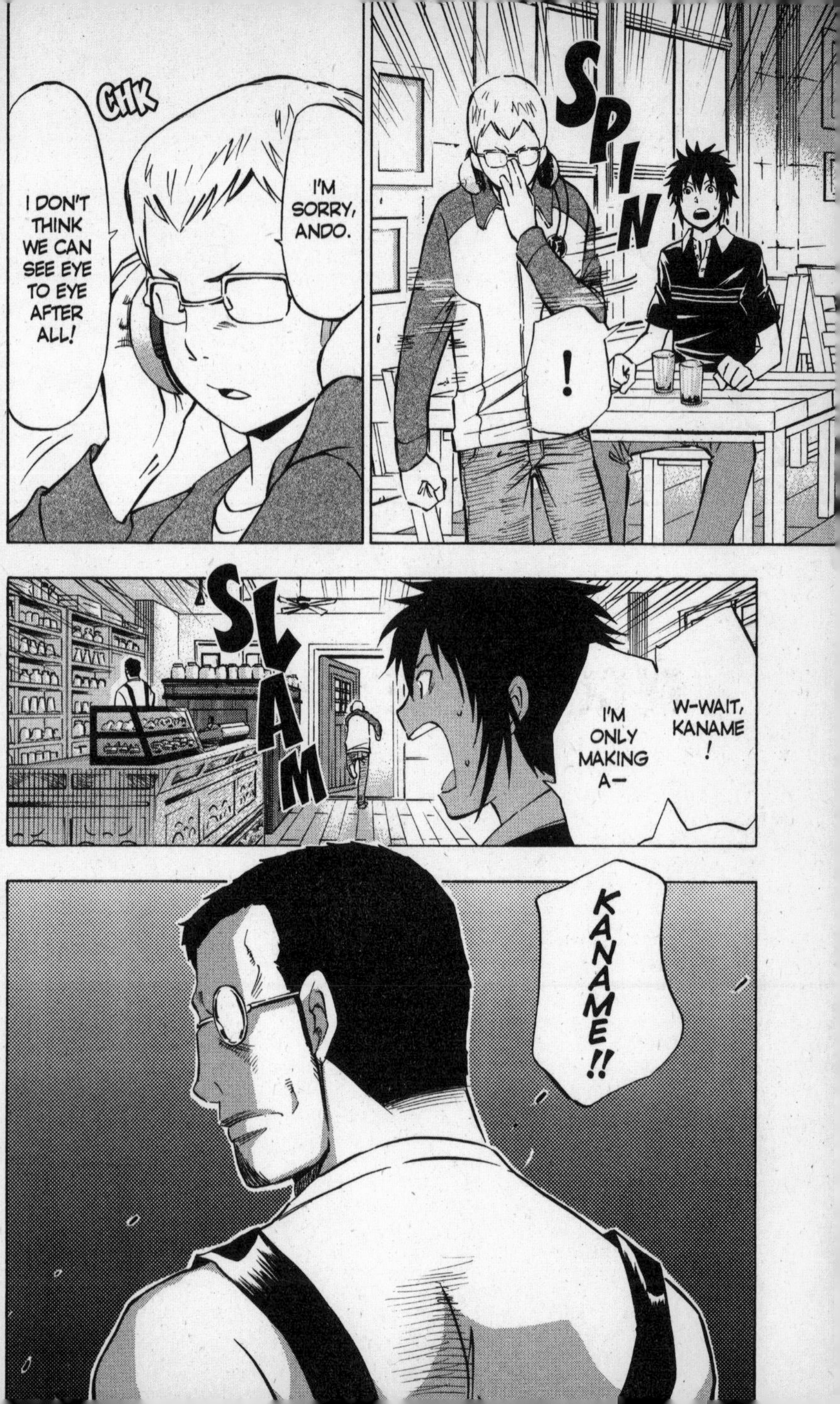
SPIN
!
I'M SORRY, ANDO.
CHK
I DON'T THINK WE CAN SEE EYE TO EYE AFTER ALL!
W-WAIT, KANAME!
I'M ONLY MAKING A—
SLAM
KANAME!!

IT CONTINUES IN Vol.02

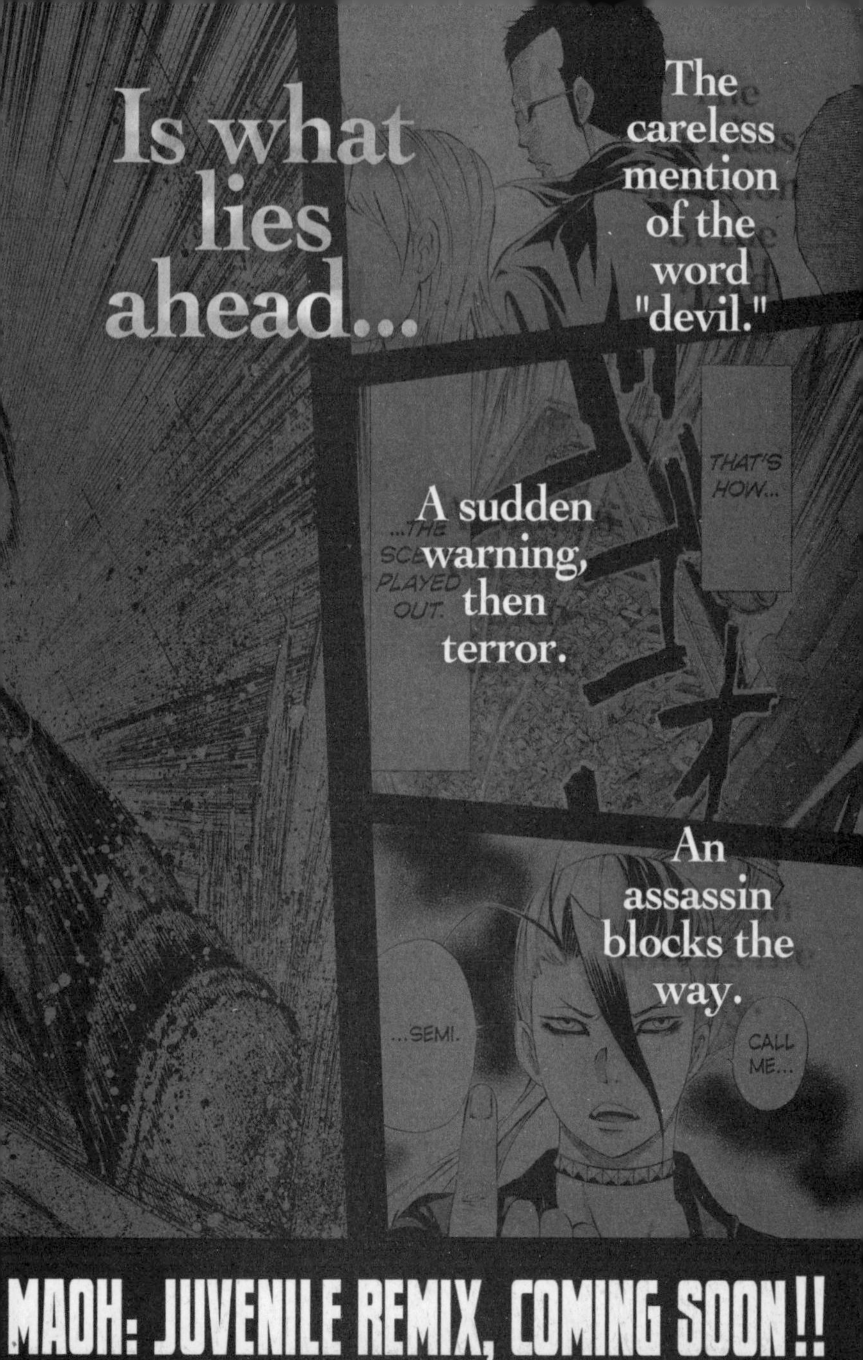
The careless mention of the word "devil."
THAT'S HOW...
A sudden warning, then terror.
...THE SC PLAYED OUT.
An assassin blocks the way.
CALL ME...
...SEMI.
Is what lies ahead...
MAOH: JUVENILE REMIX, COMING SOON!!

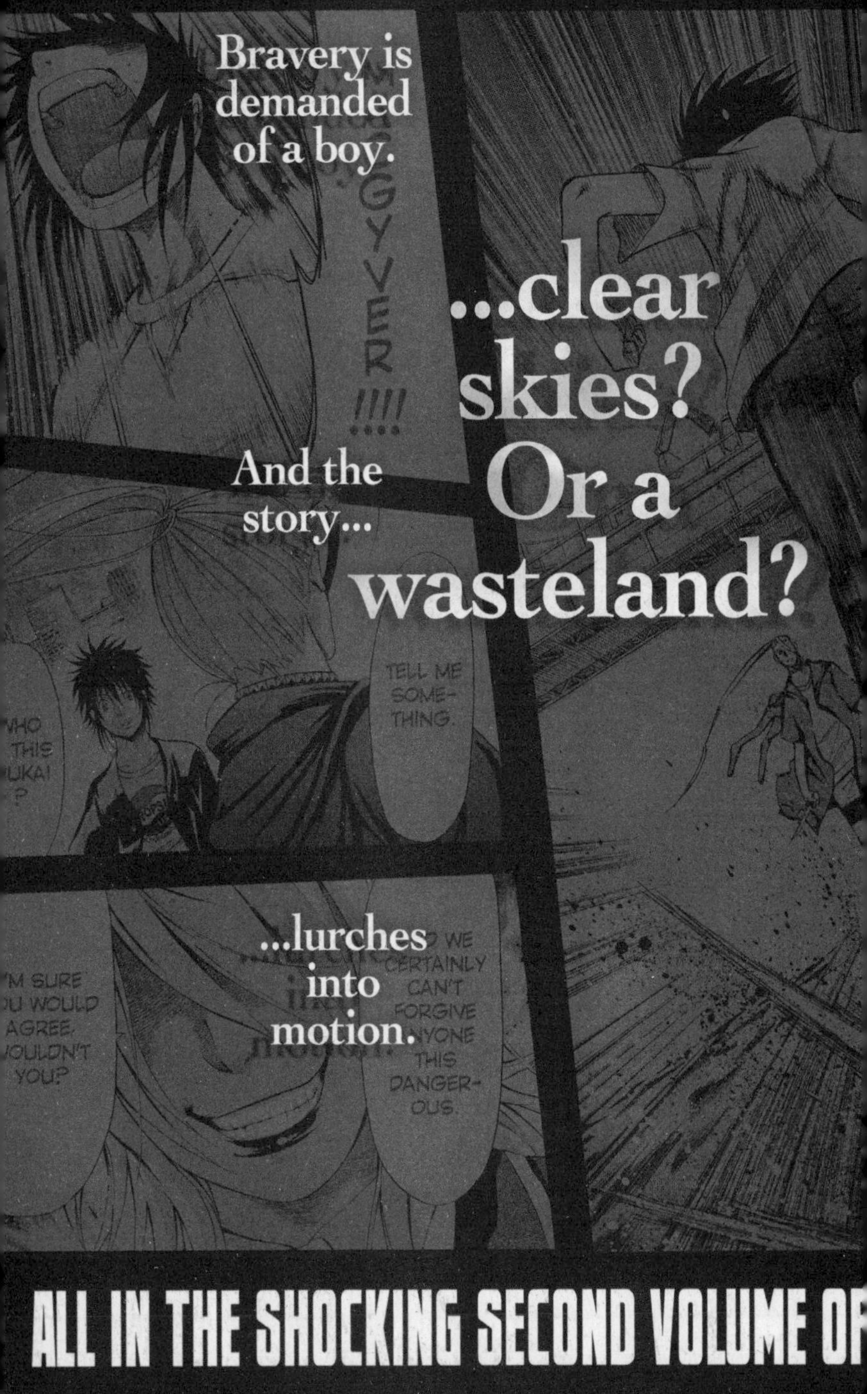
Bravery is demanded of a boy.
...clear skies? Or a wasteland?
And the story...
TELL ME SOME-THING.
...lurches into motion.
ALL IN THE SHOCKING SECOND VOLUME OF

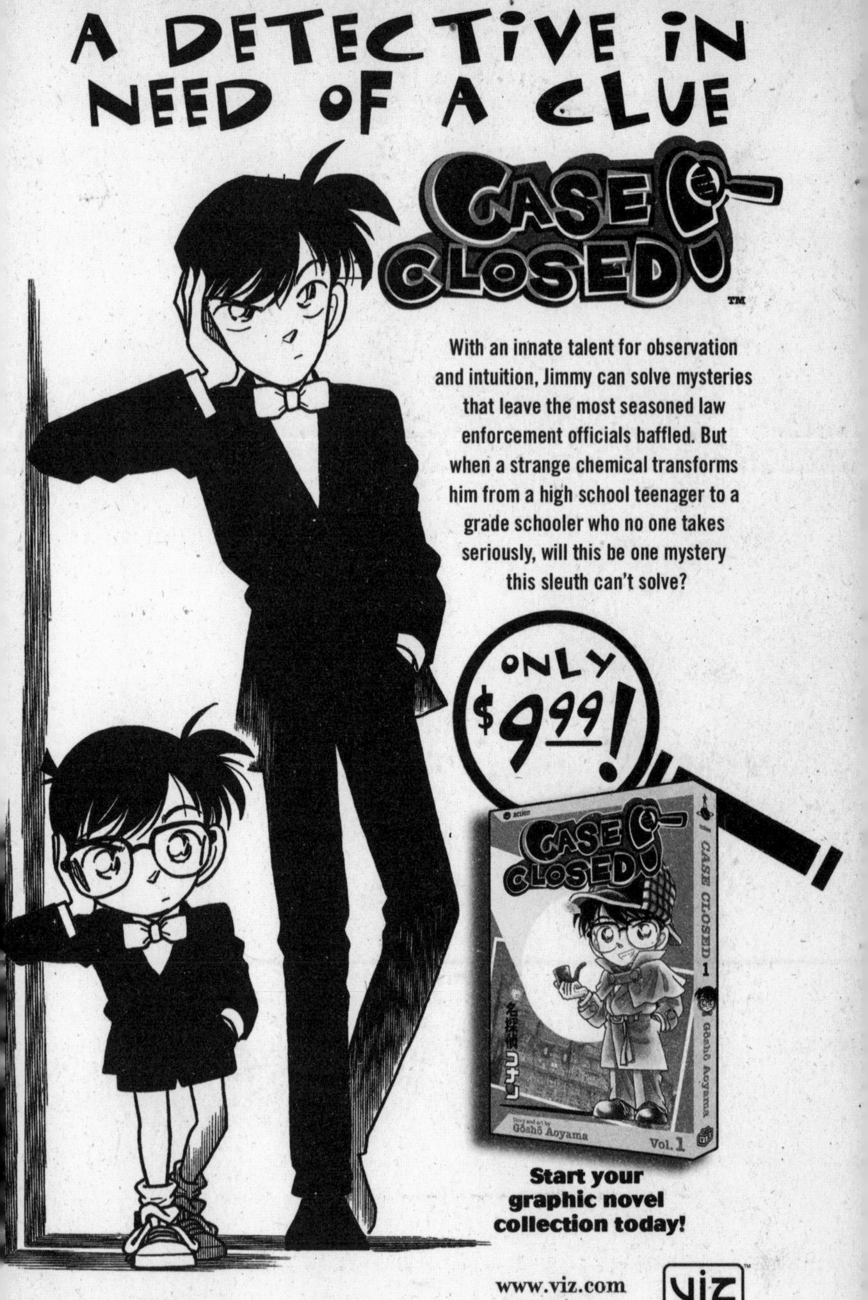
A DETECTIVE IN NEED OF A CLUE
CASE CLOSED™
With an innate talent for observation and intuition, Jimmy can solve mysteries that leave the most seasoned law enforcement officials baffled. But when a strange chemical transforms him from a high school teenager to a grade schooler who no one takes seriously, will this be one mystery this sleuth can't solve?
ONLY $9.99!
CASE CLOSED
CASE CLOSED 1
名探偵コナン
Gōshō Aoyama
Vol. 1
Start your graphic novel collection today!
www.viz.com
store.viz.com
VIZ MEDIA
©1994 Gosho AOYAMA/Shogakukan Inc.